DESCARTES
as a Moral Thinker

DESCARTES
as a Moral Thinker

Christianity, Technology, Nihilism

Gary
Steiner

BOOKS SERIES
Published in Cooperation with the
Journal of the History of Philosophy

Humanity
Books

an imprint of Prometheus Books
59 John Glenn Drive, Amherst, New York 14228–2197

Published 2004 by Humanity Books, an imprint of Prometheus Books

Inquiries should be addressed to
Humanity Books
59 John Glenn Drive
Amherst, New York 14228–2197
VOICE: 716–691–0133, ext. 207
FAX: 716–564–2711
WWW.PROMETHEUSBOOKS.COM

08 07 06 05 04   5 4 3 2 1

B
1878
.E7
S74
2004

Library of Congress Cataloging-in-Publication Data

Steiner, Gary, 1956–
    Descartes as a moral thinker : Christianity, technology, nihilism / Gary Steiner.
        p. cm. — (JHP books series)
    "Published in cooperation with the Journal of the History of Philosophy."
    Includes bibliographical references and index.
    ISBN 1–59102–212–6 (alk. paper)
    1. Descartes, René. 1596–1650—Ethics. 2. Ethics, Modern—17th century. I. Title.
II. Series.

B1878.E7S74 2004
170'.92—dc22   2004010058

Printed in the United States of America on acid-free paper

CONTENTS

ACKNOWLEDGMENTS

My work on this book was facilitated greatly by the efforts of several individuals. Richard Watson provided meticulous critiques of two preliminary versions of the manuscript; I am indebted to him for the generosity he exhibited in undertaking this task and in sharing with me his insights into Descartes and the craft of writing. Richard Wolin has offered encouragement and intellectual inspiration to me for over a decade; his work sets an example for any contemporary scholar concerned with the exigencies of our current situation.

Bucknell University provided generous ongoing support for this project, culminating in a yearlong sabbatical leave during 2000–2001. This award enabled me to spend the year in New Haven and avail myself of the remarkable libraries at Yale. That year proved to be decisive for the completion of the book. At Bucknell, Richard Fleming offered unwavering support for my work on this project; Jeff Turner made extraordinary efforts to ensure that my scholarly endeavors would be supported by the university, and he has continued to engage me in a highly productive philosophical dialogue that started over two decades ago. My many conversations with Harold Schweizer, with whom I worked closely for many years in Bucknell's humanities program, aided me in the formation of the central thesis of this book. Work on the book was also facilitated by the capable research assistance of Joel Mack in 1996 and Francis Carmen in 1998.

My editor at Humanity Books, Ann O'Hear, embraced this project enthusiastically from the very start and worked hard to ensure that my vision for the book would be realized. I very much appreciate her efforts on my behalf.

INTRODUCTION

It is still a metaphysical faith *upon which our faith in sci-*
ence rests . . . even we seekers after knowledge today, we
godless anti-metaphysicians still take our fire, too, from
the flame lit by a faith that is thousands of years old, that
Christian faith which was also the faith of Plato, that
God is the truth, that truth is divine.
—Friedrich Nietzsche, *The Gay Science*, section 344

Descartes stands at the threshold between two major epochs
in the history of Western philosophy, between the piety of
the Christian Middle Ages and the secular rationalism of
modernity. But have we truly understood Descartes's place in the
transition from the one epoch to the other? We are indebted to
Descartes more than to any other thinker for our understanding of
modernity and ourselves. If we have failed to grasp Descartes's
place in the transition from the medieval to the modern, then we
have failed to grasp something essential about ourselves.

The overwhelming tendency in contemporary scholarship, particularly in North America, has been to interpret Descartes as the
first systematically secular thinker in the European tradition. This
interpretation of Descartes is appealing because it provides a

straightforward account of the transition from medieval to modern consciousness and values, and because it appears to be supported by Descartes's emphasis on his ideal of autonomous reason and his program for marshaling scientific knowledge in the service of predicting and controlling natural processes. But on closer inspection, Descartes's writings reveal a set of underlying Christian moral commitments that stand in an uneasy tension with Descartes's insights into the power of human reason. This tension reflects a fundamental ambivalence in Descartes's thought between Christian piety and autonomous rationality.

Descartes's ambivalence is between an "angelic" ethos that takes its bearings from a relationship to the God of Christianity and an "earthly" or technological ethos that concerns itself with problems of material welfare. In the angelic ethos, truth and goodness are conceived *sub specie aeternitatis*, that is, in relation to the absoluteness and permanence of the divine intellect, while the earthly ethos is oriented on human welfare and strictly human measures, such as the ability to reproduce natural mechanisms. One of the conclusions for which I argue in this book is that Descartes's earthly or technological ethos not only is not incompatible with the angelic but in fact is derived from it. Descartes understands his turn to reason as a gift of divine inspiration, and his program for the mastery of nature as a task assigned to human beings by God. To understand Descartes in these terms is to see his entire philosophy as a project rooted in faith—not simply faith in the power of human agency to secure our existence in the face of the world's contingency but faith in a divine measure that grants us our existence and assigns us our place in the world. The ideal of human sovereignty over the earth that motivates modern technology is derived from biblical, patristic, and scholastic characterizations of the relationship between human beings, God, and nature.

But at the same time, Descartes's insights into the autonomy of reason bring the earthly ethos into a tension with the angelic. Another conclusion for which I argue is that Descartes lays the foundation for a modern ethic of unbridled mastery and human self-assertion, but he does not embrace such an ethic. Descartes makes an important step in the direction of secular technological consciousness, but he holds back from a rejection of Christian values. Descartes recognizes that the instrumental character of reason makes it useful for technological practice but that reason is incapable of grounding the moral reflection that is needed to guide practice. If, after Descartes, faith ceased to be authoritative and reason came to be the sole guide for the will, this is a sign that Descartes's insight into the power of human reason struck a responsive chord in the Promethean part of the soul of Western humanity and facilitated a detachment of reason from Christian faith that Descartes himself appears never to have advocated.

My interpretation of Descartes takes as axiomatic the theme of secularization, the idea that modernity is the product of a historical process in which devotion to sacred measures became transformed or desanctified. Over time, human reason and human will came to take the place once occupied by the authority of the Christian God. In this connection Descartes's writings on morality are especially illuminating, for they show the extent to which Descartes found himself torn between the attempt to ground general moral principles in human reason alone and the need to appeal to the Christian heritage in order to give concrete content and absolute authority to such general principles.

My interest in Descartes as a moral thinker is inspired by a set of contemporary debates about secularization, the problem of nihilism, and the power of reason to ground morality. I conclude the book with an examination of these debates and a discussion of Descartes's relevance to contemporary controversies that concern the moral status of modernity. There is vehement disagreement in the philosophical community on the question whether our culture faces a crisis in values, and, if there is such a crisis, whether reason alone is sufficient to resolve the crisis or whether instead the ascendancy of reason is the cause of the crisis. Is modernity the realization of the human capacity for self-governance and self-assertion, for the rejection as totalitarian of any extrarational authority or measure that purports to stand above the human will? Or is our age instead one whose greatest deficiency and most pressing danger is our refusal to preserve a sense of respect for the limits of human reason? Descartes struggled with precisely these questions. By reflecting on Descartes's ambivalence regarding them, we can begin to come to grips with our own ambivalence about what Jaspers called "the spiritual situation of the age."

—CHAPTER 1—

DESCARTES'S MORAL IDEAL
Between Thomism and Deontology

1. THE DISTINCTION BETWEEN THE "PROVISIONAL" AND "DEFINITIVE" MORALITIES

Even though Descartes is not thought of first of all as a moral thinker, there is a sense in which concern for the ethical motivates every aspect of Descartes's thought. Descartes is known for having hesitated to write down his thoughts on morality; in the *Conversation with Burman*, he told his interviewer that he "does not like writing on ethics, but he was compelled to include these rules" to preclude the objection that Descartes "was a man without any religion or faith."[1] The rules to which Descartes refers are the "three or four maxims" of what has come to be known as the "provisional morality," which Descartes presents in Part 3 of the *Discourse on Method*.[2] These maxims, and their relationship to Descartes's philosophy as a whole, are a central theme in the literature on Descartes's views on morality. Part of the reason for the prominence given to these maxims is that they provide the closest thing to a systematic treatment of morality to be found in Descartes's writings.

But these maxims have an even more fundamental significance

in Descartes's philosophical project. Their very status as provisional suggests that one day they will be discarded in favor of a "definitive" morality. Moreover, given the function that Descartes ascribes to the provisional maxims, they hardly seem suitable as a final or definitive morality when they are seen in the light of his philosophical project of grounding human commitments in absolute cognitive certainty. The very terms of Descartes's introduction of the provisional morality make this quite clear: he introduces the provisional morality by telling the reader that

> Now, before starting to rebuild your house, it is not enough simply to pull it down, to make provision for materials and architects (or else train yourself in architecture), and to have carefully drawn up the plans; you must also provide yourself with some other place where you can live comfortably while building is in progress. Likewise, lest I should remain indecisive in my actions while reason obliged me to be so in my judgments, and in order to live as happily as I could during this time, I formed for myself a provisional moral code consisting of just three or four maxims, which I should like to tell you about.[3]

The architectural metaphor here recalls Descartes's use of a very similar metaphor at the beginning of Part 2 of the *Discourse*. There Descartes suggests that "the will of men using reason" should give rise to works derived from a unified plan rather than spawning products in a scattered and willy-nilly fashion. Such a unified plan leads to the production of "more attractive and better planned" cities than does the ancient approach of gradually making additions to buildings already in existence, inasmuch as the ancient approach yields "ill-proportioned" towns and "crooked and irregular" streets;[4] Descartes shows the significance of the architectural metaphor when he argues for the need to dispense with the "old foundations" of learning and to replace those foundations "with the standards of reason."[5] These old foundations are objectionable on several grounds: they have spawned "many doubts and errors";[6]

they are based methodologically on syllogism, which does not permit the acquisition of new knowledge;[7] and they do not give rise to absolutely certain knowledge but force us to resign ourselves to results that are "merely probable."[8] These limitations and defects of traditional learning, which have been symbolized in the architectural metaphor by the image of ill-proportioned, crooked, and irregular streets, leave Descartes with the task of establishing a rigorous distinction between science and the "false sciences" or pseudo-sciences of alchemy, astrology, and magic.[9] Descartes devotes the first two parts of the *Discourse on Method* to sketching out the project of establishing new and solid foundations on the basis of a distinctive conception of method. He warns the reader at several points not to base his or her judgments on the inherently insecure foundation of "custom and example."[10]

Against this background, the provisional morality of Part 3 must be understood as a temporary set of measures to be relied upon until such time as the edifice of knowledge has been established upon absolutely certain foundations. The provisional morality is a necessary expedient, but in principle it is like the "moral writings of the ancient pagans," which Descartes dismisses in Part 1 of the *Discourse* as being "proud and magnificent palaces built only on sand and mud."[11] His criticism of the ancients for being unable to "explain how to recognize a virtue" is of a piece with his criticism of his forebears' inability to distinguish between science and pseudo-science: in both cases, what is needed are clear *criteria*. In morals as in science, Descartes wants knowledge, not simply the authority of "custom and example." And yet, I argue below, the basis of the provisional morality is precisely the sort of custom and example that Descartes identifies as the central failing of the tradition. This recommends the conclusion that the provisional morality is a temporary measure that will be discarded once the new foundations for knowledge have been established.

Elsewhere Descartes offers very strong support for the proposition that the provisional morality of the *Discourse* is a temporary expedient, one that will eventually be replaced by some sort of "definitive" morality. In his letter to Abbé Claude Picot, the translator of the *Principles of Philosophy*, Descartes discusses the relationship between philosophy and morality and the place of the provisional morality in the proper order of philosophical inquiry. There Descartes says that in the *Discourse*, written ten years earlier, he "summarized the principal rules of logic and of an imperfect moral code which we may follow provisionally [*par provision*] while we do not yet know a better one."[12] It is essential to establish such a provisional code *before* conducting philosophical inquiry because the acquisition of some means for regulating our conduct "tolerates no delay."[13] The exigencies of action are such that we must often make choices precisely where we lack a basis for making an absolutely secure choice. Whether our moral choices can ultimately be grounded so as to enjoy absolute security is not clear, and in the end it turns out to be doubtful. But here, as in the *Discourse*, Descartes stops short of abandoning the hope of attaining this kind of security; he leaves open the prospect of leaving behind the "imperfect" provisional morality in favor of "a better one." What sort of better one? In the letter to Picot, Descartes hints at the answer when he says that "the study of philosophy is more necessary for the regulation of our morals and our conduct in this life than is the use of our eyes to guide our steps."[14] Any moral code that is devised prior to the study of philosophy is inadequately grounded, even though the proper order of study demands the establishment of a moral code prior to the study of philosophical logic. But once the provisional morality has served its purpose as the temporary dwelling envisioned in the architectural metaphor of Part 3 of the *Discourse*, we will be in a position to gain "the satisfaction accorded by knowledge of the things which philosophy enables us to discover."[15]

Here Descartes links the study of philosophy to the attainment of a special kind of satisfaction, one grounded in *knowledge*. And it is knowledge, as I show below, that is conspicuously absent from the provisional morality. But what kind of knowledge is missing here? In the letter to Picot, Descartes outlines four

> levels of wisdom that so far have been attained. The first level contains only notions which are so clear in themselves that they can be acquired without meditation. The second comprises everything we are acquainted with through sensory experience. The third comprises what we learn by conversing with other people. And one may add a fourth category, namely what is written by people who are capable instructing us well; for in such cases we hold a kind of conversation with the authors.[16]

Descartes proceeds to add "a fifth way of reaching wisdom—a way which is incomparably more elevated and more sure than the other four," namely, "the search for first causes and the true principles which enable us to deduce the reasons for everything we are capable of knowing."[17] He says of this fifth way that "there have been great men who have tried to find" such principles, but he expresses doubt that anyone has yet adduced them, and he says that "so long as we possess only the kind of knowledge that is acquired by the first four degrees of wisdom we should not doubt the probable truths which concern the conduct of life, while at the same time we should not consider them to be so certain that we are incapable of changing our views when we are obliged to do so by some evident reason."[18]

In this statement, Descartes draws a fundamental link between "first causes and true principles" on the one hand and "truths which concern the conduct of life" on the other. If our knowledge does not exceed the first four degrees of wisdom, that is, if we lack the foundational principles that constitute the fifth degree, then we are entitled to rest content with merely probable truths in matters bearing on "the conduct of life." But what happens when we adduce the "true principles"? Descartes implies here that we will no longer be entitled to rely on merely probable truths. In the letter to Picot, he says that the first principles constituting the fifth degree of wisdom are "the clearest and most evident that the human mind can know," and "they enable all other things to be deduced from them."[19] So Descartes seems to be saying that the "truths which concern the conduct of life" will ultimately be deducible from clear and evident foundational principles; he thereby seeks to *restrict* the notion of "wisdom" by setting its limit at that of clear and distinct ideas.

This is not the first time that Descartes gives prominence to decisions regarding the conduct of life. In the earlier *Rules for the Direction of the Mind*, he recommends that anyone who "seriously wishes to investigate the truth of things" learn "how to increase the natural light of reason . . . in order that his intellect should show his will what decision it ought to make in all the contingencies of life."[20] Descartes calls the methodological basis sought in the *Rules* a *mathesis univeralis*, a universal learning or knowledge that corresponds to the first principles sought in his later writings. Just as in the later writings the first principles will serve as the foundation from which the truths concerning the conduct of life will be derived, so in the *Rules* the *mathesis universalis* will serve as the basis that leads to a *universali sapientia*, a totality of "human wisdom, which always remains one and the same" and that is identical with *scientiae omnes*, the sciences as a whole.[21] If the intellect is to guide the will in all the contingencies of life, and if the intellect is to proceed only on the basis of "certain and evident cognition" rather than on the basis of "merely probable cognition,"[22] then Descartes's aspiration in the *Rules* is the same as it is later in the letter to Picot—to ground all our choices concerning the contingencies of life in certain and evident cognition.

The same ambition is evident in the *Discourse*, where Descartes proposes to "learn to distinguish the true from the false in order to see clearly into my own actions and proceed with confidence in this life."[23] Gilson rightly sees in this statement an expression of "the moral character of Descartes's primary concerns."[24] The emphasis that Descartes repeatedly places on the importance of choices guided by the certainty of the intellect, particularly when seen in conjunction with the metaphor of the provisional morality as a temporary dwelling, lends great support to the proposition that even, and perhaps especially, moral choice will be fundamentally transformed, once the project of establishing secure foundations has been completed.

Descartes, however, never develops the definitive morality implied in the architectural metaphor of Part 3 of the *Discourse* and in his remarks in the letter to Picot. Is this because Descartes lost hope in the prospect of establishing such a morality? Or did he never have such a hope in the first place? In fact, neither one of these accounts is satisfactory, although the first is closer to the truth than the second. To suggest, as does Michèle LeDoeuff, that Descartes never really intended the provisional morality to be temporary is to make the mistake of projecting some contemporary sensibilities onto Descartes retrospectively; it is to attribute to Descartes the sense of resignation over the prospects of reason to ground morality that prevails in many minds today. As Gilson notes, not only does Descartes use the words *ad tempus* to translate *par provision* in the Latin version of the *Discourse*, but also Furetière's 1690 *Dictionnaire universel* confirms that "for the time being" (*en attendant*) was a standard meaning of the term [*par*] *provision* in the seventeenth century.[25] At least at the time of the *Discourse*, then, Descartes was committed to the ideal of a definitive morality grounded in reason.

Descartes never simply abandons this ideal, but instead begins in his later writings to express a profound *ambivalence* regarding the possibility of establishing a rigorous science of morality. It has become fairly standard in discussions of Descartes's views on morality to take the position that, whether or not he had faith in the possibility of a truly definitive morality at the time of the *Discourse on Method*, by the time of the late text *The Passions of the Soul*, Descartes had accepted the morality of the *Passions* as the most definitive one possible for human beings as a composite of mind (soul) and body. As I show below, particularly in chapter 3,

Descartes seems to have changed his thinking about the prospects for a "definitive" morality rather substantially as a result of his lengthy correspondence during the mid-1640s with Princess Elizabeth of Bohemia and Queen Christina of Sweden, and to a lesser extent with Hector-Pierre Chanut. In the course of this correspondence, Descartes found himself compelled to think more carefully than he had previously about the special problems posed by the quasi-substantial union of mind and body; during this time, Descartes seems to have gained a full appreciation of the difficulties posed for morality by the irreducible complexity of embodied experience. But even in this correspondence and in the *Passions*, there are indications of Descartes's earlier, lofty ambitions for a definitive morality, alongside his later, more tempered views. There are, then, expressions throughout Descartes's writings of a sensitivity to our fundamental limitations as finite, composite beings, together with a repeated insistence on ever-greater perfection in our moral judgments. In the *Passions of the Soul*, the ultimate basis for moral choice is virtually the same as it was in Descartes's earlier writings, namely, "firm and determinate judgments bearing upon the knowledge of good and evil."[26]

Descartes adheres to this basis for moral judgments at least as a regulative ideal in the *Passions*, but much of what he says there expresses an acknowledgment that the complexities of mind-body interaction may ultimately pose an insuperable obstacle to the realization of this ideal. This sense of resignation is a kind of second voice in Descartes's later writings that is continually in tension with the voice of confident ambitions. This sense of resignation has guided a number of influential commentators in their characterizations of Descartes's "final" views on morality. When Gilson, for example, sees the provisional morality as "destined, just as it is, to become the definitive one," he means that, if only against Descartes's intention, the morality originally presented as "provisional" in the *Discourse* would turn out to be the best that human beings could hope for.[27] Martial Gueroult suggests that the reason for this is that even though Descartes may at first have aspired to morality as an exact science, he ultimately had to recognize that the irreducible complexity of our composite mind-body existence made any such definitive morality an impossible dream.[28] Even though at the time of the *Discourse* Descartes still believed that morality would be possible as a rigorous science, the drama of Descartes's reflections and his correspondence in the mid-1640s led him to resign himself to a more modest final position—the set of techniques for controlling bodily states sketched out in the *Passions*. In other words, one is to see in the text of *The Passions of the Soul* Descartes's final conception of a "definitive" morality, but by this point the meaning of the term *definitive* has changed radically from the meaning implied in the *Discourse* and the letter to Picot.

Gueroult derives support for this interpretation from an exchange between Descartes and Elizabeth in late 1645. Elizabeth observed in a letter to Descartes that "to assess the goods [that bear upon human contentment], it is necessary to know them perfectly; and to know all those goods about which one is constrained to make a choice in an active life, it would be necessary to possess an infinite science [*une science infinie*]."[29] In his reply to Elizabeth, Descartes acknowledges that "we lack the infinite knowledge which would be necessary for a perfect acquaintance with all the goods between which we have to choose in the various situations of our lives," and he says that we must "be contented with a modest knowledge of the most necessary truths such as those I listed in my last letter [of September 15, 1645]."[30] Gueroult concludes from this that for the Descartes of the mid-1640s and later, in morality "our ignorance, as well as our uncertainty, are unavoidable. . . . This state . . . appears as having to be permanent, and must, consequently, render permanent the rules that a merely provisional certainty imposed."[31]

On Gilson's and Gueroult's interpretation, then, the views presented in *The Passions of the Soul* are a "rendering permanent" of the maxims originally presented as temporary in Part 3 of the *Dis-*

course. The program for a set of techniques to prevent our bodily states from interfering with the prudent exercise of our judgment that Descartes presents in the *Passions* is of a piece with, and simply formalizes, the basic moral principles presented in the provisional morality; it does nothing to change those principles, inasmuch as Descartes professes in one of the prefatory letters to the *Passions* to "explain the passions only as a physicist [*En Physicien*], and not as a rhetorician [*Orateur*] or even as a moral philosopher."[32] But if the *Passions* is essentially a physics (or perhaps a physiology) text, whereas Part 3 of the *Discourse* is precisely a text on morality, how can the one text be a formalization of the other? Gueroult's answer, which I examine in chapter 3, is that by the time of the *Passions*, morality for Descartes has become nothing more than a set of techniques for controlling bodily passions and procuring happiness.[33] To recognize this practical or "technological" aspiration in Descartes's writings is to see one side of the ambivalence that I discuss above, namely, the pointedly practical interests that figure so prominently in Descartes's thought. But this practical side must not be emphasized to the exclusion of what one might call, along with Jacques Maritain, the "angelic" side of Descartes's thinking.[34] To gain a sense of the full complexity of Descartes's views on morality, one must take as axiomatic the ambivalence between these two tendencies. In her book-length study of Descartes's morality, Geneviève Rodis-Lewis offers insight into this ambivalence:

> This tension in Cartesianism between the real distinction of soul and body and their no less substantial union, makes it clear why morality must assume two levels: the illumination of a soul called to a spiritual destiny, and the equilibrium of a being that lives by dominating its bodily mechanisms. Even though as a matter of right it is immediately preceded by the study of man, morality returns us to the source of all philosophical reflection: the relation between the soul and God.[35]

Gueroult fixes his attention on the second of these two levels: the substantial union of mind and body and the specific kind of morality designed to serve this union. Such a morality is, in a restricted sense, a set of techniques for facilitating the aim of domination for which Descartes is so well known. This aim of domination has as its object the human body, as Rodis-Lewis notes. But it has as its ultimate object "bodily mechanisms" in a broader sense, namely, the mechanisms of corporeal nature as a whole. Descartes has this object in mind when he sketches his program for the use of physics to render human beings "the masters and possessors of nature" in Part 6 of the *Discourse on Method*.[36] With reference to this restricted sense of "morality," Descartes wrote to Chanut that "what little knowledge of physics I have tried to acquire has been a great help to me in establishing secure foundations in moral philosophy."[37]

2. THE DEFINITIVE MORALITY

This restricted sense of morality is incomplete as a characterization of Descartes's moral project. I have shown this by examining the basic terms of the "morality" that seeks to control the human body and natural bodies in general. Descartes identifies morality in this restricted sense as one of the topmost branches of the tree metaphor in the letter to Picot. That metaphor symbolizes "the whole of philosophy" or human wisdom and represents both the scope of the sciences and the proper order of their investigation.

> Thus the whole of philosophy is like a tree. The roots are metaphysics, the trunk is physics, and the branches emerging from the trunk are all the other sciences, which may be reduced to three principal ones, namely medicine, mechanics, and morality. By 'morals' I understand the highest and most perfect morality [*la plus parfaite Morale*], which presupposes a complete knowledge of the other sciences and is the ultimate level of wisdom.[38]

Just before introducing this metaphor, Descartes defines meta-physics as containing "the principles of knowledge, including the explanation of the principal attributes of God, the non-material nature of our souls, and all the other clear and distinct notions which are in us," and he states that the proper order of study requires that we investigate metaphysics before moving on to such sciences as physics.[39] Descartes says, in effect, that the proper order of study dictates that disciplines lower on the tree be studied prior to those higher on the tree and that "metaphysics" is concerned exclusively with clear and distinct notions pertaining to God, the self, and all other areas of human knowledge in general. Taken together, these two features of the tree metaphor show that "the highest and most perfect morality" is based on a knowledge of clear and distinct ideas such as those adduced in the *Meditations on First Philosophy* through the mediation of physics, mechanics, and medicine.

This metaphor is the key to understanding the restricted sense of morality and its place in the larger enterprise of human wisdom and makes it clear why the restricted sense of morality is only *part* of the ethos of Descartes's project. Descartes certainly uses the term *morality* in a peculiar sense here; there is no entirely straight-forward sense in which morality can be understood to presuppose a knowledge of physics and medicine, unless we mean, for example, that we cannot decide whether heart bypass surgery is a reasonable choice under particular circumstances until we know the attendant risks and the chances for success. But even then we are not strictly speaking of morality but rather of something like what Kant calls counsels of prudence—we are simply contem-plating the likelihood of success in our endeavor to master bodily mechanisms, and we are doing nothing to arrive at the underlying moral *commitments*.

Gueroult recognizes this fundamental limitation of the morality that Descartes places alongside medicine and mechanics. He argues that Descartes, in adopting this as his sole approach to morality, simply dispenses with the reflection on ends that had traditionally been fundamental to ethics. Morality as traditionally understood, Gueroult observes,

> is less preoccupied with seeking to realize a certain end than to determine what this end must be, namely, to seek whether in some case we ought to act under the idea of an end.
>
> But, in fact, Cartesian morality does not deal with the latter problem; it resolves it by skipping over it [*par prétérition*]. Natural light, along with natural instinct (both guaranteed by divine veracity), reveal to us immediately, without the least doubt, that our end is happiness in the present life. It remains for morality only to furnish the technique capable of realizing this.[40]

In support of this interpretation, Gueroult cites Descartes's invocation of Seneca in a letter to Elizabeth: "all men want to live happily [*vivere beate*], but do not see clearly what makes a life happy."[41] Gueroult takes this statement to mean that for Descartes, the end of happiness is so universally accepted that it obviously must have been disclosed by the natural light of reason; all that remains is to seek the means for achieving happiness, which on Gueroult's view are to be found in techniques for manipulating natural processes, which include the human body.

On the technological or practical interpretation advanced by Gueroult, the placement of morality at the top of the tree of wisdom is a sign that Descartes has retreated from the lofty ambitions of the *Discourse* and now sees morality simply as a branch of the sciences, one concerned with the manipulation of the human body in the service of a pregiven end of human happiness. The central problem with this interpretation is that it is based on viewing Descartes too much in terms of our own contemporary, technological ethos and too little in terms of the tension that Descartes felt between the ethos of the medieval Christian world and the nascent ethos of technological modernity. To recognize this tension in Descartes is to see in the tree metaphor a concern for moral ends as much as for the means to these ends. I argue that the ends depicted in this metaphor are located at the *roots*. Descartes never speaks explicitly of ends when he speaks of metaphysics, which is represented by the roots in this metaphor; instead, he characterizes metaphysics as epistemology—as the study of God, the self, and clear and distinct insight generally. But when he says that philosophy is needed to regulate our conduct, he invites us to think of the search for wisdom as more than the search for the cognitive underpinnings of science. He himself seems to be concerned, if only confusedly, with the underlying moral context in which science and technological mastery find their motivation. Where is human reflection to arrive at an understanding of this context, if not in its contemplation of the soul and the soul's relation to God?

This question pushes one in the direction of seeking the origin of moral principles in the clear and distinct ideas that constitute the subject matter of metaphysics in the tree metaphor. At first, this seems to be an odd and counterintuitive move, given that Descartes goes to some lengths to distinguish the clear and distinct insight that is relevant to questions of material truth and falsity from the sorts of normative considerations that bear upon questions of good and evil. When in the synopsis to the *Meditations* Descartes claims not "to deal at all with sin, i.e., the error which is committed in pursuing good and evil, but only with the error that occurs in distinguishing truth from falsehood" and purports not to be dealing with "matters pertaining to faith or the conduct of life, but simply [with] speculative truths, which are known solely by means of the natural light,"[42] he seems to grant the Platonic point that wrongdoing is a matter of error, but he also seems to want to make a distinction in kind between cognitive errors (i.e., errors committed in matters of material truth and falsity) and moral errors.

This might seem to recommend the conclusion that Descartes did not conceive of clear and distinct perception as containing a moral dimension. But this may not ultimately be the case, for Descartes added the distinction between sin and material falsity in the "Synopsis" only after having read Arnauld's objections to the

Meditations, in which Arnauld warns Descartes that "the comments that [Descartes] makes [in the Fourth Meditation] on the cause of error would give rise to the most serious objections if they were stretched out of context to cover the pursuit of good and evil. Hence it seems to me that prudence requires . . . that anything which is not relevant and which could give rise to controversy should be omitted."[43] Arnauld also admonishes Descartes to make it clear that "where he asserts that we should assent only to what we clearly and distinctly know, he is dealing solely with matters concerned with the sciences and intellectual contemplation, and not with matters belonging to faith and the conduct of life."[44] Descartes heeds this advice by inserting the passage cited above and by writing to Mersenne to "put the words between brackets so that it can be seen that they have been added."[45]

It is not entirely clear what Descartes is trying to say here. Near the end of the Fourth Meditation, he *equates* the problems of sin and material error when he says that "since the will is indifferent in such cases [namely, cases in which clear understanding is lacking], it easily turns aside from what is true and good, and this is the source of my error and sin."[46] In cases of conduct as in cases of scientific judgment, in other words, the clear insight of the intellect is needed to guide the will. This reading guides such commentators as Gueroult in the *par prétérition* interpretation of the origin of moral principles: Gueroult suggests that "natural light, along with natural instinct (both guaranteed by divine veracity), reveal to us immediately, without the least doubt, that our end is happiness in the present life." Gueroult appeals to two sources of the sense of good: the *lumen naturale* that is the source of all clear and distinct insight and "natural instinct," by which Gueroult seems to mean the natural proclivity of the body to contribute to our well-being. Descartes concludes the Sixth Meditation with some remarks about this proclivity. He suggests that while as composite beings we are not infallible, we may generally rely on the coordinated efforts of our senses, memory, and intellect to promote human welfare.[47]

On this reading of Descartes's statements in the "Synopsis," reason itself is the source of normativeness. But there is another possible meaning to Descartes's statements. Arnauld admonishes Descartes to add statements to avoid controversies that would arise if Descartes seemed to be allowing reason to encroach upon the proper domain of faith, so it is possible that Descartes added the statements on merely prudential grounds. This would leave open the question whether the Fourth Meditation view of the proper relationship between will and intellect ultimately has implications for matters of conduct. Only on a superficial reading of the "Synopsis" could a reader come away with the impression that the Fourth Meditation has no implications for the problem of conduct, for if this were really indicative of Descartes's true intentions, why would he instruct Mersenne to place the added statements in the "Synopsis" in brackets? To draw the reader's attention to the fact that the statements were added later is to lend the added statements the air of an afterthought.

But if this is the case, are we to suppose that Descartes considers the natural light of reason to be capable of giving rise to normative insights, as Gueroult proposes? Descartes is largely silent on this question, but there is reason to believe that Descartes does not place this sort of confidence in the power of human reason. Instead, it seems that while Descartes locates the origin of morality in the being of God, just as he has the origin of material truth, he stops short of arguing that our access to foundational moral principles is to be found in the natural light of reason. For Descartes, the origin of both morality and scientific truth lies in God's creative will; both taken together constitute the eternal truths. Keefe demonstrates the significance of the eternal truths for Descartes's moral ethos by proposing that for Descartes, the doctrine of God's creation of the eternal truths "must form the theoretical basis of Descartes's 'morale definitive,'" that God's original determination of the good is part of the eternal truths and that it is possible for human beings to *know* the good.[48] Descartes offers strong support for this idea in the Sixth Set of Replies, where he says that "there can be nothing whatsoever which does not depend on [God]. This applies not just to everything that subsists, but to all order, every law, and every reason for anything's being true or good."[49] Here, as in the Fourth Meditation, Descartes establishes a parallel between the true and the good: both follow from the creative will of God, and from the standpoint of human experience, there are *reasons* why true things are true and good things are good. Several years after writing the *Meditations*, Descartes writes to Elizabeth that "the right use of reason . . . by giving a true knowledge of the good, prevents virtue from being false."[50]

Keefe, however, argues that Descartes would not accept the conclusion that our knowledge of the good is a matter of clear and distinct perception; even though Descartes considers "the idea of 'le bien' [to be] innate in human beings," Keefe suggests that it is not through reason but rather through some other source of knowledge— "revelation perhaps?"—that we come to know the good.[51] I leave aside for a moment this explosive suggestion about revelation and consider why for Descartes our access to the eternal truths of morality cannot be through reason. Harry Frankfurt's work on the notion of clarity and distinctness is most illuminating in this connection: for Descartes, to assent to what is "clear and distinct" or "certain and indubitable" is to be in possession of a specific kind of *evidence*:

> When Descartes considers the aim of his undertaking [in the *Meditations*] and concludes that he must assent to nothing except the 'entirely certain and indubitable,' what is presumably in his mind is that a belief has these characteristics if and only if accepting it involves no risk—no chance at all that additional evidence will ever make it reasonable for him to abandon the belief. This much can be derived from the fact that his inquiry is committed to beliefs that are solid and permanent.[52]

Finding evidence of this kind is "essentially a matter of perceiving certain logical relationships"[53]—for example, the relationship between my perceiving now and my existing now. To say that the cogito is clear and distinct is to say that no evidence could be adduced at a later time that could undermine the logical relationship between my thinking (now) and my existing (now). "It is logically impossible for there to be an occasion on which a person considers the statement *sum* and on which the statement is false."[54] The rule of evidence presented early in the Third Meditation ("So I now seem to be able to lay it down as a general rule that whatever I perceive very clearly and distinctly is true")[55] is a generalization of the principle underlying the cogito to all perceptions that exhibit this logical force: "If this conviction is so firm that it is impossible for us ever to have any reason for doubting what we are convinced of, then there are no further questions for us to ask: we have everything that we could reasonably want."[56]

The fundamental limitations of this conception of evidence derive from the nature of the standpoint that must be occupied by the rational agent. That standpoint is one of detachment and objectification. Harries calls this standpoint that of the "angelically pure or transcendental 'I' whose 'vision' of the world would be objective and a-perspectival."[57] When we adopt such a standpoint, we seek to overcome the distorting influence of our finitude, of our situatedness in a particular time and a particular place; we seek a vantage point that is transcendental in the sense that it is valid for any rational agent in any place and at any time. This is the standpoint needed for establishing a universal *mathesis*. But when we detach ourselves from the concreteness of our experience in this manner, our ideas become "formal and empty."[58] As such, they tell us about the *form* of our experience, but they necessarily fall short of the full concreteness of reality.

I now relate the fundamental limitations of reason to the problem of perceiving the eternal truths of morality. Even though Descartes draws a parallel between scientific truth and moral truth, he also seems to respect a fundamental difference between the two, for he never proposes to derive the latter truths from the light of reason. To say that the truths of morality are given *par prétérition* does not really mean that reason simply takes them for granted, as Gueroult proposes; instead it means that reason cannot give these truths to itself but must rely on a source outside itself for them. The grounding truths of morality are not reducible to clear and distinct perception. But in acknowledging the need to appeal to a source of truth other than the natural light, Descartes admits that reason *lacks* autonomy. Where the "practical" side of the Cartesian ethos depends on the sheer autonomy of reason, human finitude has serious implications for the "angelic" side. In the concluding section of this chapter as well as in the next chapter, I show that Descartes's repeated appeals to the compatability of reason and Christian faith, his conception of the human being in terms of intellect and will, and the Christian roots of his metaphysical dualism all attest to the rootedness of the technological ethos in an angelic ethos in Descartes's thought.

But why, then, does the tree metaphor contain no explicit indication of the source of normative commitments? Why, if the basis of morality is to be found at the roots of the tree rather than at the topmost branch, does Descartes not include revelation in his characterization of the roots or at least try to situate the tree metaphor in the larger Christian context out of which his thought emerged? Ultimately this is a bit of a mystery, but there are indications in Descartes's writings of the answer that he would give. The most obvious reason why revelation has no place *in* the metaphor is that Descartes conceives of the illumination of faith to be fundamentally "obscure."[59] The truths of revelation "are beyond our understanding"[60] in the sense that their content gives us a glimpse of the infinity of God and hence is not reducible to clear and distinct insight. As such, these truths are different in kind from the truths of *scientia*, and hence they have no place in a metaphor that is designed to provide an outline of rational knowledge.[61]

And yet, as I show above, Descartes frames this metaphor not simply in terms of science but in terms of *wisdom*, and he expresses a concern for the task of proceeding with confidence in this life. The emphasis and focus on "this life," both in the tree metaphor and in Descartes's writings in general, show Descartes's devotion to the emerging practical ethos of early modernity. But Rodis-Lewis's appeal to two levels of morality makes it necessary to step back from the straightforward terms of this metaphor to question the deeper context of concerns out of which it emerges: if Descartes and the Christian tradition share a concern for the soul insofar as it is essentially distinct from the body, then a concern for supernatural beatitude must be recognized as the essential background of a metaphor whose terms express a concern for the substantial union of soul (mind) and body. If Descartes does not explicitly situate the metaphor against this background, it would seem to be because his interest in developing a view of earthly existence that can be compelling for skeptics and infidels demands that he not do so. In a number of places, including the dedicatory letter to the Sorbonne at the beginning of the *Meditations* and a letter to the Curators of Leiden University, Descartes declares such an intention.[62] It is common to dismiss statements like these on the grounds that they are simply intended to supplicate theological authorities—in the case of the dedicatory letter the dean and doctors of the theology faculty of the Sorbonne and in the case of the letter to the Leiden Curators a body presiding over a disputation in which Descartes's doctrines were challenged as atheistic. To dismiss these statements on these grounds is to reject too hastily the proposition that Descartes's practical project is grounded in a more traditional one, and, as I argue in chapter 3, it is to be left with a conception of Descartes's practical intentions that is incoherent as an account of the ultimate source of meaning and value in Descartes's thought.

The absence of any appeal in the tree metaphor to a source of truth other than the natural light is not, then, a confirmation of Descartes's dismissal of such modes of illumination as faith and his invocation of moral ends *par prétérition*. Seen in the light of a Christian ethos and Rodis-Lewis's appeal to a level of morality deeper than the earthly, the metaphor refers beyond itself to what Heidegger would call the soil in which the roots of the tree take hold. Although Heidegger's concern is not the rootedness of Descartes's tree metaphor in the soil of Christianity, his reflection on the terms of the tree metaphor and the limits of Cartesian metaphysics is nonetheless instructive:

> In what soil do the roots of the tree of philosophy find their support? Out of what ground do the roots, and through them the entire tree, receive their nourishing juices and strength? What element, concealed in the ground and soil, permeates the roots which support and nourish the tree? In what does metaphysics stand and move? What is metaphysics, viewed from its ground? What fundamentally is metaphysics in general?[63]

Are we to suppose that Descartes considers metaphysics to be absolutely independent, that it is entirely presuppositionless? The more seriously we take the proposition that Descartes's ethos is, in important part, a Christian ethos, the more plausible it becomes to see the "soil" in terms of divine grace. To do this is to begin to appreciate Descartes's debt particularly to Saint Augustine and Saint Thomas Aquinas, both of whom are committed to the primacy of revelation over reason and to the ultimate dependence of reason on revelation. Notwithstanding Descartes's implicit (and sometimes explicit) criticisms of Saint Augustine and Saint Thomas, I argue in chapters 3 and 4 that neither the conception of "the sovereign good" that he develops in the mid- to late 1640s nor his program for the mastery of nature can be understood adequately without reference to the rootedness of his thinking in a deeper sense of morality that is ultimately inseparable from Christian tradition.

The guiding thread for an exploration of Descartes's underlying sense of moral existence must be, then, his ideal of a definitive morality, even if this ideal is expressed only in a vague and seemingly incoherent set of traces. Poised as it is between medieval piety and the rationalism of the Enlightenment, this ideal is an intermediate stage between Thomism and Kantian deontology. According to this ideal, God is the measure of goodness, and yet at the same time this ideal supports the self-sufficiency of human reason and drives a wedge between reason and revelation. But in the end, Descartes is at odds with Kant's goal of "religion within the limits of reason alone." Descartes's repeated invocations of God as the measure for conduct, and his implicit acknowledgment of the inability of clear and distinct insight to ground morality, underscore the extent to which, for his practical ethos, Descartes has recourse to the angelic. The practical ideal of the mastery of nature generally and the human body in particular has both its source and its measure in the ideal of recognizing and striving to live in accordance with the perfection of God, even if in the end this must remain what Kant calls a "regulative" ideal.

3. THE PROVISIONAL MORALITY

Descartes's appeal to the provisional morality of the *Discourse on Method* is best understood against the background of this regulative ideal. The temporary and ultimately inadequate character of the provisional morality is most evident in a consideration of the "three or four maxims" presented by Descartes in Part 3 of the *Discourse*. Prior to examining these maxims, I consider the source or origin of the provisional morality: Is this morality derived from reason, perhaps from the method itself? If not, then on what basis does Descartes arrive at the provisional morality, and what kind of authority can it have? One must treat with caution Descartes's suggestion in the synopsis preceding the *Discourse* that the rules of the provisional morality are "derived from [the] method."[64] The fulcrum of the rules of method is the idea of breaking problems down into their "simple" constituents, where simplicity is understood in terms of the idea of evidence.[65] Hence the rules of method invoke the notion of logical connection developed by Harry Frankfurt, and they recall Descartes's appeal to simple natures (*"naturas puras & simplices"*) in the *Rules for the Direction of the Mind*, those "certain primary seeds of truth naturally implanted in human minds" that guarantee truth because it is impossible for them to be false.[66] As I show below, there is no way that provisional rules such as respecting the religion that prevails in my country can be derived from such a logical conception of simplicity. The provisional morality is not "derived" from the method in the sense of formal logical derivation but instead functions as what Pierre Mesnard, following Lévy-Bruhl, aptly characterizes as "part of a dialectical construction that is solidly united with [Descartes's] system." The connection is not one of logical entailment; instead,

> the provisional morality responds to an absolute necessity: if the doubt were rigorously universal, it would reach to every aspect of our activity; and given the vicissitudes of practical life, it would imperil our intellectual activity by paralyzing the object of our meditations, namely 'the search for truth'. Without the provisional morality, this work itself is compromised.[67]

The provisional morality, particularly the fourth maxim, is needed "to prevent the method from devouring itself," that is, in the absence of a set of provisional rules that facilitate the ongoing activity of life while the foundations of knowledge are being reestablished, the rigorous application of the method would bring all activities of the investigator to a grinding halt. What is needed is a set of principles that, while grounded only in "sand and mud," can function temporarily to enable the investigator to address all possible contingencies in life.

The first of these principles is expressed in the first maxim of the provisional morality:

> The first was to obey the laws and customs of my country, holding constantly to the religion in which by God's grace I had been instructed from my childhood, and governing myself in all other

matters according to the most moderate and least extreme opinions—the opinions commonly accepted in practice by the most sensible of those with whom I should have to live. For I had begun at this time to count my own opinions as worthless, because I wished to submit them all to examination, and so I was sure I could do no better than follow those of the most sensible men. And although there may be men as sensible among the Persians or Chinese as among ourselves, I thought it would be most useful for me to be guided by those with whom I should have to live.[68]

Descartes then qualifies this maxim: Where different opinions are accepted equally, he will follow the "most moderate" of them; he will count "as excessive all promises by which we give up some of our freedom"; and he will strive "to make [his] judgments more and more perfect."[69]

The first principle of humanitarian common sense to which Descartes appeals is that of "conformism"[70] or "conservatism":[71] In the absence of clear, rationally informed criteria for independent choice, one does best to emulate the example of those members of one's community who appear to be the wisest and most experienced. This principle is at work throughout the history of Western thought, from Seneca's *De Vita Beata* to Ernst Tugendhat's contemporary work on communicative concensus.[72] To this extent, the principle of conformism appears to have become stabilized as part of the conventional wisdom of our humanitarian heritage, and as such a relatively stable structure, it holds the promise of providing provisional security to an investigator whose underlying moral commitments are at best unstable.

In this maxim more than in any other aspect of the provisional morality, the temporariness and inadequacy of that morality is unmistakable. Virtually everything in Descartes's writings on morality speaks against the prospect of a capitulation to moral relativism—think here first of Descartes's conception of the good as constituting part of the subject matter of the eternal truths—and yet moral relativism is precisely what the first maxim counsels.

Descartes articulates the provisional morality as the one that he himself follows. As a programmatic measure it takes on the following generalized form: One is to obey the laws and customs of one's country, follow one's inherited religion, and follow what appear to be the most moderate opinions. If the provisional morality of a Turkish Muslim should conflict with the provisional morality of a French Catholic, this is not a matter for individuals to address but rather, as Descartes's remarks elsewhere in the *Discourse* imply, is a problem to be left to princes.[73] The individual is entitled, indeed is charged, not to look outside the confines of his or her own cultural context when making choices with moral significance; the provisional morality produces moral choices with merely immanent, not transcendent, validity.

At the same time, the tension between practical and angelic ambitions in Descartes's thought manifests itself even here, in the first maxim of the provisional morality. The tension becomes evident when the first maxim is abstracted from the autobiographical to the general form. Descartes says that, in accordance with this maxim, he adhered to his inherited religion and that it was "by God's grace" that he was raised in one particular religion rather than in another. Now can the qualification "by God's grace" be coherently retained in the generalized form of the maxim? This would be to say that it is by God's grace that the Turks are raised as Muslims and the French as Catholics. Yet too much, both in Descartes's explicit pronouncements and in the Christian ethos that forms the background of his thought, speaks against such a possibility. Chief among these pronouncements is Descartes's statement in the Second Replies that "Turks and other infidels commit [a sin] by refusing to embrace the Christian religion," and in so refusing, these infidels manifest a "resistance to the impulses of divine grace within them."[74] Given the proposition that divine grace is that of a specifically *Christian* God, the first maxim of the provisional morality bears the trace of the ambivalence that is characteristic of Descartes's philosophical ethos: this maxim outwardly purports to

serve as a guideline for anyone who would embark upon an investigation into truth, and yet at the same time, it appears to anticipate
authentic enactment only by a Christian—even prior to the implementation of the method, the humanitarian background that motivates the provisional morality seems to distinguish the Christian
religion and ethos as preeminent. If "Persians or Chinese" are
directed by this maxim to follow their own inherited religion and
cultural values, the terms of Descartes's formulation of the maxim
subtly but unmistakably indicate the inferiority of these sources of
meaning. This maxim of the provisional morality is not devised in
a vacuum and is not simply a "humanitarian" measure but bears the
imprint of the Christian ethos that will guide the establishment of
its definitive replacement.

Implicit reliance on the Christian ethos, or at least on the
humanitarian background that I note above, is also evident in the
first maxim's appeal to the principle of moderation, the call to emulate the "most sensible" people, and the ideal of perfecting one's
judgment. Each of these aims presupposes a measure for judgment,
a set of preexisting values and a means available to the agent for
recognizing on the basis of those values what counts as "moderate,"
"sensible," or relatively "more perfect" under a given set of circumstances. Descartes takes these sorts of judgments to be relatively
unproblematic: he assumes that "commonly accepted" practices
tend to be the best ones to emulate, at least in the absence of a definitive morality; he takes it for granted that one can distinguish more
sensible opinions from less sensible ones, and he further assumes
that individuals have a natural ability to perfect their judgment with
regard to these matters. For all of these matters to be relatively
unproblematic, the agent must have at his or her disposal a prior
moral sense that serves as the basis for making all the relevant judgments. The terms of the first maxim give prominence to religion
and custom as the basis for making these sorts of judgments. Note
that while Descartes is extremely critical of "example and custom"
in the first two parts of the *Discourse*, he is not similarly critical of

religion. I wonder whether, particularly given his statements elsewhere to the effect that faith is beyond rational scrutiny, Descartes
sees Christian faith as the middle term that links the provisional and
definitive moralities.[75] The ideal of perfecting one's judgment presupposes orders of perfection and a measure for perfection, and
these notions are products of a medieval ethos according to which
God is *instar archetypi*, the archetype of perfection.[76] Moreover,
the premium that Descartes places on preserving one's freedom in
the formulation of the first maxim reflects the Augustinian roots of
his conception of human nature and its relation to the divine archetype of freedom.

If fundamental features of the Christian ethos form part of the
basis of the first maxim of the provisional morality, the second
maxim does not seem to be dependent on that ethos. The second
maxim "was to be as firm and decisive in my actions as I could, and
to follow even the most doubtful opinions, once I had adopted
them, with no less constancy than if they had been quite certain."[77]
This maxim, Gilson notes, is an "empirical technique" that we must
employ until theoretical certainty replaces our merely practical resolution.[78] Descartes gives the example of seeking one's way out of
a forest when one is completely lost: the best course of action is
neither to stand where one finds oneself nor to wander about aim-
lessly but rather to "keep walking as straight as [one] can, in one
direction, never changing it for slight reasons even if mere chance
made him choose it in the first place."[79] Descartes offers this as a
metaphor for the need to accept the "most probable" opinions
"when it is not in our power to discern the truest" ones.[80] But given
that the notion of probability properly pertains not to matters of ethical choice but rather to matters of material truth and falsity, the
sense of probability here cannot be a straightforwardly quantitative
one; instead it seems to signify a qualitative sense of likelihood, as
when we suppose that the expert in a given matter is "probably"
right and the comparative amateur is "probably" wrong.[81] This
returns us to the first maxim: The most probable opinions are pre-

sumably those held by what appear to be the wisest and most experienced members of one's community or by those members of the community whose opinions are most commonly accepted. It is hard to understand the sense of probability here in any other way, for if I choose one of a number of alternatives in a given set of circumstances, and I have no idea which is truly preferable, it does not make sense to suppose that the alternative I have chosen is more probably true than the others, even though I must *treat* it as if it is.

This, however, is not to recommend any sort of "irrational decisionism" or "unbridled practical irrationalism"; instead it is to "secure a minimum of rationality in a situation in which the interconnections between means and ends remain opaque" and in which action is preferable to inaction.[82] The kind of situation that Descartes has in mind is that in which inaction or indecisiveness poses a positive threat to our well-being, and while the angelic ideal requires theoretical certainty as the basis for choice, for what Röd calls "objectively correct action," the provisional morality offers the best substitute possible in the absence of such certainty.[83]

In his example of being lost in a forest, Descartes places emphasis on making decisions in conditions of more or less utter ignorance. But in a letter written shortly after the publication of the *Discourse*, he qualifies the principle of resoluteness by linking it to the first maxim's principle of perfecting our judgment. This principle does not mean that one should stubbornly adhere to one's initial decision in spite of new information that provides a basis for changing one's mind. Rather, one should adhere to one's initial decision only so long as "there are no others that one judges better or more certain"; by following such a principle, one is able to avoid "moral chaos."[84] If I am lost in the forest and initially have no idea which way I should walk, I may start out by arbitrarily picking a direction, but if while walking in that direction I gain information that appears to be relevant to my choice of a direction—say, the sounds of automobile traffic off to my left—it would be reasonable to alter my course in the direction of the traffic sounds, even though this change of direction might turn out to be a mistake. It is not the case that provisional resoluteness involves no appeal to rational criteria but only that it lacks rational *certainty*. There may be all sorts of considerations that could give me reason to change my direction—traffic sounds, the sight of familiar terrain, the spotting of trail markers left by other hikers—that would give me reason to alter my course, even though none of these considerations grant me absolute certainty. The second maxim entitles me "to change my opinions as soon as I can find better, and to lose no opportunity of looking for them." The ideal here is one of decisiveness as a virtue that lies in a mean "between its two contrary vices, indecision and obstinacy."[85] It prevents doubt from paralyzing the will in exigent circumstances, "since in everyday life we must often act without delay."

The demand for resoluteness in moral choice is a feature shared in common by the provisional and definitive moralities. The difference is that in the provisional morality, my resoluteness is not grounded in reason, whereas in the definitive, it is; only definitive sorts of resolutions are not subject to revision because they are grounded in knowledge of the truth. Descartes does not make this distinction entirely clear in the *Discourse*, but he later does so in correspondence and in *The Passions of the Soul*. In a letter written to Elizabeth in 1645, Descartes presents a set of moral maxims almost identical to those in the *Discourse*. Descartes says that "each person can make himself content by himself without any external assistance, provided he respects three conditions, which are related to the three rules of morality which I put forward in the *Discourse on the Method*." These three conditions are using the mind well "to discover what [one] should or should not do in all the circumstances of life," having "a firm and constant resolution to carry out whatever reason recommends without being diverted by [one's] passions," and divesting oneself of desires for goods that are outside our power.[86] What Descartes envisions here is an ideal according to which reason has been perfected to the point that morality is no longer beset by error: "The right use of reason . . . by giving a true knowledge of the good, prevents virtue from being false."[87] This is the most conspicuous sign of a difference between the provisional morality and the moral maxims presented in the letter to Elizabeth; to "discover what [one] should or should not do in all the circumstances of life," one ultimately needs true knowledge of the good, that one crucial possession that by definition is missing from the provisional morality. Descartes acknowledges in this letter that it is "not necessary that our reason should be free from error; it is sufficient if our conscience testifies that we have never lacked resolution and virtue to carry out whatever we have judged the best course."[88] This, however, does not undermine the appeal to true knowledge of the good as the basis for optimal moral choice; instead it is simply an acknowledgment that we are not always able to make such optimal choices, but we must often make choices under circumstances of imperfect knowledge.

The same acknowledgment is present in the *Passions*, along with a commitment to the ideal of true knowledge as the proper guide for human choice. We are told there, in a passage that recalls the example of the person lost in a forest, that if we know two possible routes to our destination, "reason insists that we choose the route which is usually the safer, and our desire in this case must be fulfilled when we have followed this route, whatever evil may befall us"—in other words, even if we choose wrongly, we may be satisfied with the knowledge that we made the best choice possible given our lack of certain knowledge about which would in fact *be* the safest route.[89] But we are also told that desire cannot be bad "when it proceeds from true knowledge" and that there is "a great difference between the resolutions that proceed from some false opinion and those that are based solely on knowledge of the truth. For, anyone who follows the truth is assured of never regretting or repenting, whereas we always regret having followed the former when we discover our error."[90] The regulative ideal for action is resolute choice informed by theoretical certainty, and while it will often be the case under particular circumstances that this ideal cannot be realized, Descartes never so much as hints that the angelic ideal of objectively correct action should ever be abandoned.

The third maxim of the provisional morality reflects what has long been considered to be a Stoic undertone in Descartes's moral thinking. That maxim is

> to try always to master myself rather than fortune, and change my desires rather than the order of the world. In general I would become accustomed to believing that nothing lies entirely within our power except our thoughts, so that after doing our best in dealing with matters external to us, whatever we fail to achieve is absolutely impossible so far as we are concerned.[91]

The implicit call to divest oneself of desires for objects that are not within one's power "is of a manifestly Stoic origin,"[92] but to see Descartes's intention here as straightforwardly Stoic is to overlook the larger context of the provisional morality and of the *Discourse*, both of which place emphasis on the end of human happiness.[93] Whereas the Stoics counsel the suppression of desire through *ataraxia*, it is in this maxim that Descartes first gestures toward the program for *regulating* desire or the passions that is his central preoccupation in *The Passions of the Soul*.

In this maxim, Descartes suggests that contentment depends on preventing oneself "from desiring in future something that [one] could not get . . . if we consider all external goods as equally beyond our power, we shall not regret the absence of goods which seem to be our birthright when we are deprived of them through no fault of our own, any more than we regret not possessing the kingdom of China or of Mexico."[94] In contrast with his statements in Part 1 of the *Discourse*, in which he disparages the morality of the Stoics,[95] Descartes here lauds the Stoics' ability "to escape from the dominion of fortune" by accustoming themselves to believing "that nothing was in their power but their thoughts."[96]

At face value this would seem to counsel Stoic resignation, but

Descartes distances himself from such an interpretation in the same letter in which he clarifies his notion of provisional resoluteness. He says that

> I did not mean that external things were not at all in our power, but that they are in our power only in so far as they can be affected by our thoughts, and not *absolutely* or *entirely* in our power because there are other powers outside us which can frustrate our designs. . . . Nothing exterior, then, is in our power except in so far as it is at the command of our soul, and nothing is absolutely in our power except our thoughts.[97]

If there appears to be a subtle sense of resignation or quietism in the third maxim, this is only because the will does not yet enjoy the secure guidance of the intellect at the time when the provisional morality is first enacted; like the principle of resoluteness, this principle will undergo a transformation once action has been theoretically grounded. In the absence of this theoretical grounding, the goal of contentment would seem to push very far in the direction of quietism because the chance of acquiring the external goods that we desire is small; the less our will enjoys the foundation of theoretical knowledge, the less control we have over our surroundings. Conversely, once the necessary theoretical grounding has been adduced, even if we may not reasonably expect total control of our surroundings we are nonetheless entitled to a much greater sense of confidence about the prospects for success in our practical endeavors. Our knowledge will make our will more efficacious by revealing to us the means for practical control over the goods of the external world; it is in this sense that external things will be in our power "in so far as they can be affected by our thoughts."

This maxim "invites us to discover the limits within which our true power extends itself, the kingdom over which our liberty can reign sovereign."[98] It both affirms our power and recognizes that this power is circumscribed within limits. If we abandon those objects of desire, those external goods in the world that lie outside our power, we can avoid the unhappiness and regret that come with the frustration of desire. To abandon such objects of desire is to turn inward to the freedom that makes us like God; in Kantian terms, it is to follow the path that "leads from the heteronomy of desires to the true autonomy of the will" and to the happiness to which the proper use of our freedom entitles us.[99] The moment of Stoic resignation in the provisional morality is counterbalanced by an affirmation of human liberty. It is the proper function of this liberty to undertake a regrounding of the sciences, to deploy scientific knowledge in the service of human welfare, and thereby to render human beings "the masters and possessors of nature."

If the place made for happiness in the third maxim is primarily negative, in the sense that the means to its attainment are characterized there primarily in terms of the suspension of the will, the positive sense of happiness anticipated in the third maxim is made quite concrete in the fourth and concluding maxim of the provisional morality. That maxim requires us "to review the various occupations which men have in this life, in order to try to choose the best."[100] In Descartes's own case, the best occupation is to "devote [his] whole life to cultivating [his] reason and advancing as far as [he] could in the knowledge of the truth."

Descartes equivocates as to whether this principle is a full-fledged maxim of the provisional morality. At the beginning of Part 3 of the *Discourse*, he says that this morality consists of "just three or four maxims." In his August 4, 1645, letter to Elizabeth, in which he presents an apparent reformulation of the provisional morality, he says that he had presented "three rules of morality" in the *Discourse*, and the reformulation that he presents in that letter outwardly appears to exclude the principle of the best occupation.[101] This has led some commentators to conclude that the principle of the best occupation is not a maxim of the provisional morality; Henri Gouhier, for example, proposes that Descartes is simply mixing his "personal itinerary" together with general principles here, and the latter have "universal import" whereas the former does not.[102] Seen in the light of the humanitarian ideals that form the background of the *Discourse* and its moral code, however, the principle of the best occupation is not so easily dismissed as Descartes's merely "personal itinerary," for it recalls the medieval Christian ideal of a vocation, of being "called" to one's proper place in the larger cosmic scheme of things. It is fully in keeping with the Christian ethos that forms the background of Descartes's thought that he would include this fourth maxim in the provisional morality. As Hamelin observes, "if the fourth [maxim] is no longer explicitly set forth [in the 1645 version of the provisional morality], its substance is retained."[103]

The key to the essence of this principle is to distinguish its general formulation from Descartes's personal enactment of it. Gouhier is right to suggest that Descartes conflates these two matters when he presents the principle; immediately after suggesting that one should choose the best occupation in life, Descartes presents compelling reasons for having devoted his life to the pursuit of truth. The force of these reasons is familiar to any reader of Descartes, indeed to such an extent that it is difficult upon reading Descartes to escape the sense that a life spent in the pursuit of truth would be an estimable vocation for *any* human being. And while in principle this might be the case, there are all sorts of reasons why in practice this would be an unreasonable expectation. Descartes says in Part 1 of the *Discourse* that "if any purely human occupation has solid worth and importance, it is the one I have chosen,"[104] but at the same time he is keenly aware that a panoply of exigencies in life "tolerate no delay" and that earthly existence is not really imaginable in the absence of civic leaders, soldiers, doctors, teachers, clergy, and the like. To suggest that the "worth and importance" of one occupation is preeminent is not to suggest that everyone should pursue that occupation to the exclusion of all others. Even Martin Luther, in proclaiming that all human beings are members of the spiritual estate, had to recognize the need for different people to occupy different "offices."

4. DESCARTES'S CONCEPTION OF THE GOOD: BETWEEN THOMISM AND DEONTOLOGY

The principle of the best occupation ties together the first three maxims by pointing toward the goal shared in common by the provisional and the definitive moralities: virtuous conduct accompanied by happiness or contentment. The two moralities differ not in terms of their respective conceptions of the highest good but rather only in terms of the demands or standards that each imposes on human beings. Where the provisional morality provides only comparatively modest guidelines for moral conduct due to its lack of a foundation in theoretical certainty, it anticipates a time when it will be superceded by a theoretically grounded morality that promises to provide us with complete assurance in the conduct of life.

But as I suggest above, Descartes never seems entirely comfortable with the idea of reducing the good to indubitable insight. He sometimes alludes to the possibility of treating the good as something that can be "clearly known."[105] And even though he states in the "Synopsis" of the *Meditations* that he does not deal in the Fourth Meditation with "sin, i.e., the error which is committed in pursuing good and evil, but only with the error that occurs in distinguishing truth from falsehood," he nonetheless in the Fourth Meditation draws a direct parallel between truth and goodness and between error and sin.[106] But at the same time, in the *Discourse* he explicitly sets aside the maxims of the provisional morality, "together with the truths of faith," as standing outside rational scrutiny.[107] And in the Fourth Replies he emphasizes the irreducibility of matters of faith and conduct to the rule of evidence.[108] The ambivalence of Descartes's approach to morality is focused clearly in the confrontation between these two sorts of statements. It must be the case either that moral choices are not really grounded in the intellect at all or that they are grounded in insights of the intellect in such a way that they are nonetheless excluded from the terms of the method.

Descartes is simply not clear as to which of these possibilities he would like to advocate. In either case, Descartes's acknowledgment of the nature and limits of cognition points toward the need to locate the basis for a reflection on ends in some *extra*rational source of value. For Descartes, that source, as I argue at length in chapter 2, is Christian faith. Descartes does not write a great deal about the relationship between faith and reason, but he writes enough to invite a comparison with Aquinas, who argues for the fundamental reliance of intellect on the illumination provided by faith. If in important respects Descartes seeks to distance himself from Aquinas's conception of the relationship between reason and revelation—significantly, Descartes refuses to treat theology as a science—it appears that the Thomistic conception of this relationship figures significantly in the Christian background that contributes to the formation of the Cartesian ethos.

But at the same time, the clear move in the direction of the self-sufficiency of reason, which has always been considered the hallmark of the Cartesian ethos, stands in a fundamental tension with this Christian background. In his many statements to the effect that moral choice is to be grounded in "firm and determinate judgments bearing upon the knowledge of good and evil," Descartes seems to want to say that it should be possible to derive such judgments from reason alone, even though the resources of reason as Descartes conceives of them appear to be incapable of serving in this capacity. Descartes is not at the point of seeking to establish "religion within the limits of reason alone," though he clearly *anticipates* Kant's move to the sheer autonomy of pure practical reason and the reduction of God to a regulative postulate. In the remainder of this chapter, I argue that Descartes's conception of the sovereign good places him midway between Thomistic piety and Kantian deontology.

The significance of the Thomistic background centers on Aquinas's belief that while reason and faith are mutually compatible modes of access to the truth, there are fundamental limits to reason that faith can and must exceed if human beings are to attain the vision of God that is necessary for beatitude. God is the source and the end (*telos*) of all things: "Now all things are ordered in various degrees of goodness to the one supreme good, which is the cause of all goodness; and so, since good has the nature of an end, all things are ordered under God as preceding ends under the last end. Therefore God must be the end of all."[109] Things in general "reach this end in so far as they have some share of likeness to Him," and the intellectual being in particular "attains to Him in a special way, namely, through its proper operation, by understanding Him."[110] The ultimate happiness or supernatural beatitude of human beings depends on such an understanding of God: "Final perfect happiness (*beatitudo*) can only come from the vision of the divine essence."[111] Moreover, our entire sense of good and evil is determined by the way in which we are ordered or referred to God: "All that man is, and can, and has, must be referred to God; and therefore every act of man, whether good or bad, acquires merit or demerit in the sight of God from the fact of the act itself."[112] Our earthly existence and conduct are referred to the divine measure, just as are our prospects for eternal salvation.[113]

The dual ends of supernatural and earthly happiness thus devolve upon the question of how we are to attain to a vision of God. For Aquinas, both ends require an appeal to revelation and divine grace. Reason is capable of making a contribution to our understanding of God, but reason has fundamental limits that make the apprehension of the divine essence inaccessible to it except by virtue of divine grace. The human intellect is capable of knowing the sorts of essences whose presence is found in material things, but "a created intellect cannot see the essence of God unless God by His grace unites Himself to the created intellect, as an object made intelligible to it"; "it is necessary that some supernatural disposition should be added to the intellect in order that it may be raised up to such a great height" that it becomes capable of seeing an essence that exceeds its own nature.[114] "It is necessary for man to receive by faith not only those things which are above reason, but also those which can be known by reason."[115] The illumination of faith roots our rational knowledge in a deeper certitude about the inner nature of things, and the objects of our faith "order us directly to eternal life."[116]

For Aquinas there is an inner compatibility between faith and reason such that these two modes of illumination cannot give conflicting insights, even though faith enjoys a fundamental priority over reason. "And even though the natural light of the human mind is inadequate to make known what is revealed by faith, nevertheless what is taught to us by faith cannot be contrary to what we are endowed with by nature. . . . So it is impossible that the contents of philosophy should be contrary to the contents of faith, but they fall short of them."[117] Philosophy necessarily falls short of the illumination of faith in this life because abstraction from our experience of material things has fundamental limitations in the attempt to attain to a vision of the immaterial God; hence, "we have a more perfect knowledge of God by grace than by natural reason."[118] Faith "follows the mode of divine realities themselves, so that they are apprehended in themselves"; faith thereby gives rise to the fundamental principles of a science of the divine, and reason proceeds "by drawing conclusions from [these] principles."[119] The objects of faith, and hence the "principles" of a science of theology, are twofold: "the secret of the Godhead, to see which is to possess happiness, and the mystery of Christ's incarnation."[120] To say that these objects are disclosed by faith and never by reason is to say that we should believe matters of faith "not because of human reasoning, but because of the divine authority."[121] This in turn means that our salvation depends on revelation and not simply on reason.[122] Because reason is limited to the contemplation of itself and of essences found in material things, the vision of the divine essence that is necessary for eternal life must be found in faith.[123]

This vision of the divine essence must remain an obscure regulative ideal for a soul united with a body. Even if earthly conduct must ultimately find its measure in the same essence the understanding of which is the cornertone of eternal salvation, the way in which we are related to that essence must be characterized somewhat differently with regard to earthly existence than with regard to eternal life. Just as in cases of faith generally we are to believe on the basis of "divine authority," so in the case of earthly conduct Aquinas appeals to a hierarchical model of *authority* according to which the faith of some takes a functional or practical priority over the faith of others and serves as the earthly guide or measure for judgments to be made about the nature of the divine and the nature of good and evil.

The conception of law developed by Aquinas in the *Summa Theologica* reflects this commitment to the notion of authority. Aquinas conceives of law as "something pertaining to reason," which "must needs concern itself with the order that is in beatitude" or "universal human happiness."[124] Human laws derive their authority from divine law by way of natural law; it is in this manner that human beings can develop laws that are in accord with the demands of divine justice and that bear the likeness of the certitude and veracity of the divine law.[125] Earthly administrators of the law are in effect executors of the divine plan.[126] If our eternal goal is supernatural beatitude in community with God, the end of earthly laws is "peace and virtue" in the community of human beings.[127]

Now with regard to the authority to promulgate earthly laws, Aquinas invokes a hierarchical model according to which the earthly lawgiver stands in a relationship to the rest of the citizenry that resembles the relationship that God has to his creatures.[128] In the *Summa Theologica*, Aquinas says that "he who is placed over a community is empowered to dispense from a human law that rests upon his authority"; and in *On Kingship*, he argues that both kings and church authorities possess this authority, although ultimately he gives primacy to the spiritual authority over the temporal.[129] Both derive their authority from God, and this means that they are dutybound to promote the common good as they understand it to have been revealed by God.

Because human beings differ in their ability to attain to a vision of the divine, they are not in an equal position to promulgate human laws or to regulate the conduct of human beings. Human laws are a matter of reason, but the divine law from which they are derived is a matter of grace. Therefore, the extent of an individual's ability to govern is directly proportional to the extent of that individual's participation in grace. Among human beings, the adequacy of one's vision of the divine varies with the degree of grace one enjoys, and since the extent of one's faith varies with the extent of grace one enjoys, and one's understanding of the principles of faith likewise varies with the extent of one's faith, it follows that different human beings do not understand the principles of faith equally.[130] In the administration of civil and ecclesiastical law, Aquinas envisions a hierarchy in which each of these forms of adminstration has just one leader—the monarch in the case of civil law, and the pope in the case of the church.[131]

A great deal of Aquinas's views of the relationship between reason and faith, as well as the nature and limits of each and the implications of these for earthly existence and moral choice, is of direct relevance to an understanding of the Christian ethos from which Descartes emerges. Some well-known deprecating remarks about Aquinas and a clear interest in departing from Aristotle and the Scholastic tradition give the impression that Descartes has little if anything in common with "the angelic doctor." But when Descartes's views concerning the basis of morality are considered against the background of Thomistic views, the nature and extent of Descartes's debt to Aquinas can be seen to be profound and unmistakable.

The most conspicuous signs of Descartes's debt to Aquinas are his conception of the relationship between faith and reason and his commitment to the primacy of faith over reason. Among Descartes's statements about the relationship between faith and reason, the most definitive is in a passage from the Second Replies:

For although it is said that our faith concerns matters which are obscure, the reasons for embracing the faith are not obscure but on the contrary are clearer than any natural light. We must distinguish between the subject-matter, or the thing itself which we assent to, and the formal reason which induces the will to give its assent: it is only in respect of the reason that transparent clarity is required. As for the subject-matter, no one has ever denied that it may be obscure—indeed obscurity itself. When I judge that obscurity must be removed from our conceptions to enable us to assent to them without any danger of going wrong, this very obscurity is the subject concerning which I form a clear judgment. It should be noted that the clarity or transparency which can induce our will to give its assent is of two kinds: the first comes from the natural light, while the second comes from divine grace. Now although it is commonly said that faith concerns matters which are obscure, this refers solely to the thing or subject-matter to which our faith relates; it does not imply that the formal reason which leads us to assent to matters of faith is obscure. On the contrary, this formal reason consists in a certain inner light which comes from God, and when we are supernaturally illumined by it we are confident that what is put forward for us to believe has been revealed by God himself.[132]

Seen against the background of Descartes's assertion in the *Discourse* that "the revealed truths which guide us [to heaven] are beyond our understanding," this statement ascribes a clear priority to faith over cognition.[133] In making this statement, Descartes is responding to Mersenne's objection that the Fourth Meditation remark assimilating sin to error seems to commit Descartes to the view that sin is to be avoided through an appeal to clear and distinct ideas; if one follows the righteous path by appealing to clear and distinct ideas, then "a Turk, or any other unbeliever, not only does not sin in refusing to embrace the Christian religion, but what is more, he sins if he does embrace it, since he does not possess clear and distinct knowledge of its truth."[134] Descartes's reply is entirely in line with Aquinas: reason can reinforce the insights disclosed by faith—and this in the Augustinian sense that "we know God through his creatures"—but reason cannot be expected to be the original source of insights into the subject matter that is of direct relevance to our beatitude. The truth disclosed in faith is obscure in principle, and this is why it exceeds the grasp of reason and is irreducible to clear and distinct insight.

Descartes's remarks about the infinity of God help to solidify this commitment and remind us of its Thomistic character:

> God cannot be taken in by the human mind, and I admit this, along with all theologians. Moreover, God cannot be distinctly known by those who look from a distance, as it were, and try to make their minds encompass his entirety all at once. This is the sense in which Saint Thomas says, in the passage quoted, that the knowledge of God is within us "in a somewhat confused manner."[135]

It is in the nature of a finite being's attempt to grasp the infinity of God that the ultimate object of our concern must remain obscure; even if we suppose that reason is capable of analyzing some elements of faith, it can never comprehend them in a way that would permit the reduction of the basis of morality to cognition.

Descartes writes to Hyperaspistes that his remarks in the Second Replies ascribe a clear priority to faith over reason, and he concludes his discussion of the provisional morality in the *Discourse* by excluding that morality and "the truths of faith, which have always been foremost among my beliefs," from subjection to the method.[136] Descartes is consistent throughout his writings in attributing this status to truths of faith. In the *Rules for the Direction of the Mind* (Rule Three), he calls revealed truths "more certain than any knowledge"; in the *Discourse on Method* (Part 1), he says that because "the revealed truths which guide us [to heaven] are beyond our understanding, I would not have dared submit them to my weak reasonings"; in the *Principles of Philosophy* (Part 1, art. 76), he says that "whatever God has revealed to us must be accepted as more certain than anything else."[137] The fundamental obscurity of objects of faith makes it easy to understand why Descartes *had* to exclude them from the method, and why, if only against the pointedly practical intentions in Descartes's thought, those intentions must have their ground and measure in a medieval view of the world from which the practically oriented Descartes was seeking to establish distance and independence. The sorts of insights that Descartes classifies as "simple" or "clear and distinct" in his writings show that the complexity of articles of faith makes them unsuitable as objects of the kind of abstraction that is characteristic of clear and evident insight; where the scientific modeling of the physical world can proceed on the basis of insights such as number, shape, extension, motion, and "I am, therefore God exists,"[138] that Descartes stops short of ever enumerating *moral* insights among simple and evident perceptions seems to be a sign of his recognition of the impossibility of reducing the moral content of revelation to logical evidence. On a number of occasions, he follows Aquinas in arguing that matters like the mystery of the Trinity are precisely irreducible to clear and distinct insight.[139]

Given these commitments, one cannot adequately characterize the overall moral standpoint advanced by Descartes as "the morality of an atheist."[140] Descartes prepares the way for the ascendancy of a technological ideal that dispenses entirely with recourse to revelation in human life, but he himself does not go that far. Maritain captures the status of Descartes's moral standpoint when he observes that "Descartes, doubtless unintentionally, but nevertheless effectively, is at the origin of the great movement by which reason is to break with the God of revealed faith and to abandon little by little the God of Metaphysics—in short, to withdraw from Him Who is."[141] Whether or not Maritain is right in suggesting that "Descartes was sincerely Catholic," it seems clear that Descartes's "fundamental principles will develop into a sheer enmity of reason against faith" through the confluence of Descartes's program for the mastery of nature with the Baconian spirit of the age.[142]

One of the most pressing questions motivating the present study is how Descartes's thought fits into the historical process of secularization. This question has been raised by a number of thinkers, but no systematic attempt has been made to answer it.[143] Descartes's commitment to the mastery of nature and the tendency in his thought to treat the earthly ends of man as ends in themselves are clear signs that Descartes is not simply an Augustinian or Thomist. He has made a decisive step in the direction of the Enlightenment ideal of the sheer autonomy of reason. But his appeal to God as the metaphysical basis for his scientific program and his recognition of the limits of reason as regards the grounding of value are clear signs that he is not yet at the point of completing the move from the transcencent to the transcendental that characterizes the thought of an Enlightenment thinker like Kant. For Descartes, it is still the case that "our mind is not the measure of reality or of truth."[144] And yet, in asserting the autonomy of reason, Descartes embarks upon a path that eventually leads to the complete divorce of reason from faith in a transcendent God. The fruits of this divorce are apparent in the thought of Kant: God is no longer the absolute measure for truth and goodness but instead has been relegated to the status of a postulate of pure practical reason, a regulative ideal for the conceptualization of our highest good and its acquisition. If we are to answer the question of Descartes's place and role in the historical process of secularization, we do best to begin by conceiving of Descartes's thought as a pivotal moment between Aquinas and Kant. Descartes serves as a bridge between the Christian orthodoxy of Aquinas and Kant's vision of deontology and "religion within the limits of reason alone."

The great distance that Kant establishes between his thought and that of Aquinas and Descartes is evident in a number of ways, particularly in Kant's subordination of the order of being to the order of knowing. In the first *Critique*, Kant begins to show the implications of this relativization for ethics when he criticizes Plato for having assumed that Ideas are "archetypes of the things themselves."[145] "On the contrary," Kant maintains, if anyone is held up as a pattern of virtue, the true original with which we compare the alleged pattern and by which alone we judge of its value is to be found only in our minds. This original is the idea of virtue . . . it is only by means of this idea that any judgment as to moral worth or its opposite is possible; and it therefore serves as the indispensable foundation for every approach to moral perfection—however the obstacles in human nature, to the degree of which there are no assignable limits, may keep us far removed from its complete achievement.[146]

In accordance with the terms of the transcendental turn, Kant sees finite human agents as incapable of deriving their ideas in any way from transcendent objects. Instead, at best we can engage in an illicit use of the pure concepts of the understanding, whereby we think the totality of an experience that is given to us as merely partial; to think this totality, we must give transcendent employment to concepts whose proper employment is merely immanent.[147] Hence for Kant, our finitude leaves us in a predicament: to give meaning and certitude to our moral reflections, we must think as a whole an experience that is given to us as necessarily partial or fragmented:

The absolute whole of all appearances—we might thus say—*is only an idea*; since we can never represent it in an image, it remains a *problem* to which there is no solution. But since, on the other hand, in the practical employment of understanding, our sole concern is with the carrying out of rules, the idea of practical reason can always be given actually *in concreto*, although only in part; it is, indeed, the indispensable condition of all practical employment of reason. The practice of it is always limited and defective, but is not confined within determinable boundaries, and is therefore always under the influence of the concept of an absolute completeness. The practical idea . . . must, as an original . . . serve as standard in all that bears on the practical.[148]

The idea of practical reason is indispensable for ethics, for the practical employment of reason, because it is only through that idea that we are able to think the totality that we never encounter in the realm of interest and inclination; we must transcend this realm if our actions are to become capable of taking on moral worth.

It is with an eye toward thinking a totality that cannot be known that transcendental Ideas of reason are to be employed. Kant sees the Ideas of freedom, God, and the immortality of the soul as corollaries or "postulates" of the pure practical reason that develops morality.[149] They are conceptual projections, fashioned out of pure concepts of the understanding in such a way as to enable us to represent to ourselves the possibility of attaining the highest good. Each of these projections seeks to supply the completeness that is fundamentally lacking in the world of sense. In the moral sphere, this completeness takes the form of a highest good for each individual understood as virtuous conduct together with happiness in proportion to the agent's worthiness to be happy.[150] But the principle of morality by itself is not sufficient for the representation of the possibility of acquiring this highest good. The Idea of freedom must be postulated to supplement the determinism of the physical; in the absence of the idea of freedom, morality would be impossible because we would be utterly subject to the determinism of causal laws.[151] The Idea of the immortality of the soul envisions "the perfect fit of the will to moral law," a fit "of which no rational being in the world of sense is at any time capable" because we are too inclined to succumb to selfish desires.[152] It is necessary to assume "an endless progress" in the conformity of our will to the moral law because in principle it would take an infinite amount of time to achieve such conformity.[153] And the Idea of God must be postulated because there is no necessary connection between virtue and reward; "there is not the slightest ground in the moral law for a necessary connection between the morality and proportionate happiness of a being who belongs to the world as one of its parts and is thus dependent on it."[154] There is no reason in the order of the material universe to suppose that virtuous people will be rewarded for their good conduct; yet, according to Kant, the wholeness of moral life makes a place for happiness, even though the prospect of happiness can never properly serve as the basis for a moral choice.[155]

That Kant's conception of the postulates is derived from Christian thought serves as a reminder of the historical process of secularization of which he is a part. He sees in Christianity the source of the insight that the moral perfection of our natures could not occur within one person's lifetime but would require "endless duration."[156] And he conceives of the highest good in terms of "the kingdom of God."[157] But in having reduced immortality and God to Ideas of reason, Kant radically transforms the meaning of religion. He does in effect what Descartes does not dare to do: he subjects morality to the rigors of method.

The conception of the highest good toward which Descartes gestures in his later correspondence more or less directly anticipates Kant's conception of the highest good as a confluence of virtue with happiness in proportion to one's worthiness to be happy. In a series of letters to Elizabeth, Descartes gives his clearest indications of a conception of the highest good in a series of reflections on Seneca's conception of the happy life. At first he proposes to embark upon a discussion of *De Vita Beata* with Elizabeth, but shortly thereafter he changes his mind and launches into a critique of Seneca for being "not sufficiently rigorous" and for being "unenlightened by faith, with only natural reason to guide him."[158] Descartes then sketches a general conception of virtue, happiness, and the relationship between the two. He accepts Seneca's view that "*vivere beate*, to live happily, is just to have a perfectly content and satisfied mind."[159] What remains to be determined is what it means for a life to be "happy." Both things within our power and things outside our power can contribute to our contentment; "virtue and wisdom" belong to the former class, and things like "honors, riches, and wealth" belong to the latter. It "would be a waste of time" to devote any concern to the latter, however, so Descartes confines his discussion of the acquisition of contentment to those things that are under our control. At this point, Descartes presents his so-called reformulation of the provisional morality. He proposes that the kind of contentment that is under our control can be attained if one employs "his mind as well as he can to discover what he should or should not do in all the circumstances of life," and if one remains resolute in his choices and divests himself of desires for objects that lie "entirely outside his power."[160]

A general picture of the highest good begins to emerge from these remarks. Descartes first distinguishes between virtue and happiness; he says that happiness is predicated upon two sorts of conditions, one being virtue and wisdom and the other being matters of fortune ("honours, riches, and health"). Even though for the purposes of his discussion with Elizabeth he dismisses the latter condition, he fully acknowledges, along with Aristotle, the influence that matters such as noble birth have on our prospects for happiness. His concern is not so much to deny the role played by matters of fortune in the happy life as to redirect our attention to matters of reason and will that are fully under our control, for he sees in this approach the prospect of minimizing (even the regulative ideal of fully eliminating) the prospect of regrets and remorse in life. Virtue is to be acquired by using our reason as well as we are able and by making resolute choices on the basis of what reason has recommended to us. Virtue itself "consists precisely in sticking firmly to this resolution"; once we have established the requisite sense of releasement toward objects of fortune, provided that "we always do whatever our reason tells us, even if events show us afterwards that we have gone wrong, we will never have any grounds for repentance, because it was not our own fault."[161]

To this extent, contentment does not depend on being right but only on our having used our judgment well and having resolutely followed the course of action recommended by our reason. In a subsequent letter, Descartes defines the "supreme good" not as this contentment but rather as "the final end or goal towards which our actions ought to tend"; contentment is a kind of reward, "the attraction which makes us seek the supreme good."[162] The final or highest

end is virtue, which Descartes now defines in a way that will characterize his writings on the highest good until the end of his life,
namely, as "a firm and constant will to bring about everything we
judge to be the best, and to use all the power of our intellect in
judging well."[163] Here it might seem as though Descartes is characterizing virtue as the highest good and the resulting contentment as
a subsidiary end, but this is not quite what he is after. He frames his
remarks about contentment and "the supreme good" by contrasting
his view with the views of the ancient pagans of whom he had been
critical in the *Discourse on Method*; in particular, he criticizes Zeno
for having made "virtue seem so severe and inimical to pleasure that
I think only depressed people, or those whose minds are entirely
detached from their bodies, could be counted among his adher-
ents."[164] These remarks are best understood in the light of the
Kantian notion of the highest good that they anticipate: if virtue and
happiness are not inimical, and if only somewhat pathological
people would consider these two ends to be opposed, then that view
is most adequate that makes room in life for both virtue and happiness. In treating happiness as a kind of reward attendant upon virtue,
Descartes gestures toward a conception of the highest good that in
broad outline is not far removed from Kant's.

But in a fundamental respect, Descartes's conception of the
highest good is rather at odds with Kant's. The entire question of the
meaning of the highest good now devolves upon the question of
how virtue is ultimately to be understood in Descartes. Much of
what Descartes writes to Elizabeth sounds as though he believes that
resoluteness and the well-intentioned use of reason are sufficient for
virtue; after all, even if we turn out to be wrong, we need have no
occasion for repentance if we did our best. But this gives only a partial picture of Descartes's views on virtue, for Descartes is not
entirely consistent in calling for nothing more than a good faith
effort on the part of our reason. Alongside those sorts of statements,
there are in his later writings repeated appeals to clear *knowledge* of
the good as the standard for virtuous conduct. In the August 4, 1645,

letter to Elizabeth, shortly after proposing that contentment depends not on judging correctly but only on "never [having] lacked resolution and virtue to carry out whatever we have judged to be the best course" and stating that contentment "in this life" depends entirely on "virtue by itself," Descartes notes that "virtue unenlightened by intellect can be false" and that "the right use of reason . . . by giving a true knowledge of the good, prevents virtue from being false." This "right use of reason," by enlightening the will with true knowledge of the good, secures "the greatest felicity of man."[165]

In these remarks, Descartes seems to commit himself to the following position: Contentment "in this life" can be secured by following the three rules of the so-called reformulation of the provisional morality, namely, by employing one's mind "as well as he can to discover what he should or should not do," by having "a firm and constant resolution" to act in accordance with what the mind thinks is right, and by confining our desires to objects in our power. We are virtuous in one sense (a practical or earthly one) if we do these things, even if we should turn out to have judged wrongly. Beyond this, there is a higher contentment, which Descartes refers to as "the greatest felicity of man"; that felicity or beatitude is to be attained not simply by following the three rules of practical conduct but by acting on the basis of a "true knowledge of the good." Descartes recognizes, in other words, that actually *doing* the right thing and doing it deliberately is better than deliberately *trying* to do the right thing but failing to do so. As a practical matter, he recognizes that it is unrealistic to demand that embodied human beings always succeed in doing the right thing, but as an ideal matter, he cannot deny that this remains the only adequate measure and regulative ideal for human conduct. That he characterizes the contentment that follows upon each of these sorts of virtue in different terms is an indication that he appeals at different times to two different conceptions of the highest good—one according to which we gain satisfaction in the knowledge that we did the best we could and the other according to which we gain the highest satisfaction from knowing that our best was the best possible. These two conceptions of virtue and contentment correspond to the practical and the angelic dimensions of Descartes's thinking.

Descartes adheres to this dual conception of virtue and contentment in his correspondence in the later 1640s and in *The Passions of the Soul*. The language of the *Passions* echoes the language of the August 4, 1645, letter to Elizabeth quite unmistakably and makes the angelic ideal a centerpiece of the doctrine of the *Passions*. In a number of places in the *Passions*, Descartes appeals to resoluteness as an essential feature of virtuous conduct. In article 49, he notes that "there is . . . a great difference between the resolutions which proceed from some false opinion and those which are based solely on knowledge of the truth. For, anyone who follows the latter is assured of never regretting or repenting, whereas we always regret having followed the former when we discover our error."[166] Here Descartes augments his view in the August 4, 1645, letter that one need not feel repentant if one should later discover that one had judged wrongly, but apart from this, his view is of a piece with the view expressed in that letter: it is not simply resoluteness but resoluteness guided by true knowledge that is the proper measure for our conduct. The resoluteness of the provisional morality will no longer suffice; what is needed is "firm and determinate judgments bearing upon the knowledge of good and evil, which the soul has resolved to follow in guiding its conduct."[167]

What keeps Descartes's conception of the highest good from being identical with Kant's is his recognition of the limits of reason and his angelic commitment to the dependence of reason on faith. In the 1645 series of letters to Elizabeth, Descartes criticizes Seneca's conceptions of wisdom and the supreme good for their "obscurity"; more importantly, Seneca rightly acknowledges that the order of things is "infallible and independent of our will," but his key failure lies in failing to employ "a Christian way of speaking," according to which "wisdom is submission to the will of God, and following it in all our actions."[168] Even though Descartes does not make an explicit appeal to faith here, the idea that God's will is the measure for our conduct is nonetheless a powerful and unmistakable invocation of the medieval formula according to which to speak truly is to repeat after God and according to which virtuous action is an *imitatio christi.*

Descartes clearly moves away from an orthodox Thomism and in the direction of what Gerold Prauss has so effectively characterized as the "practicism" of the modern age, its obsession with the technological mastery of nature.[169] And yet in Descartes this move to the practical is conditioned in an important way by the very tradition of Christianity from which he seeks to separate science and its practical application. To understand Descartes as a moral thinker is to acknowledge the fundamental tension between these two strains in his thought.

NOTES

1. René Descartes, *Conversation with Burman,* April 16, 1648, in *Oeuvres de Descartes,* ed. Charles Adam and Paul Tannery, 12 vols. (Paris: Vrin/C.N.R.S., 1964–76), 5.178; *The Philosophical Writings of Descartes,* trans. John Cottingham, Robert Stoothoff, Dugald Murdoch, and Anthony Kenny, 3 vols. (Cambridge: Cambridge University Press, 1984–1991), 3.352f. Subsequent references to *Oeuvres de Descartes* will be to "AT" plus volume and page number; references to *The Philosophical Writings of Descartes* will be to "CSM" plus volume and page number.

2. AT 6.22, CSM 1.122.

3. Descartes, *Discourse on Method,* Part 3, AT 6.22, CSM 1.122.

4. AT 6.11f., CSM 1.116.

5. AT 6.13f., CSM 1.117.

6. AT 6.4, CSM 1.113.

7. AT 6.17, CSM 1.119.

8. AT 6.8, CSM 1.115.

9. AT 6.9, CSM 1.115.

10. AT 6.10, CSM 1.10; AT 6.16, CSM 1.119.

11. AT 6.7, CSM 1.114.

12. AT 9B.15, CSM 1.186.

13. AT 9B.13, CSM 1.186 (translation altered).

14. AT 9B.3 f., CSM 1.180.

15. AT 9B.3, CSM 1.180.

16. AT 9B.5, CSM 1.181.

17. Ibid.

18. AT 9B.7, CSM 1.182.

19. AT 9B.9, CSM 1.183.

20. Descartes, Rule One, AT 10.361, CSM 1.10 (translation altered).

21. Descartes, Rule One, AT 10.360, CSM 1.9.

22. Descartes, Rule Two, AT 10.362, CSM 1.10.

23. Descartes, *Discourse*, Part 1, AT 6.10, CSM 1.115.

24. Étienne Gilson, *Discours de la Méthode: Texte et commentaire*, 5th ed. (Paris: Vrin, 1976), p. 147.

25. Ibid., p. 231; cf. Michèle Le Doeuff, *The Philosophical Imaginary*, trans. Colin Gordon (Stanford, CA: Stanford University Press, 1989), p. 62.

26. Descartes, *The Passions of the Soul*, art. 48, AT 11.367, CSM 1.347; see also arts. 49, 148, 153, 170.

27. Gilson, *Discours de la Méthode*, p. 231.

28. Martial Gueroult, *Descartes' Philosophy Interpreted According to the Order of Reasons*, trans. Roger Ariew, 2 vols. (Minneapolis: University of Minnesota Press, 1984–1985), 2.192.

29. Letter to Descartes, September 13, 1645, AT 4.289; René Descartes, *Descartes: His Moral Philosophy and Psychology*, trans. John J. Blom (New York: New York University Press, 1978), p. 149 (translation altered). Much of the key correspondence between Elizabeth and Descartes is reprinted in Descartes, *Correspondance avec Élisabeth et autres lettres*, ed. Jean-Marie Beyssade and Michelle Beyssade (Paris: Flammarion, 1989), pp. 63–237.

30. Descartes, letter to Elizabeth, October 6, 1645, AT 4.308, CSM 3.269. Descartes has included among these "truths" the "goodness of God, the immortality of our souls and the immensity of the universe," as well as the priority of the whole over the part and the consequent ideal of dwelling in a community (letter to Elizabeth, September 15, 1645, AT 4.292 f., CSM 3.266).

31. Gueroult, *Descartes's Philosophy Interpreted*, 2.206. This line of

reasoning is endorsed by a number of other commentators. See, for example, Klaus Hammacher's introduction to Descartes, *Die Leiden-schaften der Seele*, ed. and trans. Hammacher, German-French ed. (Hamburg: Meiner, 1984), p. xliv; M. H. Lefebvre, "De la morale provisoire a la générosité," in *Descartes*, Cahiers de Royamount, Philosophie no. 2 (Paris: Les Éditions de Minuit, 1957), p. 245.

32. AT 11.326, CSM 1.327 (translation altered).

33. See Gueroult, *Descartes's Philosophy Interpreted*, 2.179, 2.187.

34. See Jacques Maritain, *The Dream of Descartes Together with Some Other Essays*, trans. Mabelle L. Andison (New York: Philosophical Library, 1944), pp. 28, 183; Maritain, *Three Reformers: Luther—Descartes—Rousseau*, rev. ed. (New York: Scribner's Sons, 1929), p. 53 f.

35. Geneviève Rodis-Lewis, *La Morale de Descartes* (Paris: Presses universitaires de France, 1957), p. 27. The "matter of right" [*en droit*] to which Rodis-Lewis refers here is the priority that Descartes ascribes to sciences like physics and medicine over morality in the tree metaphor in the letter to Picot; there, in a statement to which I return below, Descartes says that the study of morality is to be the crowning achievement of human wisdom and that it presupposes a knowledge of all the other sciences (AT 9B.17, CSM 1.188).

36. AT 6.62, CSM 1.142 f. (translation altered).

37. Descartes, letter to Chanut, June 15, 1646, AT 4.441, CSM 3.289.

38. AT 9B.14, CSM 1.186 (translation altered).

39. Ibid.

40. Gueroult, *Descartes' Philosophy Interpreted*, 2.178 (translation altered).

41. Descartes, letter to Elizabeth, August 4, 1645, AT 4.263, CSM 3.257.

42. Descartes, "Synopsis of the Following Six Meditations," AT 7.15, CSM 2.11.

43. Descartes, Fourth Set of Objections, AT 7.215 f., CSM 2.151.

44. Ibid., AT 7.216, CSM 2.151 f.

45. Descartes, letter to Mersenne, March 18, 1641, AT 3.335, CSM 3.175.

46. Descartes, Fourth Meditation, AT 7.58, CSM 2.40 f.

47. AT 7.88–90, CSM 2.61 f.

48. T. Keefe, "Descartes's 'Morale Définitive' and the Autonomy of Ethics," *Romanic Review* 64 (1973): 91, 92, 90.

49. AT 7.435, CSM 2.293 f. Cf. AT 7.431 f., CSM 2.291.

50. Descartes, letter to Elizabeth, August 4, 1645, AT 4.267, CSM 3.258.

51. Keefe, "Descartes's 'Morale Définitive,'" p. 95 f. See also T. Keefe, "Descartes's 'Morale Provisoire': A Reconsideration," *French Studies* 26 (1972): 140.

52. Harry Frankfurt, *Demons, Dreamers, and Madmen: The Defense of Reason in Descartes's "Meditations"* (Indianapolis: Bobbs-Merrill, 1970), p. 26 f.

53. Ibid., p. 133; cf. p. 147.

54. Ibid., p. 105.

55. AT 7.35, CSM 2.24.

56. Descartes, Second Set of Replies, AT 7.144, CSM 2.103.

57. Karsten Harries, "Descartes, Perspective, and the Angelic Eye," *Yale French Studies* 49 (1973): 31.

58. Ibid., p. 39.

59. Descartes, Second Set of Replies, AT 7.148, CSM 2.105.

60. Descartes, *Discourse on Method*, Part 1, AT 6.8, CSM 1.114. Cf. letter to Hyperaspistes, August 1641, AT 3.426, CSM 3.191.

61. Cf. Gilson, *Discours de la Méthode*, p. 262: "Selon Descartes, le but de la religion, et de la théologie qui la formule, est de nous conduire au salut. . . . Par conséquent, la théologie et la foi concernent l'ordre pratique, dont nous savons qu'il n'exige pas nécessairement l'évidence de l'entendement et ne relève pas de la connaissance claire et distincte."

62. AT 7.3, CSM 2.4; AT 5.9, CSM 3.316 f.

63. Martin Heidegger, "Einleitung zu: 'Was ist Metaphysik?' Der Rückgang in den Grund der Metaphysik," in *Wegmarken*, 2d ed. (Frankfurt: Klostermann, 1978), p. 361; "Introduction to 'What is Metaphysics?'" in *Pathmarks*, ed. William McNeill (Cambridge: Cambridge University Press, 1998), p. 277 (translation altered).

64. "[T]irée de cette méthode" (AT 6.1, CSM 1.111).

65. The first rule requires "evident knowledge," and the third calls for the order of investigation to start "with the simplest and most easily known objects" (AT 6.18, CSM 1.120).

66. Descartes, Rule Three, AT 10.376, CSM 1.18; Rule Six, AT 10.383, CSM 1.22; Rule Eight, AT 10.399, CSM 1.32.

67. Pierre Mesnard, *Essai sur la morale de Descartes* (Paris: Boivin & Cie, 1936), p. 51. For an opposing view, according to which the provi-

sional morality is indeed derived from the method in a rigorous and direct sense, see Robert Cumming, "Descartes's Provisional Morality," *Review of Metaphysics* 9 (1955): 207–35.

68. AT 6.23, CSM 1.122.

69. AT 6.23 f., CSM 1.122 f.

70. Joseph Combès, *Le dessein de la sagesse Cartésienne* (Lyon/Paris: Emmanuel Vitte, 1960), p. 109; Wolfgang Röd, *Descartes: Die Genese des cartesianischen Rationalismus*, 2d ed. (Munich: C. H. Beck, 1982), p. 36.

71. Anthony Levi, *French Moralists: The Theory of the Passions 1585–1649* (Oxford: Clarendon, 1964), p. 291.

72. See Descartes, letter to Elizabeth, August 4, 1645, AT 4.272, CSM 3.259; Ernst Tugendhat, *Self-Consciousness and Self-Determination*, trans. Paul Stern (Cambridge, MA: MIT Press, 1986).

73. See *Discourse*, Part 6, AT 6.61, CSM 1.142.

74. Descartes, Author's Replies to the Second Set of Objections, AT 7.148, CSM 2.105 f.

75. See Descartes, *Conversation with Burman*, AT 5.176, CSM 3.350; Seventh Set of Objections with the Author's Replies, AT 7.46, CSM 2.321.

76. See Descartes, Third Meditation, AT 7.42, CSM 2.29.

77. AT 6.24, CSM 1.123.

78. "[U]n procédé empirique" (Gilson, *Discours de la Méthode*, p. 243).

79. AT 6.24, CSM 1.123.

80. AT 6.25, CSM 1.123.

81. Descartes explains the idea of moral certainty in the *Discourse on Method*, Part 5, AT 6.37 f., CSM 1.130; and in the *Principles of Philosophy*, Part 4, art. 205, AT 8A.327 f., CSM 1.289 f.

82. Röd, *Descartes: Die Genese des cartesianischen Rationalismus*, p. 38.

83. Ibid., p. 39.

84. Descartes, letter to Reneri for Pollot, April or May 1638, AT 2.35, CSM 3.97.

85. AT 2.35 f., CSM 3.97.

86. Descartes, letter to Elizabeth, August 4, 1645, AT 4.265 f., CSM 3.257 f. On the importance of resoluteness, see also *Passions of the Soul*, arts. 48, 49, 153, 170, and letter to Elizabeth, August 18, 1645, AT 4.277, CSM 3.262.

87. AT 4.267, CSM 3.258.

88. AT 4.266 f., CSM 3.258. This acknowledgment is of a piece with Descartes's concluding statement to the *Meditations*: "But since the pressure of things to be done does not always allow us to stop and make such a meticulous check, it must be admitted that in this human life we are often liable to make mistakes about particular things, and we must acknowledge the weakness of our nature" (AT 7.90, CSM 2.62).

89. Descartes, *Passions*, art. 146, AT 11.440, CSM 1.381.

90. Ibid., art. 141, AT 11.434, CSM 1.378; art. 49, AT 11.368, CSM 1.347.

91. AT 6.25, CSM 1.123.

92. Gilson, *Discours de la Méthode*, p. 248.

93. An excellent discussion of the relationship between the third maxim and Stoic thought is to be found in chap. 3 of John Marshall, *Descartes's Moral Theory* (Ithaca, NY: Cornell University Press, 1998).

94. AT 6.25 f., CSM 1.124.

95. AT 6.8, CSM 1.114.

96. AT 6.26, CSM 1.124.

97. Descartes, letter to Reneri for Pollot, April or May 1638, AT 2.36 f., CSM 3.97 f.

98. Combès, *Le dessein de la sagesse Cartésienne*, p. 113.

99. Ibid., p. 116.

100. AT 6.27, CSM 1.124.

101. AT 4.265 f., CSM 3.257 f.

102. Henri Gouhier, *Essais sur Descartes* (Paris: Vrin, 1937), p. 245.

103. O. Hamelin, *Le Système de Descartes*, 2d ed. (Paris: Alcan, 1921), p. 378.

104. AT 6.3, CSM 1.112.

105. Descartes, Replies to the Second Set of Objections, AT 7.166, CSM 2.117.

106. AT 7.15, CSM 2.11; AT 7.58, CSM 2.41.

107. AT 6.27, CSM 1.124; see also Seventh Set of Objections with Replies, AT 7.476, CSM 2.321.

108. AT 7.248, CSM 2.172.

109. Saint Thomas Aquinas, *Summa Contra Gentiles* 3, in *Basic Writings of St. Thomas Aquinas*, ed. Anton C. Pegis, 2 vols. (Indianapolis/Cambridge: Hackett, 1997), chap. 17, 2.27.

110. Ibid., chap. 25, 2.43.

111. Aquinas, *Summa Theologica* 1–2, q. 3, art. 8, in *St. Thomas Aquinas on Politics and Ethics*, trans. Paul E. Sigmund (New York: Norton, 1988), p. 42.

112. Ibid., q. 21, art. 4, in *Basic Writings*, 2.365.

113. Ibid., q. 5.

114. Aquinas, *Summa Theologica* 1, q. 12, art. 4, in *Basic Writings*, 1.97; *Summa Theologica* q. 12, art. 5, 1.98. Cf. *Summa Theologica* 1–2, q. 3, art. 8; *Summa Theologica* 1–2, q. 5, art. 3; and *Summa Contra Gentiles* 1, chap. 3.

115. Aquinas, *Summa Theologica* 2–2, q. 2, art. 4, in *Basic Writings*, 2.1079.

116. Ibid., q. 1, art. 6, 2.1064.

117. Saint Thomas Aquinas, *Exposition of the "De Trinitate" of Boethius*, q. 2, art. 3, in *On Faith and Reason*, ed. Stephen F. Brown (Indianapolis/Cambridge: Hackett, 1999), p. 36 f. See also *Summa Contra Gentiles* 1, chaps. 1, 2, 7, 9.

118. Aquinas, *Summa Theologica* 1, q. 12, art. 13, in *Basic Writings*, 1.110.

119. Aquinas, *Exposition of the "De Trinitate"*, q. 2, art. 2, in *On Faith and Reason*, p. 31. See also *Summa Theologica* 1, q. 1, art. 7, and *Summa Contra Gentiles* 2, chap. 1.

120. Aquinas, *Summa Theologica* 2–2, q. 1, art. 8, in *Basic Writings*, 2.1068.

121. Ibid., q. 2, art. 10, 2.1089.

122. Aquinas, *Summa Theologica* 1, q. 1, art. 1, in *Basic Writings*, 1.6.

123. See Saint Thomas Aquinas, *Quaestiones disputatae de veritate*, q. 14, arts. 9 and 10, in *Truth*, trans. Robert W. Mulligan, James V. Mc-Glynn, and Robert W. Schmidt, 3 vols. (Indianapolis: Hackett, 1995), 2.250f., 2.254f.

124. Aquinas, *Summa Theologica* 1–2, q. 90, art. 1 and 2, in *Basic Writings*, 2.743 f.

125. Ibid., q. 91, arts. 3 and 4, 2.751–55. Here it seems appropriate to speak first of all of the veracity rather than of the goodness of the divine law, inasmuch as in the absolute order of things the true precedes the good. See Aquinas, *de Veritate*, q. 21, art. 3, in *Truth*, 3.14.

126. Aquinas, *Summa Theologica* 1–2, q. 93, art. 3, in *Basic Writings*, 2.766.

127. Ibid., q. 95, art. 1, 2.783.

128. See Aquinas, *de Regimine principum* (*On Kingship*), chap. 12, in *Aquinas on Politics and Ethics*, p. 25.

129. Aquinas, *Summa Theologica* 1–2, q. 97, art. 4, in *Basic Writings*, 2.805; *de Regimine principum*, chaps. 12, 14, 15, in *Aquinas on Politics and Ethics*, pp. 25–29.

130. Aquinas, *Summa Theologica* 1–2, q. 112, art. 4, in *Basic Writings*, 2.1016; *Summa Theologica* 2–2, q. 5, art. 4, in *Basic Writings*, 2.1114.

131. Aquinas, *de Regimine principum*, in *Aquinas on Politics and Ethics*, chap. 1, p. 14 f.; *Summa Contra Gentiles* 4, chap. 76, in *Aquinas on Politics and Ethics*, p. 13.

132. Descartes, Author's Replies to the Second Set of Objections, AT 7.147 f, CSM 2.105.

133. Descartes, *Discourse*, Part 1, AT 6.8, CSM 1.114.

134. Descartes, Second Set of Objections, AT 7.126, CSM 2.90; cf. Fourth Meditation, AT 7.58, CSM 2.40 f.

135. Descartes, Author's Replies to the First Set of Objections, AT 7.113 f., CSM 2.81 f.; cf. Aquinas, *Summa Theologica* 1, q. 2, art. 1, in *Basic Writings*, 1.19.

136. Descartes, letter to Hyperaspistes, August 1641, AT 3.426, CSM 3.191; *Discourse on Method*, Part 3, AT 6.28, CSM 1.125.

137. AT 10.370, CSM 1.15; AT 6.8, CSM 1.114; AT 8A.39, CSM 1.221.

138. See Descartes, *Rules for the Direction of the Mind*, Rule Twelve, AT 10.418, 10.421 f.; CSM 1.44, 1.46.

139. See, for example, Descartes, Author's Replies to the Sixth Set of Objections, AT 7.443, CSM 2.299; letter to Mersenne, December 31, 1640, AT 3.274, CSM 3.166.

140. Gueroult, *Descartes's Philosophy Interpreted*, 2.189; Maritain, *Dream of Descartes*, p. 97.

141. Maritain, *Dream of Descartes*, p. 96.

142. Ibid., pp. 66, 44.

143. See, for example, Zbigniew Janowski, *Cartesian Theodicy: Descartes' Quest for Certitude* (Dordrecht: Kluwer, 1999), p. 15.

144. Descartes, letter to More, February 5, 1649, AT 5.274, CSM 3.364.

145. Immanuel Kant, *Critique of Pure Reason*, trans. Norman Kemp Smith (New York: Humanities Press, 1950), A313/B370.

146. Ibid., A315/B371 f.

147. Ibid., A295/B352, A326 f./B383.

148. Ibid., A328/B384 f.

149. Immanuel Kant, *Critique of Practical Reason*, trans. Lewis White Beck, 3d ed. (Upper Saddle River, NJ: Library of Liberal Arts/Prentice Hall, 1993), p. 139 (Ak. 133); see also p. 129 (Ak. 123).

150. Ibid., p. 116 f. (Ak. 110 f.).

151. Ibid., p. 140 f. (Ak. 134). Cf. Immanuel Kant, *Grounding for the Metaphysics of Morals*, trans. James W. Ellington, 2d ed. (Indianapolis/Cambridge: Hackett, 1985), pp. 49 ff. (Ak. 446 ff.).

152. Kant, *Critique of Practical Reason*, p. 128 f. (Ak. 122).

153. Ibid., p. 129 (Ak. 122).

154. Ibid., p. 131 (Ak. 124).

155. See ibid., pp. 36, 64 (Ak. 35, 61).

156. Ibid., p. 135 (Ak. 128); see also p. 134n (Ak. 127n).

157. Ibid., p. 137 (Ak. 130).

158. Descartes, letter to Elizabeth, July 21, 1645, AT 4.252, CSM 3.256; letter to Elizabeth, August 4, 1645, AT 4.263, CSM 3.256 f.

159. AT 4.264, CSM 3.257.

160. AT 4.265 f., CSM 3.257 f.

161. AT 4.266, CSM 3.258.

162. Descartes, letter to Elizabeth, August 18, 1645, AT 4.275, CSM 3.261.

163. AT 4.277, CSM 3.262.

164. AT 4.276, CSM 3.261.

165. AT 4.266f., CSM 3.258.

166. AT 11.368, CSM 1.347.

167. Descartes, *Passions*, art. 48, AT 11.367, CSM 1.347.

168. Descartes, letter to Elizabeth, August 18, 1645, AT 4.273, CSM 3.260.

169. Gerold Prauss, *Knowing and Doing in Heidegger's 'Being and Time,'* trans. Gary Steiner and Jeffrey S. Turner (Amherst, NY: Humanity Books, 1999).

—CHAPTER 2—

CHRISTIANITY AND DESCARTES'S ANGELIC IDEAL

1. ON READING DESCARTES AS A CHRISTIAN

I present Descartes as a thinker poised between the explicit Catholic orthodoxy of Saint Thomas and the rationalist self-assertion of Kant to illuminate an irreducible tension in the thought of Descartes. Descartes goes a long way toward embracing the Baconian ideal of submitting to nature in order to conquer her, but he stops short of positing human welfare unequivocally as the highest end; his efforts to render human beings "masters and possessors of nature" emerge from a worldview in which human beings are at the apex of creation but in which material welfare is subordinated to knowing God.[1]

Contemporary thinkers have all but lost sight of the Christian roots of Descartes's philosophy, primarily because they focus on his elimination of final causes from nature. Even though Augustine endorses the biblical wisdom that we know God through his creatures, he views the systematic investigation of nature as a temptation to be resisted. Aquinas later characterizes the investigation of nature as a proper part of the aspiration to know God, and his reliance on Aristotle's notion of the teleological ordering of being enables him to justify this link between the world of intelligences and the world of corporeality: if all things are ordered to God, then the study of the teleology of created beings has its proper place in the larger project of knowing God and our relationship to him.[2]

In contrast, Descartes's insight into the need to conceptualize nature in mathematical rather than teleological terms was as threatening to scholastic orthodoxy as it was beneficial to the interests of science and the emerging discipline of technology. This placed him at odds with the established authority of the church and the universities. Aristotelianism in natural science had long been seen to be one of the pillars of a truly Christian worldview; principles such as the centrality and immovability of the earth, and the fundamental separation of the earthly and heavenly realms, were taken to be inseparable from the nascent dualism of soul and body that emerged from the gospels and the writings of Saint Augustine.

Descartes's introduction of a mechanistic mode of explanation into natural science led to a series of attacks directed against the sincerity of his appeals to the authority of Christian orthodoxy. In his own time, Descartes was charged with atheism, and some of his opponents challenged the sincerity of his appeal to the immateriality and immortality of the human soul. These challenges to Descartes's sincerity have continued to the present, and, together with the work of a number of contemporary philosophers to understand Descartes as the father of postivism and analytic philosophy, these challenges have done a great deal to stabilize what appears to have become the prevailing conventional wisdom that Descartes is a secular atheist whose appeals to Christian concepts and the authority of Catholic orthodoxy are simply political expedients intended to shield him from the persecution of the church.

Descartes's commitment to the compatibility between faith and reason, his acknowledgment of the limits of reason, and his at least implicit awareness of the need to appeal to faith to establish the foundations of morality are all reasons for challenging this conventional wisdom. Even if as a matter of historical fact Descartes's philosophy paved the way for an irreversible cleavage between science and Christian faith, the intellectual and historical context surrounding Descartes points toward the conclusion that his philosophical endeavors become unintelligible when divorced from the Christian worldview that dominated the Christian universities of Western Europe during the first half of the seventeenth century.

Given the panoply of historical disputes concerning the precise nature of Christian orthodoxy, it is not possible to provide a clear and uncontroversial sense of the "Christian elements" of Descartes's thought. The disagreements in the early church between Augustine and the Pelagians, the claims of the semi-Pelagians, and the later conflict between the Molinists and the Jansenists over the precise status of grace, original sin, free will, and redemption suggest that the answer to the question "what is orthodox Christianity?" depends on the political will and fortunes of different factions in the Christian tradition. At the same time, the historical record of these disputes itself suggests a criterion for deciding whether and to what extent the various elements of Descartes's thought should count as Christian: the extent to which those elements exhibit conformity to the writings of the preeminent medieval Christian thinkers, Saint Augustine and Saint Thomas. Even where tribunals like the Council of Orange (529) mitigated Augustine's doctrine of divine grace in their attempts to preserve the notion of human freedom, for example, they exhibited "obvious deference" to the writings of Saint Augustine and followed his doctrine in clearly subordinating human freedom to divine grace.[3] Similarly, the writings of Saint Augustine and Saint Thomas served as crucial background for reflections on the nature of "a truly Christian life" conducted by the Council of Trent (1545–1563).[4] Their influence reflects not their absolute authority in determinations of what is "authentically Christian" but rather the extent to which they serve as a barometer of the concepts and problems characteristic of Christian thought.

In this and the following two chapters, I show that Descartes embraces a set of Christian commitments about the meaning of human life along with his commitment to the autonomy of human reason and his conception of nature as pure mechanism. Taken together, these commitments form an unstable whole in which human beings are torn between devotion to divine dictates and a spirit of earthly self-assertion. Thus Descartes both affirms grace and asserts that "since we were born men before we became Christians we cannot believe that anyone would seriously embrace opinions which he thinks contrary to that right reason which constitutes being a man, simply in order to cling to the faith which makes him a Christian."[5] To preserve and explore this tension at the core of Descartes's thought rather than to neutralize it, I examine Descartes's approach to the relationship between reason and revelation against the background of Galileo's treatment of the problem. I show, for example, why the Port-Royal school turned to Descartes for inspiration in their endeavor to develop a logic "to distinguish between those areas where the mind must submit to authority and those areas where the mind was free to draw its own conclusions."[6]

Galileo's dispute with the church is not simply a disagreement over the relative merits of the Ptolemaic and Copernican world systems, although outwardly it appears to be just that; it is ultimately a dispute about the relationship between faith and science, the rights of reason, and the proper scope of religious authority. The historical record of the Galileo affair is extensive, but its principal features are these:[7] By early 1613, Galileo had openly embraced the Copernican system and considered his own astronomical discoveries to serve as proof of it. The reception of Galileo's views was mixed in the church. Some members of the church supported Galileo and endeavored to show that the Copernican system is consistent with the Bible. Others harshly denounced Galileo, Copernicanism, and mathematics as inimical to Christianity. Early in 1615, the Carmelite priest Foscarini published a short work in which he argued for the compatibility between the Copernican view and Scripture; Foscarini's treatise was condemned by the Roman Inquisition in 1616, with the qualification that it is permissible to advance Copernicanism as a mere hypothesis. The Inquisition seems to have followed the reasoning of Cardinal Bellarmine, who wrote to Foscarini in 1615 that

> to demonstrate that the appearances are saved by assuming the sun at the center and the earth in the heavens is not the same thing as to demonstrate that in fact the sun is in the center and the earth in the heavens. I believe that the first demonstration may exist, but I have very grave doubts about the second; and in the case of doubt one may not abandon the Holy Scriptures as expounded by the holy Fathers.[8]

Galileo's stand on this matter is uncompromising. In May 1615, he wrote to his ally Piero Dini that "I should not like to have great men think that I endorse the position of Copernicus as an astronomical hypothesis which is not really true," and in notes written around this time Galileo states that "no greater truth may or should be sought in a theory than that it corresponds with all the particular appearances."[9] In other words, Galileo is unwilling to accept the position that Copernicanism is acceptable only as a hypothesis. What he demands is truth, and for him the measure of truth is the conformity of a hypothesis to observed phenomena. This may have been the roots of the young Descartes's view that the proper measure of the truth of scientific theories or models is the extent to which they enable us to reconstruct natural mechanisms.[10] In addition to demanding actual correspondence to phenomena rather than mere hypotheses in science, Galileo adheres to the orthodox view of the relationship between scientific truth and the truth that will set us free: "the Scriptures accord perfectly with demonstrated physical truth."[11] Because the moral truth of Scripture and the mathematical and observational truth of natural science proceed from the one true God, they cannot be in conflict with each other; each kind of truth has its proper domain and limits, and any apparent conflict between the two is the product of our failure to respect these limits.

Galileo's *Letter to the Grand Duchess Christina* (1615) is the

culmination of his efforts to argue for this conception of the relationship between biblical authority and natural science. The key to
Galileo's argument in the *Letter* is his suggestion that "in purely
physical matters . . . where faith is not involved . . . reason and the
evidence of the senses" are the only proper authorities; in purely
physical matters, Scripture is fundamentally ambiguous because
"under the surface meaning of its words [a given] passage [of
Scripture] may contain a different sense."[12] One should follow the
example of Copernicus, Galileo says, who

> never discusses matters of religion or faith, nor does he use argu-
> ments that depend in any way upon the authority of sacred writ-
> ings, which he might have interpreted erroneously. He stands
> always upon physical conclusions pertaining to the celestial
> motions, and deals with them by astronomical and geometrical
> demonstrations, founded primarily upon sense experiences and
> very exact observations. He did not ignore the Bible, but he knew
> very well that if his doctrine were proved, then it could not con-
> tradict the Scriptures when they were rightly understood.[13]

Galileo proposes that the meaning of the Bible is fundamentally
ambiguous in regard to physical matters, and its authority should be
subordinated to the authority of science in "purely physical" questions. It is correct to suppose that "the holy Bible can never speak
untruth," provided that "its true meaning is understood." When we
ask, for example, whether the several biblical statements that "the
sun moves and the earth stands still" are in error, we must bear in
mind that such "propositions uttered by the Holy Ghost were set
down in that manner by the sacred scribes in order to accommodate
them to the capacities of the common people, who are rude and
unlearned."[14] The aim of Scripture is not the explanation of natural
phenomena but rather "the service of God and the salvation of
souls—matters infinitely beyond the comprehension of the
common people"; hence

in discussions of physical problems we ought to begin not from the authority of scriptural passages, but from sense-experiences and necessary demonstrations; for the holy Bible and the phenomena of nature proceed alike from the divine Word, the former as the dictate of the Holy Ghost and the latter as the observant executrix of God's commands. It is necessary for the Bible, in order to be accommodated to the understanding of every man, to speak many things which appear to differ from the absolute truth so far as the bare meaning of the words is concerned. But Nature, on the other hand, is inexorable and immutable; she never transgresses the laws imposed upon her, or cares a whit whether her abstruse reasons and methods of operation are understandable to men.[15]

Galileo says that the biblical edict that the earth stands fixed in the center of creation is a metaphor intended for our moral instruction and that, properly understood, this metaphor is fully consistent with the scientific validity of the Copernican theory. "The intention of the Holy Ghost is to teach us how one goes to heaven, not how heaven goes."[16]

Galileo's analysis of the proper relationship between science and Scriptural authority has important implications for understanding Descartes. Just as Aquinas's adherence to Aristotelian final causality leads him to give teleological explanations in both the natural and the supernatural realms, Galileo's and Descartes's insight into the power of mathematics to model the physical universe leads them to separate the two domains. Galileo does much to pave the way for Descartes when he asserts the need to model nature through what later was known as a reduction from secondary to primary qualities.[17] But Galileo does not concern himself with the implications of the separation of the physical and moral realms for the traditional problems of morality; he leaves these to the church and to thinkers like Descartes.

2. THE CHRISTIAN ELEMENTS IN DESCARTES'S THOUGHT

The Christian elements in Descartes's writings are the products of a trajectory of thought that Descartes inherits in large part from Augustine and Aquinas. The problem of the interrelationship between faith and reason is a case in point. Where Augustine proposes that "understanding is the reward of faith" and that one should therefore "seek not to understand that thou mayest believe, but believe that thou mayest understand," Aquinas retreats from the strong priority of faith over reason and suggests that some articles of faith can actually be attained separately by reason even though ultimately all such articles should be confirmed by faith.[18] Aquinas thus makes a decisive step in the direction of establishing the rights of science and rigorous demonstration, a step Augustine was unwilling to make. But at the same time, Aquinas adheres to Augustine's conception of the ultimate priority of faith over reason, and he declares that we cannot have rational knowledge of articles of faith like the Trinity.[19] But even though Aquinas is careful to argue that sacred doctrine, the highest of all sciences, must depend on revelation for the basic principles that enable us to study "the truths which exceed human reason," he maintains that human beings can establish rational knowledge of angels.[20] Although Descartes is well known for his attack on Aquinas's claims about the possibility of establishing knowledge of angels, I show that his reaction to the Thomistic doctrine is not simply an attack but is in fact a refinement of the trajectory of thinking about the relationship between faith and reason that links Aquinas to Augustine and Descartes to both of these thinkers.

There are a number of obvious connections between the thought of Augustine and the thought of Descartes. Apart from the relationship between reason and revelation already discussed, there is a forerunner of Descartes's cogito in Augustine's writings, and there is a symmetry between Augustine's account of evil and Descartes's account of error. Augustine's influence is also evident in Descartes's proof of God's existence in the Third Meditation, the appeal to errors of the senses and the illusions of dreaming and madness in the First Meditation, and the demand for the certitude of mathematics in metaphysics and physics. To explore Descartes's debt to Augustine as it bears specifically upon the Christian character of Descartes's conception of morality, I focus primarily on three basic affinities: the two thinkers' shared assumptions about the nature of human freedom, the symmetry between Augustine's account of evil and Descartes's account of error, and the commitment of both thinkers to the soul's transcendence of the body and their consequent association of the sovereign good with transcendence.

Augustine starts with faith in the search for truth, but he is not satisfied to stop with it; he demands that we proceed from faith to the certitude of knowledge. The starting point for the acquisition of wisdom is faith: "We are too weak to discover the truth by reason alone and for this reason need the authority of sacred books . . . the authority of Scripture should be respected and accepted with the purest faith, because while all can read it with ease, it also has a deeper meaning in which its great secrets are locked away."[21] But the constant refrain in the *Confessions* is the imperative to "know God through His creatures," for example, to begin to grasp God through the rational reflection on the nature of time proposed in Book 11. The actions of faith and understanding converge in the project of the will to commit itself to actions that are in accordance with the will of God—subject to the qualification that because original sin makes fallen man fundamentally inclined toward evil, it is only in virtue of God's grace that the fallen will can incline toward the good.[22] Given this qualification, which seems to mitigate the possibility of genuine human freedom, Augustine examines the question of the essence of human freedom.

Augustine's struggle with this question leads him to a dual conception of freedom so powerful that even Kant cannot escape its influence. At the most elementary level, the freedom of the will is simply the ability to make one choice or another, without the influence of external necessity. In *de libero arbitrio*, Augustine introduces freedom in the sense of voluntariness to account for the possibility of evil and hence for the prospect of moral accountability: we can be held responsible for our actions only to the extent that they proceed from the determinations of our own wills rather than from the determinations of forces outside of us.[23] This spontaneity of the will is not compromised by God's omniscience; on the contrary, Augustine asserts the compatibility between human freedom and divine foreknowledge.[24] Augustine struggles to establish that the reality of human freedom is limited but not destroyed by God's supreme agency, that our actions at least to some extent proceed from the spontaneity of our own natures even though these natures proceed from an infinite God.

Augustine's conception of the freedom of the will is completed by his notion of the *good* will, the will actively directed toward an "upright and honorable" life.[25] Such a will takes its bearings from "the law that is called the highest reason, which must always be obeyed, and by which the wicked deserve misery and the good deserve a happy life."[26] This law is eternal rather than temporal: "What is evil is the turning of the will away from the unchangeable good and toward changeable goods," such as "when the will turns away from the unchangeable and common good toward its own private good."[27] The highest and most genuine freedom consists in the submission of our will to the truth; "the truth is God himself," and to attain a vision of that truth is to "enjoy the highest good."[28] In this conception of freedom, Augustine recognizes the paradox that Kant later embraces: that the extent of one's *freedom* is ultimately to be measured not in terms of the "absence of external constraint" that guides Hobbes and Hume but rather in terms of the extent to which one recognizes and accepts one's *subjection* to the moral law.

This dual conception of freedom forms the basis of Augustine's account of evil. In Book 7 of the *Confessions*, Augustine raises a complex problem that confronts any philosophy founded on Christian metaphysics: If God alone is truly substantial and therefore must be the source of all created being, and if God is supremely good, then how can there be anything evil in the world, and how can we avoid the conclusion that God is responsible for evil? First, Augustine asserts the primacy of permanence (God) over change (created being): "I considered all other things that are of a lower order than yourself [viz., God], and I saw that they have not absolute being in themselves, nor are they entirely without being. . . . It is only that which remains in being without change that truly is."[29] Following the Platonic conception, Augustine conceives of the realm of sensible particulars as a shadow play that reflects the permanence of the forms. The Christian element of this Platonism consists in Augustine's identification of God as "the unfailing Light from which I sought counsel upon all these things" and hence in his transformation of the *idea ton agathon* into the Christian God.[30] Given this conception of all things as proceeding from the one true and good source of being, "we must conclude that if things are deprived of all good, they cease altogether to be; and this means that as long as they are, they are good. Therefore, whatever is, is good; and evil, the origin of which I was trying to find, is not a sub-stance, because if it were a substance, it would be good."[31] Not only is being (God) permanence and pure goodness, but all created being participates in this goodness insofar as created being *is*.

These metaphysical commitments give rise to the paradox of evil: it is indisputable that we experience evil in the world. Is evil, then, not a being? How can it be a being if all being participates in the good? Augustine's solution to this problem is to challenge the proposition that evil has the metaphysical status of positive being. "He is God and what he wills is good and he is himself that same Good; whereas to be corrupted is not good."[32] "So we must con-clude that if things are deprived of all good, they cease altogether to be; and this means that as long as they are, they are good. There-fore, whatever is, is good; and evil, the origin of which I was trying to find, is not a substance, because if it were a substance, it would be good."[33] Strictly speaking, evil does not exist; instead, it must be conceived as a privation or defect: "Every defect comes from nothing, and that movement of turning away, which we admit is sin, is a defective movement. So you see where the movement comes from; you can be sure that it does not come from God."[34]

Nonetheless Augustine has to account for the fact that we *experience* evil, even if it cannot truly be said to exist. To account for the genesis of evil, Augustine enriches his metaphysics to make a place for the human being as an intermediary between the positive being of goodness and the nonbeing of evil. We participate in both. To the extent that we exist we participate, like all creatures, in the goodness that is God and that is being, but we must not "sink as far as that hell of error where no one confesses to you his own guilt, choosing to believe that you suffer evil rather than that man does it."[35] Evil does not simply happen to us; it is not an external affliction. "We do evil because we choose to do so of our own free will, and suffer it because your justice rightly demands that we should."[36] As spontaneous freedom of choice, our will is able to act in accordance with our nature, but it is also able to *turn away* from this good nature. "Wickedness . . . [is] not a substance but perversion of the will when it turns aside from you, O God, who are the supreme substance, and veers towards things of the lowest order, being *bowelled alive* and becoming inflated with desire for things outside itself."[37] In this sense our will is a field of spontaneity lying between God, being, and goodness on the one hand and nonbeing and evil on the other. To the extent that we allow ourselves to become absorbed in "things of the lowest order," we stray from the righteous path and descend into a kind of hell. This descent is a "hell of error" if we allow ourselves to believe that our descent is not freely chosen.

In presenting this account of the genesis of evil, Augustine portrays man as an intermediary in two distinct senses. I have already touched on the first sense: the will is an intermediary between being and nonbeing. Metaphysically, it is in principle being. But at the same time, the nature of spontaneity is such that it can turn away from being; it can modify itself so that it particpates in nonbeing. At work in this account of evil is a second, related sense in which man has the status of an intermediary: in the hierarchy or order of beings, man is an intermediary between God and pure physicality. "For I was a creature of a higher order than these things [viz., things in "the world outside . . . contained in space"], though I was lower than you. . . . I remained true to your likeness and, by serving you, became the master of my own body."[38] To devote one's will and one's life to God is at the same time to turn away from the world of embodiment. For "my soul is the better part of me, because it animates the whole of my body. It gives it life, and this is something that no body can give to another body. But God is even more. He is the Life of the life of my soul."[39] The *Confessions* is a sustained argument for the traditional Christian propositions that uncreated, permanent being is higher in the scheme of things than created, temporal beings; that soul is higher than body; and that only God is the truth and the proper measure for the striving of a created will. I show below that Descartes shares all of these commitments with Augustine. Then, I consider how and why Descartes radically departs from Augustine's intentions in proposing the systematic study and total mastery of nature.

Augustine completes his theodicy by supplementing the analysis of the genesis of evil with an explanation of how evil can be compatible with God's omnipotence and pure goodness. This explanation has as its point of departure Augustine's conception of evil as a kind of nothingness and hence as something for which God cannot be held responsible. Still, one has to ask why God did not simply prevent evil from arising in the first place. "Could [God] not have removed and annihilated the evil matter and replaced it with good, of which he could create all things?"[40] Augustine might have stated the question even more radically: If God is truly omnipotent and wholly good, then why did he not simply bring about a creation in which there is no room for evil in the first place? The very appearance of evil, even if we grant that it does not participate in being, threatens to compromise God and his creation. Augustine offers two solutions to this problem. The first is that God's judgment is inscrutable. "For you rule the universe with the utmost justice, and in the inscrutable depths of your just judgment you know what is right for [each man], because you can see the hidden merits of our souls. And let no man question the why or the wherefore of your judgment. This he must not do, for he is only a man."[41] Here Augustine addresses the question of why God allows particular men to suffer evil. I show below that Augustine's stand on this question has significant implications for the Jansenist-Pelagian controversy in which Descartes was involved. Augustine's answer to this question has important implications for his theodicy as well, for in essence he says that we cannot know why God allowed evil to manifest itself in the universe because the limits of our understanding do not allow us to penetrate into God's ultimate reasons.

Related to this argument is Augustine's second, less direct answer, which is that "though the higher things are better than the lower, the sum of all creation is better than the higher things alone."[42] Augustine is speaking specifically to the relative imperfection of earthly beings, and he proposes that a plenitude of beings that includes such imperfect beings is superior to a world in which only a few, perfect beings exist. The context of Book 7 of the *Confessions* suggests a corollary to this principle: just as being is enriched through the inclusion of lower forms of positive being, so the world in toto is somehow enriched by the inclusion of evil and of finite wills capable of doing evil. If one asks why God created corruptible natures and fallible wills, the answer must be that "our liberty is the indispensable condition for the greatest good which can fall to our lot, namely our happiness. . . . The possibility of the evil use of free will was the necessary condition for the goodness and happiness brought about by its good use."[43] At the same time, in his dispute with the Pelagians, Augustine emphasizes the necessary role of God's grace in facilitating the possibility of our redemption: man's fall from grace is due to a voluntary "turning away from that which has supreme being and towards that which has less"; "but since we cannot pick ourselves up voluntarily as we fell voluntarily, let us hold with confident faith the right hand of God—that is, our Lord Jesus Christ—which has been held out to us from on high."[44] Augustine sees original sin as man's *voluntary* fall from grace, and he sees the postlapsarian human condition as the subjection of will to corruption and sin. The prospects for our redemption depend on the dedication of our will to the righteous path, but this dedication and the capacity of our will to redirect itself toward the good depend fundamentally on the grace of God.

In the *Confessions*, Augustine recognizes our dual nature and the difficulties involved in rising above the material aspect of our being; he expresses his commitment to the transcendence of the soul over the body and the prospect for community with God that is granted by transcendence. Following the notion of inwardness expressed in the gospels, Augustine says of body and soul that "the one [is] the outer, the other the inner part of me. . . . [M]y inner self is the better of the two" because it is the "arbiter and judge" of all the data with which the body provides it.[45] Such an arbiter is needed because our relationship to material being is tortured; the same relationship to the earthly realm that can help us to approach God can also become a state of concupiscent bondage. Man "is able to *catch sight of God's invisible nature through his creatures*, but his love of these material things is too great. He becomes their slave, and slaves cannot be judges."[46]

In his account of earthly, embodied existence, Augustine characterizes the human condition as a predicament: the conditions of our mortality make it necessary to exercise dominion over the earth, and yet the corruptibility or variability of our nature as free beings poses the threat that we will become absorbed in earthly things for the sake of lust rather than for the sake of God. Augustine speaks of "our animal nature" as being characterized by needs whose gratification gives pleasure, "though I fight against it, for fear of becoming its captive. Every day I wage war upon it by fasting. Time and again I force my body to obey me, but the pain which this causes me is cancelled by the pleasure of eating and drinking." Our needs as embodied creatures can and must be satisfied by the resources of the material world, "for you have given us earth and water and sky to serve us in our weakness."[47] If the prelapsarian existence of Adam and Eve consists in a wholeness and unity with God in which toil and suffering play no role, the wages of original sin are that the world is now a wilderness in which we must struggle to satisfy our own needs. Part of this struggle consists in avoiding "the snare of concupiscence [which] awaits me in the very process of passing from the discomfort of hunger to the contentment which comes when it is satisfied."[48] For Augustine, this part of the earthly struggle most authentically characterizes our predicament. The task of turning away from evil and back toward God is the task of reclaiming our inwardness and reestablishing its primacy over the dominance of bodily desire. In this sense, the human condition consists in a struggle to gain mastery of oneself through the regulation of desire, a struggle in which we can succeed only by the grace of God.[49]

In *de immortalitate animae*, Augustine characterizes the transcendence of the soul over the body in terms of a hierarchy stretching from the pure goodness and immateriality of God to the pure materiality and changeability of the physical world. Lower things in the order of being receive their form from higher, more perfect things; the soul receives its form from God, the supreme good, and in turn gives form to body. Souls are "more excellent" than bodies because the form of soul is characterized by permanence and rationality, in contrast with the corruptibility or changeability of body.[50] The soul received its form directly from God, "the supreme Good"; in its struggle with irrationality and concupiscence, the soul or mind must turn away from the world and back "toward reason," which is "something unchangeable which is the truth that is the highest degree and primordial."[51] The soul transcends the conditions of embodiment through a contemplation of the perfection, power, and permanence of the supreme good that is God.

Descartes's Fourth Meditation is a focal point for his affinities with Augustine. Descartes's announced intention in this Meditation is to analyze the distinction between material truth and falsity and to provide a solution to the problem of error. The work undertaken in the Fourth Meditation is part of the larger goal of establishing metaphysical foundations for the conduct of modern science, a goal stated at the beginning of the First Meditation and one whose satisfaction requires a procedure for avoiding erroneous judgments. Equally important are the implications of the analysis of truth and error in this Meditation for Descartes's conception of morality, although these are less apparent because Descartes suggests in the "Synopsis" of the *Meditations* that the Fourth Meditation has no relevance to "good and evil" but concerns only the "speculative truths which are known solely by means of the natural light."[52] I examine the terms of Descartes's analysis of truth and error in the Fourth Meditation and his reasons for stating that that analysis is not to be construed as having implications for sin to show that the Fourth Meditation is essential for understanding Descartes's moral ethos.

At the end of the Third Meditation, the meditator proposes that "just as we believe through faith that the supreme happiness of the next life consists solely in the contemplation of the divine majesty, so experience tells us that this same contemplation, albeit much less perfect, enables us to know the greatest joy of which we are capable in this life."[53] What is the precise nature of such "contemplation"? Is it wholly rational? Or is rationality only one dimension of an inwardness that is ultimately completed through faith and the love of God? Descartes speaks of a contemplation that discloses "the greatest joy" of earthly existence just as it discloses "the supreme happiness" of supernatural beatitude, and in doing so he associates the possibility of the latter disclosure with faith. This association of contemplation with faith, which Descartes characterizes as an operation of the will, provides a framework for exploring the implications of his account of error for the problem of sin and evil.

Moreover, the project of the *Meditations* as a whole is not really an absolutely new philosophical beginning at all, as Descartes maintains. The form of the meditation is borrowed from a long tradition of spiritual exercises. Richard Popkin characterizes texts such as Descartes's *Meditations* and Spinoza's *Ethics* as "journeys of the mind to God," and he suggests that "Descartes's version is much like a combination of the Jesuit Ignatius of Loyola's *Spiritual Exercises*, and Bérulle's work, the two sources of Descartes's religious training."[54] Also, the two major methodological achievements leading up to the Fourth Meditation, the cogito and the Third Meditation proof(s) of God's existence, bear the imprint of medieval thought. In a variety of texts, Augustine presents an argument that bears a striking resemblance to Descartes's cogito, and he presents it in order to counter skepticism and to begin the inward movement that leads him to God.[55] At the same time, Augustine's argument is quite different from Descartes's in the respect that "it bears on life instead of thought";[56] to this extent it is "the first given of an introspective psychology" rather than "the necessary truth of a science of pure understanding."[57]

Descartes treats the relationship between the cogito and Augustine's conception of our knowledge of the existence of the self as a kind of fortuitous albeit limited coincidence. He is happy to find support in Augustine for his own ideas, but he purports not to have been aware of Augustine's anticipation of the cogito until it was brought to his attention. In a letter to Colvius, Descartes considers himself "obliged to you for drawing my attention to the passage of Saint Augustine relevant to my I am thinking, therefore I exist. I went today to the library of this town [Leiden] to read it, and I do indeed find that he does use it to prove the certainty of our existence."[58] In the Fourth Objections, written around the same time as the letter to Colvius, Arnauld takes the parallel between *de libero arbitrio*, Book 2, section 3, and the presentation of the cogito early in the Second Meditation as a clear indication "that our distinguished author has laid down as the basis for his entire philosophy exactly the same principle as that laid down by Saint Augustine."[59] And Arnauld suggests that it is from Augustine's *de animae quantitae* that Descartes inherited his commitment to "the greater certainty which attaches to what we grasp by means of reason as against what we observe by means of the bodily senses."[60]

But where Augustine establishes that we know that we exist, Descartes "show[s] that this *I* which is thinking is *an immaterial substance* with no bodily element. These are two very different things."[61] Some years later, in the *Notae in Programma*, Descartes declares that he was the first to see "that the rational soul consists solely in thought," the first "to have regarded thought as the principal attribute of an incorporeal substance, and extension as the principal attribute of a corporeal substance."[62] By deriving the cogito from the method rather than from the kind of spiritual exercise found in Augustine or Ignatius of Loyola, Descartes transforms it from a principle of life to a principle of logic that can ground an order of reasons that terminates in physics. Understood in the light of the method, Descartes's cogito serves as the point of departure for practical endeavors, such as the mastery of nature. Understood against the Christian background of spiritual exercises, however, the cogito as a purely logical tool is but one of two modes of access to the divine measure of truth and goodness. Koyré's observation that "knowledge of the self and knowledge of God are inseparably bound up with one another for Descartes, as they are for Augustine" supports the view that the project of self-knowledge is not derived from method but instead has the character of a spiritual imperative that transcends and motivates the turn to method.[63]

There are clear indications of Augustine's influence on Descartes in the notion of a hierarchy of beings that links the Third Meditation to the Fourth. In the first of two proofs from effects in the Third Meditation, in one of which the existence of God is proved on the basis of my having an idea of God and in the other on the basis of my very existence, Descartes makes central a conception of a hierarchy of causal agency that recalls the hierarchy presented by Augustine in *de immortalitate animae*. Where in Augustine's hierarchy beings closer to God give form to beings more distant from God, so that in particular soul gives form to body, the hierarchy in the Third Meditation is one in which "what is more perfect—that is, contains in itself more reality—cannot arise from what is less perfect."[64] This hierarchy relates perfection and reality to the capacity to bring about effects, that is, to power, and thereby recalls not only the discussion of a hierarchy of causal powers in *de immortalitate animae* but also the discussion of a hierarchy of perfection discussed in the *Confessions*. In Descartes as in Augustine, the ascent from earthly creatures to the divine is characterized by an order of being in which the lowest beings are purely material and inert; the next-higher beings are material and alive but lack immortal souls; the next-higher possess immortal souls and are united with bodies; and the highest are pure spirit. Lower beings in this order are less perfect, less powerful, and in an important sense less real than higher beings in this order; both Augustine and Descartes depend on this hierarchy in establishing the nature of the soul and the existence of God.

When Descartes addresses the subject of truth and error in the Fourth Meditation, his concern is twofold. He wants to understand what occurs when we make erroneous judgments so that we can avoid error, and, given that error is an imperfection that would appear to be incompatible with God's nature as wholly true, good, and non-deceptive, he wants to understand how error is possible in the first place. Thus in the Fourth Meditation, Descartes is really addressing two interrelated problems, one "epistemic-psychological" and the other "metaphysical," and the solution to the latter governs the solution to the former.[65] Augustine was concerned with both of these problems, although he did not approach the first in quite the same sense as Descartes. For Augustine, the epistemic problem is that we can make wicked choices if we turn away from the truth that is God, and his solution is that righteous conduct can be achieved by seeing the right reason and moving one's will to act in accordance with that

reason. "The power of judgment" enables us "to conquer the difficulty of acting rightly"; "the nature of reason grasps the commandment, and . . . the will is what obeys the commandment."[66] Descartes
approaches the epistemic problem in similar terms: our errors are
products of a misuse of the faculty of judgment; correct judgment
depends on clear and distinct insight, and our errors in judgment
occur when we make judgments in cases in which we lack such
insight. Like Augustine, Descartes characterizes judgment as an
activity of the will. He conceives of the will as infinite and the intellect as finite, and he sees correct judgment as occurring when the will
subjects itself to the intellect.[67] "So what then is the source of my
mistakes? It must simply be this: the scope of the will is wider than
that of the intellect; but instead of restricting it within the same limits,
I extend its use to matters which I do not understand. Since the will
is indifferent in such cases, it easily turns aside from what is true and
good, and this is the source of my error and sin."[68] I can avoid error
if "I simply refrain from making a judgment in cases where I do not
perceive the truth with sufficient clarity and distinctness."[69]

The parallel between the true and the good, and error and sin,
in the Fourth Meditation reflects Descartes's inability or unwilling-
ness to detach the problem of material truth entirely from the
problem of moral choice. Just as we feel compelled to assent to
clear perceptions, we are "drawn voluntarily and freely . . . but nevertheless inevitably, towards a clearly known good."[70] A person
"will embrace what is good and true all the more willingly, and
hence more freely, in proportion as he sees it more clearly."[71] Sin,
precisely like error, is predicated on ignorance.[72] Descartes's references to turning away, "using my free will correctly," and "a certain weakness in me," as well as his conclusion that "man's greatest
and most important perfection is to be found" in using his faculty
of judgment rightly, draw extensively on the Augustinian picture
not only of judgment but also of human life. To judge rightly, both
in matters of fact and in matters of value, is a fundamental imperative of the human vocation; we first come to God through faith,

love, contrition, and his grace, but it is through judgment that we secure our relationship to God. Descartes takes Augustine's vision one step further by seeing the power of scientific judgment and incorporating it into his ideal of righteous living. What links the scientific and moral orientations in Descartes is the foundational role of God. Descartes's God serves as the measure for truth and goodness, in accordance with the medieval adequation or correspondence model of truth. The truth of assertions is defined as *adequatio intellectus* (*humani*) *ad rem* (*creatam*), the correspondence of human ideas or assertions to the things or subject matter in our experience that we seek to describe. Human thought has its measure in the things that it seeks to grasp. Things in turn, in accordance with the terms of Augustinian metaphysics, have their measure in the creative intellect of God: *adequatio rei* (*creandae*) *ad intellectum* (*divinum*).

In the Sixth Replies, Descartes locates the roots of his conception of God and truth in Christian tradition. "The kind of knowledge possessed by the athiest . . . is not immutable and certain" because the atheist does not ground his certainty in knowledge of a nondeceptive God. It is as if the atheist were trying to satisfy himself with an accord between his thoughts and the way things appear to him to be, without regard for the ontological question whether the reality of the things has been properly derived from the creative intellect of God. The very possibility of certain knowledge depends on establishing an appropriate connection between the content of human thought and the content of the divine intellect, which is truth. In principle, God is veracity; if God were to any extent a deceiver, the connection with truth would be broken and the possibility of knowledge extinguished. Descartes frames this commitment in Augustinian terms: "The assertion that it is self-contradictory that men should be deceived by God is clearly demonstrated from the fact that the form of deception is non-being, towards which the supreme being cannot tend. On this point all theologians are agreed, and the entire certainty of the Christian faith depends on it."[73] In accordance with the Augustinian model, Descartes implicitly proposes that we participate in truth to the extent that we turn toward God, and any deception that we suffer is a product of our having turned away from God. To be an atheist is to have turned away from God and toward earthly, temporal things; toward the life of the body and concupiscence; and hence toward nonbeing. This is why an atheist "cannot be certain that he is not being deceived on matters which seem to him to be very evident"; "knowledge is conviction based on a reason so strong that it can never be shaken by any stronger reason. Nobody can have the latter unless he also has knowledge of God."[74]

These considerations return us to the second, more fundamental of the two problems addressed in the Fourth Meditation, the metaphysical problem of theodicy. The theodicy presented by Descartes in the Fourth Meditation follows that of Augustine in each of its principal features. Descartes's starting point is the axiom that God is pure truth and goodness; God is not a deceiver because "the will to deceive is undoubtedly evidence of malice or weakness, and so cannot apply to God."[75] "No cause of error or falsity" can be found in God because these do not participate in being:

> On looking for the causes of [my] errors, I find that I possess not only a real and positive idea of God, or a being who is supremely perfect, but also what may be described as a negative idea of nothingness, or of that which is farthest removed from all perfection. I realize that I am, as it were, something intermediate between God and nothingness, or between supreme being and non-being: my nature is such that in so far as I was created by the supreme being, there is nothing in me to enable me to go wrong or lead me astray; but in so far as I participate in nothingness or non-being, that is, in so far as I am not myself the supreme being and am lacking in countless respects, it is no wonder that I make mistakes. I understand, then, that error as such is not something real which depends on God, but merely a defect . . . a privation or lack of some knowledge which somehow should be in me.[76]

This account of the metaphysical possibility of error draws on the notion of a hierarchy of perfection sketched in the Third Meditation. The formal-objective reality principle presented there encompasses three basic commitments: first, "the ideas which represent substances to me amount to something more and, so to speak, contain within themselves more objective reality than the ideas which merely represent modes or accidents." Second, "the idea . . . of a supreme God, eternal, infinite, <immutable,> omniscient, omnipotent and the creator of all things that exist apart from him, certainly has in it more objective reality than the ideas that represent finite substances." And third, "something cannot arise from nothing, and also . . . what is more perfect—that is, contains within itself more reality—cannot arise from what is less perfect."[77] Taken together with the cogito and the conclusion of the Second Meditation that "my awareness of my own self is not merely much truer and more certain than my awareness of the wax, but also much more distinct and evident,"[78] these three commitments give shape to a hierarchy whose basic measures are reality, truth, power, and perfection— precisely as in Augustine. Substances possess more of each of these qualities than do modes and accidents; the infinite substance of God possesses more of these qualities than do finite substances; immaterial substances are "truer," more powerful (independent) than material substances; and beings of a given degree of perfection or reality must have as their causes beings with at least as much reality as the effect possesses. Apart from Augustine's refusal, along with Anselm and Aquinas, to characterize God as a substance, and apart from the fact that Augustine does not employ the language of modes, these commitments are entirely in line with Augustine's conception of a hierarchy of perfection.[79]

Hence for Descartes as for Augustine, everything that exists participates to a greater or a lesser extent in truth, goodness, and perfection. Positive being includes nothing defective; even the finitude of my intellect cannot be understood to be something imperfect. All imperfections must have their source in something other than the world of positive being whose order leads to God; error in particular is "a privation or lack." This characterization of error is virtually indistinguishable from Augustine's account of sin in *de libero arbitrio* as "a defective movement" that "comes from nothing."[80] Error must have its origin in the "nothingness" that is radically opposed to God, because the only alternative explanation would involve the contradiction that God is responsible for the creation of error (Descartes) or sin (Augustine). God "always wills what is best";[81] hence it cannot be the case that he wills that we err, but instead our errors must be due to our misuse of a faculty that God enables us to use properly. If we could view things not simply from our limited point of view but from the standpoint of being as a whole, this situation would presumably not appear to be imperfect: "For what would perhaps rightly appear very imperfect if it existed on its own is quite perfect when its function as a part of the universe is considered."[82] Because of his "incomprehensible and infinite" nature, God is "capable of countless things whose causes are beyond my knowledge."[83] For reasons that we can never fully grasp, a world in which we possess free will and hence the prospect of making mistakes is better than a world in which we are determined by external forces never to err. "For it is surely no imperfection in God that he has given me the freedom to assent or not to assent in those cases where he did not endow my intellect with a clear and distinct perception; but it is undoubtedly an imperfection in me to misuse that freedom and make judgments about matters which I do not fully understand."[84] The premium placed here on human freedom is a consequence of the value placed by Augustine and Descartes on our having been made in God's image and hence on the extent to which human beings are distinctive among earthly beings in possessing a power of self-determination that resembles that of God.

The primary focus of Descartes's account of the will in the Fourth Meditation is the problem of error, but both the Augustinian roots of his theodicy and his remarks about the intimate connection between error and sin or evil reveal a specifically moral concern alongside the more obvious epistemological concern of the *Medita-tions*. Descartes adds the qualification in the "Synopsis" to the *Meditations* that the Fourth Meditation does not concern sin only after Arnauld admonishes him to do so, in the interest of avoiding theological controversy: "Anything which is not relevant and which could give rise to controversy should be omitted," that is, "prudence requires that" Descartes avoid addressing any questions touching upon "the pursuit of good and evil."[85] Not only prudence but also the aims and method guiding the *Meditations* recommend avoiding the subject of good and evil to whatever extent possible; the restricted sense of wisdom at work in the *Meditations* and the *Principles* leaves little if any room for a comprehensive discussion of the ground of moral judgments, because wisdom in this restricted sense is based on a foundation of clear and distinct insight. The *Meditations* is best viewed not as an attempt to trans-form ethics into a pursuit reducible to cognition but rather as an attempt to cleave off the basis of scientific inquiry from the larger framework of Christian concerns that relate the human soul to reality, that is, to God and creation.

Descartes's restricted sense of wisdom and the specific aim of the *Meditations* to provide a foundation for modern science do nothing to alter Descartes's commitment to what is otherwise a somewhat straightforwardly Christian conception of morality and to what, as I showed in the previous chapter, is a straightforwardly Augustinian-Thomistic account of the priority of faith over reason. The human will is confronted with the dual task of judging rightly with regard to material truth and the good, and in both types of judging, the will finds its only proper measure in the divine intel-lect. Gouhier captures the point quite succinctly when he writes that the God of Descartes "is at once a Christian God and a God of the philosopher."[86] From the standpoint of the cognition that moves the method, the God who functions as the measure for material truth must remain "anonymous and indeterminate."[87] From the stand-point of value and the endeavor to understand the place of the human in the larger scheme of things, God functions as a "personal moral agent" and hence as the measure for our choices in the concrete moral exigencies of life.[88]

3. THE EMERGING CLEAVAGE BETWEEN DESCARTES AND MEDIEVAL CHRISTIANITY

Descartes's adherence to an orthodox conception of the relationship between faith and reason does not prevent him from transforming the traditional endeavor to live in the nearness of God into one in which the cognitive and physical mastery of nature figures prominently. Following Galileo's assertion of both the autonomy of science and its compatibility with the moral mission of religion, Descartes sees the prospects for a mathematically based physics to overcome the limitations of Aristotelianism and to facilitate the project of systematic control over nature. The practical aims of modernity subsequently led to a cleavage between Descartes's methodological tools and the more authentic conceptions of self, nature, and God that are his Augustinian inheritance. Louis Dupré gives the following assessment of the modern predicament, which he traces back to Descartes:

> Mind is what defines (and soon will constitute) the real in ideal categories and controls it through praxis. The modern self possesses little content of its own, and this poverty contrasts with Augustine's conception of the soul, which to him was the richest of all concepts. While Descartes's self occasionally reveals glimpses of this former richness, he has set the notion of selfhood on a course where it was to become a functional one, namely, the source of meaning and value. . . . Here begins a development that reached its final conclusion in Fichte's conception of the self as a creative act.[89]

The main motive force behind this development is the elimination of final causes from the study of nature. The consequences of this elimination for understanding the relationship between man and world are enormous. In particular, the reduction of nature to a nexus of efficient causality effectively excludes the physical world from the objects of our moral concern; it drives a wedge between material nature and the spiritual realm, which includes God, human beings, and angels. It leads Descartes to refine our understanding of science to exclude theology. And it ultimately engenders a cleavage, already anticipated by Descartes, between morality as it bears upon earthly practice and as it bears upon eternal salvation.

In embracing the modern scientific aims and methods advanced by thinkers such as Galileo and Francis Bacon, Descartes finds it necessary to make modifications in the conceptions of God, self, and nature that he inherited from Augustine and Aquinas. His departure from the trajectory of medieval Christianity is best explained in terms of two main points of divergence from the thought of Saint Thomas: the elimination of teleology from the study of material nature and the refusal to treat theology as a science.

Aquinas advocates a view of the universe as hierarchically structured and directed at God as the summum bonum, the supreme good and end of all things:

> The entire universe is constituted by all creatures, as a whole consists of its parts. Now if we wish to assign an end to any whole, and to the parts of that whole, we shall find, first, that each and every part exists for the sake of its proper act, as the eye for the act of seeing; secondly, that the less honorable parts exist for the more honorable, as the senses for the intellect, the lungs for the heart; and, thirdly, that all parts are for the perfection of the whole, just as matter is for form, since the parts are, as it were, the matter of the whole. . . . Further still, the entire universe, with all its parts, is ordained towards God as its end, inasmuch as it imitates, as it were, and shows forth the divine goodness to the glory of God. Reasonable creatures, however, have in some special and higher manner God as their end, since they can attain to Him by their own operations, by knowing and

loving Him. Thus it is plain that the divine goodness is the end
of all corporeal things.[90]

This statement shows the relationship between ethics and ontology
in Aquinas. Everything that is participates in goodness to an extent
commensurate with that thing's rank in the order of things. What is
essential to things, not just spiritual beings but corporeal beings as
well, is their participation in and contribution to the wholeness and
perfection of things. For Aquinas, as for Aristotle, things that are in
a state of becoming are to be understood as moving from a state of
lesser perfection to a state of greater perfection and hence as
moving from a state of potentiality to actuality.[91] To understand natural things is to understand their place in the plan of divine providence.[92] To the extent that God's actions are purposive, we can
understand nature only by understanding God's ends. This in turn
demands a conception of nature that inscribes natural teleology
within the larger framework of divine providence.

Aquinas is guided by a commitment to marshaling Aristotelian
metaphysics in support of biblical dogmas such as the centrality
and immovability of the earth in God's creation. Descartes, inspired
by Galileo's endeavor to separate the exploration of physical questions from the traditional treatment of moral subjects, sees the enor
mous practical potential of abandoning teleology in favor of a
mathematical treatment of nature. An important focal point for this
bifurcation of the practical and the moral realms is the mathematical "reduction" of nature that Descartes recommends in the *Rules*
and the Second Meditation.

In the *Rules*, Descartes anticipates the reduction in the Second
Meditation of material nature to pure extension and its modes when
he proposes the representation of particular degrees of qualities like
color in terms of different geometrical figures.

> We simply make an abstraction, setting aside every feature of
> color apart from its possessing the character of shape, and con-

ceive of the the difference between white, blue, red, etc. as being like the difference between the following figures or similar ones [three different geometric figures are shown]. . . . The same can be said about everything perceivable by the senses, since it is certain that the infinite multiplicity of figures is sufficient for the expression of all the differences in perceivable things.[93]

Descartes thus proposes, in 1628, a program whereby cognitive models consisting of "simple natures" and their proper combination will yield enduring and reliable knowledge of natural processes. The *"naturas puras & simplices"* of the *Rules* anticipate the conception of clear and distinct perception in Descartes's mature philosophy; they include such notions as extension, "I am," and "God exists," although at the time of the *Rules*, Descartes has not yet worked out the underlying metaphysical conceptions that later allow him to locate each of these notions in the order of reasons.[94] His conception in the *Rules* is that "the whole of human knowledge consists uniquely in our achieving a distinct perception of how all these simple natures contribute to the composition of other things." We establish knowledge by constructing models in which the simple natures are joined by necessary rather than contingent connections.[95]

The proposal to reduce all observable phenomena to distinct geometric figures is a general statement of the principle at work in Descartes's conception of cognitive models. The three concrete examples he gives of such cognitive models are the magnet, the Tantalus device, and the motion of the stars. In the case of the magnet,

someone who thinks that nothing in the magnet can be known which does not consist of certain self-evident, simple natures . . . is in no doubt about how he should proceed. First he carefully gathers together all the available observations [*experimenta*] concerning the stone in question; then he tries to deduce from this what sort of mixture of simple natures is necessary for producing all the effects which the magnet is found to have. Once he has discovered this mixture, he is in a position to make the bold claim that he has discovered the true nature of the magnet, so far as it is humanly possible to discover it on the basis of given observations.[96]

Here Descartes assumes "a relationship of ground and consequent" between the simple natures that, ideally at least, mirrors the actual relationships governing changes of state in the material world.[97] In the case of the Tantalus machine, the question concerns how to model the construction of a vessel in which a model of Tantalus sits in the center and into which water continues to flow until it reaches Tantalus's mouth, at which point all the water drains out of the vessel.[98] In both the case of the magnet and the case of the Tantalus device, the measure of the truth of the model is the extent to which it allows us to reproduce the natural mechanisms in question. In the case of the motion of the stars, the measure of the truth of a given model is, although this is only implicit in Descartes's discussion, its predictive power.[99] The presentation of the general schema for representing observable qualities with geometric shapes is in the first instance an assertion of the possibility of treating all observable phenomena in the manner in which the magnet, the Tantalus device, and the motion of the stars have been modeled; it is at the same time the anticipation of digital culture in its entirety, replete with the representation of shapes, colors, sounds, forces, and the like in terms of distinct mathematical magnitudes.

In the *Rules*, Descartes focuses on the potential for mathematical representations of nature to enhance our ability to predict and control phenomena, and he adheres to this ideal in his mature writings. Along with the avowed ideal of establishing absolute certainty in our knowledge of the world, Descartes expresses an awareness that prediction and control may suffice as practical measures of truth. In Part 6 of the *Discourse*, he says that "it is the causes which are proved by the effects."[100] We do not see the causes in nature; we do not see, for example, a force called magnetism but rather only a set of observable effects on the basis of which we deduce the necessity of the cause. This means that the order of causes in nature may not be the same as the order that we attribute to them in our conceptual models. In the *Rules*, Descartes expresses an awareness that the orders of knowing and of being may not be the same, and there he proposes a practical criterion for assessing the adequacy of mental representations: he prefaces the proposal for reducing observable phenomena to geometric figures with the qualification that "you are not obliged to believe that things are as I suggest. But what is to prevent you from following these suppositions if it is obvious that they detract not a jot from the truth of things, but simply make everything much clearer?"[101] The measure of making things clearer is the extent to which our model enables us to produce a desired effect at a given time and in a given place; it is the extent, for example, to which our model enables us to construct a magnet that works just like one that we have found.

Descartes reiterates this practical commitment in Part 3 of the *Principles of Philosophy*. There he says that "in order to come to know the true nature of this visible world, it is not enough to find causes which provide an explanation of what we see far off in the heavens; the selfsame causes must also allow everything which we see right here on earth to be deduced from them."[102] It is not enough that a scientific theory is an account consistent with the observed phenomena; the theory must enable us to "deduce" the observed phenomena in the sense of reproducing them. Even if we suppose that a given theory is false, as long as it enables us to deduce the observed effects "we shall see that our hypothesis yields just as much practical benefit for our lives as we would have derived from knowledge of the actual truth <because we shall be able to use it just as effectively to manipulate natural causes so as to produce the effects we desire>."[103] Given its emphasis on practical application rather than on truth, this approach provides a certain leeway in the construction of scientific theories; "we are . . . free to make any assumption on these matters with the sole proviso that all the consequences of our assumption must agree with our experience."[104] This principle of leeway allows Descartes to take the position that the mechanistic approach to nature is not strictly in conflict with the biblical account of creation; all that Descartes insists upon for the mechanistic model is that it enable us to reproduce natural mechanisms, although he claims that his physical principles are the simplest, the easiest to understand, and the most probable.[105] The ultimate pragmatic criterion for the acceptability of a scientific theory is not the extent to which it approaches absolute truth but rather the extent to which it suffices for the manipulation of nature. In Part 4 of the *Principles*, Descartes substitutes for absolute truth the criterion of "moral certainty": the relevant criterion for assessing hypotheses about natural phenomena is the extent to which they have "sufficient certainty for application to ordinary life, even though they may be uncertain in relation to the absolute power of God."[106]

Descartes embraces the ideal of a "practical philosophy" that provides utility, but he does not abandon the ideal of absolute truth; he simply recognizes the limits of what can be known with absolute certainty. Both in the *Principles* and in correspondence with Mersenne, he gives clear priority to absolute truth over practical application, that is, even if we cannot achieve absolute certainty regarding physical phenomena, such certainty remains the regulative ideal of inquiry. Even if physics cannot attain absolute certainty because the diverse phenomena of the natural world are not entirely reducible to mechanistic models, Descartes still claims absolute certainty for the general principles that provide the foundation for physics. In 1640, he writes to Mersenne that "I agree that a single effect can be explained in several possible ways; but I do not think that the possibility of things in general can be explained except in one way, which is the true one."[107] A year later, he writes to Mersenne that "these six Meditations contain all the foundations of my physics. But please do not tell people, for that might make it harder for supporters of Aristotle to approve them. I hope that readers will gradually get used to my principles, and recognize their truth, before they notice that they destroy the principles of Aristotle."[108] In the Fourth Meditation, Descartes pronounces "the customary search for final causes to be totally useless in physics,"on the grounds that God "is capable of countless things whose causes are beyond my knowledge."[109] Descartes repeats this reasoning in Part 3 of the *Principles*, where he says that "it would be the height of presumption if we were to imagine that all things were created by God for our benefit alone, or even to suppose that the power of our minds can grasp the ends which he set before himself in creating the universe."[110] In the *Conversation with Burman*, Descartes derides "this constant practice of arguing from ends [as] Aristotle's greatest fault"; and he makes a distinction between "purposes which are known through revelation," in connection with which final causes are entirely appropriate, and matters that fall under the rubric of philosophy.[111] Philosophy here is to be understood in the terms in which it is explained in the letter to Picot and specifically in terms of the tree metaphor, in which philosophy provides the foundations for disciplines with practical applications. The ultimate roots of morality, on the other hand, derive from revelation and contemplation of God's purposes.

The reduction of nature to pure mechanism follows from a conception of knowledge and logical evidence that leaves no room for the Thomistic treatment of theology as a science. It is precisely because our relationship to God is not simply a cognitive one that Descartes must take recourse to faith. Shortly after writing the *Meditations*, Descartes expresses to Mersenne his conviction that faith plays an indispensable role in human life:

> One should note that what is known by natural reason—that [God] is all good, all powerful, all truthful, etc.—may serve to prepare infidels to receive the Faith, but cannot suffice to enable them to reach heaven. For that it is necessary to believe in Jesus Christ and other revealed matters, and that depends on grace.[112]

The ultimate source or measure of meaning in human life is tacitly skipped over in this statement, which links faith to the prospect of eternal salvation. But here Descartes's words remind us that our relationship to God is incomplete if we attempt to understand him solely through cognition. They help us to understand how Descartes, in the *Meditations*, is able to introduce into his discussions of God attributes that are not products of reason alone. From the standpoint of pure rational reflection, the idea of the infinite must remain entirely formal and empty, as must the idea of our relationship to the infinite, and yet Descartes characterizes God in more than a merely formal and empty way, and he proposes a relationship to God that is more than formal and empty. In the Third Meditation, he characterizes God not simply as *causa sui* and *instar archetypi* but more specifically as an intelligent creator who offers us life after our earthly existence.[113] In an early letter to Mersenne, he says that "all those to whom God has given the use of this reason have an obligation to employ it principally in the endeavor to know him and to know themselves."[114] And in the Second Replies, he explicitly characterizes God and our obligations toward him in specifically Christian terms:

> The sin that Turks and other infidels commit by refusing to embrace the Christian religion does not arise from their unwillingness to assent to obscure matters (for obscure they indeed are), but from their resistance to the impulses of divine grace within them, or from the fact that they make themselves unworthy of grace by their other sins. Let us take the case of an infidel who is destitute of all supernatural grace and has no knowledge of the doctrines which we Christians believe to have been revealed by God. If despite the fact that these doctrines are obscure to him, he is induced to embrace them by fallacious arguments, I make bold to assert that he will not on that account be a true believer, but will instead be committing a sin by not using his reason correctly. And I think that all orthodox theologians have always taken a similar view on this matter.[115]

For Descartes, the claim of the Christian God is universal, and it imposes on us specific obligations that are matters of divine revelation. To use one's reason correctly in this connection is to arrive at clarity about specifically Christian truths that are obscure from the standpoint of reason. Descartes's statement that one *commits a sin* by failing to employ reason in this manner recalls his statement in the *Discourse on Method* that he could not have kept his physics a secret "without sinning gravely against the law which obliges us to do all in our power to secure the general welfare of mankind." Even though Descartes does not link this idea directly to Christian faith in the *Discourse*, he makes this statement in the course of presenting a program for the development of "a practical philosophy" that will "render us . . . the masters and possessors of nature,"[116] and he does so immediately after asserting the earthly authority of "those whom God has set up as sovereigns over his people," which frames his statement about mastery in terms of the relationship between divine, natural, and human law proposed by Aquinas in the *Summa Theologica*.[117] The appeal to reason alone could never provide the basis for a sense of obligation to master nature, but to the extent that the law that "obliges us to do all in our power to secure the general welfare of mankind" is part of natural law, its legitimacy consists in its being derived from God's eternal law. Such a view of the relationship between human beings and nature is entirely consonant with the commitment, shared by Cartesian and Christian metaphysics, that the realm of nature is of a lower order of existence than the human soul and that the value of nature consists primarily if not exclusively in its contribution to human material welfare.

In Descartes's later writings, namely, the *Principles of Philosophy*, *The Passions of the Soul*, and his correspondence of the mid- to late 1640s, the question of our access and obligations to God is of fundamental concern. Descartes makes several very strong assertions concerning the primacy of faith in the *Principles of Philosophy*. In Part 1, as I note above, Descartes gives a clear priority to revelation over the natural light; there he also says that God can reveal things to us "about himself or others which [are] beyond the natural reach of our mind—such as the mystery of the Incarnation or of the Trinity."[118] Our relationship to the infinity of God is not simply abstract but instead gives rise to concrete, Christian content, even if that content is inaccessible through the natural light of reason alone, and even if that content is ultimately irreducible to cognitive insight.

Both our endeavor to secure ourselves in our earthly estate and our prospects for supernatural beatitude are grounded in divine veracity. Divine veracity is at once the foundation of the truth of clear and distinct insight and "of faith and all our belief."[119] Not only do we find ourselves compelled to assent to clear and distinct insights, but we also find ourselves compelled to act in accordance with clearly known goods, at least in those cases where goods can be clearly known. The primary difference between the scientific and the moral domains in this connection is simply that the truths of *scientia* are demonstrable, whereas "we must not in any way subject [the truths of theology] to critical examination."[120] By recognizing the power of human reason to base its conclusions on logical evidence, Descartes establishes a rigorous distinction between the domains of faith and reason. While the two domains are essentially compatible inasmuch as they refer back to the creative agency of God, faith refers to an order that is irreducibly obscure from the standpoint of human understanding, while reason refers to an order that is amenable to clear analysis.

This distinction leads Descartes to make a sharp attack on Aquinas's conception of theology. The fact that, as Maritain puts it, "the philosophy of clear ideas . . . is essentially repugnant to the idea of supra-rational mystery, of divine mystery, as the object of a *science* made possible by revelation" makes it incumbent upon Descartes to repudiate the Thomistic ideal of theology as a science.[121] Aquinas distinguishes between two senses of theology: sacred doctrine, which is a science rooted in revelation and surpassing the intellect, and "that theology which is part of philosophy."[122] Sacred doctrine is ultimately concerned with "those things that are in themselves of faith, which order us directly to eternal life," namely, "the secret of the Godhead, to see which is to possess happiness, and the mystery of Christ's Incarnation, *by Whom we have access* to the glory of the sons of God."[123] Philosophical theology, on the other hand, is a speculative endeavor that, while it ultimately needs the support of revelation and is intended to provide support of its own to faith, has a kind of quasi autonomy in virtue of which it can reflect on the traces of the divine in the world and establish abstract knowledge of God. Speculation in general has the character of moving progressively from a confused acquaintance with the objects of sense to an increasingly clear grasp of the principles underlying things; Aquinas describes this movement as one "from potentiality to act."[124] With regard to the objects of theology, this means that the intellect can arrive at abstract knowledge of God, which, while incomplete in itself, can supplement and reinforce the truths disclosed by faith. In the specific case of the endeavor of the intellect to know God, Aquinas says that

> our intellect cannot be led by sense so far as to see the essence of God; because sensible creatures are effects of God which do not equal the power of God, their cause. . . . But because they are His effects and depend on their cause, we can be led from them so far as to know of God *whether He exists*, and to know of Him what must necessarily belong to Him, as the first cause of all things, exceeding all things caused by Him.[125]

Hence, while matters like the Trinity are disclosed only through faith, the intellect can demonstrate the existence of God on the basis of our experience of the created world.[126]

Descartes's well-known attack on Aquinas's treatment of theology as a science has as its object the discipline of sacred doctrine. Descartes's acceptance of a philosophical or speculative theology is evident in his proofs of God's existence in the *Meditations*. His refusal to treat theology as a science is directed at Thomistic claims to possess knowledge of such supernatural beings as angels; it is a consequence not so much of a turn against Aquinas as of an attempt to refine the terms of the Thomistic distinction between faith and reason and the objects proper to each. For Descartes, the problem is not theology per se but rather the traditional association between theology and Aristotle. In an early letter to Mersenne, Descartes complains that theology "has been so deeply in the thrall of Aristotle that it is almost impossible to expound another philosophy without its seeming to be directly contrary to the Faith."[127] Subsequently, in the letters in which Descartes takes up the question of the creation of the eternal truths, he expresses an interest in confining his attention to philosophical questions and in leaving theology to the theologians; he says that "I do not want to involve myself in theology," on the grounds that "when truths depend on faith and cannot be proved by natural argument, it degrades them if one tries to support them by human reasoning and mere probabilities."[128] Theology "in the strict sense" concerns matters "dependent on revelation," and it needs to be as unencumbered by philosophical arguments as philosophical arguments need to be by revelation.[129] While the two domains need to be kept separate, they are nonetheless mutually compatible; moreover, to the extent that the restricted sense of wisdom sketched in the letter to Picot falls short of the whole sense of wisdom in human life, there is nothing inappropriate about the expectation that the fundamental limits of philosophy will be redressed through an appeal to theology "in the strict sense."

In the *Conversation with Burman*, Descartes brings his views on the relationship between philosophy and theology into sharper focus. There he reiterates the mutual compatibility of faith and reason, and he distinguishes the proper form of explanation in the two disciplines:

> This rule—that we must never argue from ends—should be carefully heeded. For, firstly, the knowledge of a thing's purpose

never leads us to knowledge of the thing itself; its nature remains just as obscure to us. Indeed, this constant practice of arguing from ends is Aristotle's greatest fault. Secondly, all the purposes of God are hidden from us, and it is rash to want to plunge into them. I am not speaking here of purposes which are known through revelation; it is purely as a philosopher that I am considering them. It is here that we completely go astray.[130]

The chief target of Descartes's attack on Aquinas in this connection is Aquinas's extensive writings on the possibility of establishing knowledge of angels. In the Third Meditation, Descartes introduces a passing reference to the idea we have of angels, and in the Second Replies he says that such an idea "can be put together from the ideas which we have of God and of man."[131] When Burman asks Descartes how it is possible for us to have an idea of an angel, Descartes modifies his answer somewhat: "As far as the idea of an angel goes, it is certain that we form it from the idea we have of our own mind: this is the sole source of our knowledge of it. And this is so true that we can think of nothing in an angel *qua* angel that we cannot also notice in ourselves."[132] Descartes alters his explanation of the genesis of our idea of an angel to lay emphasis on the transgression of the limits of human understanding in Aquinas's angelology:

Saint Thomas wanted every angel to be of a different kind from every other, and he described each one in as much detail as if he had been right in their midst, which is how he got the honorific title of the "Angelic Doctor." Yet although he spent more time on this question than on almost anything else, nowhere were his labours more pointless. For knowledge about angels is virtually out of our reach, when we do not derive such knowledge from our own minds, as I have said. We just do not know the answers to all the standard questions concerning angels, for example whether they can be united with a body, or what the bodies were like which they frequently took in the Old Testament, and so on. It is best for us to follow Scripture and believe they were young men, or appeared as such, and so forth.[133]

Aquinas argues that angels are beings whose existence can be proved and whose place in the order of things can be specified in detail.[134] Aquinas attempts to give *rational arguments*, for example, that angels "exist in exceeding great number, far beyond all material multitude"; that they "have not bodies naturally united to them" but can "sometimes assume bodies"; that angels can communicate with one another by means of "interior speech," which "expresses metaphorically the angel's power by which he manifests his mental concept"; and the like.[135] Descartes criticizes such angelology for failing to respect the limits of human reason and for failing to pay proper respect to the power of revelation. He says that "it is not clear by natural reason alone whether angels are created like minds distinct from bodies, or like minds united to bodies. I never decide about questions on which I have no certain reasons, and I never allow room for conjectures."[136] Even if this is a bit of a distortion of Aquinas's position—he never suggests that our knowledge of angels is derived exclusively from natural reason—it nonetheless highlights what for Descartes is a serious flaw in Thomistic theology: its commingling of revelation and reason, where a rigorous distinction between the two is needed. Descartes's derision of Aquinas's angelology is meant to draw attention to this flaw and to draw out the logical consequences of the Thomistic distinction between revealed theology (sacred doctrine) and speculative or philosophical theology.

In the *Notae in Programma*, Descartes clarifies his view of the proper relationship between philosophy and theology. He distinguishes three sorts of questions: those "believed through faith alone—such as the mystery of the Incarnation"; those which, "while having to do with faith, can also be investigated by natural reason," such as "the existence of God, and the distinction between the human soul and the body"; and those "which have nothing whatever to do with faith, and which are the concern solely of human reasoning, such as the problem of squaring the circle, or of making gold by the techniques of alchemy, and the like."[137] Philosophy can aid theology in questions of the first sort by showing that such questions are not incompatible with the natural light; and in questions of the second sort, the function of philosophy is "to demonstrate them to the best of their ability by arguments which are grounded in human reason."[138] In general, Descartes takes the position that as a philosopher he prefers not to take a stand on truths of revelation.[139] One particular concern in this connection is the doctrine of the Trinity, which even Aquinas acknowledges to be irreducible to rational insight.[140] Descartes treats in comparable terms the doctrine of the immortality of the human soul. In the preface and synopsis of the *Meditations*, Descartes intimates that he can at least "attempt" a rational demonstration of immortality; in the synopsis he notes that such a demonstration presupposes "an account of the whole of physics."[141] But in the Second Replies he repudiates the idea that reason can establish the immortality of the soul, maintaining that immortality is an article of faith and even claiming that "he wrote nothing concerning the immortality of the soul" in the *Meditations*.[142]

Descartes's position that reason cannot establish knowledge of such matters as the Trinity, immortality, or angels follows directly from his insistence on maintaining a rigorous distinction between faith and reason. One key consequence of that distinction is the autonomy of reason in questions bearing upon natural science and the manipulation of natural mechanisms; another equally important consequence is the implicit consignment of fundamental questions of value to the realm of faith. Descartes's assertion that he would be committing a "sin" by failing to share with the world his program for the mastery of nature is of a piece with his conviction that "Turks and other infidels" commit a "sin . . . by refusing to embrace the Christian religion"—these statements inscribe the idea of righteous conduct within the framework of a Christian conception of value, and they acknowledge the impossibility of deriving either the mandate to master nature or the supremacy of the Christian religion from the natural light of reason.[143] When it comes to the question of giving an account of the metaphysics of transubstantiation, however, Descartes makes an important and ultimately fateful exception to his demand for a strict separation of reason and revelation.

4. DISPUTES CONCERNING THE ORTHODOXY OF DESCARTES'S CHRISTIANITY

Descartes was willing to address the question of transubstantiation because it was widely viewed as the definitive litmus test for the "Christianity" of a philosopher's views. Shortly after the publication of the *Meditations*, Descartes wrote to Mersenne of his interest in demonstrating the special compatibility of his philosophy with Christian faith. There he expresses a recognition of the need to address the question of the Eucharist:

> You will see that in [the Fourth Replies] I reconcile the doctrine of the Councils about the Blessed Sacrament with my own philosophy—so much that I maintain that it is impossible to give a satisfactory explanation of the doctrine by means of the traditional philosophy. Indeed, I think that the latter would have been rejected as clashing with the Faith if mine had been known first. . . . So I have decided not to keep silent on the matter, and to fight with their own weapons the people who confound Aristotle with the Bible and abuse the authority of the Church in order to vent their passions—I mean the people who had Galileo condemned. They would have my views condemned likewise if they had the power; but if there is ever any question of that, I am confident that I can show that none of the tenets of their philosophy accords with the Faith so well as my doctrines.[144]

The purpose of giving a philosophical account of transubstantiation is not to revise or correct any biblical dogma but rather to address a question of the second kind outlined in the *Notae in Programma* and to do so in a way that makes a compelling case to such authorities as the theology faculty of the Sorbonne that they should endorse Descartes's philosophical writings.

But this was not the only problem Descartes faced in his endeavor to gain acceptance for his philosophy. The intellectual climate in which Descartes worked was one in which the question of a philosopher's fidelity to Christian doctrine was one of paramount importance. Yet there was no one settled view of orthodoxy; instead, the reception of Descartes's thought was influenced by the fortunes of schools of thought that include Jansenism and Molinism, which in the seventeenth century were engaged in heated disputes concerning grace, original sin, predestination, and ultimately human freedom. By making an account of human freedom central to his metaphysics, Descartes found his ideas implicated in the disputes between the Jansenists and the Molinists, and the eventual placement of Descartes's philosophy on the *Index librorum prohibitorum* in 1663 and the prohibition of the teaching of his works in Paris in 1671 may have had as much to do with the outcome of the Jansenist-Molinist dispute as with the perceived failure of his account of transubstantiation. I next examine Descartes's attempt to reconcile transubstantiation with his metaphysics and then outline the nature of his disputes in the Netherlands and their implications for the Jansenist-Molinist debate.

Descartes addressed the problem of reconciling transubstantiation with his philosophy as early as 1630, and by 1638 he claims to have arrived at a satisfactory solution to the problem.[145] The need to address this question is made incumbent upon Descartes by his rejection of Aristotelianism, specifically by his rejection of substantial forms and real accidents. Descartes wrote to Regius in 1642 that

> the denial of substantial forms can be reconciled with Holy Scripture. . . . [W]hen we deny substantial forms, we mean by the expression a certain substance joined to matter, making up with it a merely corporeal whole, and which, no less than matter and even more than matter—since it is called an actuality and matter

only a potentiality—is a true substance, or self-subsistent thing. Such a substance, or substantial form, present in merely corporeal things but distinct from matter, is nowhere, we think, mentioned in Holy Scripture.[146]

A review of the intrigues surrounding Descartes's attempt to gain ecclesiastical support for his philosophy shows that departures from strict Aristotelianism were generally received as prima facie signs of hostility toward Christian orthodoxy. People such as Voetius based their attacks on Descartes principally on the anti-Aristotelian tenets of Cartesian physics, and it is specifically in response to a challenge from Voetius that Descartes asserts the compatibility between theology and the metaphysics of the *Meditations*.[147]

But not everyone who challenged Descartes to reconcile the dogma of transubstantiation with mechanistic physics was his enemy. Arnauld was a Sorbonne theologian and a member of the Port-Royal circle, a group of Jansenists who sought to vindicate an Augustinian sense of the dependence of salvation on divine grace. Arnauld accepts Descartes's Christianity without question; he issues his challenge to Descartes concerning the Eucharist in the spirit of defending Cartesian philosophy and physics against its detractors.[148] Arnauld challenges Descartes in the concluding section of the Fourth Objections, "Points Which May Cause Difficulty to Theologians." He writes that the implications of Descartes's metaphysical views for the traditional doctrine of transubstantiation are "likely to give the greatest offense to theologians" because "according to the author's doctrines it seems that the Church's teaching concerning the sacred mysteries of the Eucharist cannot remain completely intact."[149] Arnauld defends the orthodox view, according to which "we believe on faith that the substance of the bread is taken away from the bread of the Eucharist and only the accidents remain."[150] This would mean that qualities such as "shape, extension, and mobility remain" in the bread after the consecration of the sacrament but without any substance in which to inhere. This is unacceptable for Descartes, because he rejects the notion of real accidents and instead believes that accidents must inhere in a substance. In the Fourth Replies, he attempts to avoid recourse to real accidents by giving the following explanation:

> the surface of the bread or wine or any other body should not in this context be taken to be a part of the substance or the quantity of the body in question, nor should it be taken to be a part of the surrounding bodies. It should be taken to be simply the boundary that is conceived to be common to the individual particles and the bodies that surround them; and this boundary has absolutely no reality except a modal one.[151]

For Descartes, this is sufficient for concluding that "the new substance must affect all our senses in exactly the same way as that in which the bread and wine would be affecting them if no transubstantiation had occurred," and Arnauld eventually accepts it as sufficient.[152]

It is difficult to understand Descartes's position simply by reading Arnauld's objection and Descartes's reply. Several years later, Descartes spells out the terms of the controversy in a way that makes his position somewhat clearer. The controversy over transubstantiation involves two questions: "One is how it can come about that all the accidents of the bread remain in a place where the bread is no longer present, and where another body is taking its place. The other is how the body of Jesus Christ can exist within the same dimensions where the bread was."[153] Scholastics had attempted to argue that the substance of the bread is either converted into (Aquinas) or replaced by (Scotus) the substance of Christ's body, and that

> the "accidents" of the bread (i.e., its non-essential qualities, including its sensible appearance) remain, although *not* inhering in Christ's body as substratum. Moreover, Christ's body is really underneath the appearances of the bread not with its own dimensions (that is, not as an extended human body) but solely with its substantiality. . . . There is a *real presence* only of the substance

of Christ's body in the Eucharist; its dimensions are there by a "natural concomitance."[154]

In the Fourth Objections, Arnauld addresses one of the two questions that Descartes poses in his 1646 letter. Arnauld points out that an account of the Eucharist that appeals to the notion of real accidents is precluded by Descartes's theory of matter inasmuch as the observer dependence of sensible qualities makes it impossible for the accidents to be self-subsistent.[155]

Descartes's remarks in the Fourth Replies are intended to provide an answer to both of the questions posed in his letter of March 1646. By the time of writing that letter, Descartes had conducted a correspondence for several years with Mesland on the question of the Eucharist, although that correspondence was cut off abruptly when the Jesuits banished Mesland to Canada for showing too much sympathy to Descartes's approach.[156] Of decisive importance here is the fact that Descartes's theory of matter makes it difficult for him to give an explanation of the Eucharist that will be satisfactory to anyone accustomed to the traditional account, which appeals to the Aristotelian notion of substantial forms.

In the letter to Father Dinet, Descartes reaffirms his resolution of the problem of the Eucharist and asserts the rights of his philosophy against the increasingly vitriolic attacks lodged by Gisbertus Voetius, professor of theology (and later rector) of Utrecht University. Descartes goes so far in this letter as to claim that the articles of Christian faith are preeminently compatible with his philosophy:

> As far as theology is concerned, since one truth can never be in conflict with another, it would be impious to fear that any truths discovered in philosophy could be in conflict with the truths of faith. Indeed, I insist that there is nothing relating to religion which cannot be equally well or even better explained by means of my principles than can be done by means of those which are commonly accepted.[157]

In his remarks on the Eucharist, Descartes proceeds on the implicit assumption that if he can account for transubstantiation in terms of his philosophy, then there can be absolutely no question concerning the compatibility between his philosophy and Christian doctrine. Descartes encountered opposition in this connection from both Voetius and from Bourdin, the author of the Seventh Objections. Descartes makes reference to both of these disputes in the letter to Dinet;[158] he appends the letter to the Seventh Replies because Dinet was Bourdin's superior in the Jesuit order and hence was a potential ally in Descartes's endeavor to vindicate himself and his philosophy in these disputes with exponents of orthodox Scholasticism.

These disputes reach an extreme in Descartes's conflict with Voetius. This conflict was initiated by Regius, who sought to promote Descartes's philosophy in the Netherlands; to this end, Regius undertook a series of three disputations at Utrecht University in 1641, in which he attempts to defend Cartesian physics.[159] The third of these disputations became quite heated, as a result of Regius's attempt to argue to the theology faculty that the union of mind and body is accidental rather than substantial; this "directly compromised the dogma of the resurrection of the body" and hence was received by the theology faculty as tantamount to atheism.[160]

Voetius responded to this by launching a protracted and vitriolic attack on Descartes; in particular, Voetius attacks Descartes's proofs of the existence of God, and he defends the Aristotelian notion of substantial forms. Voetius's basic intent is to show that Descartes's philosophy has not been proved to be an adequate substitute for the Aristotelian philosophy that was canonical in Utrecht and hence that Descartes's thought should not be taught or discussed there at all. In March 1642, Voetius succeeded in moving the Utrecht academic senate to issue a formal condemnation of Cartesian philosophy, partly on the grounds that it conflicts with orthodox theology.[161] Around the same time, as a further means to promote this end, and in response to Descartes's attack on him in the letter to Father Dinet, Voetius enlisted his student Martinus

Schoock to write the bitterly anti-Cartesian *Admiranda Methodus*, which was published in 1643. In it Schoock undertakes a general attack on Descartes's conceptions of reason and method, and in particular he argues that Descartes's method leads to atheism.[162]

In response, Descartes wrote the two-hundred-page *Epistola ad Voetium* in 1643.[163] Descartes believes that Voetius is really the author of the *Admiranda Methodus* and directs his response to Voetius rather than to Schoock. In this response, Descartes vehemently rejects the criticisms of his metaphysics presented in the *Admiranda*, and in particular he denies the charge of atheism.[164] Voetius, who by this time was rector of Utrecht University, brought charges of libel against Descartes for having claimed that Voetius had written the *Admiranda* and for lodging these charges against him. Ultimately Descartes had to appeal to the Prince of Orange to intervene on his behalf.

Regius's actions following the dispute with Voetius led to a break between Descartes and Regius that culminated in the *Notae in Programma*. It is clear already in Regius's Utrecht disputations that he is interested entirely in vindicating Cartesian physics and that theological or metaphysical foundations are of relatively little interest to him. In 1645, within a year of the publication of Descartes's *Principles of Philosophy*, Regius sent Descartes the manuscript of his *Fundamenta Physice*, a text on natural philosophy that exhibits, in Descartes's opinion, an utter failure to comprehend the nature and importance of metaphysical foundations. Descartes wrote to Regius, strongly advising against publishing the *Fundamenta*. In his letter, Descartes admonishes Regius that those who read the proofs in the *Fundamenta* "will make fun of them and hold them in contempt"; Descartes says that he "was astounded and saddened" by Regius's insistence on publishing views that are both incorrect and dangerous and that "I find it necessary to declare once and for all that I differ from you on metaphysical questions as much as I possibly could."[165] Descartes is clearly afraid that his prior association with Regius, and the fact that for some years Regius had been playing the role of self-appointed defender of Descartes, would lead people to attribute Regius's objectionable and poorly thought-out ideas to Descartes.

In spite of this admonition, Regius published the *Fundamenta Physice* in 1646. In the letter to Picot, Descartes responds by making a clear break with Regius:

> I am well aware that there are some people who are so hasty and use so little circumspection in what they do that even with very solid foundations they cannot construct anything certain. . . . I recently had some experience of this from one of those who were reckoned to be particularly anxious to follow me. . . . Last year he published a book entitled The Foundations of Physics in which, as far as physics and medicine are concerned, it appears that everything he wrote was taken from my writings. . . . But because he copied down the material inaccurately and changed the order and denied certain truths of metaphysics on which the whole of physics must be based, I am obliged to disavow his work entirely.[166]

Here Descartes notes that in his 1643 letter to Voetius he expressed complete confidence in Regius's intelligence and had seen complete accord between Regius's ideas and his own; by 1647, however, Descartes completely disavows any connection with Regius's ideas. Central to Descartes's disavowal is Regius's complete rejection of Descartes's metaphysics.[167]

Just which "certain truths of metaphysics" Descartes has in mind here becomes clear in Regius's response to these remarks. Shortly after the publication of the French edition of the *Principles*, Regius anonymously published a *programma* or broadsheet in 1648 titled *Explicatio Mentis Humanae*, in which he argues against the idea that soul is necessarily independent of body and also argues against the view that having an idea of God suffices to prove that God exists.[168] Descartes responded to the *Explicatio* with his *Notae in Programma*, in which he sharply criticizes both of these points immediately after offering the vehement defense of the place of faith and Christian dogma in the foundations of his philosophy that I examine above.[169]

As for Descartes's fortunes in the Netherlands, Verbeek's analysis makes several things clear: even though Cartesianism was suppressed by law in Utrecht in 1642, the law went largely unenforced; even though the regulations in Leiden and Utrecht prohibited the *teaching* of Descartes's ideas, the Utrecht law stopped short of prohibiting *disputations*, which proved instrumental in the dispute with Regius and Voetius; even in spite of the prohibitions, in Utrecht at least, by the mid-1650s, "Cartesian philosophy had become a normal part of university routine."[170] Verbeek shows that the prohibition in Utrecht was intended not so much to suppress the spread of Descartes's thought as to moderate the increasingly violent disagreements fomented by Voetius.[171]

Verbeek's analysis of Descartes's reception in the Netherlands also makes clear just how common it was in the seventeenth century for opponents in religico-metaphysical disputes to charge one another with atheism. Verbeek shows just how vitriolic Voetius's attacks were on the Remonstrants, who subscribed to an anti-Calvinist view of the reality of human freedom and repentance, and it shows how Voetius's attacks on Descartes were due to the similarity of Descartes's views to those of the Remonstrants, even though "most Cartesians were perfectly orthodox from a religious point of view."[172] And Verbeek shows how Descartes's piety was impugned by Jacobus Revius, who found Descartes's conception of God as *causa sui* to be so inconsistent with orthodox Calvinism as to smack of Pelagianism.[173]

The charge of Pelagianism raises the question of Descartes's relationship to the context of religious controversies in the seventeenth century that concern the role of human freedom in good works and eternal salvation. These controversies have their roots in Augustine's own dispute with the Pelagians over the question whether man's redemption is dependent primarily on grace or on human striving. In his study of the rise of Jansenism, Alexander Sedgwick focuses the controversy in the following terms:

> While some Catholics may be described as having a comparatively optimistic view of human nature, others, influenced by Augustinian theology, were more pessimistic about man's natural inclinations. In his later years, Saint Augustine had vigorously attacked what he perceived to be the heretical convictions of Pelagius and his followers. Influenced by the ethical principles of Stoicism as well as of Christianity, the Pelagians emphasized the human potential for good, at the expense of original sin. Augustine, on the other hand, insisted that man's nature had been seriously impaired by original sin, for which reason man on his own had no potential for good. Only by means of God's healing grace was man able to achieve salvation.[174]

Whereas Augustine viewed eternal salvation as a matter of grace, the Pelagians viewed salvation as something to be earned by human striving. Pelagianism was condemned at the Council of Carthage in 418, but different versions of the controversy manifested themselves almost immediately thereafter and persisted into the seventeenth century. Near the end of Augustine's life, the semi-Pelagians proposed a sort of middle position between Augustine and the Pelagians, according to which human freedom is subject to divine grace but can nonetheless contribute to salvation; the semi-Pelagians rejected the Augustinian doctrine of predestination, according to which part of grace is the determination of which souls will be saved and which will not. Much of the semi-Pelagian view was rejected by the second Council of Orange (529), which decreed that "grace brings one to baptism, but the grace conferred in baptism restores the freedom of the will. One can hereafter choose either good or evil."[175]

The question of the relationship between grace and human agency was revisited at the Council of Trent (1545–1563) in response to the Lutheran Reformation. Luther argued that original sin destroyed freedom of the will, so that our subjection to original sin means that we are incapable of doing good. The council decreed that "free will, weakened as it was in its powers and downward bent, was by no means extinguished."[176] In keeping with Augustinian orthodoxy, grace is still required for salvation, but man's "justification" requires a voluntary acceptance of grace:

> This disposition or preparation [for justification] is followed by justification itself, which is not only a remission of sins but also the sanctification and renewal of the inward man through the voluntary reception of the grace and gifts whereby an unjust man becomes just and from being an enemy becomes a friend, that he may be an heir according to hope of life everlasting.[177]

The Council of Trent thus decreed that grace alone is not sufficient for salvation and that human efforts such as following the commandments are both possible and necessary.[178]

In the sixteenth and seventeenth centuries, the long-standing controversies over the relative merits of grace and human freedom were focused in the dispute between the Molinists and the Jansenists. In the sixteenth century, Ignatius of Loyola affirmed the role of human freedom in eternal salvation and the compatibility of freedom with divine grace. In the *Spiritual Exercises* (1548), he says that

> in our discourse we ought not to emphasize the doctrine that would destroy free will. We may therefore speak of faith and grace to the extent that God enables us to do so, for the greater praise of His Divine Majesty. But, in these dangerous times of ours, it must not be done in such a way that good works or free will suffer any detriment or be considered worthless.[179]

This became a canonical Jesuit line of thinking; in 1588 the Jesuit Luis de Molina reaffirmed it in *Liberi arbitrii cum gratiæ donis, divina præscientia, prædestinatione et reprobatione concordia*

(*The Concord of Free Will with the Gift of Grace*, generally known as the *Concordia*), in which he argues that "sufficient grace for salvation is never denied to man, and that the factual efficacy of grace depends upon free human consent, although its infallibility depends upon God, the mode of whose prescience includes and transcends human indetermination."[180]

Conceived in broad terms, the dispute that Molina addresses is between an Augustinian position that gives fundamental primacy to divine grace and predestination and a Pelagian position according to which human freedom is real and makes some sort of independent contribution to salvation. Molina and the Jesuits fall generally on the side of the Pelagians in this dispute but not without some important qualifications. Molina is severely critical of the determinism of the Manichaeans and what he takes to be the Pelagians' practical denial of providence. Molina's position is that "fallen man . . . is capable of positing the act of saving faith with prevenient grace, but not without."[181] Molina sees the apparent conflict between divine predestination and human free will: how can my efforts have any bearing on my salvation if the eventual disposition of my soul is known to God from eternity? Molina offers a solution that anticipates Leibniz's attempt to reconcile divine foreknowledge and free will: Molina argues that "predestination includes a condition of foreknowledge of the way in which man will use his free will in certain circumstances; this foreknowledge distinguishes predestination from providence."[182] In this way, Molina and the Jesuits thought that they could reconcile free will and predestination in a way that would preserve the notion of moral accountability.

Cornelius Jansen sees the Jesuit position as a perversion of Augustinian orthodoxy, and in 1640 he published *Augustinus* as an attack on the Jesuits and on neo-Scholasticism generally. Jansen calls Molina's position a kind of Pelagianism, and he argues for the primacy of grace by maintaining that the exercise of human freedom apart from grace can lead only to sin. Moreover, Jansen maintains that where grace does manifest itself, human will is never in a position to resist it, nor does grace require human cooperation to succeed. The publication of Jansen's *Augustinus* occurred at a time when disputes between the Jesuits and the Augustinians had been going on for some time. In 1611 Cardinal Bérulle founded the Oratory, an order devoted to a reform of the priesthood on the basis of adherence to the writings of Augustine; Bérulle, in a famous meeting in 1628, is said to have encouraged Descartes to pursue his researches, and Gouhier believes that Bérulle may specifically have encouraged Descartes to read Augustine.[183] Guillaume Gibieuf was another member of the Oratory whose views seem to have influenced Descartes. In 1630, Gibieuf published *De libertate Dei et Creaturae*, which defended a strict Augustinian conception of will that Descartes considers to be at least compatible with his own views on divine liberty.[184]

Another group that supported the Augustinian position and explicitly endorsed Jansenism is the Port-Royal circle, which includes Pascal and Descartes's ally Antoine Arnauld. In 1643, Arnauld published *De la fréquente communion*, in which he reasserts the Jansenist view of the primacy of grace; he also attacks the Jesuit view of the will as anti-Catholic Pelagianism and condemns the Jesuit formula for repentance as unduly lax. The Jesuits reponded by launching a campaign of strong opposition to Jansenism. The political implications of the Molinist-Jansenist dispute are such that in 1653, Pope Innocent X issued the bull *Cum occasione*, in which he condemns the main tenets of Jansen's *Augustinus*. In particular, the *Cum occasione* defends the principle of man's voluntary acceptance of grace rather than his necessary subjection to it and defends the Jesuits against the charge of Pelagianism. Shortly thereafter, in 1655, Arnauld was expelled from the Sorbonne.

Descartes's rejection of Aristotelianism and his views on the will placed him, if only entirely against his own intention, in the middle of these theological disputes. In calling for a return to Augustinian orthodoxy, the Jansenists placed themselves in opposition to the Aristotelian Thomism of the Jesuits. Descartes's attempt at a mechanistic explanation of the Eucharist, with its explicit rejection of substantial forms and real qualities, must have invited the association of Descartes's philosophy with Jansenism.[185] Moreover, the close associations between Descartes's and Augustine's conceptions of the soul, the will, and the soul's relationship to God could well have reinforced the Jesuits' sense that there is a special compatibility between Descartes's philosophy and Jansenism.

On the other hand, Descartes's clear departure from Augustine has fundamental implications that preclude any facile association between Descartes and Jansenism. Notwithstanding his deep conceptual indebtedness to Augustine, Descartes makes a decisive departure from Augustine in asserting the rights of practical philosophy in human life, and in doing so, he at least partly detaches the project of earthly existence from the ideal of eternal salvation. Most importantly, as I argue below in chapter 4, Augustine would have found it impossible to endorse a view of human agency the goal of which is the systematic study and mastery of nature. Jansenist opponents of Descartes could point to his views on the will and his advocacy of a program for the mastery of nature as grounds for leveling the charge of Pelagianism against him.

Descartes's careful separation of the prospect of eternal salvation from questions of earthly practice puts him in a strong position to repudiate this charge. In a letter to Mersenne written several years before the publication of Jansen's *Augustinus*, Descartes addresses the question whether the human will is capable of doing good. He says that when "well-doing . . . [is] understood in a theological sense," that is, when what is at stake is our salvation, he cannot take a philosophical stand because "there grace comes into the question." Descartes refuses to address such a purely "theological" question, implicitly leaving it to the theologians to examine. But when it comes to action "in the sense of moral and natural philosophy, where no account is taken of grace," Descartes's position is that "in order to do well it is sufficient to judge well," that is, acting well is a genuine possibility for us in our earthly condition and requires only that we use our faculty of judgment properly. Human willing can do good things within the context of earthly existence, but our salvation is entirely in the hands of divine grace; therefore, Descartes points out, he "cannot be accused . . . of the error of the Pelagians."[186]

Descartes's position on the efficacy of the will ultimately makes him more Molinist than Jansenist, but he nonetheless stops short of Pelagianism. Descartes treats earthly good works as oriented entirely on the material welfare and peaceful existence of mankind. He sees earthly existence as an anticipation of eternal salvation, and he considers grace to be an absolute prerequisite for eternal salvation. Descartes's interest in the Jansenist-Molinist dispute is limited to a desire to show that his conception of the will should not be offensive to either side in the dispute. In the *Principles*, he adopts what appears to be a Molinist stand on the question of preordination, but when it comes to the problem of reconciling preordination with the freedom of the will, Descartes simply notes the difficulties involved, implicitly leaving the resolution of these difficulties to theologians.[187]

Descartes's real interest is not in taking a stand on any of these disputes but rather in developing the foundations of modern science and arguing for their compatibility with Christianity. The fact that Descartes was charged by the Jansenists with Pelagianism is of a piece with the fact that Voetius and others charged Descartes with atheism. In both cases, Descartes's antagonists are unable to see that his devotion to the new science and his belief that this science is entirely consistent with the Christian faith are born of a pure interest in truth that transcends the religico-political disputes in which these antagonists are embroiled. Descartes sees the potential for a mechanistic physics to facilitate a systematic understanding of nature and to enhance human welfare. He is convinced of the potential to incorporate such a physics into the Christian worldview that he has inherited from Augustine and Aquinas, and in the spirit of Galileo, he tries to find ways to accommodate the interpretation of Christian dogma to the incontrovertible conclusions of philosophical method and natural science. His interest in avoiding theological disputes is not a sign of cowardice or pragmatism but rather is a consequence of his desire to maintain a clear separation between his personal devotion to Catholicism and his professional vocation as a natural philosopher.

5. CHARGES OF DISSIMULATION AND THE QUESTION OF DESCARTES'S SINCERITY

Although many leading interpreters of Descartes have acknowledged the sincerity of his appeals to Christianity and the systematic place of Christian concepts in his philosophy, there is also a prominent countertendency, extending back into Descartes's own time, to view him as a secular atheist interested entirely in the development of a physics with practical applications. Certainly the actions of Regius did much to popularize the thesis that Descartes was an atheist, as did the reciprocal charges of atheism issued by various opponents in the seventeenth-century debates over grace, original sin, free will, and transubstantiation. The terms of the debate have not changed much in the intervening centuries. Given the profound influence that this debate has had on our historical reception of Descartes, particularly regarding his views on the compatibility between his philosophy and Christianity, I now examine the terms of this debate in some depth.

   In the twentieth century, Maritain declares that "Descartes was sincerely Catholic," and Jaspers proposes that Descartes's Catholicism "was essential to the meaning of his entire philosophy and to the practical grounding of his life,"[188] but the suggestion has also been made that Descartes's

   moral philosophy is non-religious in principle and perhaps deliberately hostile to religion. . . . He feigns submission to the

Church and pretends to possess a metaphysics which upholds the existence of God and the immortality of the soul. This pretense is made necessary by his understandable desire to avoid persecution for heterodox opinions.[189]

Caton offers an extreme statement of what has come to be known as "the dissimulation thesis," the thesis that Descartes concealed or "dissimulated" his true intentions due to fear of persecution by religious and political authorities who would certainly have persecuted Descartes if he were to admit that his philosophy has no relevance to nor any need of religious concepts whatsoever. According to the dissimulation thesis, Descartes's appeals to God and perhaps even to the soul are disingenuous attempts to conceal the atheistic underpinnings of the new science. The advocates of this thesis also call into question Descartes's appeals to faith and his expressions of respect for church authority.

I have shown that Descartes makes numerous appeals to the primacy of revelation or faith over the natural light of reason throughout his writings, and that faith performs the function of providing a substantive ground for concrete ethical commitments, where reason can do no more than clarify the logical consequences or implications of the fundamentally obscure subject matter first disclosed by faith. Hence on a prima facie reading of Descartes's thought, faith is indispensable in the endeavor to ground concrete norms for human action.

But are Descartes's statements about the importance of faith and God to be taken at face value? Advocates of the most extreme form of the dissimulation thesis insist not only that Descartes is not a sincere Christian but also that he is a strict metaphysical materialist who reduces God to extension and really believes that human beings are purely material, without an immortal soul. This view has had its vigorous exponents ever since Descartes's own time. Descartes's contemporary Henry More characterizes him as "a pleasant and abundantly cunning and abstruse Genius" who must be "either Delirant and Crazed, or else Plays Tricks" when he proposes the immateriality of the mind."[190] La Mettrie maintains that "whatever he recounts about the distinction between the two substances, it is obvious that it was only a trick, a cunning device to make the theologians swallow the poison hidden behind an analogy that strikes everyone and that they alone cannot see."[191] Maxime Leroy believes that "Descartes dissimulated his true thought" behind a public mask that he hoped would conceal "the consequences of his thought that were irreligious, or at any rate those that were destructive to Catholic theology."[192] And Charles Adam maintains that Descartes "wants to gain acceptance for [his physics] by advancing their principles under the cover of an orthodox metaphysics. The flag, if one dare say so, was to cover the goods; and Descartes cherished the goods at least as much as the flag."[193]

Not everyone who entertains the possibility of dissimulation arrives at such an extreme conclusion. Elizabeth Haldane takes a more modest approach in her biography of Descartes when she suggests that whereas Descartes was alarmed by the sanctions imposed on Galileo for advocating the Copernican hypothesis, and whereas Descartes's conduct does exhibit a certain "moral weakness," he "was a scholar much more than a reformer" and simply suppressed his more controversial views rather than engage in outright dissimulation.[194] Whether this interpretation holds for all of Descartes's writings and actions is a difficult question; at any rate, there is ample support in Descartes's early correspondence with Mersenne that it holds without qualification for the publication of *Le Monde*, composed during 1629–1633 but published only in 1664. In 1629, Descartes writes to Mersenne that he is preparing to publish a treatise on sublunary phenomena and that he will "hide behind the scene [*tableau*] in order to hear what people will say about it."[195] Shortly thereafter, Descartes again writes to Mersenne that he has "decided not to put my name to the work" and that he wants Mersenne and others to examine it prior to publication "mainly on account of theology, which has been so deeply in the thrall of Aristotle that it is almost impossible to expound another philosophy without its seeming to be directly contrary to the Faith."[196] The central problem that Descartes faces here is how to avoid creating the impression that his mechanistic physics, which promises to overcome the failure of Aristotelianism, is incompatible with true Christian faith; in essence the problem is the same as that faced by Galileo, namely, how to embrace Copernicanism without seeming impious. Descartes writes to Mersenne at the end of 1630 that he wants "to find a device [*biais*] for giving a true account without doing violence to anyone's imagination or shocking received opinion."[197]

By late in 1633, Descartes seems to have lost confidence that this would be possible. He writes to Mersenne that the burning of all available copies of Galileo's *Dialogue Concerning the Two Chief World Systems* and the conviction and punishment of Galileo left Descartes

> so astonished . . . that I almost decided to burn all my papers or at least . . . let no one see them. . . . I must admit that if the [Copernican] view is false, then so too are the entire foundations of my philosophy, for it can be demonstrated from them quite clearly. . . . I did not want to publish a discourse in which a single word could be found that the Church would have disapproved of; so I preferred to suppress it rather than to publish it in a mutilated form.[198]

A few months later, Descartes writes to Mersenne that "I would not wish, for anything in the world, to maintain [my views] against the authority of the Church. . . . I desire to live in peace and to continue the life I have begun under the motto 'to live well you must live unseen.'"[199] This appears to be the motive that led Descartes to suppress the publication of *Le Monde* for the rest of his life, and it lends support to Haldane's view that Descartes suppressed his more controversial views rather than dissimulating them, at least as concerns *Le Monde*.

This series of letters to Mersenne demonstrates something even more decisive for the assessment of the dissimulation thesis. It shows that Descartes is entirely unafraid to express his views candidly to Mersenne, even to the point of expressing his support of Copernicanism. This lends support to the proposition that Descartes's entire correspondence with Mersenne, and the Second Replies as well, should be read in the light of candor and sincerity rather than concealment and duplicity. This, in turn, should lend credibility to Descartes's professed devotion to Christianity, both in his later correspondence with Mersenne and in the Second Replies, which were addressed to Mersenne. To take Descartes at his word is to support the position taken not only by commentators like Maritain and Jaspers but also by Jean Laporte, who rejects altogether the proposition that Descartes's appeals to Christian faith are anything less than completely sincere.[200] Descartes's candor in his writings to Mersenne, and in particular his willingness to express even his most heterodox views to Mersenne, seems to constitute at least an important part of the basis for a coherent hermeneutics of *sincerity*. In this connection, Jaspers notes that "in his letters, when there was no need for it, [Descartes] attested to his zeal for the Catholic faith, his veneration for its dignitaries, and his unshaken faith in the infallibility of the Church to which he belonged."[201]

Naturally, one is inclined to wonder whether Descartes dissimulates his views on at least some occasions. In particular, we may never know whether his words should be taken at face value when in the *Principles* he presents the biblical account of creation as the truth disclosed both by Christian faith and by reason and offers an evolutionary account of the genesis of created beings as a mere hypothesis, even though it possesses greater explanatory power than the biblical account.[202] It must forever remain a matter of speculation whether Descartes intended this pronouncement sincerely, or whether he really equated explanatory power with truth and purported to separate the two simply as a conciliatory gesture toward the church.[203] What is not a matter of speculation is the central place that Descartes makes in his metaphysics for concepts and commitments derived from Christian tradition.

What we are left with if we denude Descartes's thought of this inheritance is a brand of positivism that dominated European consciousness only some time after the seventeenth century. Nonetheless, the forces that led to a complete separation of reason from faith are already at work in the thought of Descartes, best understood as a thinker who operated within a largely traditional moral ethos but whose insight into the autonomy of reason led irretrievably if unwittingly to the divorce of science from faith. In an important sense, "Descartes's intentions were entirely orthodox. . . . [His] philosophy was used, as he intended it, to support the authority of the church (even though some churchmen entertained grave suspicions about its orthodoxy) . . . by separating matter from spirit so drastically, Descartes unintentionally opened the door to a mechanistic materialism."[204] The task of understanding Descartes's thought as a whole, then, consists in recognizing the essential Christianity of its foundational concepts and seeking to understand Descartes's vision of the inner compatibility between the traditional ideal of salvation and the emerging practical ethos of modernity. The recognition of Descartes's Christian inheritance makes anything more than a fairly weak version of the dissimulation thesis implausible; whether a weak version of the thesis should be endorsed or whether the entire question of dissimulation should simply be dismissed is a question in which little is ultimately at stake.

NOTES

1. Saint Thomas Aquinas, *Summa Contra Gentiles* 3, in *Basic Writings of St. Thomas Aquinas*, ed. Anton C. Pegis, 2 vols. (Indianapolis/Cambridge: Hackett, 1997), chap. 25, 2.43 f.

2. Saint Augustine, *Confessions*, trans. R. S. Pine-Coffin (London: Penguin, 1961), bk. 7, sec. 17, p. 151, and bk. 10, sec. 31, p. 235; Aquinas, *Summa Theologica* 1, q. 65, art. 2, resp., in *Basic Writings*, 1.612.

3. Rebecca Harden Weaver, *Divine Grace and Human Agency: A Study of the Semi-Pelagian Controversy* (Macon, GA: Mercer University Press, 1996), pp. 13, 237.

4. See Hubert Jedin, *A History of the Council of Trent*, trans. Dom Ernest Graf, 2 vols. (Saint Louis: B. Herder, 1961–1963), 1.366 f., 1.377 f.

5. Descartes, "Comments on a Certain Broadsheet," AT 8B.353 f., CSM 1.301.

6. Alexander Sedgwick, *Jansenism in Seventeenth-Century France: Voices from the Wilderness* (Charlottesville: University Press of Virginia, 1977), p. 100 f.

7. See Galileo, *Discoveries and Opinions of Galileo*, trans. Stillman Drake (New York: Anchor/Doubleday, 1957), pp. 145–71. See also Richard J. Blackwell, *Galileo, Bellarmine, and the Bible: Including a Translation of Foscarini's Letter on the Motion of the Earth* (Notre Dame, IN: University of Notre Dame Press, 1991).

8. Galileo, *Discoveries and Opinions*, p. 164.

9. Ibid., pp. 166, 169.

10. See Descartes, *Rules for the Direction of the Mind*, Rule Fourteen, AT 10.439, CSM 1.57.

11. Galileo, *Discoveries and Opinions*, p. 168.

12. Galileo, *Letter to the Grand Duchess Christina*, in *Discoveries and Opinions*, p. 179.

13. Ibid., p. 179 f.

14. Ibid., p. 181.

15. Ibid., p. 182. These laws are to be known by reason: "That man will indeed be fortunate who, led by some inner light, can turn from dark and confused labyrinths in which he might have gone perpetually winding with the crowd and becoming ever more entangled" (Galileo, *The Assayer* [*Il Saggiatore*], in *Discoveries and Opinions*, p. 240). Cf. Descartes, *Rules for the Direction of the Mind*, Rule Five, AT 10.379 f., CSM 1.20, where Descartes assimilates method to "the thread of Theseus" in the labyrinth.

16. Galileo, *Letter to the Grand Duchess Christina*, in *Discoveries and Opinions*, p. 186. Galileo attributes this dictum to Cardinal Baronius. Galileo similarly treats Aquinas's statement that physical space is "void" or "empty"; see p. 201.

17. Galileo, *Assayer*, p. 276 f.; see also *The Starry Messenger*, in *Discoveries and Opinions*, p. 56.

18. Saint Augustine, *Tractates on the Gospel of John 28–54*, in *Fathers of the Church*, vol. 88, trans. John W. Rettig (Washington, DC: Catholic University of America Press, 1993), tractate 29, section 6, p. 18 (translation altered). Aquinas, *Summa Theologica* 1, q. 1, art. 2, and *Summa Theologica* 2–2, q. 2, art. 4.

19. Aquinas, *de Trinitate*, in *Truth*, trans. Robert W. Mulligan, James V. McGlynn, and Robert W. Schmidt, 3 vols. (Indianapolis: Hackett, 1995), q. 10, art. 13; q. 14, art. 9.

20. Aquinas, *Summa Theologica* 1, q. 1, art. 2, in *Basic Writings*, 1.6 f. Aquinas presents his reflections on angels principally in q. 50–64, and *de Veritate*, in *Truth*, q. 8.

21. Augustine, *Confessions*, bk. 6, sec. 5, p. 117.

22. See, for example, Saint Augustine, *Enchiridion*, 30–32, in *The Essential Augustine*, ed. Vernon J. Bourke, 2d ed. (Indianapolis: Hackett, 1974), pp. 181–83; *The City of God against the Pagans*, ed. R. W. Dyson (Cambridge: Cambridge University Press, 1998), bk. 10, chap. 22, p. 424.

23. See Augustine, *On Free Choice of the Will*, trans. Thomas Williams (Indianapolis/Cambridge: Hackett, 1993), bk. 1, sec. 1 and 12, pp. 1 and 19 f.

24. Augustine, *City of God*, bk. 5, chap. 9, p. 201 f.; *On Free Choice of the Will*, bk. 3, sec. 4, p. 78. Descartes follows Augustine in asserting this compatibility; see letter to Elizabeth, January 1646, AT 4.352 f., CSM 3.282.

25. Augustine, *On Free Choice of the Will*, bk. 1, sec. 13, p. 22.

26. Ibid., bk. 1, sec. 6, p. 11.

27. Ibid., bk. 2, sec. 19, p. 68.

28. Ibid., bk. 2, sec. 13, p. 56 f. On "the true eternity of truth" as the measure for human judgment, see Augustine, *Confessions*, bk. 7, sec. 17, p. 151.

29. Augustine, *Confessions*, bk. 7, sec. 11, p. 147.

30. Ibid., bk. 10, sec. 40, p. 249.

31. Ibid., bk. 7, sec. 12, p. 148.

32. Ibid., bk. 7, sec. 4, p. 137.

33. Ibid., bk. 7, sec. 12, p. 148.

34. Augustine, *On Free Choice of the Will*, bk. 2, sec. 20, p. 69.

35. Augustine, *Confessions*, bk. 7, sec. 12, p. 137.

36. Ibid., bk. 7, sec. 3, p. 136.

37. Ibid., bk. 7, sec. 16, p. 150.

38. Ibid., bk. 7, sec. 7, p. 143.

39. Ibid., bk. 10, sec. 6, p. 213.

40. Ibid., bk. 7, sec. 5, p. 139.

41. Ibid., bk. 7, sec. 6, p. 142.

42. Ibid., bk. 7, sec. 13, p. 149.

43. Étienne Gilson, *The Christian Philosophy of Saint Augustine*, trans. L. E. M. Lynch (New York: Random House, 1960), p. 146 f.

44. Augustine, *City of God*, bk. 10, sec. 8, p. 508; *On Free Choice of the Will*, bk. 2, sec. 20, p. 69. See also *Confessions*, bk. 10, sec. 31, p. 236.

45. Augustine, *Confessions*, bk. 10, sec. 7, p. 212. The emergence of this notion of inwardness can be seen in Matt. 5:28, 6:25, 10:28, 15:19; Mark 7:5 ff., 7:15, 7:21; Rom. 1:20, 2:29, 7:14, 7:22.

46. Augustine, *Confessions*, bk. 10, sec. 6, p. 213 (citing Rom. 1:20, italics in original).

47. Ibid., bk. 10, sec. 31, p. 235.

48. Ibid.

49. Ibid., p. 235 f.

50. Saint Augustine, *The Immortality of the Soul*, in *Fathers of the Church*, vol. 4, trans. John A. Mourant and William J. Collinge, introd. and notes by Collinge (Washington, DC: Catholic University of America Press, 1992), chap. 1, p. 16; chap. 8, p. 32; chap. 16, p. 45 f.

51. Augustine, *Confessions*, bk. 10, sec. 6, p. 235 f.

52. Descartes, "Synopsis of the Following Six Meditations," AT 7.15, CSM 2.11.

53. AT 7.52, CSM 2.36.

54. Richard Popkin, "The Religious Background of Seventeenth-Century Philosophy," *Journal of the History of Philosophy* 25 (1987): 41.

55. See Augustine, *Enchiridion*, in *Essential Augustine*, bk. 7, sec. 20; *de trinitate*, bk. 15, chap. 12, sec. 21–22; *de beata vita*, bk. 2, chap. 2, sec. 7; *de libero arbitrio*, bk. 2, sec. 3; *de civitate dei*, bk. 11, chap. 26. Cf. *de vera religione*, 39, 73, where Augustine presents the related argument that doubting is a sufficient basis for knowing that there is such a thing as truth, and *contra academicos*, 3.11.25–26, where Augustine

argues that neither sleep, madness, nor the unreliability of the senses undermines the certainty of forms of knowledge such as mathematics.

56. Gilson, *Christian Philosophy of Saint Augustine*, p. 268n17.

57. Martial Gueroult, *Descartes's Philosophy Interpreted According to the Center of Reason*, trans. Roger Ariew, 2 vols. (Minneapolis: University of Minnesota Press, 1984–1985), 1.34.

58. Descartes, letter to Colvius, November 14, 1640, AT 3.247, CSM 3.159. See also letter to [Mesland], May 2, 1644, AT 4.113, CSM 3.232.

59. Descartes, Fourth Set of Objections, AT 7.197 f., CSM 2.139.

60. Ibid., Fourth Set of Objections, AT 7.205, CSM 2.144; cf. Augustine, *Magnitude of the Soul*, in *Fathers of the Church*, 4:87.

61. AT 3.247 f., CSM 3.159.

62. Descartes, "Comments on a Certain Broadsheet," AT 8B.347 f., CSM 1.296 f.

63. Alexandre Koyré, *Descartes und die Scholastik* (Bonn: Bouvier Verlag Herbert Grundemann, 1971), p. 63.

64. Descartes, Third Meditation, AT 7.40 f., CSM 2.28.

65. See Gueroult, *Descartes's Philosophy Interpreted*, 1.212.

66. Augustine, *On Free Choice of the Will*, bk. 3, sec. 20, p. 110; bk. 3, sec. 24, p. 119.

67. On the infinitude of the will and the finitude of the intellect, see Augustine, *De diversis quaestionibus 83* (*Answers to Eighty-Three Different Questions*), quest. 15.

68. Descartes, Fourth Meditation, AT 7.58, CSM 2.40 f.

69. AT 7.59, CSM 2.41.

70. Descartes, Second Set of Replies, AT 7.166, CSM 2.117; see also *Discourse on Method*, Part 3, AT 6.28, CSM 1.125.

71. Descartes, Sixth Set of Replies, AT 7.432, CSM 2.292.

72. Descartes, *Conversation with Burman*, AT 5.159, CSM 3.342; letter to [Mesland], May 2, 1644, AT 4.117, CSM 3.234.

73. Descartes, Sixth Set of Replies, AT 7.418, CSM 2.289. See also letter to Mersenne, April 21, 1641, AT 3.359 f., CSM 3.179.

74. Descartes, Second Set of Replies, AT 7.141, CSM 2.101; letter to Regius, May 24, 1640, AT 3.65, CSM 3.147. Cf. Augustine, *Magnitude of the Soul*, chap. 30, sec. 58, p. 125, and *Advantage of Believing*, chap. 11, sec. 25, in *Fathers of the Church*, 4:425 f.

75. AT 7.53, CSM 2.37.

76. AT 7.54, CSM 2.38.

77. AT 7.40, CSM 2.28 (bracketed clause added in French translation approved by Descartes).

78. AT 7.33, CSM 2.22.

79. Augustine, *The Trinity*, trans. Stephen McKenna, in *Fathers of the Church*, vol. 45, bk. 5, chap. 2, sec. 3, p. 177, and bk. 7, chap. 5, sec. 10.

80. Augustine, *On Free Choice of the Will*, bk. 2, sec. 20, p. 69.

81. AT 7.55, CSM 2.38.

82. AT 7.55 f., CSM 2.39.

83. AT 7.55, CSM 2.39.

84. AT 7.61, CSM 2.42.

85. Arnauld, Fourth Set of Objections, AT 7.215 f., CSM 2.151.

86. Henri Gouhier, "Descartes et la religion," in *Cartesio nel terzo centenario nel "Discorso del Metodo"* (Milan: Societa Editrice "Vita e Pensiero," 1937), p. 421.

87. Jean-Luc Marion, *Sur la théologie blanche de Descartes: Analogie, création des vérités éternelles et fondement* (Paris: Presses universitaires de France, 1981), p. 450.

88. Norman Smith, *Studies in the Cartesian Philosophy* (New York: Russell and Russell, 1962), p. 59n.

89. Louis Dupré, *Passage to Modernity: An Essay in the Hermeneutics of Nature and Culture* (New Haven/London: Yale University Press, 1993), p. 118.

90. Aquinas, *Summa Theologica* 1, q. 65, art. 2, resp., in *Basic Writings*, 1.612.

91. See ibid., q. 115, arts. 3, 4.

92. Ibid., q. 22, art. 2, resp., and q. 116, art. 1, resp.; *Summa Contra Gentiles* 3, chaps. 64, 67.

93. Descartes, *Rules for the Direction of the Mind*, Rule Twelve, AT 10.413, CSM 1.41.

94. Descartes, Rule Six, AT 10.383, CSM 1.22; Rule Twelve, AT 10.421 f., CSM 1.46.

95. Descartes, Rule Twelve, AT 10.427, 10.421; CSM 1.49, 1.45 f.

96. Ibid., AT 10.427, CSM 1.49.

97. See Wolfgang Röd, *Descartes: Die Genese des Cartesianischen Rationalismus*, 2d ed. (Munich: C. H. Beck, 1982), p. 124. See also

Descartes's letter to Mersenne, November 13, 1629, AT 1.70, CSM 1.7, in which Descartes pronounces "all the phenomena of nature" to be reducible to "the whole of physics."

98. Descartes, Rule Thirteen, AT 10.436, CSM 1.55.

99. Ibid.

100. AT 6.76, CSM 1.150.

101. Descartes, Rule Twelve, AT 10.412, CSM 1.40. On the distinction between "things in the order that corresponds to our knowledge of them" and things "in accordance with how they exist in reality," see Rule Twelve, AT 10.417, CSM 1.43 f., and Rule Nine, AT 10.398, CSM 1.32.

102. Descartes, *Principles of Philosophy*, Part 3, art. 42, AT 8A.98, CSM 1.255.

103. Ibid., art. 44, AT 8A.99, CSM 1.255 (bracketed clause added in French translation approved by Descartes).

104. Ibid., art. 46, AT 8A.101, CSM 1.256 f.

105. See ibid., art. 46, AT 8A.101, CSM 1.257, and art. 47, AT 8A.102, CSM 1.257.

106. Ibid., Part 4, art. 205, AT 8A.327, CSM 1.289 f.

107. Descartes, letter to Mersenne, September 30, 1640, AT 3.212, CSM 3.154.

108. Descartes, letter to Mersenne, January 28, 1641, AT 3.298, CSM 1.173.

109. AT 7.55, CSM 2.39.

110. Descartes, *Conversation with Burman*, art. 2, AT 8A.81, CSM 1.248.

111. Ibid., AT 5.158, CSM 3.341.

112. Descartes, letter to Mersenne, March 1642, AT 3.544, CSM 3.211.

113. Descartes, Third Meditation, AT 7.50, 7.42, 7.52; CSM 2.34, 2.31, 2.36.

114. Descartes, letter to Mersenne, April 15, 1630, AT 1.144, CSM 3.22.

115. Descartes, Author's Replies to the Second Set of Objections, AT 7.148, CSM 2.105 f.

116. Descartes, *Discourse on Method*, Part 6, AT 6.61 f., CSM 1.142 f. (translation altered); cf. Descartes's appeal to "the true religion" in Part 2, AT 6.12, CSM 1.117.

117. AT 6.61, CSM 1.142; cf. Aquinas, *Summa Theologica* 1–2, q. 91, 94, in *Basic Writings*, 2.748 ff., 2.772 ff.

118. Descartes, *Principles of Philosophy*, Part 1, sec. 25 and 76, AT 8A.14, 8A.39; CSM 1.201, 1.221.

119. Descartes, letter to Mersenne, April 21, 1641, AT 3.360, CSM 3.179.

120. Descartes, *Conversation with Burman*, AT 5.176, CSM 3.151.

121. Jacques Maritain, *The Dream of Descartes Together with Some Other Essays*, trans. Mabelle L. Andison (New York: Philosophical Library, 1944), p. 76 f.

122. Aquinas, *Summa Theologica* 1, q. 1, art. 1, repl. obj. 2.; q. 1, art. 2, resp., in *Basic Writings*, 1.6 f.

123. Aquinas, *Summa Theologica* 2–2, q. 1, art. 6, repl. obj. 1; q. 1, art. 8, resp., in *Basic Writings*, 2.1064, 2.1068.

124. Aquinas, *Summa Theologica* 1, q. 85, art. 3, resp., in *Basic Writings*, 1.819.

125. Ibid., q. 12, art. 12, resp., 1.109 (italics in original).

126. On the Trinity as an article of faith, see Aquinas, *Summa Theologica* 1, q. 12, art. 13, repl. obj. 1; cf. *Quaestionaes disputatae de veritate*, in *Truth*, q. 10, art. 13. On proving God's existence, see *Summa Theologica* 1, q. 2.

127. Descartes, letter to Mersenne, December 18, 1629, AT 1.85 f., CSM 3.14.

128. Descartes, letter to Mersenne, May 6, 1630, AT 1.150, CSM 3.25; letter to [Mersenne], May 27, 1630, AT 1.153, CSM 3.26.

129. Descartes, letter to Mersenne, April 15, 1630, AT 1.144, CSM 3.22.

130. Descartes, *Conversation with Burman*, AT 5.158, CSM 3.341.

131. Descartes, Third Meditation, AT 7.43, CSM 2.29; Second Set of Replies, AT 7.139, CSM 2.99.

132. AT 5.157, *Descartes' Conversation with Burman*, trans. John Cottingham, (Oxford, UK: Clarendon, 1976), p. 18 f.

133. Ibid., p. 19.

134. See Aquinas, *Summa Theologica* 1, q. 50–65, 106–13, in *Basic Writings*, and *Quaestiones disputatae de veritate*, q. 7–9. For a summary of Aquinas's views on angels, see Étienne Gilson, *The Philosophy of St.*

Thomas Aquinas, trans. Edward Bullough (New York: Dorset, 1948), chap. 8.

135. Aquinas, *Summa Theologica* 1, q. 50, art. 3, resp.; q. 51, art. 1, resp.; q. 51, art. 2, resp.; q. 107, art. 1, repl. obj. 2, in *Basic Writings*, 1.486, 1.492, 1.493, 1.990.

136. Descartes, letter to More, August 1649, AT 5.402, CSM 3.380.

137. Descartes, "Comments on a Certain Broadsheet," AT 8B.353, CSM 1.300. The circumstances surrounding the composition of this text are discussed later in this chapter.

138. AT 8A.353, CSM 1.300 f.

139. See Descartes, letter to Mersenne, April 15, 1630, AT 1.143 f., CSM 3.22; letter to [Mesland], May 2, 1644, AT 4.117, CSM 3.234.

140. Descartes, letter to Mersenne, October 28, 1640, AT 3.215 f., CSM 3.155; letter to Mersenne, December 31, 1640, AT 3.274, CSM 3.166. Cf. Aquinas, *Summa Theologica* 1, q. 32, art. 1, resp., in *Basic Writings*, 1.316.

141. AT 7.3, CSM 2.4; AT 7.13 f., CSM 2.9 f.

142. AT 7.153 f., CSM 2.108 f.

143. Descartes, Second Set of Replies, AT 7.148, CSM 2.105.

144. Descartes, letter to Mersenne, March 31, 1641, AT 3.349 f., CSM 3.177.

145. See Descartes, letter to Mersenne, November 25, 1630, AT 1.179, CSM 3.28, and letter to [Vatier], February 22, 1638, AT 1.564, CSM 3.88.

146. Descartes, letter to Regius, January 1642, AT 3.502, CSM 3.207. On Descartes's rejection of real qualities or accidents, see Sixth Set of Replies, AT 7.434, 7.441–43; CSM 2.292 f., 2.297 f.; and letter to Mersenne, April 26, 1643, AT 3.648, CSM 3.216. See also *Principles of Philosophy*, Part 4, art. 198, AT 8A.322, CSM 1.285.

147. AT 3.503, CSM 3.208.

148. See Elmar J. Kremer, "Arnauld's Interpretation of Descartes as a Christian Philosopher," in *Interpreting Arnauld*, ed. Elmar J. Kremer (Toronto: University of Toronto Press, 1996), pp. 76–90.

149. Descartes, Fourth Set of Objections, AT 7.217, CSM 2.152 f.

150. AT 7.217, CSM 2.153.

151. AT 7.250 f., CSM 2.174.

152. AT 7.251, CSM 2.175.

153. Descartes, letter to ?, March 1646?, AT 4.374 f., CSM 3.284. The nature of the problem and Descartes's proposed solution is discussed in depth in Jean-Robert Armogathe, *Theologica Cartesiana: L'explication physique de l'Euchariste chez Descartes et Dom Desgabets* (The Hague: Nijhoff, 1977). See also Henri Gouhier, *La pensée religieuse de Descartes*, 2d ed. (Paris: Vrin, 1972), pp. 221 ff.

154. Steven M. Nadler, "Descartes, Arnauld, and Transubstantiation: Reconciling Cartesian Metaphysics and Real Presence," *Journal of the History of Ideas* 49 (1988): 230 f. (referring to Aquinas's account in the *Summa Theologica*, italics in original).

155. Descartes, Fourth Set of Objections, AT 7.217 f., CSM 2.152 f.

156. See Descartes, letter to [Mesland], May 2, 1644, AT 4.120, CSM 3.235 f.; letter to Mesland, February 9, 1645, AT 4.163–70, CSM 3.241–44; letter to Mesland, May 1645, AT 4.216, CSM 3.248 f.; letter to Mesland, 1645 or 1646, AT 4.346 f., CSM 3.278 f. On Descartes's views on the Eucharist, see also letter to Mersenne, January 28, 1641, AT 3.296, CSM 3.172; letter to Mersenne, March 1642, AT 3.545, CSM 3.211 f.; letter to Clerselier, March 2, 1646, AT 4.372 f., CSM 3.284.

157. Descartes, letter to Father Dinet, AT 7.581, CSM 2.392.

158. See AT 7.582, 7.596; CSM 2.393.

159. See Theo Verbeek, *Descartes and the Dutch: Early Reactions to Cartesian Philosophy, 1637–1650* (Carbondale/Edwardsville: Southern Illinois University Press, 1992), pp. 13 ff.

160. Ibid., p. 17.

161. Descartes gives an account of this dispute in the letter to Father Dinet, and he quotes the Senate's decree. See AT 7.592 f., CSM 2.393n.

162. For a more precise account of the *Admiranda Methodus*, see Verbeek, *Descartes and the Dutch*, pp. 20 ff.

163. AT 8B.1–194; an excerpt is translated at CSM 3.220–24. Descartes had already written at length of the dispute with Voetius in the letter to Father Dinet, AT 7.582–601; a few pages of these remarks are translated at CSM 2.393–96. He also discusses it in the letter to the Magistrates of Utrecht, AT 8B.201–73. French translations of the *Admiranda Methodus* and the letter to Voetius are presented, together with a historical outline, the letter to Father Dinet, and Descartes's letter of apology to the Magistrates of Utrecht, in René Descartes and Martin Schoock, *La*

Querelle d'Utrecht, ed. Theo Verbeek, preface by Jean-Luc Marion (Paris: Les impressions nouvelles, 1988).

164. AT 8B.175 f., 8B.193; CSM 3.223 f.

165. Descartes, letter to Regius, July 1645, AT 4.249 f., CSM 3.254 f.

166. AT 9B.19, CSM 1.189.

167. See Verbeek, *Descartes and the Dutch*, p. 54.

168. Henricus Regius, *Brevis explicatio mentis humanae*, new ed. (Utrecht: Th. ab Ackersdijck and G. à Zyll, 1657), pp. 18 ff., cited in Verbeek, *Descartes and the Dutch*, p. 59 f.

169. Descartes, *Notae in Programma*, AT 8B.354 ff., CSM 1.301 f. On Descartes's criticism of Regius's view of the soul and of the human being as *ens per accidens*, see letter to Regius, December 1641, AT 3.460 f., CSM 3.200.

170. Verbeek, *Descartes and the Dutch*, p. 88; see also Stephen Gaukroger, *Descartes: An Intellectual Biography* (Oxford: Clarendon, 1995), p. 480.

171. Verbeek, *Descartes and the Dutch*, p. 31.

172. Ibid., p. 5; cf. p. 70.

173. Ibid., pp. 40 ff.

174. Sedgwick, *Jansenism in Seventeenth-Century France*, p. 5. Cf. Nigel Abercrombie, *The Origins of Jansenism* (Oxford: Clarendon, 1936), p. 32.

175. Weaver, *Divine Grace and Human Agency*, p. 230. See also Abercrombie, *Origins of Jansenism*, pp. 48 ff.

176. *Canons and Decrees of the Council of Trent*, trans. H. J. Schroeder, O. P. (Rockford, IL: Tan Books and Publishers, 1978), sixth session, chap. 1, p. 30.

177. Ibid., chap. 7, p. 33.

178. Ibid., chap. 11, p. 36. Nonetheless, the council was clear in stating that the capacity to resist sin depends on "the grace of Jesus Christ" (fifth session, "Decree Concerning Original Sin," p. 23). In the thirteenth session, pp. 72 ff., the council reaffirmed the doctrine of transubstantiation first adopted by the Fourth Lateran Council in 1215.

179. Saint Ignàcio de Loyola, "Rules for Thinking with the Church," in *The Spiritual Exercises of Saint Ignatius*, trans. Anthony Mottola (Garden City, NY: Image Books, 1964), no. 17, p. 141.

180. Abercrombie, *Origins of Jansenism*, p. xi.

181. Ibid., p. 97.

182. Ibid., p. 111.

183. See Gouhier, *La pensée religieuse de Descartes*, p. 261.

184. See Descartes, letter to [Mersenne], May 27, 1630, AT 1.153, CSM 3.26; letter to Mersenne, April 21, 1641, AT 3.360, CSM 3.179.

185. See Tad M. Schmaltz, "What Has Cartesianism To Do with Jansenism?" *Journal of the History of Ideas* 60 (1999): 43 ff.

186. Descartes, letter to Mersenne, end of May 1637, AT 1.366, CSM 3.56. See also letter to Mersenne, March 1642, AT 3.544, CSM 3.211.

187. Descartes, *Principles of Philosophy*, Part 1, art. 40, AT 8A.20, CSM 1.206.

188. Maritain, *Dream of Descartes*, p. 44; Karl Jaspers, *The Great Philosophers*, vol. 1, *The Disturbers: Descartes, Pascal, Lessing, Kierkegaard, Nietzsche. Philosophers in Other Realms: Einstein, Weber, Marx*, ed. Michael Ermarth and Leonard H. Ehrlich (New York: Harcourt Brace, 1995), p. 8.

189. Hiram Caton, *The Origin of Subjectivity: An Essay on Descartes* (New Haven: Yale University Press, 1973), p. 12; see also Caton, "The Problem of Descartes' Sincerity," *Philosophical Forum* 2 (1971): 355–70.

190. Henry More, *Philosophical Writings of Henry More*, ed. Flora Isabel Mackinnon (New York: AMS Press, 1969), pp. 184, 197.

191. Julian Offray de la Mettrie, *Man Machine and Other Writings*, ed. Ann Thomson (Cambridge: Cambridge University Press, 1996), p. 35.

192. Maxime Leroy, *Descartes, le philosophe au masque*, 2 vols. (Paris: Éditions Rieder, 1929), 2.75, 1.16. Leroy's title is a play on Descartes's statement in the *Cogitationes Privatae* (1619–1622) that "Actors, taught not to let any embarrassment show on their faces, put on a mask. I will do the same. So far, I have been a spectator in this theatre which is the world, but I am now about to mount the stage, and I come forward masked" (AT 10.213, CSM 1.2).

193. Charles Adam, *Vie et oeuvres de Descartes. Étude historique*, AT 12.306.

194. Elizabeth S. Haldane, *Descartes: His Life and Times* (London: John Murray, 1905), p. 154 f.

195. Descartes, letter to Mersenne, October 8, 1629, AT 1.23 f., CSM 3.6 (translation altered).

196. Descartes, letter to Mersenne, December 18, 1629, AT 1.85 f., CSM 3.14.

197. Descartes, letter to Mersenne, December 23, 1630, AT 1.194, CSM 3.29 (translation altered).

198. Descartes, letter to Mersenne, end of November 1633, AT 1.270 f., CSM 3.40 f.

199. Descartes, letter to Mersenne, April 1634, AT 1.285, CSM 3.42 f. Descartes takes the expression *Bene vixit, bene qui latuit* from Ovid, *Tristia*, 3.4.25.

200. Jean Laporte, *Le rationalisme de Descartes*, rev. ed. (Paris: Presses universitaires de France, 1950). On Laporte's view that Descartes's morality and Catholicism are complementary, see pp. 437, 452, 464–68; on Laporte's rejection of the dissimulation thesis, see pp. 299 f., 465.

201. Karl Jaspers, *Three Essays: Leonardo, Descartes, Max Weber*, trans. Ralph Manheim (New York: Harcourt, Brace, & World, 1964), p. 148.

202. Descartes, *Principles of Philosophy*, Part 3, art. 45, AT 8A.99 f., CSM 1.256.

203. See ibid., art. 44.

204. Margaret C. Jacob, *The Radical Enlightenment: Pantheists, Freemasons, and Republicans* (London: George Allen & Unwin, 1981), pp. 42, 43, 45.

—CHAPTER 3—

DESCARTES'S EARTHLY MORALITY

1. THE SUBSTANTIAL UNION OF MIND AND BODY AND THE IDEAL OF A PRACTICAL MORALITY

Descartes's ambivalence between angelism and earthly practicism is an ambivalence between two different ways of understanding the relationship between the subjectivity of human experience and what lies beyond the limits of that experience. It is, in Jaspers's estimation, an ambivalence "between a thinking without foundation and obedience without understanding."[1] If on the angelic side Descartes submits the human condition to the absolute authority of revealed truth, on the practical side he denies a place for faith and demands that the basis of morality be adduced entirely by means of rational reflection. But if reason as Descartes conceives it is incapable of adducing moral commitments, it must remain "a thinking without foundation," and the human freedom that corresponds to it must remain "astonishingly devoid of substance."[2]

To this extent it is impossible simply "to reject all authority and the prejudices of faith, and to proceed to live by pure reason, in the naïve conviction that everything will come out all right. . . . Actually philosophy faces an enormous task: instead of exercising

151

reason in a vacuum, it must strive, through reason, to apprehend the positive sources of authority."[3] For Descartes, this striving takes the form of a struggle to reconcile the demands of faith and reason, rather than sacrificing one for the sake of the other. Descartes's thought is torn between "two irreconcilable modes of the Encompassing,"[4] that of reason staring blankly into the inherent meaninglessness of a mechanistic universe and that of faith anticipating the supernatural beatitude promised by the Christian God. As Jaspers recognizes, this commingling of the religious and the secular "accounts for the ambiguities and contradictions that characterize [Descartes's] whole system."[5]

The secular dimension of Descartes's thinking about morality is evident particularly in his later writings in his repeated insistence on rational knowledge as the basis of moral conduct. In the letter to Picot, he stresses the idea of a "highest and most perfect moral system [*Morale*], which presupposes a complete knowledge of the other sciences and is the ultimate level of wisdom."[6] And in a letter to Chanut, he says that "what little knowledge of physics I have tried to acquire has been a great help to me in establishing sure foundations in moral philosophy."[7] These statements, particularly in the light of Descartes's discussion of virtue as a set of techniques for controlling psycho-physiological states in *The Passions of the Soul*, invite the conclusion that Descartes conceives of earthly morality as having a "technological" character, that is, that morality becomes nothing more than a set of techniques for mastering natural processes in general and for mastering the human body's tendency to interfere with the rational pursuit of the good life in particular. This impression is reinforced by Descartes's many references to the ideal of "firm and determinate judgments respecting the knowledge of good and evil." One begins to suspect that if Descartes had lived perhaps ten years longer, he would have written a formal treatise on morality that would have included a clear explanation of the precise role of reason in the determination of the ultimate goods that should serve as the goals of moral striving.

Had he done so, the irreducible contradictions in his thinking might have become more apparent. For as I argue above, in connection with earthly morality Descartes employs a restricted conception of "wisdom" that he marks very clearly as such in the letter to Picot. The entire discussion of morality and the goals of philosophy in that letter have an unambiguously technological character: Descartes defines the "supreme good, considered by natural reason without the light of faith" as "nothing other than the knowledge of the truth through its first causes, that is to say, wisdom, of which philosophy is the study."[8] Such a characterization of the supreme good suggests that there is alongside it another, richer conception of the supreme good considered *with* the light of faith; for any consideration of the supreme good that is conducted exclusively from the standpoint of reason will be subject to the fundamental limitation of reason, namely, that its insights are confined to logical abstractions such as the cogito. In the letter to Picot, Descartes says that there are "greater good[s]" than "the objects of the senses"; he does not enumerate these "greater goods" explicitly, but the implication is that goods like "the regulation of our morals and our conduct in this life" are higher than material goods like "health, honour and riches."[9] The problem here is clear: How, exactly, can the natural light of reason provide us with the moral grounds for regulating our conduct? The light of reason discloses insights such as the cogito, the necessary priority of God's existence over my own, and the mathematical equivalence of "$2 + 3$" and "5," but Descartes never provides any account of how this kind of reason can arrive at clear and determinate insights about whether, for example, it is ever permissible to tell a lie. An answer to this sort of question would seem to require recourse to some extrarational source of meaning; the best that reason alone can do is to determine under what sorts of circumstances a lie can be told successfully, that is, without damaging the fortunes of the liar.

Answers to questions about whether certain actions can be performed successfully are characteristic of the restricted conception of wisdom that Descartes develops in the letter to Picot. But this restricted conception is troublingly inadequate in its fundamental inability to answer questions about the ultimate moral legitimacy of certain actions. The restricted sense of wisdom in the letter to Picot is best understood as a "technological" conception, inasmuch as it reduces notions such as "good" and "virtue" to straightforwardly practical questions; it measures good and virtue strictly with reference to "this life," specifically with reference to the extent to which given actions enhance the material conditions of this life.[10] For Descartes, with regard to this life, those actions are "good" that facilitate the mastery of nature and promote a general sense of human welfare; such mastery includes applied physical science in general and applied sciences such as medicine in particular, inasmuch as the ability both to reproduce natural mechanisms and to regulate the health of the body are necessary if we are "to render ourselves, as it were, the masters and possessors of nature."[11]

This commitment to the mastery of nature is not derived *par prétérition* but instead has its roots in a Christian moral ethos whose terms I have examined in the previous chapter. In this chapter, I examine Descartes's program for the regulation of bodily states so that they help to promote the mind's endeavor to make sound judgments regarding good and evil, and in the next chapter, I examine Descartes's broader program for the mastery of nature generally. Descartes provides his most sustained discussion of the substantial union of mind and body in *The Passions of the Soul*; there and in correspondence from the mid- to late 1640s he presents his clearest views on the importance of an understanding of the substantial union for leading a moral life. To the extent that Descartes conceives of earthly existence as inscribed within the larger traditional Christian framework of a relation to God that includes the prospect of supernatural beatitude, it is of fundamental importance to examine the project of mastery (of both nature and the human body) against this background rather than in strictly technological terms. If God serves as the measure and source of *all* truth and

goodness, then this has fundamental implications for earthly existence as well as for the prospect of eternal salvation. To suppose
that a Christian thinker would radically divorce earthly existence
from supernatural beatitude is to suppose that such a thinker could
in all seriousness propose that this life has no relevance whatsoever
to eternal life; it is to assimilate Descartes's practical interests to
something like the pneumatic freedom of libertine Gnosticism,
which found a way to rationalize earthly voluptuousness and excess
as being compatible with our eventual union with God.[12]
Descartes's commitment to treating nature and grace as separate
realms thus stands in an irreducible tension with his more orthodox
Christian metaphysical commitments, according to which the
things of the created world are reflections of God's goodness and
beauty and hence are not radically separable from the divine.

Descartes is led by his correspondence with Elizabeth in the
mid-1640s to take very seriously the implications of mind-body
interaction for the problem of living a good life. This correspondence inspired Descartes to write a draft of the first two parts of the
Passions and to send them to Elizabeth, who expressed approval
"of the entire moral part of the treatise."[13] Descartes writes to
Chanut that his "little treatise on the nature of the passions" constitutes part of his "thinking about particular problems in ethics," even
though in the preface to the *Passions*, Descartes states that he is
writing about the passions "only as a natural philosopher [*en Physicien*], and not as a rhetorician [*en Orateur*] or even as a moral
philosopher."[14] The key to understanding the significance of the
doctrine of the *Passions* for Descartes's thinking about morality
lies in making a clear distinction between those portions of the treatise in which Descartes treats the passions as a physicist (*en Physicien*) and those in which he moves beyond a mechanistic account
of the passions and treats them as a moral philosopher (*en
philosophe moral*). If Descartes purports not to be treating the passions as a moral philosopher, then this is simply to place himself at
a distance from the Stoics, who "saw in *pathos*, passion, a *patho-*

logical phenomenon, which the sage was required to quash in aspiring to *apatheia.*"[15] The Stoics, in other words, believe that the passions must be denied or suppressed to achieve satisfaction or tranquility. Descartes's primary objection to this view is that "in principle it presents a theory of morals for disembodied beings."[16] If morality is to be meaningful on the earthly plane of existence, then it must affirm the passions by recognizing their proper place in the good life. Cassirer notes that Descartes is led to this conclusion by his mechanistic orientation, which makes him recognize the "factical character" of the affects; this is why "Descartes does not speak first of all as the teacher of a specific morality, but rather as a physicist and physiologist."[17]

But for all that I oppose Gueroult's influential claim that Descartes, at the time of the *Passions*, transforms morality into "a technique, an applied science" whose end is "domination over things."[18] The conception of wisdom that Descartes develops in the *Passions* and in his later correspondence includes the recognition that the senses provide us with information that is crucial to our material welfare. But the conception of wisdom articulated in these writings, as in the letter to Picot, is centered on a commitment to goods higher than goods of the senses, and in these writings Descartes specifies the precise nature of these goods. The conception of wisdom that emerges in these late writings is one according to which material welfare is not an end in itself but instead serves the pursuit of virtues that are derived largely from Christian tradition.

2. THE USE OR FUNCTION OF THE PASSIONS IN HUMAN LIFE

Descartes's turn away from teleology in favor of a mechanistic understanding of nature is motivated by an interest in the systematic domination of natural phenomena. By divesting nature of a sense of inherent meaning, that turn effectively reduces nature from a reflection of God's nobility to "an impersonal and abstract world of mechanical particle interactions."[19] Where the Stoics and the Christian philosophers idealize the prospect of human beings living in harmony with nature, Descartes's mechanistic conception of materiality alienates man from nature. Even though as a substantial union we are linked to nature through our embodiment, the Second Meditation makes it clear that embodiment is not part of our essence and that authentic humanity consists in asserting the primacy of the soul over the body. The body can assist us in our endeavor to secure goods like health, but the pursuit of the good life is to be conducted by that part of us that makes us most like God—our free will, informed by our intellect.

Descartes's correspondence with Elizabeth leads him to recognize mind-body interaction as a special focal point for the problem of mastery. Given that mind and body exert reciprocal causality over one another, and given that the body is subject entirely to the laws of mechanics,[20] the key to controlling the influence that the body exercises over the mind must lie in understanding that influence in mechanistic terms. This endeavor to control bodily influences on the mind would not be necessary if the body always gave us reliable information about the world. But Descartes recognizes that the body has the capacity to distort the magnitude of the material goods and evils that confront us, and that part of the task of morality is to regulate the influence that the passions have on our will so that the will is not impeded in its endeavor to choose genuine goods. Descartes distinguishes between actions (volitions) and passions, and he further distinguishes between passions of the body and of the soul. A bodily passion is any "movement that we make without any contribution from our will—as often happens when we breathe, walk, eat and, indeed, when we perform any action which is common to us and the beasts"; such movements depend "solely on the arrangement of our limbs and on the route which the spirits, produced by the heat of the heart, follow naturally in the brain, nerves, and muscles."[21] Passions of the body include not only autonomic phenomena like pulse and insulin production but also any involuntary physical reaction to external stimuli, such as blinking when an object is unexpectedly thrust before our eyes or cringing at the sounds of cannonballs on the battlefield. Passions of the soul, on the other hand, are "the various perceptions or modes of knowledge present in us"; these may be "perceptions of our volitions and of all the imaginings or other thoughts which depend on them," or they may be representations caused by our bodily states.[22] In either case, passions of the soul are intentional states that take the form of conscious awareness, either of our own acting or of our being acted upon.

The passions of the soul play an indispensable role in life inasmuch as they function as representations of external goods and evils and thereby influence us to pursue or avoid the things in our environment that can enhance or harm the welfare of the substantial union. In general, "the function of the passions consists solely in this, that they dispose our soul to want the things which nature deems useful for us, and to persist in this volition."[23] For example, the sight of something harmful first causes a feeling of pain in us, which in turn causes us to feel sadness and then hatred of the object with which we associate the feeling of pain; similarly, exposure to something beneficial first causes a feeling of pleasure, which in turn produces a feeling of joy and then a desire to take measures to prolong the feeling of joy.[24] In each case, an initial sensation of pleasure or pain gives rise to a particular passion, such as fear or courage. "Thus the feeling of fear moves the soul to want to flee, that of courage to want to fight, and similarly with the others."[25] But Descartes recognizes that the passions are not entirely reliable indices of external goods and evils and that the passions must therefore be subjected to rational scrutiny and control.

> There are many things harmful to the body which cause no sadness initially (or which even produce joy), and . . . other things are useful to the body, although at first they are disagreeable. Furthermore, the passions almost always cause the goods they repre-

sent, as well as the evils, to appear much greater and more important than they are, thus moving us to pursue the former and flee
from the latter with more ardour and zeal than is appropriate. . . .
That is why we must use experience and reason in order to distinguish good from evil, and know their true value, so as not to
take the one for the other or rush into anything immediately.[26]

Our body "is only the lesser part" of our being, and hence we must
subordinate it to our soul, which "is much nobler than the body."[27]
The more we submit unreflectively to those passions of the soul
that bear upon external goods and evils, the more likely we are to
go astray.

The example that Descartes offers most frequently in this connection is that of the inclination to run in the face of danger, when
the nobler part of our nature demands that we stand and fight:

We may . . . acknowledge a kind of conflict, in so far as the same
cause that produces a certain passion in the soul often also produces certain movements in the body, to which the soul makes
no contribution and which the soul stops or tries to stop as soon
as it perceives them. We experience this when an object that
excites fear also causes the spirits to enter the muscles which
serve to move our legs in flight, while the will to be bold stops
them from moving.[28]

The problem posed by the flight response is symbolic of the entire
problem of regulating the passions; if we remain attentive to the fact
that "all our passions represent to us the goods to whose pursuit they
impel us as being much greater than they really are," then "when we
feel ourselves moved by some passion we [will] suspend our judgment until it is calmed, and [will] not let ourselves be easily
deceived by the false appearance of the goods of this world."[29]

Thus the entire problem of subordinating the inclinations of the
body to the considered judgments of the soul resolves itself into the
regulation of desire or what Mesnard refers to as a "psycho-

physiological hygiene."[30] "Because these passions cannot lead us to perform any action except by means of the desire they produce, it is this desire which we should take particular care to control; and here lies the chief utility of morality. . . . [D]esire is always good when it conforms to true knowledge; likewise it cannot fail to be bad when based on some error."[31] This subordination of bodily impulses to rational judgment follows the program for the subjection of natural impulses to reason anticipated in the Third Meditation and sketched out more explicitly in the Sixth, and it sheds light on a statement made by Descartes in a letter to Mersenne written some years prior to the beginning of Descartes's correspondence with Elizabeth:

> For my part, I distinguish two kinds of instinct. One is in us *qua* human beings, and is purely intellectual: it is the natural light or mental vision. This is the only instinct which I think one should trust. The other belongs to us *qua* animals, and is a certain impulse of nature towards the preservation of our body, towards the enjoyment of bodily pleasures, and so on. This should not always be followed.[32]

Although the sort of physical instinct that we share with animals is generally reliable, Descartes notes in article 138 of the *Passions* that "animals are often deceived by lures, and in seeking to avoid small evils they throw themselves into greater evils."[33] Whereas animals are governed entirely by their physiological constitutions, which include autonomic functioning and inclinations caused by exposure to external stimuli, because human beings are rational the task of morality is to "transform the necessity [of our sensual nature] into freedom."[34]

Descartes's conception of a hierarchy of goods in earthly existence helps us to see why not only physics but also medicine and "the highest and most perfect morality" located at the top of the tree of wisdom must ultimately be in the service of higher ends.

Descartes says in the *Discourse* that "the maintenance of health . . . is undoubtedly the first [*premier*] good and the foundation of all the other goods in this life. For even the mind depends so much on the temperament and disposition of the bodily organs that if it is possible to find some means of making men in general wiser and more skilful than they have been up to now, I believe we must look for it in medicine."[35] Descartes lays stress on the *utility* of medicine, and the conception of wisdom to which he alludes here is the restricted, technological sense that he sketches out more completely in the letter to Picot. Good health is essential for the acquisition of "all the other goods in this life" because the proper exercise of our free will depends crucially on our health.[36]

At one point in her correspondence with Descartes, Elizabeth suggests that the proper evaluation of these sorts of goods would require "an infinite science" [*une science infinie*], and at another point she observes that the "infinite knowledge" [*une connaissance infinie*] required here cannot be attained by human beings.[37] The sort of regulation of the affects that would be necessary for the promotion of earthly wisdom would seem to demand a science governing every possible contingency, and this is too much to demand of beings possessing a finite intellect. Descartes responds by acknowledging that "it is true that we lack the infinite knowledge which would be necessary for a perfect acquaintance with all the goods between which we have to choose in the various situations of our lives. We must, I think, be contented with a modest knowledge of the most necessary truths," such as that God is supremely good and that the interests of the community take precedence over the interests of the individual.[38]

It is with an eye toward living in accordance with these sorts of truths that Descartes develops his theory for the regulation of the passions. This discipline is to be a science of means whose improvement will know no limit and whose application will be guided by reason in a twofold sense. In the most immediate sense, "it is *reason*, and reason alone, which determines the legitimate domain of [the passions]" by assessing the true value of the goods that they represent to us.[39] And in a more fundamental sense, reason must guide the entire enterprise of regulating the passions by reflecting on the proper ends of human conduct; the psycho-physiological hygiene that is concerned with material welfare is finally subject to a "spiritual hygiene" concerned with virtue or the proper exercise of our freedom.[40] This means that Descartes's program for regulating the passions is concerned only indirectly with virtue. Its immediate object is the study and alteration of our psycho-physiological responses to stimuli. Descartes recognizes that in general, the passions "dispose the soul to want the things for which they prepare the body,"[41] but he also recognizes that because the passions tend to distort the magnitude of material goods and evils, it is necessary to alter or "correct" our response patterns so that our passions dispose us to want the right sorts of things. He also recognizes that by studying the mechanisms of stimulus and response, we can learn how to modify these responses.

Descartes sees the potential for restructuring physical responses as early as 1630, when he writes to Mersenne that "if you whipped a dog five or six times to the sound of a violin, it would begin to howl and run away as soon as it heard that music again."[42] This remarkable anticipation of Pavlov's conditioned reflex contains the germ of an idea that Descartes later applies to the problem of human psycho-physical responses. In the *Passions*, Descartes again offers an example that focuses on altering the response patterns of dogs: "When a dog sees a partridge, it is naturally disposed to run towards it; and when it hears a gun fired, the noise naturally impels it to run away. Nevertheless, setters are commonly trained so that the sight of a partridge makes them stop, and the noise they hear afterwards, when someone fires at the bird, makes them run towards it."[43] The significance of this example, Descartes says, is that it can

encourage each of us to make a point of controlling our passions. For since we are able, with a little effort, to change the move-

ments of the brain in animals devoid of reason, it is evident that
we can do so still more effectively in the case of men. Even those
who have the weakest souls could acquire absolute mastery over
all their passions if we employed sufficient ingenuity in training
and guiding them.[44]

Because animals experience only bodily passions, the only effective way to restructure their physiological responses is to make
them associate pleasure with the responses that we desire of them
and to make them associate pain with the responses that we do not
desire of them. When we turn to human *psycho*-physiological
responses, the principle of habituation remains the same, but the
precise mechanism whereby the restructuring occurs is different.
Specifically, because we are rational, the process of habituation
depends on the use of mental representations and not simply on
exposure to the physical stimuli of pleasure and pain.

Descartes sketches the role of habituation in the project of mastering the passions in articles 44 and 45 of *The Passions of the Soul*.
In article 45, he says that our passions

> cannot be directly aroused or suppressed by the action of our will,
> but only indirectly through the representation of things which are
> usually joined with the passions we wish to have and opposed to
> the passions we wish to reject. For example, in order to arouse
> boldness and suppress fear in ourselves, it is not sufficient to have
> the volition to do so. We must apply ourselves to consider the rea-
> sons, objects, or precedents which persuade us that the danger is
> not great; that there is always more security in defence than in
> flight; that we shall gain glory and joy if we conquer, whereas we
> can expect nothing but regret and shame if we flee; and so on.[45]

It is not sufficient simply to "will" to be courageous; one must
instead contemplate the goods that are at stake, and the representation of these goods will cause the desired bodily response. As I
show below, the goods that Descartes has in mind here are oriented

not on the safety of the individual in question but rather on that of the community of which he or she is a part. Even the individual's worthiness to feel glory is measured by the extent of his or her service to the community.

3. THE IDEAL OF GENEROSITY AND THE LOVE OF GOD

Descartes offers his technological approach to the manipulation of bodily states against the background of deeper moral considerations that place emphasis on the proper use of the will. In the previous chapter, I show that Descartes characterizes the proper use of the will in terms that recall Saint Augustine's treatment of the will: just as truth must find its measure in the creative will of God, so must the proper exercise of human freedom. If, in connection with matters of moral choice, this measure must ultimately be disclosed by faith, Descartes, like Aquinas, sometimes treats the good as reducible to rational insight. Thus in his August 4, 1645, letter to Elizabeth, Descartes states that "the right use of reason . . . by giving a true knowledge of the good, prevents virtue from being false. . . . So we must conclude that the greatest felicity of man depends on the right use of reason; and consequently the study which leads to its acquisition is the most useful occupation one can take up."[46] In his dedicatory letter to Elizabeth at the beginning of the *Principles*, Descartes links this conception of felicity to acting in accordance with God's dictates: those who "make a firm and faithful resolution to do their utmost to acquire knowledge of what is right, and always to pursue what they judge to be right . . . find great favour with God."[47]

I note above that Elizabeth challenges Descartes on the question whether a finite mind is capable of the "infinite science" that would be required for a complete knowledge of the good. It is particularly in Descartes's dedicatory letter to Elizabeth that the complete terms of his response to this challenge become clear. A complete knowledge of every contingency is admittedly impossible, but it is also unnecessary for earthly felicity; all that is required is a resolute intention to act in accordance with the good, together with a resolute endeavor to determine the good as it bears upon the case at hand. At the same time, as I note in chapter 1, Descartes's conception of the highest good is founded on the conviction that the resolution to act well together with success in the endeavor is to be preferred to the mere intention to act well. In this respect, Descartes's conception of righteous action is almost identical to the terms in which Gilson characterizes Aquinas's conception of such action: "A moral act, therefore, always gains by being inspired by good intention, for, even if failing in the accomplishment of its object, it retains none the less the merit of having intended to do good, and often even deserves more than it accomplishes. Still, a morally perfect act is nevertheless an act which fully satisfies the demands of reason, in its end no less than in each of its parts, and, not content with merely willing the good, actually achieves it."[48]

The terms of Descartes's characterization of resoluteness in the *Passions* closely follow his remarks in the August 4, 1645, letter to Elizabeth and the Dedicatory Letter to Elizabeth at the beginning of the *Principles*. Again he places emphasis on knowledge of the truth: "There is . . . a great difference between the resolutions which proceed from some false opinion and those which are based solely on knowledge of the truth. For, anyone who follows the latter is assured of never regretting or repenting, whereas we always regret having followed the former when we discover our error."[49] Descartes's association of repentance with poor judgment and his association of God's favor with good judgment is significant. What begins to emerge is a set of subtle but ultimately unmistakable references to the Christian background that Descartes purports to have put aside in his endeavor to characterize morality in wholly rational terms. Repentance is a Christian virtue, as is the submission to divine Providence of which Descartes so often speaks. In fact, the entire overarching ideal of generosity that Descartes develops in the *Passions* is to a remarkable degree characterized in Christian terms.

Descartes identifies generosity as the highest of the passions; it "causes a person's self-esteem to be as great as it may legitimately be," and it

> has only two components. The first consists in [one's] knowing that nothing truly belongs to him but the freedom to dispose his volitions, and that he ought to be praised or blamed for no other reason than his using this freedom well or badly. The second consists in his feeling within himself a firm and constant resolution to use it well—that is, never to lack the will to undertake and carry out whatever he judges to be best. To do that is to pursue virtue in a perfect manner.[50]

There is a distinction in principle between legitimate and illegitimate self-esteem; legitimate self-esteem depends on the "good" use of one's free will, whereas illegitimate self-esteem involves a turn away from the good and a consequent "highly blameworthy vanity."[51] Legitimate self-esteem depends first of all upon a recognition and acceptance of the limits of our freedom:

> And we must recognize that everything is guided by divine Providence, whose eternal decree is infallible and immutable, to such an extent that, except for matters it has determined to be dependent on our free will, we must consider everything that affects us to occur of necessity and as it were by fate, so that it would be wrong for us to desire things to happen in any other way. But most of our desires extend to matters which do not depend wholly on us or wholly on others, and we must therefore take care to pick out just what depends only on us, so as to limit our desire to that alone.[52]

The influence of Stoic thinking on Descartes is evident in his recognition that our persistence in "vain desires" compromises our ability to achieve earthly satisfaction.[53] This appeal to Providence recalls Descartes's more straightforwardly Stoic formulation in the provisional morality of the *Discourse* of the requirement that we limit our desires to what is in our power. But Providence here is different from the πρόνοια of the Stoics. These thinkers' abstract and impersonal understanding of the divine leads them to conceive of providence along the lines of fate; their materialist conception of the divine leads them to a conception of providence as wholly immanent, in contrast with the transcendent conception of divine Providence in Christianity. Descartes's commitment to the Christian conception of an immaterial and personal God and his Augustinian commitments concerning the relationship between the human and divine wills show why he goes out of his way to characterize Providence as "a fate or immutable necessity, which we must set against Fortune in order to expose the latter as a chimera, which arises solely from an error of our intellect."[54] The link between the ideal of generosity and the acceptance of divine Providence is a restatement of the endeavor to inscribe human striving within a larger metaphysical context in which human freedom both is subject to the divine will and has its proper measure in that will. With regard to the relationship between human and divine will, Descartes writes to Elizabeth that

> if we think only of ourselves we cannot help regarding ourselves as independent; but when we think of the infinite power of God, we cannot help believing that all things depend on him, and hence that our free will is not exempt from this dependence. For it involves a contradiction to say that God has created human beings of such a nature that the actions of their will do not depend on his. . . . But just as the knowledge of the existence of God should not take away our certainty of the free will which we experience and feel in ourselves, so also the knowledge of our free will should not make us doubt the existence of God. The independence which we experience and feel in ourselves, and which suffices to make our actions praiseworthy or blameworthy,

is not incompatible with a dependence of quite another kind, whereby all things are subject to God.[55]

As I show in the previous chapter, Descartes attempts to steer a middle course between the extremes of Jansenism and Pelagianism; he wants to defend the reality of human freedom, but he wants to subject it to the dual priority of God as our supremely powerful creator and as the measure for all judgments about the "good" use of our free will.

Thus the two components of generosity that Descartes specifies in article 153 of the *Passions* are systematically related to one another. The "firm and constant resolution to use [one's free will] well" presupposes a conception of good use that includes a respect for proper limits. Outwardly these limits concern the dividing line between what is and what is not in our power, and to this extent Descartes incorporates a Stoic impulse into his thinking. But at a deeper level, Descartes subjects human choice to the divine dictates. We must *not* "think only of ourselves" but instead must be mindful of the difference between thinking of things entirely in relation to ourselves and in absolute terms. Descartes addresses this difference in the Second Replies:

> As everyone knows, there are two quite distinct ways of speaking about God. The first is appropriate for ordinary understanding and does contain some truth, albeit truth which is relative to human beings; and it is this way of speaking that is generally employed in Holy Scripture. The second way of speaking comes closer to expressing the naked truth—truth which is not relative to human beings; it is this way of speaking that everyone ought to use when philosophizing.[56]

In his later correspondence, Descartes draws out the significance of this distinction for earthly morality. Descartes distinguishes between relative goods (such as glory and riches) and absolute goods (such as virtue, knowledge, and health), and he associates absolute goods with membership in "a more perfect whole" than can be achieved exclusively on the basis of relative goods.[57] And he makes a distinction between the "supreme good" understood in absolute terms and in relation to the individual:

> The goodness of each thing can be considered in itself without reference to anything else, and in this sense it is evident that God is the supreme good, since he is incomparably more perfect than any creature. But goodness can also be considered in relation to ourselves. . . . Thus the ancient philosophers, unenlightened by the light of faith and knowing nothing about supernatural beatitude, considered only the goods we can possess in this life.[58]

For those enlightened by faith, earthly striving is seen against the background of God's absolute supremacy and the prospect of "supernatural beatitude"; only one who commits a sin "by refusing to embrace the Christian religion" sees human existence in wholly secular terms.[59] To exercise one's will properly is to strive to act in accordance with God's dictates and therefore to be deserving of the reward of contentment, which only God can bestow upon us. "Nothing except virtue really deserves praise. All other goods deserve only to be esteemed and not to be honoured or praised, except in so far as they are supposed to have been acquired or obtained from God by the good use of free will. For honor or praise is a reward, and only what depends on the will provides grounds for reward or punishment."[60]

Descartes's emphasis on seeing our existence within the larger scheme of things has two important consequences that provide part of the background for his conception of generosity. One is that we should not make the mistake of supposing that human beings are necessarily the center of created existence; the other is that we should not make the mistake of supposing that earthly existence is the end or telos of human existence. The aspiration to use scientific knowledge to control natural processes must be tempered by a clear awareness that "it would be childish and absurd for a metaphysician to assert that God, like some vainglorious human being, had no other purpose in making the universe than to win men's praise; or that the sun, which is many times larger than the earth, was created for no other purpose than to give light to man, who occupies a very small part of the earth."[61] To suppose that sublunary things were made for the sake of human beings is to commit the sin of hubris: "We may say that all created things are made for us in the sense that we may derive some utility from them; but I do not know that we are obliged to believe that man is the end of creation. On the contrary, it is said that all things are made for his (God's) sake."[62] Moreover, this supposition distorts the significance of earthly goods in the larger scheme of things by treating earthly existence as the highest state that human beings can achieve. "For if we imagine that beyond the heavens there is nothing but imaginary spaces, and that all the heavens are made only for the service of the earth, and the earth only for man, we will be inclined to think that this earth is our principal abode and this life our best."[63]

These statements about the importance of finding one's proper place in the larger scheme of things bear directly upon Descartes's ideal of generosity. The hallmarks of the generous person are an acknowledgment of divine Providence and the resolve to use one's will well, where the measure for the good use of the will is conformity to the divine dictates. If we fail to respect our status as a mere part in a larger cosmic scheme, "we might arrive at the absurdity of wishing to be gods, and thus make the disastrous mistake of loving divinity instead of loving God."[64] The ideal of a generous person is that of an individual who "esteem[s] nothing more highly than doing good to others and disregarding [his or her] own self-interest," is "always perfectly courteous, gracious and obliging to everyone," and has "mastery over [his or her] desires."[65] In virtue of loving God rather than divinity, the generous individual relates himself or herself to that transcendent measure that alone can confer legitimacy on one's choices.[66] Descartes's conception of love makes it clear that generosity is concerned with the establishment of a human community characterized by devotion to God and mutual respect between human beings. It has its full expression through the Christian virtues of charity, humility, and compassion.[67]

Descartes sketches an increasingly sophisticated account of love in the *Passions*. Initially he defines love as a passion that we experience "when we think of something as good with regard to us, i.e., as beneficial to us."[68] A few articles later, he defines joy in precisely the same terms: consideration of any "present good arouses joy in us, and consideration of a present evil arouses sadness."[69] Descartes's initial definition of love is sufficiently broad to include regard for things that promote our self-interest—*anything* that is beneficial to me, according to this definition, is suitable as an object of "love," be it another person or a good meal. But when he turns to a more rigorous examination of the passion of love in articles 79 to 83, Descartes explains that the objects of love form a hierarchy that recalls the hierarchy of perfections delineated in the Fourth Meditation. Love "is an emotion of the soul . . . which impels the soul to join itself willingly to objects that appear to be agreeable to it"; in contrast, hatred "impels the soul to want to be separated from objects which are presented to it as harmful."[70] The feeling of joy that we experience in connection with beneficial objects of desire moves us to form a bond with those objects. What is at stake here is not, however, simply an individualistic endeavor to secure one's material health or happiness; Descartes qualifies the term *willingly* by stating that it signifies "the assent by which we consider ourselves henceforth as joined with what we love in such a manner that we imagine a whole, of which we take ourselves to be only a part, and the thing to be loved the other."[71]

This qualification needs to be read against the background of Aquinas's conception of community. Aquinas's adherence to teleology in his efforts to conceptualize creation makes his characterization of earthly government as a hierarchical structure relatively straighforward. Descartes's abandonment of teleology in favor of mechanism tends to obscure the fact that he views not earthly community but rather only material processes in mechanistic terms. Descartes's appeal to love as the passion that can help us find our place in the larger scheme of mutual caring is a clear indication of his fidelity to some unmistakably Thomistic commitments about the proper order of things. Descartes clarifies his conception of a hierarchy of objects of love in article 82, where he refers to

> the passions which an ambitious man has for glory, a miser for money, a drunkard for wine, a brutish man for a woman he wants to violate, an honourable man for his friend or mistress, and a good father for his children. . . . [T]he men in the first four examples have love only for the possession of the objects to which their passion is related, and not for the objects themselves: for these objects they have merely desire mingled with other particular passions. Whereas the love of a good father for his children is so pure that he desires to have nothing from them, and he wants neither to possess them otherwise than he does, nor to be joined to them more closely than he already is. . . . For he imagines that he and they together form a whole of which he is not the better part, and so he often puts their interests before his own and is not afraid of sacrificing himself in order to save them.[72]

All forms of love, even the "concupiscent love" that we have for wine and the like, involve benevolence.[73] But the "benevolence" that we feel toward objects of concupiscent love is simply the desire that the object of our desire continue to be available to us for our consumption. The benevolence that we feel toward higher objects of love, particularly other people and the community of which we are a part, is of a different kind; it is the kind of regard in connection with which we see ourselves as relatively insignificant in comparison with the object of our affection. That we place a higher value on the objects of this higher kind of love than we place on ourselves puts us in a position to be willing to sacrifice ourselves for the sake of the whole.

The significance of the passion of love is therefore that it awakens and reinforces an awareness of the fact that

> none of us could subsist alone and that each one of us is really one of the many parts of the universe, and more particularly a part of the earth, the state, the society and the family to which we belong by our domicile, our oath of allegiance and our birth. And the interests of the whole, of which each of us is a part, must always be preferred to those of our own particular person . . . if someone saw everything in relation to himself, he would not hesitate to injure others greatly when he thought he could draw some slight advantage; and he would have no true friendship, no fidelity, no virtue at all. On the other hand, if someone considers himself part of a community . . . he would even be willing to lose his soul to save others.[74]

The willingness to see oneself as part of a community whose significance transcends one's own is an absolute precondition for virtue and hence for the life of the generous individual. Part of the task of using one's free will well consists in working to promote the interests of the community, and in being ready to sacrifice oneself for others when the circumstances dictate it. In the letter to Elizabeth in which he asserts the primacy of this notion of community, Descartes presents the principle "that the interests of the whole . . . must always be preferred to those of our own particular person" as one of four "truths most useful to us" on which we may rely in the absence of the perfect knowledge of which only God is capable. The other three truths are "the goodness of God, the immortality of our souls and the immensity of the universe."[75]

These four "useful" truths are systematically interrelated with one another. They reflect an overarching ethos that sees earthly existence against the background of the promise of eternal salvation and that sees even earthly existence as "ordered to God" in a way reminiscent of Aquinas. God is the highest possible object of love, and the love of God puts us in a position to integrate ourselves in the most virtuous possible way into our community. Descartes distinguishes between love for objects that are below us, for those that are equal to us, and for those that are higher than us in the scheme of things; the higher the object with which we unite ourselves in love, the more adequate our capacity for dwelling becomes, so that our union with God becomes the ideal of emotional commitment:

> We may, I think, more reasonably distinguish kinds of love according to the esteem which we have for the object we love, as compared with ourselves. For when we have less esteem for it than for ourselves, we have only a simple affection for it; when we esteem it equally with ourselves, that is called 'friendship'; and when we have more esteem for it, our passion may be called 'devotion'. Thus, we may have affection for a flower, a bird, or a horse; but unless our mind is very disordered, we can have friendship only for persons. . . . As for devotion, its principal object is undoubtedly the supreme Deity, for whom we cannot fail to have devotion when we know him as we ought. But we may also have devotion for our sovereign, our country, our town, and even for a particular person when we have much more esteem for him than we have for ourselves.[76]

All these forms of love are goods, and they are goods of different degrees of significance for the virtuous life. Friendship is a good whose significance is greater than that of the joy we feel for a flower or an animal, but inasmuch as it is a relationship between equals, its significance for life is inferior to that of our devotion to the community.[77] And in turn, our devotion to earthly community (our family, our town, or our state) is a union with a lesser perfection than is our devotion to God.

In placing God at the apex of a hierarchy of perfections, Descartes applies to the problem of the substantial union a principle that he articulates in the Third and Fourth Meditations: that a comprehension of our finite condition presupposes a relation to the infinite God. As I note above, Descartes recognizes that we can speak of the "sovereign good" either in absolute or in relative terms and that the good in relation to the individual (the effort to use one's will well, together with the contentment that follows on this) is founded on the true supreme good that is God, who "is incomparably more perfect than any creature."[78] Following the principle of the Third Meditation, this means that any assessment of finite, earthly goods must proceed on the basis of a prior relation to the infinite perfection of God. So it is not surprising when Descartes identifies the love of God as "the most delightful and useful passion possible" in this life.

> If a man meditates on these things [viz., the priority of God and the role of Providence] and understands them properly he is filled with extreme joy. Far from being so injurious and ungrateful as to want to take [God's] place he thinks that the knowledge with which God has favoured him is enough by itself to make his life worth while. Uniting himself willingly entirely to God, he loves Him so perfectly that he desires nothing at all except that His will should be done.[79]

Like all passions, our love of God disposes us to will those things that arc beneficial to us. Corresponding to the distinction that Descartes makes between volitions that terminate in the soul ("as when we will to love God") and those that terminate in the body, there is a distinction between passions that move us to will things good for the soul and those that move us to will things good for the body.[80] Descartes's appeal to the primacy of the love of God among all the passions reflects his commitment to the priority of goods of the soul over goods of the body. Our material well-being serves our spiritual well-being, and our spiritual well-being is ultimately for the sake not of ourselves but of God. "The true object of love is perfection," and only God is perfect without limit or qualification.[81] To realize our freedom is, on this view, not simply to exercise a capacity for unbridled mastery but is instead to realize a capacity to act that is inseparable from a sense of responsibility to a higher authority.

The passion of generosity is inspired through the realization of this responsibility. In turn, generosity reciprocally inspires the right kind of conduct:

> Those who are generous in this way are naturally impelled to do great things and at the same time to undertake nothing of which they do not feel themselves capable. And because they do not hold anything more important than to do good to other men and to disdain their individual interests, they are for this reason always perfectly courteous, affable and obliging towards everyone.[82]

The imperative to act this way is not disclosed by cognition, since the light of nature is oriented on logical evidence and hence is incapable of disclosing a sense of good and evil. The recognition that our sense of commitment to others must be derived from an extra-rational source of meaning is of a piece with Descartes's belief that our love of God is not ultimately a product of cognition.

> I pass to your second question, whether the natural light by itself teaches us to love God, and whether one can love him by the power of that light alone.
>
> I see two strong reasons for doubting that one can. The first is that the attributes of God most commonly considered are so high above us that we do not see at all how they can be fitting for us, and so we do not join ourselves to them willingly. The second is that nothing about God can be visualized by the imagination, which makes it seem that although one might have an intellectual love for him, one could not have any sensuous love, because it would have to pass through the imagination if it were to reach the senses by way of the intellect. Consequently I am not surprised that some philosophers are convinced that the only thing which makes us capable of loving God is the Christian religion, which teaches the mystery of the Incarnation. . . . Nevertheless, I have

no doubt at all that we can truly love God by the sole power of our nature.[83]

Here Descartes stops short of accepting the proposition that Christianity alone is capable of moving us to love God. Instead he recommends a process of meditation whereby we apprehend God's infinity by degrees. Descartes describes this process in terms that recall God's infinity in the Third Meditation. Here, as in the Third Meditation, he leaves unanswered the question how such a process of cognitive reflection can terminate in a conception of God that includes a concrete sense of meaning and moral obligation. And yet, in the *Passions* and the later correspondence, Descartes links the love of God to human virtues possessing Christian content.

4. SOCIAL AND POLITICAL IDEALS

The ideal of the generous individual brings together two aspects that at first seem to be incompatible: independence and self-reliance on the one hand and dependence on and devotion to God on the other. Alongside statements to the effect that our happiness is entirely within our own power, Descartes places emphasis on an orthodox commitment to the dependence of the "free" will of human beings on God. In the absence of this commitment, there appears to be no content and no measure for human desire other than material welfare. The generous individual is concerned first of all with the well-being of a whole greater than himself, and this whole is ultimately a spiritual whole rather than a material one. The generous individual does not fall prey to the temptation to interpret "the independence which we experience and feel in ourselves" as genuine independence but instead recognizes that this "felt" independence is in fact "not incompatible with a dependence of quite another sort, whereby all things are subject to God."[84] The generous person gives priority to "intellectual or rational" love over "the love which is a passion," and is thereby able to give priority to goods of the soul over goods that concern the union of soul and body.[85]

In the *Passions* and the later correspondence, Descartes appeals to a notion of hierarchy in his discussion of earthly government that recalls Aquinas's teleological conception of earthly government and its relation to divine government. The centerpiece of Descartes's discussion is a theory of sovereignty that takes into account the differing degrees of rational sophistication possessed by different human beings. Even though he is committed to the idea that all individuals are in principle equally rational, as he states in the first sentence of the *Discourse*, when it comes to political matters he advocates an aristocracy of minds. In the *Rules* he opposes "mediocre" minds and "great minds," and in the Dedicatory Letter to Elizabeth at the beginning of the *Principles*, he says that "whereas what depends on the will is within the capacity of everyone, there are some who possess far sharper intellectual vision."[86] Even in the *Discourse* he notes that "there are those who have enough reason or modesty to recognize that they are less capable of distinguishing the true from the false than certain others by whom they can be taught; such people should be content to follow the opinions of these others rather than seek better opinions themselves."[87]

These sorts of statements, in which Descartes acknowledges as a practical fact the difference between human intelligences, have led some commentators to conclude that Descartes is deliberately advocating a traditional model of political authority when he says in the *Discourse* that Sparta was prosperous at one time "not because each of its laws in particular was good . . . but because they were devised by a single man and hence all tended to the same end."[88] Others have seized upon statements about reform in Part 2 of the *Discourse* as evidence for Descartes's commitment to a hierarchically structured conception of political authority. In particular, Descartes implies that those who are "called neither by birth nor by fortune to the management of pubic affairs" are not the best suited to undertake social reforms, and Gouhier sees in this an endorsement of Richilieu's imperative that the sovereign do everything in his power to preserve his authority.[89] Yet others have focused on what might be considered Descartes's own political actions, such as his appeal to the theology faculty of the Sorbonne to support his work, as evidence that Descartes placed particular esteem on political consensus and not simply on truth; Rainer Specht argues that such appeals reflect Descartes's recognition that universal consensus cannot be achieved by free insight alone but instead requires an appeal to political authority.[90]

Specht is right to attribute to Descartes a recognition of the need for unified political will to be achieved not through broad consensus but rather through the imposition of sovereign decision that is respected by society; such a recognition is expressed in Descartes's remark about Sparta, and it accords with the reasoning that Hobbes offers in *Leviathan* regarding the need for prompt and decisive political choice in exigent circumstances.[91] But there are fundamental differences between Descartes and such political thinkers as Hobbes that concern the precise nature of *legitimate* political authority. In particular, Descartes, unlike Hobbes, conceives of legitimate political authority as having a special relationship to the truth; it is this relationship to the truth that recommends certain people, by "birth" or "fortune," for political leadership. Descartes is not simply being ironic at the beginning of the *Discourse* when he says that all men are equally capable of distinguishing the true from the false; instead, he has in mind a distinction that he makes clear only later in a letter to Elizabeth: "For although many people are incapable of finding the right path on their own, yet there are few who cannot recognize it well enough when somebody else clearly points it out to them."[92] There is, in other words, a fundamental distinction between the ability to see that a given truth is true, and the ability to find the truth; "all men are capable of distinguishing the truth, [but] a very small number are capable of discovering it."[93] Discovering the truth requires a vision or facility that simply distinguishing the truth does not; those who can discover the truth are something like Hegel's world-historical figure or Kant's genius, who possesses an insight into the nature of things that others can be helped to appreciate but which they cannot arrive at on their own.

The tension between the egalitarian and aristocratic moments in Descartes's thought mirrors the tension between rational order and the concrete historical order of things. In the abstract, human beings share equal access to truth, as the rational exercises of the *Meditations* are designed to demonstrate, but in practice, differences of birth and fortune give rise to differences in the actual extent to which different individuals succeed in realizing the truth. This distinction between equality in principle and inequality in practice recommends a model of political authority in which those capable of the most independent insight into the truth, presumably because they are subject to the most favorable birth and fortune, should govern society. If such a principle of political authority outwardly appears to be at odds with the egalitarian strain in Descartes's thought with which we are more familiar, the appearance of conflict disappears when we consider that Descartes's model of political authority is inseparable from his ideal of generosity. The sovereign is not to be the sort of absolute authority exalted by Hobbes; for Descartes the guiding principle of political sovereignty is not *Authoritas, non veritas, facit legem* but instead is a principle according to which the legitimacy of a sovereign's actions is to be judged according to the extent to which those actions exhibit the devotion to the good of the community and the devotion to God that are characteristic indices of generosity. Descartes's later writings even lend support to Mesnard's contention that Descartes's ideal of political sovereignty is that of "a very Christian king."[94]

The text of the *Passions* contains some subtle indications of the link between the notion of generosity and Descartes's ideal of political leadership. In the *Discourse* he links the ability to undertake "the management of public affairs" to gifts of "birth" and "fortune."[95] In the *Passions* he says that there is "no virtue so dependent on good birth as" generosity.[96] Even though Descartes believes that virtue and wisdom are subject only to the proper exercise of our free will and hence can be attained by those of low birth as well as by those of high birth, he also believes that circumstances ("like honors, riches and health") can enable some people to "enjoy a more perfect contentment" than others.[97] His remark in the *Passions* about the advantages of good birth for the cultivation of generosity establishes a parallel between the pursuit of contentment and the endeavor to realize the best kind of community: in both cases, some people will be blessed by circumstances in a way that others are not. In particular, Descartes says that "a good upbringing is a great help in correcting defects of birth."

I show above that Descartes conceives of the sovereign as superior to other human beings in the hierarchy of value in terms of which he sees the human community. God is the "principal object" of devotion, and in the earthly order of things the hierarchy runs from "our sovereign, our country, [and] our town" to "particular person[s]."[98] There is a clear order here: one's sovereign is closest to God and therefore is worthy of the greatest devotion among earthly beings. And while one should extend the greatest respect to one's sovereign, one should not think of one's sovereign as being more important than the state to which the individual and his sovereign both belong. Regarding the execution of Charles I (Princess Elizabeth's uncle) in London on February 9, 1649, Descartes writes to Elizabeth that "there is great glory in dying for a reason which ensures that one is universally pitied, praised and missed by everyone with any human feeling," suggesting in effect that a greater social good may ultimately be derived from this regicide.[99] Thus, in accordance with natural law tradition, what is ultimately at stake in political existence is the good of the state, and devotion to one's sovereign has a special status among earthly goods in the promotion of this end. In his letter to Chanut regarding the nature of love, Descartes makes a special place for one's devotion to one's prince or one's country. Such devotion makes an individual regard himself as only a tiny part of the whole which he and they constitute. He should be no more afraid to go to certain death for their service than one is afraid to draw a little blood from one's arm to improve the health of the rest of the body. Every day we see examples of this love, even in persons of low condition, who give their lives cheerfully for the good of their country or for the defence of some great person they are fond of.[100]

Even those who have not been blessed by circumstances can recognize the importance of the community and of certain individuals whose capacities and achievements render them worthy of our respect. And the more cultivated our own soul, the more likely we will be to give our respect to our society and the special individuals in it. "For the more noble and generous our soul is, the more we are inclined to render to each person that which belongs to him; thus, not only do we have a very deep humility before God, but also we are not reluctant to render to each person all the honour and respect due to him according to his position and authority in the world."[101] Preeminent among these authorities is the individual who alone has the prerogative to make human laws and to direct human affairs: the sovereign.

In several places Descartes draws an analogy between the sovereign's relation to his or her subjects and God's relation to humanity that recalls the natural law tradition of thinking about political absolutism. Descartes conceives of God as having "laid down [the laws of nature] just as a king lays down laws in his kingdom," that is, in each case the legislator establishes *lex* (law) through an absolutely free edict.[102] But in accordance with the natural law tradition, against the background of which Descartes develops his model of earthly sovereignty, the absolute prerogative of the earthly sovereign to legislate is subject in principle to a higher authority, namely, the exclusive authority of God to define *ius* (right). Bodin articulates the classical formula for the legitimacy of the earthly sovereign's legislation when he states that the divine lawgiver defines *ius* and the earthly lawgiver endeavors to legislate *lex* so as to realize the divinely ordained *ius*.[103] The earthly sovereign's responsibility is to set aside selfish interest and work toward the realization on earth of God's decrees by means of generous political leadership. In Part 2 of the *Discourse*, Descartes leaves the management of public affairs to individuals of suitable birth and fortune; in Part 6, he leaves both reform and matters of conduct generally to "those whom God has set up as sovereigns over his people or those on whom he has bestowed sufficient grace and zeal to be prophets."[104] "I believe only sovereigns, or those authorized by them, have the right to concern themselves with regulating the morals of other people."[105] In principle, only sovereigns possess the divine right, the requisite vision, and the devotion to the community as a whole that are prerequisites to the kind of leadership that is most likely to bring about God's will on earth. With regard to this last quality, Descartes says that "as it is a nobler and more glorious thing to do good to others than to oneself, it is the noblest souls who have the greatest inclination thereto and who make least account of the goods they possess. Only weak and base souls value themselves more than they ought."[106] Here Descartes is lauding a sovereign, Elizabeth, for her efforts to "be useful to those she loves." In doing so, he is implicitly emphasizing the link between the qualities characteristic of generosity and the image of an ideal sovereign.

This relationship certainly appears to hold for the case of an ideal sovereign. But what about a sovereign who is not generous, who does not maintain the sort of relationship to divine *ius* that is the measure of *legitimate* sovereignty? Descartes makes his answer to this question clear in two letters to Elizabeth in which he contrasts his views on sovereignty with the views articulated by Machiavelli in *The Prince*. The focal point of Descartes's critique is Machiavelli's failure to "distinguish [sufficiently] between princes who have come to power by just means and those who have usurped it by illegitimate methods," a failure that leads Machiavelli to recommend "indiscriminately maxims that are suitable only for the latter."[107] Machiavelli dedicated *The Prince* to Cesare Borgia in an attempt to ingratiate himself to Borgia and return from political exile; his focal point in *The Prince* was not the administration of a just state but rather the acquisition and maintenance of power. Thus Machiavelli anticipates the political absolutism of Louis XIV and Hobbes rather than Descartes's ideal of the generous monarch; he articulates a version of what Carl Schmitt calls "the politics of the exception." The politics of the exception is the idea that the goal of political existence is sheer survival and that this goal is to be served by giving absolute primacy to "the exception," that is, to the irreducible, concrete particularity of the current circumstances; by giving such primacy to the exception, we leave no room for general principles or the rule of law to take precedence over the constant imperative to secure our existence at all costs. By embracing the politics of the exception, Machiavelli abandons the concept of legitimation through the appeal to a transcendent measure, and he instead adopts a model according to which the measure for legitimation becomes a merely immanent distinction between "friend" and "enemy." Here the political is oriented not on unity, harmony, and tranquility, as in Descartes, but instead on irreducible antagonisms between sovereign states. Machiavelli makes the survival of the state a necessary concomitant of or prerequisite for the prince's ultimate goal of maintaining his hold on power.

By focusing on the case of the unjust usurper, Machiavelli makes the norm the case of "those who have gained power by crime" and who "would be unable to remain in power if they took to virtue."[108] Descartes sets up a fundamental contrast between tyranny and generosity; tyranny, and the methods the tyrant employs in order to preserve his hold on power (such as being "willing to ruin a whole country in order to remain master of it," trying "to appear good rather than to be good in reality," and the like) exhibit none of the piety and devotion to the larger whole that are characteristic of noble or generous souls.[109] At the same time, Descartes includes in his discussion of Machiavelli a sober recognition of the need for sovereigns to take extraordinary measures when the circumstances dictate them. The guiding principle, derived from the classical theory of sovereignty, is that "justice between sovereigns does not have the same bounds as justice between individuals. . . . In this instance God gives the right to those to whom he gives power."[110] Sovereigns have a special political status among human beings; even though in principle all individuals are equal, the well-being of a political state demands that sovereigns be given special prerogatives. Under ideal circumstances, the sovereign merits this special status because of his or her preeminent generosity. This means that when the sovereign employs artifice to conquer his or her enemies, his or her actions have their measure and limit in the principles of devotion to God and community. Hence even though Descartes at first seems difficult to distinguish from Machiavelli when he endorses Machiavelli's call for the prince to be both fox and lion (i.e., both cunning and vicious), "provided that some advantage to oneself or one's subjects ensues," there is finally this fundamental difference: that "I rule out one type of deception which is so directly hostile to society that I do not think it is ever permissible to use it," namely, "pretending to be a friend of those one wishes to destroy, in order to take them by surprise. Friendship is too sacred a thing to be abused in this way."[111] The premium that Descartes places on the integrity of society over the welfare even of a sovereign, together with his invocation of the category of the sacred, places him at a pronounced distance from the Machiavelli of *The Prince*. The sort of friend-enemy distinction at work in Descartes's conception of the political is not the immanent conception in Machiavelli and Schmitt but rather is a conception that has its measure in a transcendent conception of divine will and the good. Descartes's conception of friendship is not simply a conception of blind political solidarity but instead is part of a larger conception of devotion that envisions a unified human community living in the service of God.[112]

What we are to envision in a sovereign, on Descartes's view, is a special capacity for judgment and for devotion to God and the community. Generosity, legitimacy, and justice are ideal norms, even for princes; we should expect of a good political sovereign that he or she is "the most humble" and "esteem[s] nothing more highly than doing good to others and disregarding [his or her] own self-interest."[113] While the sovereign may have to suspend these ideal norms in dealing with his or her enemies, it is with an eye toward the restoration of peace and the promotion of these norms that Descartes considers extraordinary measures against the sovereign's enemies to be permissible. In contemplating such measures, the sovereign is left to consult his or her own conscience, with an eye toward the demands of community and generosity.[114] What we are to envision in the best kind of sovereign is not a tyrant but instead the kind of benevolent monarch who acts in the interest of his or her subjects, sets an example for those subjects, and who so esteems the interests of his or her subjects that the interests of sovereign and community coincide as much as possible. In these respects, Descartes's image of the sovereign anticipates the ideal of monarchy to which the early German Romantics give prominence a century and a half later.

5. THE ROLE OF CHRISTIAN VIRTUES IN THE GENEROUS LIFE

Descartes's conceptions of generosity and community are characterized by an explicit and almost systematic appeal to classically Christian virtues. This appeal goes together with the special place that Descartes makes for divine Providence in his earthly morality. In an early letter to Mersenne, Descartes invokes Christian virtues as a necessary corrective to natural tendencies such as the spirit of revenge:

> As for your question how the Christian virtues accord with the natural virtues, I would not tell you anything but this: just as we

do not straighten a bent stick simply by putting it back in line but instead bend it in the opposite direction, because our nature is so directed toward vengeance God does not command us simply to pardon our enemies but instead commands us to do good to them, and to others as well.[115]

Here Descartes makes an implicit appeal to the Christian virtue of charity as the necessary corrective to our lower tendencies. This appeal anticipates the prominence that Descartes gives to "the Christian virtue called charity" in his October 6, 1645, letter to Elizabeth. There he makes reference to charity in the context of a discussion of the importance of community, which he sees as being held together by a love that is implicitly Christian in nature:

> Evil is nothing real, but only a privation. When we are sad on account of some evil which has happened to our friends, we do not share in the defect in which this evil consists; and whatever sadness or distress we feel on such occasions cannot be as great as the inner satisfaction which always accompanies good actions, and especially actions which proceed from a pure affection for others which has no reference to oneself, that is, from the Christian virtue called charity.[116]

The terms of this discussion recall Augustine's conception of devotion to God and Descartes's reliance on Augustine in formulating his own conception of the way in which human beings are related to God as the measure for truth and goodness. Charity is nothing but a "pure affection for others" that is founded on our pure affection for God; it takes the form of a turning toward other human beings, just as in the Augustinian formula the love of God takes the form of turning toward him. There is nothing of selfish individualism here but rather an authentic turning toward. Later in the same letter, Descartes makes this clear when he says that it is only "base souls [who] cannot be persuaded to take trouble for others unless you can show them that they will reap some profit for themselves."[117]

Descartes's thinking about charity in this letter continues a line of thought that he introduced in the letter to Voetius, in which he quoted the following passage from 1 Corinthians 13:1–6:

> I may speak in tongues of men or of angels, but if I have no love, I am a sounding gong or a clanging cymbal. I may have the gift of prophecy and the knowledge of every hidden truth; I may have faith enough to move mountains; but if I have no love, I am nothing. I may give all I possess to the needy, I may give my body to be burnt, but if I have no love, I gain nothing by it.
>
> Love is patient and kind. Love envies no one, is never boastful, never conceited, never rude; love is never selfish, never quick to take offence. Love keeps no score of wrongs, takes no pleasure in the sins of others, but delights in the truth.

To speak of the notion of love, Paul follows the Old Testament tradition of using the term ἀγάπη, which Jerome translates as *caritas* in the Vulgate. In English translations, the term is rendered variously as "charity" (King James Version) and "love" (New and Revised English Bibles), and the difficulty of settling on one of these terms or the other reflects the complexity of the notion of love in the context of Christianity. Descartes uses the French *charité* in translating the passage. He incorporates into his ethical views the foundational character of *caritas* when he says that "it is clear from this passage that all the other gifts that man can receive from God have value only to the extent that they are joined together with charity."[118] The entire conception of love or devotion that Descartes articulates in his later writings must be seen in this unequivocally Christian light. Our devotion to others is to take the form of Christian charity, and this earthly devotion is based on our love of God. This rootedness of generosity in our devotion to God is an expression of the rootedness of the "highest and most perfect morality" in the metaphysics that discloses to us our divine measure.

Descartes's appeal to such Christian virtues as charity is intimately bound up with his departure from the Stoic conception of providence. For Descartes, the task of humanity is to get into the right relation to God and not simply to an anonymous "nature." Although he incorporates a moment of Stoic resignation into his thinking, he does not stop there but instead inscribes resignation within a larger scheme of human action that includes a positive ideal of satisfaction. Descartes is critical of Seneca's conception of wisdom for being "very obscure" and for misunderstanding what it means to get into the right relationship to nature. To correct Seneca's misconceptions, we must "use a Christian way of speaking" and say that "wisdom is submission to the will of God, and following it in all our actions."[119] It is against the background of this explicit invocation of Christianity that we best understand not only Descartes's appeal to charity but also his references to the virtues of repentance, humility, and compassion.

A reading of the provisional morality might lead one to suppose that Descartes leaves no room in his ethical thought for a moment of repentance, for he says that the proper exercise of resoluteness will allow us to "free [ourselves] from all the repentance [*repentirs*] and remorse which usually trouble the consciences of those weak and faltering spirits who allow themselves to set out on some supposedly good course of action which later, in their inconstancy, they judge to be bad."[120] In this connection, the difference between the provisional and definitive moralities is illuminating. When in his later writings Descartes makes a place for repentance in his ethical thought, he has in mind the prospect of resoluteness being guided by knowledge, so that our resolutions can be "corrected" or improved progressively by the increasing store of our knowledge. This prospect of improvement or correction is not absent from the provisional morality but is reliant there on example and custom— even if experience may make me a better judge of circumstances and the prevailing customs and mores of my society, this sort of acquaintance with the circumstances and traditions that happen to prevail does not satisfy the requirements of rigorous knowledge.

In the context of a definitive morality, repentance inspires us to improve our judgment and to strive to control our passions so they do not prevent us from doing what we judge to be best. Descartes writes to Elizabeth that "nothing can impede our contentment except desire and regret or repentance; but if we always do whatever our reason tells us, even if events show us afterwards that we have gone wrong, we will never have any grounds for repentance, because it was not our own fault."[121] Virtue, as I show in chapter 1, is a matter of resolutely following what reason presents as the best course of action; contentment is a reward that follows upon virtue. The problem of acting well is a problem of striving to acquire knowledge and of striving to exercise our will in conformity with what reason dictates; with regard to the substantial union of mind and body, the problem of ethical conduct becomes that of regulating our desires so that they promote rather than impede conformity to the dictates of reason. In this connection repentance can play a crucial corrective role. "I think that there is nothing to repent of when we have done what we judged to be best at the time when we had to decide to act, even though later, thinking it over at our leisure, we judge that we made a mistake. There would be more ground for repentance if we had acted against our conscience, even though we realized afterwards that we had done better than we thought."[122] Descartes recognizes the Aristotelian problem of ακρασία or weakness of the will: Knowing the right thing to do is not sufficient for acting in accordance with this knowledge, because passion can get in the way. Failing to do the right thing when we know what is right is worse than failing to do the right thing due to ignorance that is no fault of our own. When we repent, we reflect on our failure and recognize that it was entirely within our power. We recognize that our failure was due to a deliberate turning away from God and the good and that it is in our power to turn again toward the good.

In response to Descartes's remarks about repentance, Elizabeth writes that in dodging repentance concerning the faults we have committed, as though it is an enemy to our happiness, one could run the risk of losing the desire to correct oneself, principally when some passion has produced those faults—for we have a natural love to be roused by our passions and to follow their movements, and it is only the inconvenience proceeding from them that teaches us they can be harmful.[123]

Descartes replies that he "would not venture to contradict what Your Highness writes about repentance." He recognizes the possibility that a person could surrender to the prospect of bodily enjoyment; too much in the world testifies to the dominance of carnal impulses over spiritual ones for Descartes or anyone else to suppose that a simple reflection on the nature of things will automatically turn a person into a righteous member of the divine community. But he goes on to say that repentance "is a Christian virtue which serves to make us correct our faults—not only those committed voluntarily, but also those done through ignorance, when some passion has prevented us from knowing the truth."[124] In stressing that repentance is a Christian virtue, Descartes subtly acknowledges the limits of rational insight in the endeavor to move oneself to act in accordance with God's will. He gestures toward the traditional Christian commitment that reason must be supplemented by a more direct connection to God if we are to "join ourselves entirely willingly to Him." Descartes is careful to avoid appealing to faith in this connection, but he is aware that rational reflection and the systematic rehabituation of our bodily responses are never sufficient to move us to the kind of devotion that forms the crux of his ideal of society. Repentance is not simply a technique or a mechanism but instead is founded on a spiritual reflection on one's dependence on, obligation to, and love of God that performs the positive function of turning us back toward God whenever the temptations of the world entice us to turn away from him. Repentance is part of a life project in which we seek to close the gap between our fallen state and an original state of unity with God. It presupposes a sense of loss and a desire to retrieve or establish the wholeness of which Descartes speaks when he develops his notion of community. Repentance "is a kind of sadness, which results from our believing that we have done some evil deed; and it is very bitter because its cause lies in ourselves alone. But this does not prevent its being very useful when the action of which we repent is truly evil and we know this for certain, because then our repentance prompts us to do better on another occasion."[125] Repentance functions against the background of an Augustinian conception of evil as a privation and a turning away from God; as such, it presupposes the priority of a whole union with God over the fragmentation of fallen, individual existence.

The virtue of humility is incorporated implicitly into Descartes's earthly morality in the emphasis he places on acknowledging our limits and our dependence on God, and it is explicitly incorporated in several articles of the *Passions*. In article 54, Descartes associates self-esteem with humility and self-contempt with abjectness.[126] Given the identification of self-esteem with generosity in articles 152 and 153, Descartes is clearly calling for the generous individual to exercise a certain modesty. In article 154, he characterizes generous individuals as those who "never have contempt for anyone" and who "do not have much more esteem for themselves than for those whom they surpass. For all these things seem to them to be very unimportant, by contrast with the virtuous will for which alone they esteem themselves, and which they suppose also to be present, or at least capable of being present, in every other person."[127] Legitimate self-esteem is based exclusively on the proper exercise of one's free will (art. 152). In comparison with this, such matters as one's superior station in worldly affairs are of little consequence in the generous individual's estimations of moral worth, both of himself or herself and of others. "Thus the most generous people are usually also the most humble. We have humility as a virtue when . . . we do not prefer ourselves to anyone else and we think that since others have free will just as much as we do, they may use it just as well as we use ours."[128]

If generous individuals possess legitimate self-esteem, one must be careful to contrast the case of individuals who possess unjustified self-esteem. The difference, Descartes writes to Elizabeth, is one between individuals who know their true worth and those who overestimate it:

> Besides, the vanity which makes a man think better of himself than he deserves is a vice which only weak and base souls display; but this does not mean that the strongest and most noble souls have a duty to despise themselves. We must do ourselves justice, and recognize our perfections as well as our faults. Propriety forbids us to boast of our good qualities, but it does not forbid us to be aware of them.[129]

Descartes puts the point slightly differently in the *Passions*: "All who conceive a good opinion of themselves for any other reason" than that they exercise their free will properly "do not possess true generosity, but only a vanity which is always a vice, and is all the more so the less justification such people have for esteeming themselves highly."[130] Unjustified self-esteem manifests itself in two ways: in overestimating our worth and in basing our sense of self-worth on qualities that are not properly relevant to considerations of self-worth. The only appropriate basis for such considerations is the proper exercise of our freedom. In such considerations, the generous person employs modesty but is not self-effacing.

The generous person must strive, then, for a middle course between the extreme of "a highly blameworthy vanity," which takes the form of valuing ourselves for our "intelligence, beauty, riches, honours, etc.," and the opposite extreme of "abjectness, or humility as a vice," which "consists chiefly in a feeling of weakness or irresolution, together with an incapacity to refrain from actions which we know we shall regret later on, as if we lacked the full use of our free will. It involves also the belief that we cannot subsist by ourselves or get along without many things whose acquisition depends on others."[131] The vain individual evaluates gifts of Providence as though they were products of his or her own industry. Moreover, "vain people attempt to humble everyone else; being slaves to their desires, they have souls which are constantly agitated by hatred, envy, jealousy, or anger."[132] The vain person believes that human worth is based on such things as beauty and wealth and wants to assert superiority over others on the basis of possessing such goods. In the other case, abject or inappropriately humble people fail to acknowledge the gift of free will, and they therefore consider themselves to be at the utter mercy of forces outside their control. The attitude that enables the generous individual to avoid these two extremes is that of Christian humility, "which is the total subjection of creature to creator, and the acknowledgment that the human being 'has nothing that he has not been given.'"[133]

This appeal to humility is a corollary to Descartes's fidelity to Augustine and Aquinas on matters of the relationship between free will and divine Providence. Aquinas argues that

> A thing moved by another is forced if it is moved against its natural inclination. But if it is moved by another which gives to it its natural inclination, it is not forced. Thus, a heavy body, made to move downward by that which produced it, is not forced. In like manner God, while moving the will, does not force it, because He gives the will its own natural inclination.[134]

Descartes follows this formula when he explains the "middle course" that the generous person needs to steer between the extremes of vanity and abjectness:

> As for free will, I agree that if we think only of ourselves we cannot help regarding ourselves as independent; but when we think of the infinite power of God, we cannot help believing that all things depend on him, and hence that our free will is not exempt from this dependence. For it involves a contradiction to

say that God has created human beings of such a nature that the actions of their will do not depend on his. . . . But just as the knowledge of the existence of God should not take away our certainty of the free will which we experience and feel in ourselves, so also the knowledge of our free will should not make us doubt the existence of God. The independence which we experience and feel in ourselves, and which suffices to make our actions praiseworthy or blameworthy, is not incompatible with a dependence of quite another kind, whereby all things are subject to God.[135]

Because the generous person recognizes this founded character of human freedom, the extent to which he or she values his or her own accomplishments will always be couched in reverence for the fact that our will has been created by and depends upon God. This reverence moves the generous individual to a feeling of humility before the greatness of God, and it reminds him or her that in a deep sense he or she is essentially no different (and hence no better) than any other human being. In comparison with the greatness of God, even what one accomplishes through the proper exercise of freedom is quite insignificant. At the same time, because generous individuals recognize that freedom is compatible with our dependence on God, they do not succumb to hopelessness or irresoluteness but instead endeavor to exercise their will and to do so in accordance with their best understanding of God's decrees.

As a complement to the virtue of charity, the virtue of pity or compassion goes together quite naturally with the ideal of generosity. The open-heartedness and community spirit of the generous includes "good will towards everyone." The most generous individuals

are not free from compassion when they see the infirmities of other men and hear their complaints. . . . [T]he chief object of the pity of the greatest men is the weakness of those whom they see complaining. For they think that no misfortune could be so great an evil as the timidity of those who cannot endure it with forbearance. And although they hate vices, they do not on that account hate those whom they see prone to them: they merely pity them.[136]

The feeling of pity is a natural concomitant of the Christian love that aspires to a universal community of humanity. Ordinary people who feel compassion for others are generally "moved to pity more by the love they bear towards themselves than by the love they have for others," that is, they feel compassion because "they think of the evil affecting others as capable of befalling themselves."[137] Generous individuals, in contrast, feel pity for others not out of self-love but out of genuine charity. Those who completely fail to feel pity are either "evil-minded and envious" misanthropists or "so brutish and so thoroughly blinded by good fortune or rendered desperate by bad fortune, that they do not think any evil could possibly befall them."[138] What makes the generous individual preeminently capable of feeling compassion is an underlying sense of love or devotion, together with the basic characteristic of generosity specified in article 153 of the *Passions*, namely, the recognition "that nothing truly belongs to him but [the] freedom to dispose his volitions." When one proceeds from this knowledge and maintains a firm resolution to use his or her will properly, Descartes believes, an individual will never run the risk of being "blinded by good fortune or rendered desperate by bad fortune," because the goods of fortune play a relatively insignificant role in the evaluations of goods that the generous person makes. The love or charity that fundamentally moves the generous person leaves absolutely no room for evil-mindedness or envy.

Descartes's incorporation of the Christian virtues of charity, repentance, humility, and compassion or pity into his ideal of generosity reflects his vision of a society whose sovereign is "a legitimate and probably a Christian prince," a "very Christian king."[139] Mesnard offers this as a "hypothesis" because Descartes nowhere presents this conclusion straightforwardly. But it is supported by the cumulative force of his views about devotion, generosity, community, and Christian virtues, particularly in the light of his debt to Augustine and Aquinas. Descartes sees the relationship between an earthly sovereign and his or her subjects as modeled on that between the divine sovereign and his creatures. At the same time, Descartes makes a decisive step in the direction of separating earthly government from divine government when he asserts that sovereigns alone may regulate the morals of human beings.[140] There is no reference to the authority of Scripture or the church here. Instead, a sovereign is to consult his or her conscience in matters bearing upon human morals. And while Descartes envisions an appeal to specifically Christian conscience in this connection, he does not tether the sovereign's prerogative to any specific ecclesiastical authority nor explicitly and formally to the guidance of Scripture. Even though Descartes is, in the words of Jaspers, "a pious Catholic," it is not difficult to see the influence of the Lutheran Reformation on his thinking about the nature of spiritual inwardness in matters of earthly morality.

6. THE LIMITS OF A "TECHNOLOGICAL" READING OF DESCARTES'S LATER WRITINGS

The interpretation of Descartes as a fundamentally Christian thinker has met with widespread opposition, particularly when consideration is given to his "earthly" morality. Even if one grants that in an absolute sense Descartes believes that we find our measure in God, one might still suppose that in a sense relative to earthly existence we find our measure in the practical ability to master nature, particularly to the extent that mastery promotes good health and our general material prosperity. Many commentators have focused on the practical orientation of the *Passions* and the later correspondence and have seen in these writings clear indications of such a practical orientation. Gueroult and Maritain see a wholly secular morality in the later writings; Gueroult considers the earthly morality to be "a technique, an applied science," while Maritain sees it as involving "a radical negation of the notion of Christian philosophy."[141]

Gueroult and Maritain provide us with a highly influential view of Descartes as a secular thinker for whom the mastery of self and nature are the guiding teloi of human development and for whom these ends are to be attained through the autonomous exercise of human reason. Such a "technological" voice is certainly at work in Descartes's writings. But as I have shown, this voice speaks against the background of another call, a transcendent one that assigns us an earthly vocation subject to the prospect of supernatural beatitude. The ethos or sense of belonging according to which we concern ourselves with the *saeculum*, with our earthly estate, has its measure and its completion in what I have called an "angelic" ethos that summons us to a higher vocation.

Therefore any reading of Descartes as an exclusively "secular" or "technological" thinker is necessarily incomplete. Descartes does establish a fundamental distance from such thinkers as Aquinas in detaching the *form* of earthly authority (be that authority one's conscience, one's sovereign, or some form of "reason") from our divine measure. But in fundamental respects, the *content* of Descartes's ideal of earthly existence is derived from the same underlying sense of belonging that guided Augustine and Aquinas. This incommensurability between form and content leads Descartes to an untenable resolution: he continually claims that reason is sufficient to guide the will in all the contingencies of life, thereby supplanting the provisional morality of the *Discourse* with the certainty of *scientia*. For all that, however, Descartes never abandons the certainty of salvation and the devotion to God that are central to Christianity. His "definitive" view, even if he does not acknowledge it explicitly, is that anyone who reflects and strives properly will recognize the reality and authority of the Christian God and will thereby find a secure basis for following the dictates of religion. On this basis, Descartes boldly asserts that "the sin that

Turks and other infidels commit by refusing to embrace the Christian religion . . . [arises] from their resistance to the impulses of divine grace within them."[142] The conception of adherence to religion that Descartes envisions here is far removed from the formulation of the first rule of the provisional morality, according to which each individual should follow, inter alia, the religion of his or her birth. A properly conceived definitive morality is, for Descartes, a morality rooted in Christianity.

The idea of the certainty of salvation is inseparable from the entire apparatus of divine and created beings that Descartes makes central to his metaphysics. But our access to those fundamental truths of Christianity that can give content to human existence is not cognitive; moral truths are not reducible to cognition. Hence, while Descartes sometimes hints that he will demonstrate the immortality of the soul rationally, in the end he acknowledges that it is not reason but *faith* that "teaches us . . . the promise of eternal life for our bodies, and consequently for the world in which they will exist, after the Resurrection."[143] Elsewhere he appeals to an undefined notion of conscience that falls somewhere between faith and cognition that terminates in clear and distinct perception. He seems to recognize that form comes from cognition and content from faith, but his interest in realizing a unified, harmonious human community leads him to recognize that there is no way to prove the unique truth of Christianity.

In this connection, several commentators provide important insights about the predicament in which Descartes finds himself. Röd observes that Descartes postulates but does not rationally ground the priority of social interests over individual interests because such a priority cannot be derived from clear insight. Röd suggests that this fundamental limitation of reason forces Descartes to derive the content of his moral commitments from religion.[144] Boutroux notes that the close alliance between science and morality in Descartes's thought should not lead us to the misconception that Descartes's morality is in any way derived from science; Descartes places a "morals of ends" above a "morals of means," and science is confined to the realization of the means.[145] Rodis-Lewis stresses the significance of the roots of the tree of wisdom for the fruit: the doctrine of the *Passions* has a limited scientific aim and does not establish but instead presupposes "the first causes and the true principles" of knowledge that Descartes identifies in the letter to Picot as the fifth degree of wisdom.[146] If the "morality" of the *Passions* does not even reach as far as the foundational principles of truth disclosed by cognition, and if those foundational principles themselves do not establish but instead presuppose moral content, then a fortiori the "morality" of the *Passions* falls short of adducing the essential content of morality as well. It is not really a morality at all but rather a set of techniques for attaining practical ends that have been posited by a discipline that is prior to the doctrine of the *Passions*. That discipline in turn is extrarational and the source of guidance for liberty that is not indifferent but instead depends upon and is ordered to the will of God.

To conceive of the will as absolutely independent or autonomous is therefore "to think only of ourselves" and not to inscribe the operation of our will in the larger metaphysical context that refers us to supernatural beatitude. To acknowledge the subordinate or relative status of earthly existence is to see it against the background of the eternal life in which we can enjoy supernatural beatitude. Descartes makes implicit reference to this distinction when he notes that the passions are relevant to satisfaction only in *this* life.[147] Our existence as a substantial union of mind and body is not our only existence. Descartes expresses his commitment to the primacy of eternal life over earthly existence in several pieces of correspondence. He writes to Colvius in 1637 that "the time during which we live on earth is such a small thing in comparison to eternity" that it is a relatively insignificant matter exactly how long we live.[148] And in the letter to Elizabeth in which he outlines the four "most useful truths," Descartes says that a reflection on the nature of the soul leads us to the conclusion that it is much nobler than the body, and that it is capable of enjoying countless satisfactions not to be found in this life. This prevents us from fearing death, and so detaches our affections from the things of this world that we look upon whatever is in the power of fortune with nothing but scorn.

. . . [I]f we imagine that beyond the heavens there is nothing but imaginary spaces, and that all the heavens are made only for the service of the earth, and the earth only for man, we will be inclined to think that this earth is our principal abode and this life our best.[149]

Descartes's interest in medicine and the mastery of the body is subsidiary to a more fundamental interest in the life of the soul after its deliverance from the world of embodiment. He cautions us not to let ourselves believe that "this life is our best" and that the earth exists "only for man," and he finds in the promise of a higher life the basis for overcoming our fear of death.[150] Naturally this does not mean that we should consider this life to be without value, nor should we seek death; instead we must see and affirm the true value of earthly existence, which is finally outstripped by the significance of eternal life.[151]

This is why Descartes's earthly morality must be interpreted against the background of his "angelic" aspirations and why any interpretation of Descartes's earthly morality as wholly secular distorts his significance as a moral thinker. To interpret Descartes's appeal to generosity as an appeal to "self-affection" with no reference to any higher measure than the individual's autonomous ability to represent his or her highest possible perfection to himself or herself is to break the fundamental link that our representations and feelings have to God. It is to posit autonomous self-determination where there is at best an ambivalence between self-determination and subjection to divine dictates.[152] The self on Descartes's view is not ultimately independent but instead belongs to a community that is higher in principle than any finite individual or community of finite individuals. The passion of generosity is less a sign of the independence of the self than of the devotion to community that is incumbent upon every individual. In the end, this community is not merely a human one. Community, like truth, is *sub specie aeternitatis*; the content and meaning of human existence, both earthly and supernatural, are derived from a transcendent source, not an immanent one. The technology of virtue in the later writings, like all the sciences on the tree of wisdom, derives its legitimacy from the roots of the tree. These roots, in turn, are based on moral imperatives disclosed by the soul's contemplation of its relation to God. What outwardly appears to be a self-sufficient program for the pursuit of wisdom, depicted by the tree metaphor, is grounded in an extrarational Christian mandate. I show in the next chapter that this holds as much for Descartes's program to master nature as it does for the program of the *Passions* to regulate bodily affects.

NOTES

1. Karl Jaspers, *Three Essays: Leonardo, Descartes, Max Weber*, trans. Ralph Manheim (New York: Harcourt, Brace, & World, 1964), p. 152.

2. Ibid., p. 153.

3. Ibid., p. 150.

4. Ibid., p. 152.

5. Ibid., p. 149.

6. AT 9B.14, CSM 1.186.

7. Descartes, letter to Chanut, June 15, 1646, AT 4.441, CSM 3.289.

8. AT 9B.4, CSM 1.180 f.

9. AT 9B.3 f., CSM 1.180.

10. Descartes, *Discourse on Method*, Part 6, AT 6.62, CSM 1.143.

11. Ibid., AT 6.62, CSM 1.142 f. (translation altered).

12. On libertine Gnosticism, see Hans Jonas, *The Gnostic Religion: The Message of the Alien God and the Beginnings of Chrisitanity*, 2d ed. (Boston: Beacon Press, 1991), pp. 47, 270 ff.

13. Letter to Descartes, April 25, 1646, AT 4.404, in *Descartes: His*

Moral Philosophy and Psychology, trans. John J. Blom (New York: New York University Press, 1978), p. 178.

14. Descartes, letter to Chanut, June 15, 1646, AT 4.442, CSM 3.289; Descartes's reply to the second prefatory letter to the *Passions*, AT 11.326, CSM 1.327.

15. Geneviève Rodis-Lewis, introduction to *The Passions of the Soul*, by René Descartes, trans. Stephen Voss (Indianapolis/Cambridge: Hackett, 1989), p. xvi.

16. Ernst Cassirer, *Descartes: Lehre—Persönlichkeit—Wirkung* (Stockholm: Bermann-Fischer, 1939), p. 107.

17. Ibid., p. 241.

18. Martial Gueroult, *Descartes' Philosophy Interpreted According to the Order of Reasons*, trans. Roger Ariew, 2 vols. (Minneapolis: University of Minnesota Press, 1984–1985), 2.187 f.

19. John Cottingham, *Philosophy and the Good Life: Reason and the Passions in Greek, Cartesian and Psychoanalytic Ethics* (Cambridge: Cambridge University Press, 1998), p. 71 f. Cf. *Principles of Philosophy*, Part 4, art. 188, AT 8A.315, CSM 1.279: "I have described the earth and indeed the whole visible universe as if it were a machine."

20. See Descartes, *Passions of the Soul*, art. 6, AT 11.330 f., CSM 1.329 f., where Descartes compares the body of a live man to a fully wound watch; cf. art. 16 and *Treatise on Man*, AT 11.166, CSM 1.104, where Descartes compares the mechanical control of muscular motion to the functioning of a church organ.

21. Descartes, *Passions*, art. 16, AT 11.341 f., CSM 1.335.

22. Ibid., arts. 17 and 19, AT 11.342 f., CSM 1.335 f.

23. Ibid., art. 52, AT 11.372, CSM 1.349

24. Ibid., art. 137, AT 11.430, CSM 1.376.

25. Ibid., art. 40, AT 11.359, CSM 1.343.

26. Ibid., art. 138, AT 11.431, CSM 1.377.

27. Ibid., art. 139, AT 11.432, CSM 1.377; letter to Elizabeth, September 15, 1645, AT 4.292, CSM 3.265.

28. Descartes, *Passions*, art. 47, AT 11.366, CSM 1.346 f.; see also arts. 36, 40, 45, 48, and the Dedicatory Letter to Elizabeth at the beginning of the *Principles*, AT 8A.2, CSM 1.191.

29. Descartes, letter to Elizabeth, September 15, 1645, AT 4.295, CSM 3.267.

30. Pierre Mesnard, *Essai sur la morale de Descartes* (Paris: Boivin & Cie, 1936), p. 141.

31. Descartes, *Passions*, art. 144, AT 11.436, CSM 1.379.

32. Descartes, letter to Mersenne, October 16, 1639, AT 2.599, CSM 3.140.

33. AT 11.431, CSM 1.377.

34. Cassirer, *Descartes: Lehre—Persönlichkeit—Wirkung*, p. 249.

35. Descartes, *Discourse*, Part 6, AT 6.62, CSM 1.143 (translation altered). Cf. AT 6.78, CSM 1.151; letter to Elizabeth, May or June 1645, AT 4.220, CSM 3.250; and letter to Picot, AT 9B.14, 9B.17; CSM 1.186, 1.188.

36. Descartes, letter to Elizabeth, September 1, 1645, AT 4.281 f., CSM 3.262; letter to Elizabeth, October or November 1646, AT 4.528 f., CSM 3.296. Cf. letter to Elizabeth, August 4, 1645, AT 4.264 f., CSM 3.257.

37. Letter to Descartes, September 13, 1645, AT 4.289, in *Descartes: His Moral Philosophy and Psychology*, p. 149 (translation altered); letter to Descartes, April 25, 1646, AT 4.405, in *Descartes: His Moral Philosophy and Psychology*, p. 179.

38. Descartes, letter to Elizabeth, October 6, 1645, AT 4.308, CSM 3.269; see also letter to Elizabeth, May 1646, AT 4.411, CSM 3.287.

39. Geneviève Rodis-Lewis, "Maîtrise des passions et sagesse chez Descartes," in *Descartes*, Cahiers de Royaumont, Philosophie no. 2 (Paris: Les éditions de minuit, 1957), p. 224.

40. Mesnard, *Essai sur la morale de Descartes*, p. 204.

41. Descartes, *Passions*, art. 40, AT 11.359, CSM 1.343.

42. Descartes, letter to Mersenne, March 18, 1630, AT 1.134, CSM 3.20.

43. Descartes, *Passions*, art. 50, AT 11.370, CSM 1.348.

44. Ibid.

45. AT 11.362 f., CSM 1.345. Cf. letter to Elizabeth, July 1647, AT 5.65, in *Descartes: His Moral Philosophy and Psychology*, p. 226.

46. Descartes, letter to Elizabeth, August 4, 1645, AT 4.267, CSM 3.258.

47. AT 8A.3, CSM 1.191.

48. Étienne Gilson, *The Philosophy of St. Thomas Aquinas*, trans. Edward Bullough (New York: Dorset, 1948), p. 319 f.

49. Descartes, *Passions*, art. 49, AT 11.368, CSM 1.347.

50. Ibid., art. 153, AT 11.445 f., CSM 1.384.

51. Ibid., art. 158, AT 11.158, CSM 1.386.

52. Ibid., art. 146, AT 11.439, CSM 1.380.

53. Ibid., art. 145, AT 11.437 f., CSM 1.379 f.

54. Ibid., art. 145, AT 11.438, CSM 1.380. Cf. Phil. 2:12–14.

55. Descartes, letter to Elizabeth, November 3, 1645, AT 4.332, CSM 3.277; cf. *Principles*, Part 1, art. 37, 40, 41.

56. AT 7.142, CSM 2.102.

57. Descartes, letter to Chanut, June 6, 1647, AT 5.55 f., CSM 3.321 f.

58. Descartes, letter to Christina, November 20, 1647, AT 5.82, CSM 3.324.

59. Descartes, Author's Replies to the Second Set of Objections, AT 7.148, CSM 2.105.

60. Descartes, letter to Christina, November 20, 1647, AT 5.84, CSM 3.325.

61. Descartes, letter to Hyperaspistes, August 1641, AT 3.431, CSM 3.195. Cf. *Conversation with Burman*, AT 5.168, CSM 3.349, and *Principles*, Part 3, arts. 2–3, AT 8A.80 f., CSM 1.248 f.

62. Descartes, letter to Chanut, June 6, 1647, AT 5.54 f., CSM 3.321.

63. Descartes, letter to Elizabeth, September 15, 1645, AT 4.292, CSM 3.266.

64. Descartes, letter to Chanut, February 1, 1647, AT 4.608, CSM 3.309.

65. Descartes, *Passions*, art. 156, AT 11.447 f., CSM 1.385.

66. See Geneviève Rodis-Lewis, *La morale de Descartes* (Paris: Presses universitaires de France, 1957), p. 81.

67. In art. 161 of *Passions*, Descartes endeavors to distinguish generosity from the notion of magnanimity used in the schools (AT 11.453, CSM 1.388). But there are important affinities between generosity and Thomistic magnanimity that help place Descartes's conception into proper context; see Rodis-Lewis, *La morale de Descartes*, pp. 74, 85n1, and François Heidsieck, "Honor and Nobility of Soul: Descartes to Sartre," *International Philosophical Quarterly* 1 (1961): 579.

68. Descartes, *Passions*, art. 56, AT 11.374, CSM 1.350.

69. Ibid., art. 61, AT 11.376, CSM 1.351.

70. Ibid., art. 79, AT 11.387, CSM 1.356.

71. Ibid., art. 80, AT 11.387, CSM 1.356.

72. Ibid., art. 82, AT 11.388 f., CSM 1.356 f.

73. Ibid., art. 81, AT 11.388, CSM 1.356.

74. Descartes, letter to Elizabeth, September 15, 1645, AT 4.293, CSM 3.266.

75. AT 4.293, CSM 3.266.

76. Descartes, *Passions*, art. 83, AT 11.390, CSM 1.357.

77. Descartes, letter to Chanut, February 1, 1647, AT 4.609 ff., CSM 3.309 ff.

78. Descartes, letter to Christina, November 20, 1647, AT 5.82, CSM 3.324.

79. Descartes, letter to Chanut, February 1, 1647, AT 4.609, CSM 3.309 f.

80. Descartes, *Passions*, art. 18, AT 11.343, CSM 1.335.

81. Descartes, letter to Elizabeth, September 15, 1645, AT 4.291, CSM 3.265.

82. Descartes, *Passions*, art. 156, AT 11.447 f., CSM 1.385.

83. Descartes, letter to Chanut, February 1, 1647, AT 4.607 f., CSM 3.308 f.

84. Descartes, letter to Elizabeth, November 3, 1645, AT 4.333, CSM 3.277.

85. Descartes, letter to Chanut, February 1, 1647, AT 4.602 f., CSM 3.306.

86. Descartes, Rule Eight, AT 10.399, CSM 1.32; Rule Thirteen, AT 10.433, CSM 1.53; AT 8A.3, CSM 1.191.

87. Descartes, *Discourse*, Part 2, AT 6.15, CSM 1.118.

88. Ibid., AT 6.12, CSM 1.117.

89. AT 6.14 f., CSM 1.118; Henri Gouhier, *Essais sur Descartes* (Paris: Vrin, 1937), p. 266 f.

90. Descartes, Dedicatory Letter to the Sorbonne, AT 7.5 f., CSM 2.5 f.; Rainer Specht, "Über Descartes's politische Ansichten," *Der Staat* 3 (1964): 288 f.

91. See Thomas Hobbes, *Leviathan* (Harmondsworth: Penguin, 1985), Part 2, chap. 19, pp. 241 ff.

92. Descartes, letter to Elizabeth, August 15, 1645, AT 4.272, CSM 3.259.

93. Étienne Gilson, *Discours de la Méthode: Texte et commentaire*, 5th ed. (Paris: Vrin, 1976), p. 178.

94. Mesnard, *Essai sur la morale de Descartes*, p. 210.

95. Descartes, *Passions*, Part 2, AT 6.14, CSM 1.118.

96. Ibid., art. 161, AT 11.453, CSM 1.188.

97. Descartes, letter to Elizabeth, August 4, 1645, AT 4.264, CSM 3.257.

98. Descartes, *Passions*, art. 83, AT 11.390, CSM 1.357.

99. Descartes, letter to Elizabeth, February 22, 1649, AT 5.282, CSM 3.367.

100. Descartes, letter to Chanut, February 1, 1647, AT 4.612, CSM 3.311.

101. Descartes, *Passions*, art. 164, AT 11.455 f., CSM 1.388 f.

102. Descartes, letter to Mersenne, April 15, 1630, AT 1.145, CSM 3.23. Cf. Sixth Replies, AT 7.436, CSM 2.294, where Descartes calls God "the supreme legislator" of the laws of nature; and letter to Elizabeth, January 1646, AT 4.353, CSM 3.282.

103. Jean Bodin, *Six Books of the Commonwealth* (1594), abridged and trans. Michael Tooley (New York, Barnes and Noble, 1967), bk. 1, chap. 9, p. 36.

104. AT 6.61, CSM 1.142.

105. Descartes, letter to Chanut, November 20, 1647, AT 5.87, CSM 3.326.

106. Descartes, letter to Elizabeth, October 6, 1645, AT 4.317, CSM 3.273.

107. Descartes, letter to Elizabeth, September 1646, AT 4.486, CSM 3.292. Elizabeth responds that "to instruct in the governing of a state, [Machiavelli] chooses to consider the one most difficult to govern, where the prince is a new usurper, at least in the opinion of the people" (letter to Descartes, October 10, 1646, AT 4.520, in *Descartes: His Moral Philosophy and Psychology*, p. 193).

108. Descartes, letter to Elizabeth, September 1646, AT 4.486, CSM 3.292.

109. AT 4.487, CSM 3.292.

110. AT 4.487, CSM 3.293.

111. AT 4.488, CSM 3.293; cf. Niccolò Machaivelli, *The Prince*, trans. Harvey C. Mansfield, Jr. (Chicago: The University of Chicago

Press, 1985), chap. 18, p. 69: "A prince . . . needs to be a fox to recognize the snares and a lion to frighten the wolves."

112. John Marshall is therefore mistaken when he attributes to Descartes the view that "one's community and one's state, aside from their considerable instrumental value, are not such objects of love and joy as to be greater goods than one's friends" and that God is "not an exception but rather an exceptional friend" (*Descartes's Moral Theory* [Ithaca, NY/London: Cornell University Press, 1998], pp. 145, 147).

113. Descartes, *Passions*, art. 155, 156; AT 11.447 f.; CSM 1.385.

114. See Descartes, letter to Elizabeth, October 6, 1645, AT 4.307 ("conscience"); letter to Elizabeth, October or November 1646, AT 4.530, CSM 3.297 ("le conseil de son génie").

115. Descartes, letter to Mersenne, January 1630, AT 1.110.

116. AT 4.308 f., CSM 3.269 f.

117. AT 4.317, CSM 3.273.

118. Descartes, letter to Voetius, May 1643, AT 8B.112.

119. Descartes, letter to Elizabeth, August 18, 1645, AT 4.273, CSM 3.260.

120. Descartes, *Discourse*, Part 3, AT 6.25, CSM 1.123 (translation altered).

121. Descartes, letter to Elizabeth, August 18, 1645, AT 4.266, CSM 3.258. Cf. *Passions*, art. 49, AT 11.368, CSM 1.347: Anyone who follows "resolutions which . . . are based solely on knowledge of the truth . . . is assured of never regretting or repenting, whereas we always regret having followed [resolutions that proceed from some false opinion] when we discover our error." On the distinction between regret and repentance, see *Passions*, art. 177, AT 11.464, CSM 1.392: "Remorse of conscience is a kind of sadness which results from our doubting that something we are doing, or have done, is good. . . . [I]f we were certain that what we have already done was bad, we would feel repentance for it, not simply remorse."

122. Descartes, letter to Elizabeth, October 6, 1645, AT 4.307, CSM 3.269.

123. Letter to Descartes, October 28, 1645, AT 4.322, in *Descartes: His Moral Philosophy and Psychology*, p. 165 f.

124. Descartes, letter to Elizabeth, November 3, 1645, AT 4.331, CSM 3.276.

125. Descartes, *Passions*, art. 191, AT 11.472, CSM 1.396.

126. AT 11.373 f., CSM 1.350.

127. AT 11.446 f., CSM 1.384.

128. Descartes, *Passions*, art. 155, AT 11.447, CSM 1.385.

129. Descartes, letter to Elizabeth, October 6, 1645, AT 4.307 f., CSM 3.269.

130. Descartes, *Passions*, art. 157, AT 11.448, CSM 1.385.

131. Ibid., art. 158, AT 11.449, CSM 1.386; art. 159, AT 11.450, CSM 1.386.

132. Ibid., art. 158, AT 11.449, CSM 1.386.

133. Jean Laporte, *Le rationalisme de Descartes*, rev. ed. (Paris: Presses universitaires de France, 1950), p. 451.

134. Aquinas, *Summa Theologica* 1, q. 105, art. 4, repl. obj. 1, in *Basic Writings of Saint Thomas Aquinas*, ed. Anton C. Pegis, 2 vols. (Indianapolis/Cambridge: Hackett, 1999), 1.975; cf. *De veritate*, q. 24, art. 1, ad 3, 5, in *Truth*, trans. Robert W. Mulligan, James V. McGlynn, and Robert W. Schmidt, 3 vols. (Indianapolis/Cambridge: Hackett, 1995), 3.139 f.

135. Descartes, letter to Elizabeth, November 3, 1645, AT 4.332 f., CSM 3.277.

136. Descartes, *Passions*, art. 187, AT 11.470, CSM 1.395.

137. Ibid., art. 186, AT 11.469, CSM 1.395.

138. Ibid., art. 188, AT 11.470 f., CSM 1.396.

139. Mesnard, *Essai sur la morale de Descartes*, p. 209 f.

140. Descartes, letter to Chanut, November 20, 1647, AT 5.87, CSM 3.326. This may be an additional reason why Descartes did not articulate his views on sovereignty and community in a systematic and straightforward way: it is not the proper place of a mere philosopher to do so.

141. Gueroult, *Descartes' Philosophy Interpreted*, 2.187; Jacques Maritain, *The Dream of Descartes Together with Some Other Essays*, trans. Mabelle L. Andison (New York: Philosophical Library, 1944), p. 97.

142. Descartes, Second Replies, AT 7.148, CSM 2.105 f.

143. Descartes, letter to Chanut, June 6, 1647, AT 5.53, CSM 3.320. Cf. letter to Mersenne, March 1642, AT 3.544, CSM 3.211: In order "to reach heaven . . . it is necessary to believe in Jesus Christ and other revealed matters."

144. Wolfgang Röd, *Descartes: Die Genese des cartesianischen Rationalismus*, 2d ed. (Munich: C. H. Beck, 1982), p. 170.

145. Émile Boutroux, *Historical Studies in Philosophy*, trans. Fred Rothwell (London: MacMillan, 1912), pp. 254, 252.

146. Rodis-Lewis, "Maîtrise des passions et sagesse chez Descartes," pp. 217, 211; cf. AT 9B.5, CSM 1.181.

147. Descartes, *Passions*, art. 212, AT 11.488, CSM 1.404; letter to Chanut, November 1, 1646, AT 4.538, CSM 3.300.

148. Descartes, letter to Colvius, June 14, 1637, AT 1.379f: "Le temps que nous vivons en ce monde est si peu de chose en comparaison de l'éternité que nous ne devons pas fort nous soucier si nous sommes pris quelques années plus tôt ou plus tard."

149. Descartes, letter to Elizabeth, September 15, 1645, AT 4.292, CSM 3.265 f.

150. See Descartes, letter to Mersenne, January 9, 1639, AT 2.480, CSM 3.131; letter to Huygens, October 10, 1642, AT 3.798, CSM 3.215; letter to Elizabeth, September 1, 1645, AT 4.282, CSM 3.263.

151. See Descartes, letter to Elizabeth, November 3, 1645, AT 4.333, CSM 3.277.

152. See Jean-Luc Marion, "Generosity and Phenomenology: Remarks on Michel Henry's Interpretation of the Cartesian *Cogito*," in *Essays in the Philosophy and Science of René Descartes*, ed. Stephen Voss (New York: Oxford University Press, 1993), p. 65.

—CHAPTER 4—

THE MASTERY OF NATURE

1. MASTERY AND WISDOM

In previous chapters, I show how an underlying tension or ambivalence in Descartes's sense of meaning in human life supports my thesis that his basic morality has a theological foundation. We fail to grasp Descartes's aspirations fully if we characterize the motive force of his philosophy in terms of earthly self-assertion on the part of human beings. Nowhere is the interpretation of Descartes's thought more susceptible to this secular interpretation than in his call in the *Discourse on Method* to marshal scientific knowledge in the service of human dominion over the earth. In Part 6 of the *Discourse*, he describes his insight into the power of science in the following way:

> But as soon as I had acquired some general notions in physics and had noticed, as I began to test them in various particular problems, where they could lead and how much they differ from the principles used up to now, I believed that I could not keep them secret without sinning gravely against the law which obliges us to do all in our power to secure the general welfare of mankind. For they opened my eyes to the possibility of gaining knowledge which would be very useful in life, and of discovering a practical

philosophy which might replace the speculative philosophy
taught in the schools. Through this philosophy we could know
the power and action of fire, water, air, the stars, the heavens and
all the other bodies in our environment, as distinctly as we know
the various crafts [*métiers*] of our artisans; and we could use this
knowledge—as the artisans use theirs—for all the purposes for
which it is appropriate, and thereby render ourselves the masters
and possessors of nature [*et ainsi nous rendre comme maîtres et
possesseurs de la nature*].[1]

Many commentators, particularly in the wake of Nietzsche, argue
that Descartes is here inaugurating a distinctively modern approach
to the human condition by asserting the self-sufficiency of human
reason and industry and by rejecting all authorities other than sheer
human willing. This view of Descartes's aspirations leads Gueroult
to his *par prétérition* account of Descartes's turn to technological
practice. But as I show in previous chapters, Gueroult ignores the
Christian basis of Descartes's conception of human life. That basis
is of vital importance in understanding the source of Descartes's
commitment to the mastery of nature. The ideal of human mastery
over nature has its roots in the book of Genesis and was advocated
explicitly as a Christian vocation over a hundred years before the
time of Saint Thomas Aquinas by Hugh of Saint Victor:

For, in truth, God the Creator first made the world, and then made
man as the possessor and Lord of the world [*possessorem et
dominum mundi*], so that man might rule over all other things by
right of his foundation, being subject with free will to Him alone
by whom he had been made. Whence it is clear that the creation
of man was certainly posterior in time to the creation of all visible things, but prior in cause, because all things were made for
his sake who was made after all things.[2]

The ideal of human mastery over nature was originally conceived
as part of a Christian worldview, which makes it possible to see

Descartes's statement in Part 6 of the *Discourse* as more than the expression of a secular intention. Descartes sees the program of mastery as a human obligation. He says that he would be "sinning gravely against the law which obliges us to secure the general welfare of mankind" if he did not publish his "general notions in physics." At stake here is more than simply the publication of Descartes's achievements. The "law" to which Descartes alludes is more than an injunction to speak; it is an injunction to act in ways that improve our material welfare, not simply for the sake of that welfare but for the sake of living in accordance with the place that God has assigned to us. That the project of mastery has important implications "for the maintenance of health, which is undoubtedly the chief [*premier*] good and the foundation of all the other goods in this life," does not mean that material welfare is the highest good in this life.[3] Instead, as I show in chapter 3, the mastery of material processes serves higher, spiritual goods in this life. Descartes does not explain what he has in mind when he speaks of "sin" and when he appeals to the "law" in this connection, but the Christian context here suggests the interpretation that he is invoking God's law, if only indirectly, by way of the Thomistic conception of natural law.

The ideal sketched by Descartes in Part 6 of the *Discourse* is one of applied science in the service of human welfare. It is like the program of cognitive mastery in the *Rules for the Direction of the Mind*. The "general notions in physics" that admit of practical application are like the cognitive models such as the magnet or the Tantalus device that facilitate the reproduction of observed natural phenomena. The ideals of health and general human welfare in the *Discourse* correspond to the ideal in the *Rules* of establishing knowledge that can guide the will "in all the contingencies of life." Descartes's suggestion in Part 6 of the *Discourse* that health is "the foundation of all the other goods in this life" shows that he develops a hierarchy of earthly goods subsequent to abandoning the project of the *Rules*. The goods to be served by health are, for Descartes, not simply material. The notion of "the contingencies of life" to which

Descartes appeals, if only implicitly in the *Discourse*, is not exhausted by the notion of material welfare but instead raises the question of the higher ends to be served by such welfare.

Marx's ideal of "species-being"[4] is illuminating in this connection. Marx is aware that being human involves more than the pursuit of material security; it involves a capacity to exercise freedom and creativity in ways that depend on but are not confined to considerations of material welfare. In appealing to the notion of species-being, Marx implicitly asks what life would be like once economic exploitation were done away with and technological capacity were marshaled in the service of procuring leisure for human beings. Are we to imagine a world in which people find genuine satisfaction simply by "enjoying the fruits of the earth," that is, by maintaining health and consuming natural resources? The premium that Marx places on the human ability to produce or create, and the emphasis that he places on the way in which this ability is systematically perverted through class-based economy, points toward a different answer. Marx has in mind something like Aristotle's distinction between material welfare and virtue, and he seems to follow Aristotle in locating at the core of human "capacity" the ability to transcend the conditions of mere materiality toward the prospect of creating for the sake of a higher kind of satisfaction. What binds Marx and Descartes is their shared faith in the power of technology to contribute to the liberation of human beings from the lodestone of Αναvκη, "the pressure of vital needs," which for the Hobbesian Freud is the defining feature of the human condition and the foundational impetus for the mastery of nature.[5] In his conception of the place or significance of the mastery of nature in human life, Descartes anticipates Marx rather than Freud. Given Marx's quasi-eschatological reading of history, according to which time progresses toward an έσχατος, or moment of fruition, whereupon human beings become freed from the destructive aspects of time, this affinity between Descartes and Marx should not be surprising. Descartes's understanding of the significance of the program of mastery is also founded on an eschatological conception of time and of the relationship of time to the human condition as a whole. He anticipates a time when "all the truths that can be deduced from these principles are actually so deduced," even if that time lies in a distant future.[6] Given Descartes's subordination of bodily goods to goods of the soul, the precise nature of the "perfection and felicity [in] life" that acquisition of these truths will make possible is implicitly to be found in the ideal of generosity. The mastery of nature is the material prerequisite for a spiritual ideal of earthly community.

2. THE IDEA OF LORDSHIP OVER NATURE IN AUGUSTINE AND AQUINAS

Descartes follows Augustine and Aquinas in conceiving of nature as the lowest order of created being, and this evaluation of nature makes it possible for modern thinkers such as Descartes to take seriously the prospect of marshaling theory in the service of earthly practical endeavors. In recent years, a great deal of controversy has arisen over the question whether and to what extent Christian tradition endorses human dominion over nature. After examining Augustine's and Aquinas's views regarding the moral status of nature and the relationship of these views to the programs for mastery advanced by Bacon and Descartes, I return to this question to show how Christian metaphysics entails a system of moral evaluations that grants human beings license to use nature in the name of furthering human welfare.

I show in chapter 2 that Saint Augustine is committed to a metaphysics according to which the divine is eternal and the highest degree of being, and the temporal or changeable is the lowest degree of being. Everything in creation, even animals and natural landscapes, participate in their heavenly creator. This is why it is possible for us to learn about God by contemplating "his creatures."

Even though the earth is "the lower part of creation," being lower than created souls, earthly beings are beautiful because they are creations and hence reflections of God's beauty.[7] But for all that, the beauty of created things is of a lower order than the beauty of God. In particular, the beauty of purely corporeal things is of the lowest order of all. "The body also is a creature of God and is adorned in its own beauty, although of the lowest kind."[8] The relationship between corporeal things, God, and the human condition as a middle station between these two extremes reflects the idea of a hierarchy of being and perfection. The lower end of this hierarchy, the purely corporeal, is the focal point for questions bearing on the mastery of nature. One might suppose that because Augustine warns us against succumbing to the temptations of the flesh, he associates aspirations to mastery with an inappropriate lust for material enjoyment. "Man, [in contrast with animals], can question nature. He is able to *catch sight of God's invisible nature through his creatures*, but his love of these material things is too great. He becomes their slave, and slaves cannot be judges."[9] In the *City of God*, Augustine expressly classifies the will to mastery as a vice.[10] But it is revealing that when he does so, he expresses concern not for the welfare of nature but instead for the problem of the corruption of the human soul. The examples he gives involve "the vices of cruelty and luxury" committed when people succumb to the desire to dominate other people or to amass great wealth. Anything like the welfare or the interests of corporeal beings is left out of consideration here, because Augustine considers purely material, changeable beings to be of such a low order of being that they "cannot be either blessed or wretched."[11] If human beings are obligated to treat nature in certain ways, for example, to refrain from gratuitous consumption, this is not because such consumption is an affront to nature but because it is predicated on the turning away from God that constitutes sin. Gratuitous consumption is an affront to the potential of human beings to cultivate a relationship to God of which other earthly beings are incapable.

Human beings, then, stand in a dual relationship to nature. On the one hand, Augustine believes that God has "given us earth and water and sky to serve us in our weakness," but on the other hand, this gift is not accompanied by the license to use nature in any way we wish.[12] The Cambridge theologian C. F. D. Moule characterizes the use of nature informed by self-mastery in terms of a duty on man's part to "use nature, not to abstain from using it; but . . . he must use it as a son of God and in obedience to God's will. . . . Man is placed in the world by God to be its lord. . . . He is meant to have dominion over it and to use it and to use it up—but only for God's sake."[13]

Aquinas affirms Augustine's commitment to human dominion over nature, and he incorporates this commitment into his conception of cosmic teleology. Everything in the universe is "ordained toward God as its end," with "the less noble" creatures existing "for the [sake of the] nobler, as those creatures that are less noble than man exist for the sake of man."[14] In *de veritate*, Aquinas explains the notion of nobility in the following terms: "That which is active is always more noble than that which is passive. Now, among superior creatures, the closest to God are those rational ones that exist, live, and understand in the likeness of God."[15] By "superior creatures," Aquinas means those creatures that "have not only that by which they are good in themselves, but also that by which they are the cause of goodness for other things which participate the least in God's goodness."[16] Even inert matter, being created by God, participates in God's goodness and is "good in itself," but more active creatures are closer to the active agency of God. Thus bees, which pollinate flowers, are more noble than rocks or plants, and even though they play a crucial role in "causing" the propagation of flowers, bees are less noble than human beings because bees cannot reflect on the ends that they pursue. Rational creatures are "more active" and hence more noble than nonrational creatures. "The intellectual agent acts for an end, as determining for itself its end; whereas the natural agent, though it acts for an end . . . does not determine its end for itself, since it knows not the nature of end, but is moved to the end determined for it by another."[17] Thus the more noble, active creatures govern the lower creatures, and among "superior creatures" the more rational govern the less rational. Among earthly beings, this hierarchy has the following character: "In natural things species seem to be arranged in a hierarchy: as the mixed things are more perfect than the elements, and plants than minerals, and animals than plants, and men than other animals; and in each of these one species is more perfect than others."[18]

Because "rational nature alone is immediately ordered to God, since other creatures do not attain to the universal, but only to something particular," rational beings have license to exercise dominion over lower, nonrational creatures.[19] Natural, nonrational beings lack the "freedom to follow or not to follow the impressions produced by heavenly agents."[20] Reason gives human beings the freedom to reflect on the impressions with which they are confronted and to choose which of these impressions they will pursue. Natural beings—animals, plants, and minerals—lack this ability, hence human beings are "more noble" than other creatures, and the less noble creatures exist for the sake of the more noble ones. "The last end of all generation is the human soul, and to this does matter tend as its ultimate form. Consequently, the elements are for the sake of the mixed body, the mixed body for the sake of living things, and of these plants are for the sake of animals, and animals for the sake of man. . . . [T]he end of the movement of the heavens is directed to man as its last end in the genus of things subject to generation and movement."[21] Nature, then, exists for the sake of human beings, and, within the limits imposed by Providence, we may use nature as we see fit. "Man is not the author of nature, but he uses natural things for his own purposes in his works of art and virtue."[22]

These commitments concerning the order of nature and its overall significance in the scheme of being reinforce the connection between ontology and ethics in Augustine and Aquinas. What emerges in the thinking of these figures is the clarification and stabilizing of a metaphysical and moral dualism derived from the Gospels, which lies at the core of Descartes's philosophical project. Even those inclined to see in Descartes's aspiration to mastery the Promethean self-assertion of a secular technophile must recognize the continuity between Descartes's ideal of human beings as the masters of nature and the theological view of Augustine and Aquinas concerning the supremacy of human beings in the natural realm.

3. THE BACONIAN IDEAL AND ITS INFLUENCE ON DESCARTES

A consideration of Descartes's conception of the relationship between scientific knowledge and power in the context of the intellectual climate of the early seventeenth century shows that his program for mastery has important antecedents, particularly the work of Francis Bacon.[23] Consideration of Bacon's program for the mastery of nature does a great deal to shed light on the nature and aims of Descartes's program because the programs of the two thinkers exhibit many key affinities—not least among them the inscription of the program of mastery within a specifically Christian ethos. It has become a commonplace in historical scholarship to distinguish the programs of Bacon and Descartes on the grounds that Bacon advocates an empirical, piecemeal approach to the acquisition of knowledge, whereas Descartes marshals mathematics in the service of a rational, systematic approach. While this is clearly a fundamental difference between the two thinkers, it is important to recognize the extent to which Descartes's thinking is influenced by and maintains continuity with Bacon's.

The best-known focal point for Bacon's program for the mastery of nature is his assertion early in the *New Organon* that "human knowledge and human power come to the same thing, because ignorance of cause frustrates effect. For Nature is conquered only by obedience; and that which in thought is a cause, is like a rule in practice."[24] Bacon recognizes that power over nature is obtained through an understanding of the unseen causes that produce observed effects. In this regard, Bacon says, we are to emulate the example of God. "On the first day of creation God made only the light, and devoted the whole day to this work, and made no material that day. We too need first to elicit the discovery of true causes and axioms from every kind of experience."[25] Bacon, writing in 1620, presents a conception of the relationship between theory and practice that anticipates what Descartes articulates almost ten years later in the *Rules*. Where Descartes proposes a model of scientific understanding according to which the measure of knowledge is our ability to reproduce observed effects, Bacon says that an adequate conceptualization of the unseen cause of a phenomenon will function as a guideline for practical application—"that which in thought is a cause, is like a rule in practice."

In the *New Organon*, Bacon conceives of scientific knowledge in terms familiar to any reader of Descartes. In particular, he articulates a conception of simple natures at the methodological center of his program. Practical application presupposes the discovery of "the true and perfect precept of operation" at work in the phenomenon in question. This discovery depends on a "transformation of bodies" into "a company or combination of simple natures. . . . [T]his mode of operation . . . proceeds from what is constant, eternal and universal in nature, and affords us opportunities to human power."[26] To get from these simple natures to practical efficacy, we need the further abstraction of "forms," which are laws governing "pure individual acts" experienced in nature. These "laws of act" are "figments of the human mind" inductively derived from experimentation.[27] Forms are figments in the respect that they can mislead us into supposing "that things which are in flux are unchanging." Nonetheless, "he who knows forms comprehends the unity of nature in very different materials. And so he can uncover and bring forth things which have never been achieved. . . . Hence true Thought and free Operation result from the discovery of

Forms."[28] In constructing forms, we reduce nature from a multitude of observed phenomena to "laws of act" that represent mechanistic interactions. The "causes and axioms" that hold the key to mastering nature leave no room whatsoever for Aristotelian final causes, which are "a long way from being useful" and "actually [distort] the sciences except in the case of human actions."[29]

The key to understanding the "fictive" nature of forms is to recognize the limits of human knowledge, which make it impossible for us to observe what Hume calls "hidden powers" in nature. Our mental constructions must proceed from observed phenomena. But because we cannot penetrate beyond sensible appearances, we can never be in a position to confirm our hypotheses with absolute certainty. Instead we must satisfy ourselves with a pragmatic criterion of truth. "This then will have to be our declaration of the true and perfect precept of operation: it should be certain, free and favorable to, or tending towards, action. And this is the same as the discovery of true Form. . . . [W]hat is most useful in operating is truest in knowing."[30] Does this mean that Bacon is not interested in truth in the traditional sense but only in power? Bacon often speaks as if he is. In the *Valerius Terminus*, for example, he says that

> it is not the pleasure of curiosity, nor the quiet of resolution, nor the raising of the spirit, nor victory of wit, nor faculty of speech, nor lucre of profession, nor ambition of honour or fame, nor inablement for business, that are the true ends of knowledge . . . but it is a restitution and reinvesting (in great part) of man to the sovereignty and power . . . which he had in his first state of creation.[31]

Bacon seems to see our postlapsarian condition as one in which we are obliged not simply to contemplate the wonders of the world but also to "dissect nature" in order to put ourselves in a position to exercise sovereignty over it.[32]

In certain respects, Bacon's utopian tract *The New Atlantis* would appear to support this interpretation of Bacon as a pragmatist. In that text, which appears to have been written shortly after the publication of *The New Organon*, Bacon illustrates his technological aspirations through the image of the island of Bensalem, the "new Atlantis" contrasted with the "old Atlantis" of Platonic lore. The lost sailors in the story are granted temporary refuge on the island, where they learn of the House of Salomon, the purpose of which is to acquire "the knowledge of Causes, and secret motions of things; and the enlarging of the bounds of Human Empire, to the effecting of all things possible."[33]

In spite of the fact that the Father of the House of Salomon gives "thanks to God" for directing human labors to "good and holy uses," the historical reception of Bacon has been dominated by a tendency to see in his work a clear priority of secular technophilia over any kind of traditional religious reverence.[34] The flaw in this interpretation is diagnosed by Paolo Rossi. He examines the famous passage in the *New Organon* in which Bacon appears to reduce "knowledge" to the acquisition of power:

> We declare that the inept models of the world (like imitations by apes), which men's fancies have constructed in philosophies, have to be smashed. And so men should be aware (as we said above) how great is the distance between the *illusions* of men's minds and the ideas of God's mind. The former are simply fanciful abstractions [*abstractiones ad placitum*]; and the latter are the true marks of the Creator on his creatures [*vera signacula Creatoris super creaturas*] as they are impressed and printed on matter in true and meticulous lines. Therefore truth and usefulness are (in this kind) the very same things [*ipsissimae res sunt veritas et utilitas*], and the works themselves are of greater value as pledges of truth than for the benefits they bring to human life.[35]

In translating *ipsissimae res* as "the very same things," Spedding notes that "I think that this must have been Bacon's meaning, though not a meaning which the word can properly bear."[36] Rossi explains why Spedding should have had misgivings about this interpretation. "(1) Bacon knew Latin well enough to use *idem* correctly in place of *ipse*," if he meant to proclaim an identity between knowledge and power, and "(2) the phrase *ipsissimae res*, or the term *ipsissimus*, which were widely used in scholastic terminology, recur in other passages of the *Novum organum* with a precise, technical meaning."[37] *Ipsissimae res* in the *New Organon* refers not to identity but to "'the objective reality of things,' or to 'things in their reality,' or simply to 'essence.'"[38] A more accurate translation of "*ipsissimae res sunt veritas et utilitas*" is "truth and utility are in this kind the very things we seek for" or "the chief things of all are, in this kind, truth and usefulness."[39] Bacon is not trying to replace the traditional notion of truth with a modern ideal of utility, but he instead is asserting that

> *things as they really are, considered not from the viewpoint of appearance but from that of existence, not in relation to man but in relation to the universe, offer conjointly truth and utility.* In other words, only where the human mind forsakes its state of arbitrary freedom (i.e., the state of being 'left to itself') and learns to make use of specific techniques of inquiry, will it be able to arrive at the knowledge of natural facts in their objective form. Furthermore, it is only from this point of view (which, moreover, is that of science and method, in contrast to that of the various 'fantastic' philosophies) that theoretical truths and operative rules are united and identical.[40]

Even though Bacon makes the distinctively modern turn to what Hans Jonas calls "the practical uses of theory," he still believes that "practicality without truth is arbitrary and casual, and thus incapable of progress and development"; Rossi observes that Bacon's endeavor to elevate modern science above such idols as alchemy and magic presupposes a distinction in principle between the two things, knowledge and power, that he seeks to unite in practice.[41]

This interpretation of the relationship between knowledge and power illuminates the relationship between Bacon's utilitarianism and the premium he places on truth at the beginning of Book 1, aphorism 124, of the *New Organon*. "The contemplation of truth is worthier and higher than any utility or power in effects." Contemplation holds the promise of a "serenity and tranquillity of detached wisdom" that constitutes a "much more godlike condition" than seeking nothing but power "in a Tartarus of confusion and turmoil."[42] Bacon associates the subordination of power to the pursuit of truth with nearness to God, whereas in characterizing the unbridled pursuit of power he invokes the image of Tartarus, the lowest region of the Greek underworld, in which the most abject sinners are punished for their transgressions. Those condemned to this region of the underworld are individuals such as Ixion, who have sinned against the gods themselves. Bacon's admonition shows why the association between truth and power cannot be one of simple identity but instead places utilitarian aims within a larger framework of value—just as in Descartes.

In Book 1, aphorism 124 of the *New Organon*, Bacon invokes the model of truth thought *sub specie aeternitatis* that guides Descartes. He says that "men should be aware . . . how great is the distance between the illusions of men's minds and the ideas of God's mind."[43] The ideas of God's mind are "the true marks of the Creator on his creatures as they are impressed and printed on matter in true and meticulous lines," that is, to arrive at the truth about natural phenomena is to find the divine ideas hidden in the flux of earthly events. Briggs proposes that, on Bacon's view, there is a

> divine code in nature [that] reveals, to an audience that has submitted to its reduction, the instrumentality of the world in the hands of its maker. It is a mere device. Yet the very idea that it is God's highly wrought riddle intimates the possibility that it hides divine purpose in nature and history, and therefore offers a glimpse of Providence and the chance of acting in its favor.[44]

Given Bacon's demand that we eliminate final causes from our scientific understanding of nature, this cannot mean that Bacon expects us to decipher God's moral intentions through our investigation of nature. Rather, we are to discover ways in which nature can be used to satisfy our material needs, and this equation between knowledge and power will confirm to us God's desire that we use nature for our purposes. As in Aquinas and Descartes, such use must be subordinated to our best understanding of God's higher moral dictates. Bacon seeks to understand nature in terms different from those in which we endeavor to understand God but still based on the idea that God has assigned human beings the right and the obligation to "dissect" nature and thereby to establish "empire" over it.

This science is secular, but the values guiding it are not. As Brian Vickers observes in connection with Bacon's *Advancement of Learning*, "the Middle Ages had made philosophy as a whole subordinate to theology; Bacon exempted natural philosophy from that position but allowed moral philosophy to remain there—evidently because he found the other-centred Christian ethics superior to anything in the classical tradition."[45] This is the crucial link between Bacon and Descartes: the moral whole into which Bacon inscribes science and technology is, as for Descartes, a *Christian* whole. Christianity has a twofold significance in connection with the mastery of nature. First, such thinkers as Bacon and Descartes believe that it has an advantage over "heathen" religions because it involves a distinction between the study of the divine and the study of nature. This is a virtual requirement for the progress of science in the service of religion. Compared to religions such as that "of the Turks . . . the singular advantage which the Christian religion hath towards the furtherance of true knowledge, [is] that it excludeth and interdicteth human reason, whether by interpretation or anticipation, from examining or discussing the mysteries and principles of faith."[46] Second, "the right over nature" is given to man "by God's gift," that is, the project of mastery is not first of all an act of human self-assertion but is given to us by divine bequest.[47] The "Plan of the Work" that precedes the main text of *The New Organon* concludes with a prayer to God to "protect and govern this work, which began in your goodness and returns to your glory. . . . [I]f we labour in your works, you will make us to share in your vision and in your sabbath."[48] Bacon explains this sentiment at the end of Book 2: "By the Fall man declined from the state of innocence and from his kingdom over the creatures. Both things can be repaired even in this life to some extent, the former by religion and faith, the latter by the arts and sciences."[49] Augustine condemned the aspirations of theoretical curiosity as *concupiscentia oculorum*, as a covetous leering at what is best contemplated for the truth that it can disclose to us about God. Bacon sees in the contemplation of nature the prospect of securing the human condition in complete accordance with the dictates of Christianity.[50] His proposition that "the new science reflects a Christian love for humanity" entails a rejection of the Augustinian view that the systematic investigation of nature is contrary to God's dictates.[51] Bacon is committed to a view that is distinctively modern, namely, that "natural philosophy, after the word of God, is the strongest remedy for superstition and the most proven food of faith. Therefore it has deservedly been granted to religion as its most faithful handmaid; for one manifests the will of God, the other his power."[52]

Bacon's technological project is derived from a Christian ethos. It brings with it a sense of humility and a respect for limits. In this respect, there is a basic affinity between the technological project of Bacon and Descartes and the religious program of Saint Augustine. Bacon acknowledges that "the angels fell because of an appetite for power, and men fell because of an appetite for knowledge."[53] The occasion for the Fall, however, was not the desire for scientific knowledge but rather "the ambitious and demanding desire for moral knowledge, by which to discriminate good from evil, to the end that Man might turn away from God and give laws to himself."[54] Bacon, Descartes, and Augustine share a commitment to an ideal of humility. In *The Advancement of Learning*, Bacon links the pursuit of knowledge and power to "that admonition of St. Paul, that 'we be not seduced by vain philosophy,'" and he calls on mankind to respect "the true bounds and limitations whereby human knowledge is confined and circumscribed; and yet without any such contracting or coarctation [restriction], but that it may comprehend all the universal nature of things."[55] The pursuit of scientific knowledge must be tempered by Christian humility that respects certain limits, particularly that "we do not presume by the contemplation of nature to attain to the mysteries of God."[56] In *de sapientia veterum*, Bacon invokes the image of Prometheus to illustrate his critique of hubris. Prometheus's failing is not that he created man and appropriated fire but that in doing so, he sought to assert complete independence and thereby to deny any dependence on the divine.[57]

Bacon's discussion of Prometheus brings into focus the ideal of mastery within limits. Bacon advocates the mastery of nature, but he warns against selfish egoism. He proposes that we can use science to recover from the Fall, provided that we remain mindful of our mortality and respectful of divine mystery. Bacon appeals to the Christian charity that guides Descartes. Charity keeps the desire for knowledge in check: "There is no danger at all in the proportion or quantity of knowledge, how large soever, lest it should make it swell or out-compass itself; no, but it is merely the quality of knowledge, which be it in quantity more or less, if it be taken without the true corrective thereof . . . this corrective spice, the mixture whereof maketh knowledge so sovereign, is Charity."[58] As Descartes does twenty years later, Bacon draws the meaning of charity from 1 Corinthians, where Paul subordinates knowledge to the *caritas* that is the key to pious devotion. Charity guarantees that our endeavor to master nature will not lead to blind hubris. Whereas "the desire of power in excess caused the angels to fall" and "the desire of knowledge in excess caused man to fall . . . in charity there is no excess; neither can angel or man come in danger by it."[59] Bacon elects to call the institution responsible for scientific knowledge in *The New Atlantis* "Salomon's House." This links the enterprise of modern science to the wisdom of Solomon and expresses Bacon's conviction that, directed by pious moral convictions, science is not only permissible but also fundamental to the vocation of fallen man. Laurence Berns aptly frames the relationship between piety and the will to mastery in the following terms: "The true temper of Baconian charity . . . evidently must combine the spirit of compassion with the spirit of domination" to arrive at "something like the grand passion of generosity" that Descartes makes central in his later thought.[60]

There are a number of systematic and historical connections between Bacon and Descartes that make a consideration of Bacon's program important for understanding Descartes's ideal of mastery. There are several indications that Descartes read and was influenced by Bacon's thought. Baillet writes that Bacon's death in 1626 moved Descartes, who admired Bacon and his work.[61] In January 1630, Descartes thanks Mersenne "for the qualities that you have derived from Aristotle; I had already made another, larger list of them, taken in part from Verulamius [viz., Bacon, Baron Verulam] and in part from out of my head, and this is one of the first things that I will try to explicate" in the treatise (*Le Monde*) that he is about to start writing.[62] Near the end of 1630, on the question of scientific experimentation, Descartes writes to Mersenne that "I have nothing to add to what Verulamius has written, except that the main thing is to make a general collection of all the most common things, without being too curious about examining all the minute particulars pertaining to a matter."[63] And the first of the prefatory letters to *The Passions of the Soul*, written "by one of the Author's friends," includes the statement that "I've also seen the *Instauratio Magna* and the *Novus Atlas* of Chancellor Bacon, who seems to me to be, of all those who wrote before you, the one with the best thoughts concerning the Method that should be followed to guide Physics to its perfection."[64] Lüder Gäbe says that "Descartes went so far as to maintain that his *Regulae* are superior to Bacon's *New Organon*."[65]

There are also a large number of systematic parallels between the work of the two thinkers. André Lalande demonstrates more than a dozen direct and fundamental similarities in Bacon and Descartes, including the basic equality of human intellects, the need to overcome opinion or prejudice in the pursuit of truth, the inadequacy of syllogism as a basis for scientific inquiry, the immateriality of the rational soul and the corporeality of the animal (sensitive) soul, and the importance of medicine within the project of mastery.[66] Notwithstanding Bacon's failure to see the prospect of representing nature systematically in mathematical terms, Lalande points out a striking parallel between Descartes's proposal in Rule 12 to reduce qualities such as colors to geometric representations and a passage from Bacon's *Valerius Terminus*, in which Bacon proposes the following reduction in the service of

> a contriving of directions and precepts for readiness of practice. . . . Let the effect to be produced be whiteness . . . all bodies or parts of bodies which are unequal equally, that is in a simple proportion, do represent whiteness. . . . It is then to be understood, that absolute equality produceth transparence, inequality in simple order or proportion produceth all other colours, and absolute or orderless inequality produceth blackness; which diversity, if so gross a demonstration be needful, may be signified by four tables; a blank, a chequer, a fret, and a medley; whereof the fret is evident to admit great variety. Out of this assertion are satisfied a multitude of effects and observations . . . the reduction must be, that the bodies or parts of bodies so intermingled . . . be of a certain grossness or magnitude.[67]

Bacon presents this concept of reduction almost thirty years before Descartes wrote the *Rules*. It serves as a methodological tool in Bacon's "universal science," which he conceives in terms of a tree metaphor in the *de dignitate*:

> Philosophy may therefore be conveniently divided into three branches of knowledge; knowledge of God, knowledge of

Nature, and knowledge of Man, or Humanity. But since the divisions of knowledge are not like several lines that meet in one angle; but are rather like branches of a tree that meet in one stem . . . therefore it is necessary before we enter into the branches of the former division, to erect and constitute one universal science, to be as the mother of the rest. . . . This science I distinguish by the name of *Philosophia Prima* . . . or *Sapience*.[68]

It is striking how much of the thinking that we associate with Descartes is anticipated by Bacon. In particular, Bacon articulates a practical conception of wisdom that presupposes the guidance of a Christian moral ethos, and he advocates a strictly mechanistic conception of nature for the purposes of scientific inquiry.

Bacon and Descartes share an interest in establishing a rigorous distinction between science and pseudo-sciences such as alchemy, magic, and astrology.[69] Lüder Gäbe argues that Bacon's interest in establishing such a distinction moved the young Descartes to abandon the project of the *Rules* and seek a secure and systematic metaphysical grounding for the pursuit of scientific knowledge. Gäbe notes that for both thinkers, this interest is subservient to the interest in mastering nature.[70] Bacon's notion of *Idola tribus* (idols of the tribe) appears to have led Descartes to recognize the need to overcome the sorts of basic prejudices that hinder the progress of science. Descartes recognizes the problem of prejudice in the *Rules*, but there he does not yet see it as a *systematic* obstacle to the acquisition of truth.[71] Hence there is nothing in the *Rules* comparable to Descartes's admonitions in the Sixth Replies and the *Principles* regarding preconceived opinions, and there is nothing like the hyperbolic doubt of the *Meditations*.[72] But when Descartes develops the mature method of the *Meditations*, he gives a place to mathematics that Bacon precisely denies: in *The New Organon*, Bacon classifies geometry along with final causes among the idols of the tribe that debilitate the progress of science. Both are "plainly derived from the nature of man rather than of the universe," and for this reason we must derive simple natures not from the mind but from induction performed on observed events.[73] Bacon recognizes that "natural inquiry succeeds best when the physical ends in the mathematical" and that "all things in both natural powers [should] be (as far as possible) numbered, weighed, measured and determined." But he never seizes upon the idea that mathematics can be employed as a basic tool in the systematic representation of nature.[74] Gäbe believes that a comparison of the *Rules* and the *New Organon* led Descartes to revise his early standpoint, and specifically that Book 1, aphorism 48, of the *New Organon* must have been objectionable to Descartes. For Descartes as for Bacon, teleological explanations have no proper place in natural science. But the mature Descartes admits talk of infinite magnitudes and infinite divisibility precisely where Bacon forbids it.[75]

Thus while both thinkers offer the image of the thread of Theseus as a symbol of the power of scientific knowledge, only Descartes takes the step of making a truly mathematical physics the foundation of the other sciences.[76] Bacon's sensitivity to the dangers of undue philosophical abstraction leaves him unwilling to endorse the proposition, put forth by Galileo three years after the publication of *The New Organon*, that

> philosophy is written in this grand book, the universe, which stands continually open to our gaze. But the book cannot be understood unless one first learns to comprehend the language and read the letters in which it is composed. It is written in the language of mathematics, and its characters are triangles, circles, and other geometric figures without which it is humanly impossible to understand a single word of it; without these, one wanders about in a dark labyrinth.[77]

Descartes formalizes the systematic connection between theory and practice to provide a path through what Comenius calls "the labyrinth of the world."[78] At the same time, Descartes follows Galileo and Bacon in separating the endeavor to understand sublunary phenomena from the contemplation of divine purposes. Bacon rejects final causes in natural science not only because they are "a long way from being useful," but also because "the ways and proceedings of God with spirits are not included in nature, that is, in the laws of heaven and earth; but are reserved to the law of his secret will and grace: wherein God worketh still, and resteth not from the work of redemption, as he resteth from the work of creation; but continueth working till the end of the world."[79] When Descartes speaks of the need to dispense with final causes, he offers both lines of reasoning as well. In the Fourth Meditation, he says "the customary search for final causes [is] totally useless in physics," and in the Fifth Replies, he rejects final causes on the grounds that in "the direction of the universe . . . God's purposes . . . are equally hidden in the inscrutable abyss of his wisdom."[80] Both Bacon and Descartes recognize that if scientific knowledge is to be useful, if it is to improve the human condition with an eye toward the possibility of "a restitution and reinvesting (in great part) of man to the sovereignty and power . . . which he had in his first state of creation," then it is necessary to adopt a new conception of theory according to which the object of contemplation is not the divine or the eternal but rather the temporal and earthly. Of signal importance from a moral standpoint is the fact that both Bacon and Descartes present this new conception of theory, oriented as it is on practice, as subordinate to a traditional conception of contemplation as the proper source of meaning and the measure for human choice. The link between the moral and the practical, or between the angelic and the earthly, is the Christian God, who is both the ultimate end toward which all earthly beings are ordered and the creator of a nature that permits explication and mastery through recourse to mathematics.

4. THE SIGNIFICANCE OF THE PRACTICAL TURN

In radically revising the ancient conception of theory to make theory applicable to nature in a manner that facilitates human mastery, Bacon and particularly Descartes contribute to a revolution in thinking that inaugurates the modern age. Hans Jonas gives a concise definition of the sense in which the modern turn to practice is a revolution: it is "a collective change in human affairs which is radical, comprehensive, and of a certain rapid pace; and . . . it concerns man's environment, behavior, and thought." Moreover, "the change [is] man-made [and] ultimately [has] its source in ourselves."[81] The precise nature of the change in our relation to theory that marks the onset of modernity has to do with the significance of theory for human life:

> Relation to an objective transcendence lies today outside theory by its rules of evidence, whereas formerly it was the very life of theory.
>
> "Transcendence" (whatever else the term comprises) implies objects higher than man, and about such was classical theory. Modern theory is about objects lower than man: even stars, being common things, are lower than man. No guidance as to ends can come from them. The phrase "lower than man," implying a valuation, seems to contradict the asserted "value-freedom" of science. But this value-freedom means a neutrality as much of the objects as of the science: of the objects, their neutrality (indifference) toward whatever value may be "given" them. And that which lacks intrinsic value of its own is lower than that by reference to which alone it may receive value, namely, man and human life, the only remaining source and referent of value.[82]

The "objects" of ancient theory are eternal and immutable and are by their very nature higher than man. For a thinker like Aristotle, "theory" is the product of contemplating objects that in principle have no relevance to "art" or skillful manipulation of the environment. Reflection on them involves an irreducible component of respect for an order of being in which human beings and their practical concerns have but a subordinate place. In the *Metaphysics*, Aristotle characterizes the contemplation that leads to theory as superior to knowledge that admits of practical application. Speculative knowledge is good for its own sake, and "of the sciences . . . that which is desirable on its own account and for the sake of knowing it is more of the nature of Wisdom than that which is desirable on account of its results."[83] Aristotle presents the relationship between pure theory and sciences that lead to practice in accordance with the teleological principle that "that which is best" presupposes inferior antecedents, the capacity for contemplation presupposes leisure, and leisure presupposes the satisfaction of material needs. Thus the contemplation of "divine objects" presupposes the establishment of "sciences which . . . aim at giving pleasure [and] at the necessities of life" through a reflection on changeable and mutable things.[84] This conception of the relationship between theory and practice corresponds to Aristotle's position in the *Politics*: the aims of political life are conjointly the satisfaction of material needs and the collective pursuit of virtue. But only the pursuit of virtue is "the final cause and end" of society, for which the satisfaction of material needs is a necessary condition. This is why Aristotle spends so much time in Book 1 of the *Politics* warning us against the gratuitous acquisition of wealth and in Book 10 of the *Nicomachean Ethics* arguing that the "end" of society is not pleasure or leisure. The highest end of social existence would be pure contemplation of eternal things, if such contemplation were ultimately possible for human beings.[85]

This classical conception of the relationship between theory and practice is inverted in the modern age. Jonas says that "among the benefits that knowledge grants through power over things is relief from toil: leisure, then, but not the scientist's own, is here a fruit of knowledge. The classical pattern was the opposite: leisure was a condition of theory, antecedently assured to make theory possible, not something to be achieved by its exertions."[86] Bacon's dream of a multitude of inventions in *The New Atlantis* and Descartes's promise of "the invention of innumerable devices which would facilitate our enjoyment of the fruits of the earth" in Part 6 of the *Discourse* confirm Jonas's analysis of the modern revolutionization of theory. No longer concerned with the eternal and immutable and no longer predicated on freedom from toil, theory is henceforth concerned with an understanding and manipulation of changeable things with an eye toward the provision of longevity, health, and leisure. "Self-sufficiency" is no longer conceived as liberation from practical concerns but instead signifies human mastery of the domain in which these concerns present themselves. "Theory" is no longer related to the kind of transcendence that assigns man a place in the larger scheme of things; now "only efforts to alter reality contribute to its explanation, and the patience [*Insistenz*] of reposeful contemplation is useless."[87]

The redirection of theory from divine transcendence to earthly practice corresponds to the restricted sense of wisdom advanced by Descartes in the letter to Picot, and it coincides with the elimination of final causes from our understanding of nature. An ontological reduction of nature in mathematical terms takes the place of a teleological conception of nature according to which all natural things are necessarily referred to God. This reduction leaves us with a conception of nature devoid of measures or guidelines for our conduct with regard to it, because the "nature" of scientific inquiry no longer contains any reference to God:

Nature is not a place where one can look for ends. Efficient cause knows no preference of outcomes: the complete absence of final causes means that nature is indifferent to distinctions of value. It cannot be thwarted because it has nothing to achieve. It only proceeds—and its process is blind. Its "necessity" is not that of compulsion but the mere absence of alternatives to the type of inter-connection by which all things operate—and by which they can be known. Thus the object of knowledge—the whole ceaseless drama of creation, be it the universe, terrestrial nature, or living things—is divested of any "will" of its own. The regularity which makes it knowable makes it meaningless at the same time. With the last trace of anthropomorphism expunged, nature retains no analogy to what man is aware of in himself, namely, that one direction is preferred to another, and that outcomes make a difference, some being fulfillments and others failures. In the working of things there are no better or worse results—indeed there is no "good" or "bad" in nature, but only that which must be and therefore is.[88]

The predicament posed by the bifurcation of the divine and earthly realms is one that did not confront the ancients or medievals, namely, how to establish a direct connection between divine dictates and our treatment of nature. As long as one maintains fidelity to Christianity, the predicament has a solution. But as soon as our Promethean tendency gains ascendancy through its empowerment by modern science, the situation changes into one in which the "end" of practice becomes the endless progress or perfectibility of the human condition. Such was the ideal of progress advocated by Comte. The Cambridge historian J. B. Bury sees the roots of this ideal in Descartes's mechanization of nature: "The Cartesian mechanical theory of the world and the doctrine of invariable law, carried to a logical conclusion, excluded the doctrine of Providence. . . . [I]t was just the theory of an active Providence that the theory of Progress was to replace; and it was not till men felt independent of Providence that they could organise a theory of Progress."[89]

Jonas says that the ultimate consequence of this elimination of purposiveness from our understanding of nature is a fundamental lack of reverence:

What has neither will nor wisdom and is indifferent to itself solicits no respect. Awe before nature's mystery gives way to the disenchanted knowingness which grows with the success of the analysis of all things into their primitive conditions and factors. The powers that produce those things are powerless to impart a sanction to them: thus their knowledge imparts no regard for them. On the contrary, it removes whatever protection they may have enjoyed in a prescientific view. . . . If nature sanctions nothing, then it permits everything.[90]

When the nature we behold does not contain reflections of the divine, when God is no longer "known through his creatures," but instead we confront a realm of inert matter acted upon by anonymous laws and forces, there is nothing in nature that would remind us of our dependence upon divine transcendence. Nature is now so radically divorced from the divine that we are left with no reason to display any reverence toward nature, no reason to observe limits in our exploitation of nature.

Both Bacon and Descartes recognize that if we are to establish systematic control over nature, we must first have a systematic understanding of nature. The radical moment in their thinking is not their advocacy of the ideal of human lordship over nature but instead their insight into the power of human reason to provide the kind of systematic understanding of nature that promises to facilitate systematic mastery. Bacon and Descartes consider such mastery to be fully consonant with God's expectations about our conduct. Both treat it, at least implicitly, as a divine mandate. In their Christian worldview Augustine and Aquinas do not advocate the wholesale subjection of nature, but they do see nature as an appropriate object of human use. This evaluation of nature paves the way for the Baconian-Cartesian ideal. What remains to be explained in the historical advent of technology is not how it emerged from the Christian worldview, but rather how it became detached from the regulative guidance of such a worldview.

5. THE MORAL STATUS OF NATURE IN THE CHRISTIAN TRADITION

The Christian doctrine of human lordship over nature, as articulated by Augustine and Aquinas, gives human beings moral prominence in nature in virtue of their godlike capacity for rational reflection and their capacity to relate to God through faith. Nonhuman natural beings, such as plants and animals, have dual status as objects for the satisfaction of human needs and occasions for reflection on God's divine nature. As such, plants and animals exist for the sake of human beings. But this does not mean that we are permitted to engage in acts of wanton destruction or abject neglect. What is permissible is to be determined through reflection on the divine will. Thus Augustine and Aquinas are ambivalent regarding the moral status of nature: nature may, in fact, it must, be used by postlapsarian humanity for the sake of preserving mortal existence. At the same time, nature may not be exploited capriciously but must be seen as a living testimonial to the creative power of God. Nature is not an end in itself, inasmuch as it exists for the sake of humanity. But neither is it a mere means, inasmuch as it stands fundamentally in the light of the divine majesty. The moral status of nature consists in its being the creation and reflection of a morally perfect creator, not in being something that possesses the dignity of an end in its own right.

The elimination of final causes from natural science removes a conceptual obstacle that stands in the way of the systematic exploitation of nature. Even if nature is God's creation, Descartes no longer understands it in Augustinian terms as a reflection or symbol of the divine. Descartes's view of the material world leaves no room for a romanticized nature that retains traces of a prelapsarian paradise. But is this departure from the Augustinian conception of nature indicative of a fundamental departure from the grounding moral outlook of Christianity, or is it instead a logical extension of sentiments that date back to the origins of Christianity? To answer this question, and thereby to explain the relationship between Descartes's program for the mastery of nature and the Christian ideal of lordship over nature, I consider a more fundamental question: What precise moral status does nature enjoy in the traditional Christian conception of human dominion or lordship over nature?

The moral status of nature in Christianity has been hotly contested, particularly since Lynn White published "The Historical Roots of Our Ecological Crisis" in 1967. White argues that the book of Genesis includes numerous indications of a commitment to the proposition that all of creation was made "explicitly for man's benefit and rule" and that man "is not simply a part of nature [but] is made in God's image."[91] Christianity "not only established a dualism of man and nature but also insisted that it is God's will that man exploit nature for his proper ends. . . . By destroying pagan animism, Christianity made it possible to exploit nature in a mood of indifference to the feelings of natural objects."[92] White sees the development of modern science as a consequence of the "voluntarist orientation" of the Latin Church, which, in contrast with the "intellectualist orientation" of the Greek Church, grounds salvation in right conduct rather than in spiritual illumination. On this view, human transcendence over nature makes it incumbent on us to adopt not a position of resignation or quietism but rather one of active self-assertion in the name of God.[93] This self-assertion takes the form of treating nature as inert matter that may be used for the satisfaction of human desires. "To a Christian a tree can be no more than a physical fact. The whole concept of the sacred grove is alien to Christianity and to the ethos of the West."[94]

Although he briefly acknowledges heterodox tendencies in the Christian tradition, such as the Franciscan regard for nature, on the whole White treats Christianity as if it were a monolithic cultural institution with a univocal meaning, an unequivocal stand on the relevance of human effort to the prospect of salvation, and a settled view regarding the moral status of nature. White ignores debates between the Augustinians and the Pelagians (the Jansenists and the Molinists), and he makes too little of the reflections of early church figures such as Saint Augustine regarding the significance of natural beauty. But White does recognize the metaphysical "dualism of man and nature" that is characteristic of Christianity and that the reduction of nature to the status of mere resource is a consequence of that dualism.

White's essay has drawn a great deal of criticism, much of it from environmentally concerned members of the Christian community who wish to see in Christianity the elements of a responsible environmental ethic. Many of White's critics maintain that the Bible does not sanction the wanton use or abuse of nature, and in fact the Bible contains all the necessary elements for a responsible environmental ethic. These critics shift the focus of the controversy from the Christian thought of the Middle Ages to passages in the Bible and particularly in the Old Testament. For these critics, the central question in the controversy over the moral status of nature in the Bible is not whether human beings are entitled to exercise dominion over nature but what the meaning of dominion is supposed to be in the Bible—whether it signifies stewardship or despotism. If it can be shown that passages in the Bible counsel reverence for nature, or at least that they assign to humanity a stewardship rather than a despotic role vis-à-vis nature, then any interpretation that holds Christianity responsible for the technological exploitation and degradation of nature can be challenged.

The most fruitful work done on the question whether the Bible counsels a reverential or stewardship relation to nature is focused on the early books of the Old Testament. When this work is marshaled in defense of Christianity, the operative assumption is that any passages in the Old Testament not superceded or contradicted by passages in the New Testament remain binding and constitute part of the fabric of orthodox Christian doctrine. This assumption is significant, because almost all the Biblical passages bearing on the question of human dominion over nature are in the Old Testament and particularly in the book of Genesis. In Genesis 1:26, God creates human beings in his own image and grants them "dominion over the fish in the sea, the birds of the air, the cattle, all wild animals on land, and everything that creeps on the earth." Some have seen in Adam's naming of creatures in Genesis 2:19–20 a symbol of this dominion. Other passages bearing on the moral status of nature occur subsequent to the Fall and to the flood and the tower of Babel. In passages subsequent to these events, there are signs of a change in the moral status of nature. The first reference to the sacrifice of live animals comes after the flood, in Genesis 8:20–21, where Noah makes a burnt offering to God, the smell of which causes God to say to himself that he will "never again . . . put the earth under a curse because of mankind, however evil their inclination may be from their youth upwards." And whereas before the flood God gave human beings only plants to eat (Gen. 1:29), after the flood God tells Noah that "every creature that lives and moves will be food for you; I give them all to you, as I have given you every green plant" (Gen. 9:3).

Yet at the same time, when God makes his covenant with Noah after the flood, he extends this covenant not only to Noah's descendants but also to "every living creature that is with you, all birds and cattle, all the animals with you on earth, all that have come out of the ark" (Gen. 9:10). That is, God's covenant is not simply with human beings but with "all that lives on earth" (Gen. 9:19). Thus it cannot be said without further ado that the book of Genesis sketches an unambiguous ethic of human despotism over nature, for if living nature is mere resource, then it is difficult to understand why it should be included in God's covenant. Inert things such as rocks are not included in the covenant, but all living creatures are. Does this mean that Genesis attributes to man a stewardship role with regard to nature?

Research conducted into the so-called Yahwist conception of nature points toward an affirmative answer to this question. Biblical scholarship shows that the early books of the Old Testament were based on sagas or narratives attributed to three ancient sources. Who these sources were is not known, and it is not even known whether they were individual persons or groups of people. By convention they are referred to as the Yahwist (or "J," following the German spelling *Jahwist*), who names God as Yahweh; the Elohist, who uses the general term *elohim* or *God*; and the Priestly Writer(s). The Yahwist is of special significance in the attempt to find a sense of environmental responsibility in the book of Genesis, because the Yahwist is considered to be the source of some of the key passages just cited, and because historical research has shown that the Yahwist exhibited a much greater sense of reverence for nature than the Elohist or the Priestly Writer(s). In a masterful study of the Yahwist controversy and its significance for environmental ethics, Theodore Hiebert argues that the conventional wisdom, that the early Israelite culture devalued nature because of the culture's beginnings in the desert, is mistaken. Hiebert has assembled impressive evidence in support of the contrary thesis that "the Yahwist's landscape" consisted of "agricultural highlands," and he proposes that "it is within this agrarian environment that biblical values toward the natural world arose and were shaped."[95] Moreover, Hiebert observes that "the Biblical Hebrew language possesses no terms comparable to the modern words 'nature' and 'history', which divide reality into two independent and unified realms." This feature of the language reflects the absence of the distinction between culture and nature or between spirit and matter that is a fixture of later cultural consciousness.[96] Thus the fact that the name for man (*'adam*) is etymologically related to the term for arable land (*'adama*) is not accidental but reflects an underlying moral outlook in the Yahwist epic, in which the first human being is literally fashioned from topsoil. Facts like this undermine the credibility of the traditional claim that Israelite religion devalued nature.[97]

What emerges from this research into the early Israelite experience of nature is the conclusion that there is no one definitive attitude toward nature in that early experience. Instead, the Old Testament contains conflicting views, particularly those of the Priestly Writer(s) and the Yahwist. The view of the Priestly Writer(s) "is conspicuously hierarchical" and ascribes to human beings absolute "dominion over other animate life," whereas that of the Yahwist "conceives of this relationship in more communal terms" and sees animals "as helpers" rather than as mere resources.[98] Commentators who use the Old Testament as the basis of a genuine environmental ethic tend to ignore or play down the voice of the Priestly Writer(s) and treat the voice of the Yahwist as definitive to come to such conclusions as the following: "The [Jewish] Bible upholds as its millennial ideal a symbiosis of animals and people in which all living creatures dwell in peace."[99]

One must look to the New Testament to determine whether or not the Yahwist sensibility is preserved intact there or instead becomes superceded by an emerging distinction between spirit and matter. Consideration of Christian attitudes toward nature requires that the earth-friendly sentiments in select Old Testament passages be considered not simply in relation to early Israelite experience but also in the light of those New Testament passages that place emphasis on the idea of spiritual inwardness. The idea of faith as inwardness is developed extensively in the Gospels and in Paul's letter to the Romans, and it is a fundamental presupposition of the ethic of *caritas*. The suggestion that "life is more than food" in the book of Matthew is a first indication of the emerging split between spirit and matter. To "set [one's] mind on God's kingdom and his justice before everything else" is to place a premium on the life of the spirit over the life of the mortal body.[100] The criticism of the Pharisees in Mark 7 for their undue emphasis on outward ritual over inward spirituality illustrates the primacy of inwardness: "Nothing that goes into a person from outside can defile him; no, it is the things that come out of a person that defile him" (Mark 7:15–16).

Paul's letter to the Romans echoes this criticism of the Pharisaical emphasis on outward ritual. Regarding Jewish law, Paul says that "the real Jew is one who is inwardly a Jew, and his circumcision is of the heart, spiritual not literal; he receives his commendation not from men but from God" (Rom. 2:29). Paul goes on to draw a distinction between spirit and nature that figures prominently in the tradition of Christian thought leading from Saint Augustine to Descartes: "Those who live on the level of the old nature have their outlook formed by it, and that spells death; but those who live on the level of the spirit have the spiritual outlook, and that is life and peace. For the outlook of the unspiritual nature is enmity with God; it is not subject to the law of God and indeed it cannot be; those who live under its control cannot please God" (Rom. 8:5–8). The Jews' lack of such an inward relation to God constituted a fundamental limitation in their effort to find redemption: "Israel made great efforts after a law of righteousness, but never attained to it. Why was this? Because their efforts were not based on faith but, mistakenly, on deeds" (Rom. 9:31–32). It is not in the Old Testament but in the New that there is talk of the role of "conscience" in relating properly to God (Rom. 13:5). The turn to inwardness marks a decisive step toward the formal development of a dualistic metaphysics in medieval Christian thought. It leads Saint Augustine to declare that "my soul is the better part of me, because it animates the whole of my body" and to conclude that earthly things are morally inferior to spiritual beings.[101]

6. THE IDEAL OF MASTERY AS THE NEXUS BETWEEN THE "ANGELIC" AND "EARTHLY" MORALITIES

In chapter 1, I show that Descartes stands midway between Aquinas's scholasticism and Kant's deontology. On the side of content, he exhibits a fundamental commitment to the Christian God as the source and measure of being and truth. But on the side of form, he makes a decisive step away from the authority of the divine and toward the authority of autonomous human reason. He sometimes speaks as if reason alone is adequate to ground a sense of meaning and value in human life, and yet he has recourse to an inherently extrarational measure in establishing a sense of propriety or belonging for human beings. We gain our bearings not through any immanent considerations but through an underlying relation to the same transcendent ground that gives shape to the ethos of the Christian Middle Ages. At the same time, Descartes inspires a move away from Scholastic humility before God and toward the self-assertion of rational autonomy that is completed by the time of Kant. How are we to understand the hybrid character of Descartes's project, tensed as it is between respect for the transcendent God and a self-reliance that many of Descartes's contemporaries branded as Pelagianism?

Descartes's project exhibits the peculiar innovation of inscribing a Promethean tendency within a Christian worldview. The abandonment of final causes in favor of mechanistic explanations signifies a change not only in the nature of science but also in the conceptualization of the underlying ethos that motivates scientific inquiry. For Bacon and Descartes, not only is there no conflict between Christian charity and rational self-reliance, but these two ideals mutually reinforce one another. Their ideal of human prudence is predicated on the idea that the world for postlapsarian humanity is a wilderness and that fallen humanity is charged with the responsibility to carve out an existence in that wilderness by dint of nothing but its own industry. The world is no longer a reflection of the divine majesty, as it still appears to have been in Aquinas and Hugh of Saint Victor, but is mere matter. The reduction of nature from a teleological whole to a mathematically describable nexus of matter and forces is as much a moral reduction as it is a cognitive one.

This attitude constitutes a step toward the unqualified ascendancy of reason in the Enlightenment, even though it retains many basic affinities with the moral sensibilities of the Middle Ages.

Augustine's pronouncement that we need care little (if at all) for
the suffering of dying animals does not outwardly appear to be far
removed from Descartes's enthusiasm over the prospects of vivi-
section. To this extent, one might suppose that Descartes's views
on the mastery of nature are different from Augustine's not in kind
but merely in degree.[102] But Descartes's ideal of "possessing"
nature is decisive in this connection because it is indicative of a
fundamental shift in the conception of how human beings may
properly relate to nature. This shift is Promethean in the sense that
it appropriates for human beings prerogatives previously reserved
to God. Augustinian-Thomistic morality makes a place for using
natural beings such as animals to preserve human life, but it stops
short of the "morality of expansion and conquest that aims at domination over things."[103] Augustine's contemptus mundi, inspired
by biblical passages such as 1 John 2:15 and James 4:4, is not
intended to give human beings license to use the world as a set of
resources for the satisfaction of human desires but instead is
intended to devalue earthly existence in relation to eternal salvation. Augustine's disregard for the welfare of earthly beings such
as animals is motivated not by an interest in justifying the use of
those beings but instead by the conviction that human beings are
the only earthly beings subject to divine judgment and the prospect
of salvation. Descartes's commitment to the development of a
mechanistic physics in the service of human welfare reflects an
expanded conception of the significance of earthly existence
according to which the systematic cultivation of our earthly estate
need not pose any threat to our piety.

Exemplary in this regard is Descartes's preoccupation with pro-
longing human life. Descartes writes that our contemplation of the
immortality of the soul should put us in a position not to fear death.
He thus expresses his commitment to the traditional promise of
eternal life, in which we will enjoy "pleasures and felicities much
greater than we enjoy in this world."[104] For Descartes, this promise
in no way mitigates the need to take our earthly existence as some-

thing real and significant in its own right. The premium he places on medicine reflects a bifurcation of the earthly and supernatural realms in spite of the fact that he sees the earthly against the background of the supernatural. Medicine is needed to promote health, which is "the first [*premier*] good and the foundation of all the other goods in this life." Through advancements in medicine, "we might free ourselves from innumerable diseases, both of the body and of the mind, and perhaps even from the infirmity of old age."[105] Medicine holds the promise not simply of curing and preventing illness but of "slowing down the ageing process."[106] Descartes had a congenitally weak physical constitution and appears to have been unusually preoccupied with his own mortality. In a letter written to Huygens not long after the publication of the *Discourse*, Descartes uses a reflection on his own mortality as a way to envision the prospect of a hundred-year life span for healthy human beings:

> I have never taken greater care in looking after myself than I am doing at the moment. Whereas I used to think that death could deprive me of only thirty or forty years at the most, I would not now be surprised if it were to deprive me of the prospect of a hundred years or more. I think I see with certainty that if only we guard ourselves against certain errors which we are in the habit of making in the way we live, we shall be able to reach without further inventions a much longer and happier old age than we otherwise would.[107]

The goal of extending the limits of the human life span is a primary indication of the transformation of the old ideal of human lordship over nature. Not only do we use nature to preserve our health, but we now begin to have a share in what was formerly conceived as the divine prerogative to determine how long our earthly existence is to last. Nature is no longer conceived as God's possession but instead is understood as the proper possession of human beings. This shift in understanding and valuing earthly existence sanctions activities such as animal research, which according to Descartes is of instrumental value in the exercise of our prerogative to extend the limits of human life.[108]

Descartes's program for the prolongation of life through medical art presupposes a higher value on earthly goods than Augustine or Aquinas permitted. These thinkers embrace what Gilson refers to as the "Christian optimism" that God's creation is fundamentally good and that the only real prospects for perfecting existence lie in the endeavor to overcome moral evil.[109] These thinkers do not conceive of earthly "goods" as true goods because earthly goods pertain to the realm of embodiment, which is metaphysically and morally inferior to the realm of spirit. Descartes, too, considers earthly or bodily goods to be inferior to spiritual goods. But he recognizes the promise of medicine and other sciences opened up by Copernicus and Vesalius, and the emerging sense that the mastery of nature is practicable leads him to join Bacon in rethinking the moral status of earthly goods in a way unacceptable to Augustine and Aquinas. Augustine repeatedly cautions his reader to master or control bodily desires. But whereas Descartes counsels mastery of the body in the affirmative sense of promoting health and happiness, Augustine places stress on the need to renounce bodily desires.[110]

Aquinas similarly devalues earthly pleasures and worldly endeavors. In the *Summa Contra Gentiles*, he writes that

> the highest perfection of man cannot consist in his being united to things lower than himself, but consists in his being united to something above him; for the end is better than that which tends to the end. Now the above pleasures consist in man's being united through his senses to things beneath him, certain sensible things. Therefore we must not assign happiness to such pleasures.[111]

Aquinas's teleology leads him to see earthly goods as being for the sake of higher ends, and like Augustine he warns against the pursuit of bodily pleasures for their own sake.[112] And he subtly echoes Augustine's quietism when he suggests that "human power is most imperfect, for it is based on human will and opinion, which are full of inconstancies." Hence we should not seek happiness in "external" goods at all, but we should instead seek it only in the contemplation of truth, that is, God.[113] Thus Aquinas, like Augustine, sees the earth as existing for the sake of human beings. But at the same time, because he sees the earth in the light of divine nobility, he respects a dividing line between using the earth for the preservation of human life and exploiting the earth to serve Promethean prerogatives.

In his study of nihilism, Stanley Rosen traces the shift in human thinking about the use of nature to a "split between the useful and the noble which developed in the seventeenth century."[114] When final causes are eliminated from natural science, nature loses the nobility that medieval Christianity had attributed to it in virtue of its being ordered to God. Even if nature does not possess the intrinsic value that human beings possess, and even if on the Augustinian account human beings should generally shun earthly things in the mode of a contemptus mundi, nature is still God's creation and hence is a reflection (albeit an imperfect one) of the absolute perfection of its creator. As a matter of historical understanding, if not of systematic necessity, once nature is no longer thought to be ordered to God, even though it is still recognized to be God's creation, the final obstacle to the human appropriation of nature in the service of earthly self-assertion is removed. The replacement of teleology with mechanism has become appropriated in the service of our Promethean tendency. Thus the distinction between the mastery of nature in the (indirect) service of God and the mastery of nature in the service of sheer human self-assertion arises because the turn to mechanism in the seventeenth century is not the motivational basis for the mastery of nature but is instead itself motivated by an anterior commitment to the supremacy of human beings in the order of creation. With this turn, the ancient conception of the relationship between theory and practice is inverted so that theory now serves practical motives rather than being the "end" of human life. The subordination of theory to practice does not logically necessitate an abandonment of God, and yet the power that it granted plays an instrumental role in the articulation of a new conception of human self-sufficiency.

Thus even though Bacon and Descartes pave the way for a usurpation of prerogatives that had formerly been reserved to God, they remain committed to Christian ideals that impose a sense of measure and propriety on earthly existence. Reason was detached from faith, and the "end" of mastery was reconceived as the satisfaction of human desire, without any reference to higher measures or considerations. Louis Dupré gives the following diagnosis of the philosophical forces at work in this process:

> The modern self possesses little content of its own, and this poverty contrasts with Augustine's conception of the soul, which to him was the richest of all concepts. While Descartes's self occasionally reveals glimpses of this former richness, he has set the notion of selfhood on a course where it was to become a functional one, namely, the source of meaning and value. . . . Here begins a development that reached its final conclusion in Fichte's conception of the self as a creative act. . . . In becoming pure project, the modern self has become severed from those sources that once provided its content. The metaphysics of the ego isolates the self. It narrows selfhood to individual solitude and reduces the other to the status of object.[115]

Alongside his proclamations of Christian faith and his adherence to a Christian worldview in articulating an earthly ethic, Descartes makes a fateful step toward the Fichtean ideal of an absolutely self-constituting self. Christianity and rational self-assertion are mutually compatible sources of authority for Descartes, and yet they stand in an inner tension with one another. Descartes outwardly seeks to resolve this tension in purely rational and practical terms, but in its foundations his thought is unmistakably religious and irreducible to rational criteria.

NOTES

1. AT 6.61 f., CSM 1.142 f. (translation altered).

2. Hugh of Saint Victor, *De sacramentis Christianae fidei* (ca. 1134), bk. 1, Part 2, chap. 1, in *Patrologia Latina*, vol. 176 (Paris: J-P Migne, 1854), p. 205, and *On the Sacraments of the Christian Faith*, trans. Roy J. Deferrari (Cambridge, MA: The Medieval Academy of America, 1951), p. 28; cf. bk. 1, Part 1, chap. 25, *Patrologia Latina*, vol. 176, p. 203, and *On the Sacraments of the Christian Faith*, p. 25, where Hugh invokes Genesis 1 in support of the proposition that "man was made, not as an adornment of the earth, but as its lord and possessor [*ergo factus est homo non quasi ornatus terrae, sed dominus et possessor*], so that his creation, for whose sake the earth was made, should not be referred to the earth."

3. AT 6.62, CSM 1.143.

4. See Karl Marx, "Estranged Labour," *The Marx-Engels Reader*, ed. Richard C. Tucker, 2d ed. (New York: Norton, 1978), p. 75.

5. See Sigmund Freud, Lecture 23, in *Introductory Lectures on Psycho-Analysis*, trans. James Strachey (New York: Norton, 1989), p. 441; cf. Freud, *Civilization and Its Discontents*, trans. James Strachey (New York: Norton, 1984), pp. 27, 37 f.

6. Descartes, letter to Picot, AT 9B.20, CSM 1.189.

7. Saint Augustine, *Confessions*, trans. R. S. Pine-Coffin (London: Penguin, 1961), bk. 7, sec. 13, p. 149; bk. 7, sec. 7, p. 143; bk. 2, sec. 5, p. 48.

8. Saint Augustine, *On Music*, in *Fathers of the Church*, vol. 4, trans. John A. Mourant and William J. Collinge, introd. and notes Collinge (Washington, DC: Catholic University of America Press, 1992), p. 368.

9. Augustine, *Confessions*, bk. 10, sec. 6, p. 213 (citing Rom. 1:20).

10. Saint Augustine, *The City of God against the Pagans*, ed. R. W. Dyson (Cambridge: Cambridge University Press, 1998), bk. 5, chap. 19, p. 224 f.

11. Saint Augustine, Letter 18, to Coelestinus, in *The Essential Augustine*, ed. Vernon J. Bourke, 2d ed. (Indianapolis: Hackett, 1974), p. 46.

12. Augustine, *Confessions*, bk. 10, sec. 31, p. 235.

13. C. F. D. Moule, *Man and Nature in the New Testament* (Philadelphia: Fortress Press, 1967), pp. 2, 14.

14. Saint Thomas Aquinas, *Summa Theologica* 1, q. 65, art. 2, resp., in *Basic Writings of St. Thomas Aquinas*, ed. Anton C. Pegis, 2 vols. (Indianapolis/Cambridge: Hackett, 1997), 1.612.

15. Saint Thomas Aquinas, *Quaestiones disputatae de veritate*, q. 5, art. 8, resp., in *Truth*, trans. Robert W. Mulligan, James V. McGlynn, and Robert W. Schmidt, 3 vols. (Indianapolis: Hackett, 1995), 1.233.

16. Ibid.

17. Aquinas, *Summa Contra Gentiles* 3, chap. 3, in *Basic Writings*, 2.8.

18. Aquinas, *Summa Theologica* 1, q. 47, art. 2, in *Basic Writings*, 1.461.

19. Aquinas, *Summa Theologica* 2–2, q. 2, art. 3, resp., in *Basic Writings*, 2.1078.

20. Aquinas, *Summa Theologica* 1, q. 115, art. 6, resp., in *Basic Writings*, 1.1066.

21. Aquinas, *Summa Contra Gentiles* 3, chap. 22, in *Basic Writings*, 2.36 f.

22. Aquinas, *Summa Theologica* 1, q. 22, art. 2, repl. obj. 2, in *Basic Writings*, 1.233.

23. Other antecedents include Giordano Bruno, who proclaims in *Spaccio de la bestia trionfante* (1584) that "the gods had given intellect and hands to man" so that "he would succeed in preserving himself as god of the earth" (*The Expulsion of the Triumphant Beast*, trans. Arthur D. Imerti [New Brunswick, NJ: Rutgers University Press, 1964], p. 205).

24. Francis Bacon, *The New Organon*, ed. Lisa Jardine and Michael Silverthorne (Cambridge: Cambridge University Press, 2000), bk. 1, aph. 3, p. 33. Cf. bk. 1, aph. 129, p. 100: "For one does not have empire over nature except by obeying her." Cf. also "The Plan of the Work," p. 24: "Therefore those two goals of man, knowledge [*scientiae*] and power [*potentiae*], a pair of twins, are really come to the same thing, and works are chiefly frustrated by ignorance of causes."

25. Bacon, *New Organon*, bk. 1, aph. 70, p. 58.

26. Ibid., bk. 2, aphs. 4 and 5, p. 104 f.

27. Ibid., bk. 2, aph. 2, p. 103; bk. 1, aphs. 50 and 51, p. 45.

28. Ibid., bk. 1, aph. 51, p. 45; bk. 2, aph. 3, p. 103.

29. Ibid., bk. 1, aph. 99, p. 81; bk. 2, aph. 2, p. 102.

30. Ibid., bk. 2, aph. 4, p. 104.

31. Francis Bacon, *Valerius Terminus of the Interpretation of Nature*, in *The Works of Francis Bacon*, ed. James Spedding, Robert Leslie Ellis, and Douglas Denon Heath, 14 vols. (London: Longman and Co., 1857–1874), 3.222. Cf. 3.232: "For I find that even those that have sought knowledge for itself, and not for benefit or ostentation or any practical enablement in the course of their life, have nevertheless propounded to themselves a wrong mark, namely satisfaction (which men call truth) and not operation."

32. See Bacon, *New Organon*, bk. 1, aph. 51, p. 45.

33. Francis Bacon, *The New Atlantis*, in *Francis Bacon*, ed. Brian Vickers (Oxford/New York: Oxford University Press, 1996), p. 480.

34. Ibid., p. 488.

35. Bacon, *New Organon*, bk. 1, aph. 124, p. 96.

36. Bacon, in *Works of Francis Bacon*, 4.110n.

37. Paolo Rossi, *Philosophy, Technology, and the Arts in the Early Modern Era*, trans. Salvator Attanasio, ed. Benjamin Nelson (New York: Harper Torchbooks, 1970), p. 157 f.

38. Ibid., p. 159.

39. Ibid., p. 158.

40. Ibid., p. 160 (italics in original).

41. Ibid., p. 162 f.; cf. p. 171 f.

42. Bacon, *New Organon*, bk. 1, aph. 124, p. 96. Cf. bk. 1, aph. 129, p. 101: "The very contemplation of things as they are, without superstition or deceit, error or confusion, is more valuable in itself than all the fruits of discoveries." See also *Cogitata et visa* (*Thoughts and Conclusions*), where Bacon says that "in nature practical results are not only the means to improve well-being but the guarantee of truth" (Benjamin Farrington, *The Philososophy of Francis Bacon: An Essay on Its Development from 1603 to 1609 with a New Translation of Fundamental Texts* [Liverpool: Liverpool University Press, 1964], p. 93).

43. Bacon, *New Organon*, p. 96.

44. John C. Briggs, *Francis Bacon and the Rhetoric of Nature* (Cambridge, MA: Harvard University Press, 1989), p. 26.

45. Brian Vickers, notes to *Francis Bacon*, p. 656.

46. Bacon, *Valerius Terminus*, in *Works of Francis Bacon*, 3.251. Cf. *Of the Dignity and Advancement of Learning*, bk. 9, chap. 1, in *Works of Francis Bacon*, 5.113: Islam "interdicts argument altogether."

47. Bacon, *New Organon*, bk. 1, aph. 129, p. 101.

48. Ibid., p. 24.

49. Ibid., bk. 2, aph. 52, p. 221.

50. Cf. Augustine, *Confessions*, bk. 10, sec. 35, p. 241, with Bacon, *Valerius Terminus*, in *Works of Francis Bacon*, 3.222, 3.232.

51. Ian Box, "Bacon's Moral Philosophy," in *The Cambridge Companion to Bacon*, ed. Markku Peltonen (Cambridge: Cambridge University Press, 1996), p. 276.

52. Bacon, *New Organon*, bk. 1, aph. 84, p. 75.

53. Bacon, "Preface to 'The Great Renewal,'" in *Works of Francis Bacon*, p. 13.

54. Ibid., p. 12; cf. bk. 1, aph. 89, p. 75.

55. Bacon, *Advancement of Learning*, in *Francis Bacon*, p. 124 (citing Col. 2:8).

56. Ibid.

57. Bacon, *de sapientia veterum*, in *Works of Francis Bacon*, 6.748 ff. Cf. 6.753, where Bacon asserts an affinity between the lesson of the Prometheus myth and the moral tenets of Christianity.

58. Bacon, *Advancement of Learning*, in *Francis Bacon*, p. 124.

59. Bacon, "Of Boldness" (Essay 12), in *Francis Bacon*, p. 363; see also *Advancement of Learning*, in *Francis Bacon*, p. 263, and *Valerius Terminus*, in *Works of Francis Bacon*, 3.217.

60. Laurence Berns, "Francis Bacon and the Conquest of Nature," *Interpretation* 7 (1978): 23.

61. Adrien Baillet, *La vie de Monsieur Des-Cartes*, 2 vols. (New York/London: Garland, 1987), 1.144.

62. Descartes, letter to Mersenne, January 1630, AT 1.109.

63. Descartes, letter to Mersenne, December 23, 1630, AT 1.195. Descartes later writes to Mersenne that "it would be very useful if some such person were to write the history of celestial phenomena in accordance with the Baconian method, and to describe the present appearances of the heavens without any explanations or hypotheses, reporting the position of each fixed star in relation to its neighbors, listing their differ-

ences in size and colour and visibility and brilliance and so on" (letter to Mersenne, May 10, 1632, AT 1.252, CSM 3.38).

64. Descartes, *The Passions of the Soul*, trans. Stephen Voss (Indianapolis/Cambridge: Hackett, 1989), p. 14. Ross notes that the *New Atlantis* "was republished in Latin as Nova Atlantis in 1643 in Holland, where Descartes then resided. An edition published in 1648 has the same misspelling of the title that appears here."

65. Lüder Gäbe, *Descartes' Selbstkritik: Untersuchungen zur Philosophie des jungen Descartes* (Hamburg: Meiner, 1972), p. 101.

66. André Lalande, "Sur quelques textes de Bacon et de Descartes," *Revue de Métaphysique et de Morale* 19 (1911): 296–311.

67. Bacon, *Valerius Terminus*, in *Works of Francis Bacon*, 3.233, 3.236 ff.; cf. Lalande, "Sur quelques textes," p. 310 f.

68. Bacon, *Advancement of Learning*, bk. 3, chap. 1, in *Works of Francis Bacon*, 3.337.

69. See Descartes, *Discourse*, Part 1, AT 6.9, CSM 1.115; Bacon, *Advancement of Learning*, bk. 3, in *Works of Francis Bacon*, 4.349 ff.; *Valerius Terminus*, in *Works of Francis Bacon*, 4.223.

70. Gäbe, *Descartes's Selbstkritik*, p. 98.

71. Ibid., p. 102 f.

72. See Descartes, Sixth Set of Replies, AT 7.441 ff., CSM 2.297 f.; *Principles*, Part 1, art. 71–72, AT 8A.35 ff., CSM 1.218 ff.

73. Bacon, *New Organon*, bk. 1, aph. 48, p. 44; bk. 2, aph. 52, p. 220.

74. Ibid., bk. 2, aph. 8, p. 108; bk. 2, aph. 7, p. 229.

75. Cf. Bacon, *New Organon*, bk. 1, aph. 48, p. 44, with Descartes, *Principles*, Part 1, art. 26–28, AT 8A.14 ff., CSM 1.201 ff. See also Gäbe, *Descartes's Selbstkritik*, p. 107.

76. In his "Preface to the Work" and bk. 1, sec. 82, of *New Organon*, Bacon speaks of the need for "a thread to guide our steps," lest we remain trapped "as in a labyrinth" [*tanquam in labyrintho*], pp. 10, 68 (translation altered). Cf. Descartes, Rule Five, AT 10.380, CSM 1.20.

77. Galileo, "The Assayer," in *Discoveries and Opinions of Galileo*, trans. Stillman Drake (New York: Anchor/Doubleday, 1957), p. 237 f.

78. Johannes Comenius, *The Labyrinth of the World and the Paradise of the Heart* (1631), trans. Howard Louthan and Andrea Sterk (New York/Mahwah, NJ: Paulist Press, 1998).

79. Bacon, *New Organon*, bk. 2, aph. 2, p. 102; "A Confession of Faith," in *Francis Bacon*, p. 108 f.

80. Descartes, Fourth Meditation, AT 7.55, CSM 2.39; Fifth Set of Replies, AT 7.375, CSM 2.258. On the latter reason for rejecting final causes, see also *Conversation with Burman*, AT 5.158, CSM 3.341, and *Principles*, Part 1, art. 28, AT 8A.15 f., CSM 1.202.

81. Hans Jonas, "Seventeenth Century and After: The Meaning of the Scientific and Technological Revolution," in *Philosophical Essays: From Ancient Creed to Technological Man* (Chicago/London: The University of Chicago Press, 1974), p. 47.

82. Hans Jonas, "The Practical Uses of Theory," in *The Phenomenon of Life: Toward a Philosophical Biology* (Chicago/London: The University of Chicago Press, 1982), p. 195.

83. Aristotle, *Metaphysics*, bk. 1, chap. 2 at 982a15 ff., in *Introduction to Aristotle*, ed. Richard McKeon (New York: Modern Library, 1992), p. 260; cf. 981b15 ff., p. 259.

84. Aristotle, *Physics*, bk. 2, chap. 2 at 194a30 ff., in *Introduction to Aristotle*, p. 127; *Metaphysics*, bk. 1, chap. 2 at 983a5–10, p. 262, 981b20 ff., p. 259.

85. Aristotle, *Nicomachean Ethics*, bk. 10, chap. 7 at 1177b18–30, in *Introduction to Aristotle*, p. 568 f.

86. Jonas, "Practical Uses of Theory," p. 194.

87. Hans Blumenberg, *Die Legitimität der Neuzeit*, rev. ed. (Frankfurt: Suhrkamp, 1988), p. 449; *The Legitimacy of the Modern Age*, trans. Robert M. Wallace (Cambridge, MA/London: MIT Press, 1983), p. 385.

88. Jonas, "Seventeenth Century and After," in *Philosophical Essays*, p. 69.

89. J. B. Bury, *The Idea of Progress: An Inquiry into Its Origin and Growth* (London: Macmillan, 1924), p. 73; cf. p. 29.

90. Jonas, "Seventeenth Century and After," in *Philosophical Essays*, p. 70.

91. Lynn White Jr., "The Historical Roots of Our Ecological Crisis," *Ecology and Religion in History*, ed. David Spring and Eileen Spring (New York: Harper Torchbooks, 1974), p. 24.

92. Ibid., p. 24 f.

93. Ibid., p. 26 f.

94. Ibid., p. 28.

95. Theodore Hiebert, *The Yahwist's Landscape: Nature and Religion in Early Israel* (New York/Oxford: Oxford University Press, 1996), p. 141 f. Hiebert provides a useful appendix in which he shows which passages of the Pentateuch are supposed to have come from each of the three ancient sources; see pp. 163 ff.

96. Ibid., pp. 17 ff., 27.

97. Ibid., pp. 33, 150; cf. p. 142.

98. Ibid., p. 157.

99. Jeanne Kay, "Concepts of Nature in the Hebrew Bible," *Environmental Ethics* 10 (1988): 326.

100. Matt. 6:25, 33. Cf. Matt. 10:28: "Do not fear those who kill the body, but cannot kill the soul. Fear him rather who is able to destroy both soul and body in hell."

101. Augustine, *Confessions*, bk. 10, sec. 6, p. 213.

102. Saint Augustine, *The Catholic and Manichaean Ways of Life*, trans. Donald A. Gallagher and Idella J. Gallagher (Washington, DC: Catholic University Press, 1966), pp. 102, 105; Descartes, letter to Plempius, February 15, 1638, AT 1.523–527, CSM 3.80–82; "Description of the Human Body," AT 11.241 ff., CSM 1.317f. See also Gary Steiner, "Descartes on the Moral Status of Animals," *Archiv für Geschichte der Philosophie* 80 (1998): 268–91.

103. Martial Gueroult, *Descartes' Philosophy Interpreted According to the Order of Reasons*, trans. Roger Ariew, 2 vols. (Minneapolis: University of Minnesota Press, 1984–1985), 2.188.

104. Descartes, letter to Huygens, October 10, 1642, AT 3.798, CSM 3.216; see also letter to Elizabeth, September 1, 1645, AT 4.282, CSM 3.263, and letter to Elizabeth, November 3, 1645, AT 4.333, CSM 3.277.

105. Descartes, *Discourse*, Part 6, AT 6.62 f., CSM 1.143 (translation altered).

106. Descartes, "Description of the Human Body," AT 11.223 f., CSM 1.314.

107. Descartes, letter to Huygens, December 4, 1637, AT 1.649, CSM 3.76

108. See Descartes, letter to [The Marquess of Newcastle], October 1645, AT 4.329, CSM 3.275, where Descartes says that "the treatise on animals which I plan and which I have not yet been able to complete is only a prolegomenon" to the science of medicine.

109. Étienne Gilson, *The Spirit of Mediaeval Philosophy*, trans. A. H. C. Downes (Notre Dame, IN/London: University of Notre Dame Press, 1991), pp. 110 ff.

110. Augustine, *Confessions*, bk. 10, sec. 31, p. 235.

111. Aquinas, *Summa Contra Gentiles* 3, in *Basic Writings*, chap. 27, 2.52.

112. Ibid., chap. 37, 2.59.

113. Ibid., chap. 31, 2.56; chap. 37, 2.60.

114. Stanley Rosen, *Nihilism: A Philosophical Essay* (New Haven/London: Yale University Press, 1969), p. 78.

115. Louis Dupré, *Passage to Modernity: An Essay in the Hermeneutics of Nature and Culture* (New Haven/London: Yale University Press, 1993), p. 118 f.

—CHAPTER 5—

DESCARTES AND THE PROBLEM OF NIHILISM

1. MODERNITY AND NIHILISM

My interest in examining Descartes as a moral thinker is inspired by contemporary controversies about secularization, nihilism, and what Hans Blumenberg calls "the legitimacy of the modern age." I now explore the implications of Descartes's conception of the moral life for the task of thinking through these controversies. The two main focal points in the following considerations are Descartes's adherence to metaphysical dualism and his appeal to the disclosive power of faith. I examine a lineage of thinking about nihilism inaugurated by Nietzsche, who seizes upon dualism as one of the root causes of nihilism and argues that ultimate meaning must be sought not in a transcendent beyond but rather in earthly existence. I then examine Hans Blumenberg's claim that reason alone is sufficient to guide the will by situating Blumenberg's claim against the background of Descartes's recognition that reason must be grounded in an extrarational source of meaning. As enamored as he was with the power of instrumental reason, Descartes was unwilling to dispense with faith as our primary route of access to meaning. But Descartes was ambivalent about the need to appeal to faith as the source of meaning and value in life. This ambivalence is a sign of an underlying tension in Descartes's philosophical project that was subsequently resolved in favor of reason; Kant, for example, resolves this tension by bringing faith under the yoke of practical reason. Today, as in the seventeenth and eighteenth centuries, the power of reason to establish fundamental values is highly controversial. Hans Blumenberg's critic Karl Löwith suggests reasons why the confidence in reason advocated by Blumenberg may not simply be misguided but may also be the source of the problem of nihilism. The contemporary debate about nihilism and the power of reason raises many of the key concerns that motivated Descartes's reflection on the respective roles of reason and faith in life. Thus the contemporary debate about nihilism can benefit greatly from a reflection on its relationship to Descartes. In this debate, the voices of Blumenberg and Löwith each mirror one side of Descartes's own ambivalence.

"The true world—unattainable, indemonstrable, unpromisable; but the very thought of it—a consolation, an obligation, an imperative. . . . [H]ow could something unknown obligate us?"[1] With these words, Nietzsche reinverts the "inverted world" offered to us by the philosophical tradition from Plato to Hegel. In his critique of European nihilism, Nietzsche calls into question the traditional conviction that truth and value can be conceived as stable foundations that underlie the world of changing phenomena, that is, that permanence is the substrate of change. His lack of faith in what postmodern thinkers call "the metaphysics of presence" leads Nietzsche to propose the project of "a revaluation of all values." For Nietzsche, the decline of European culture is reflected in a loss of faith in transcendent values that are absolutely binding on the human will. The decline of the West is to be understood in terms of the image of the death of God, which Nietzsche introduces in *The Gay Science*:

The madman jumped into their midst and pierced them with his eyes. "Whither is God?" he cried; "I will tell you. We have killed him—you and I. All of us are his murderers. But how did we do this? How could we drink up the sea? Who gave us the sponge to wipe away the entire horizon? What were we doing when we unchained this earth from its sun? Whither is it moving now? Whither are we moving? Away from all suns? . . . Is there still any up or down? Are we not straying as through an infinite nothing?"[2]

In *The Will to Power*, Nietzsche clarifies the terms of this nihilistic decentering, this loss of bearings, and the turn away from "all suns" to the abyss of nothingness. "Nihilism as a psychological state will have been reached, *first*, when we have sought a 'meaning' in all events that is not there . . . *secondly*, when one has posited a totality, a systematization, indeed any organization in all events, and underneath all events, and a soul that longs to admire and revere has wallowed in the idea of some supreme form of domination and administration."[3] But it is not our demand for meaning in events that are ultimately meaningless, nor our projection of wholeness onto the flux of time, that is constitutive of nihilism. Instead nihilism is a consequence of our underlying sense that there are no such meaning and wholeness in the world. The insights "that becoming has no goal and that underneath all becoming there is no grand unity in which the individual could immerse himself completely as in an element of supreme value" lead "the human being [to lose] faith in his own value" because he has presupposed that his own value depends on some "infinitely valuable whole [that] works through him; i.e., he conceived such a whole in order *to be able to believe in his own value*."[4]

These two conditions specified by Nietzsche in section 12 of *The Will to Power* characterize the philosophy of Aristotle, who seeks a meaning in worldly events and posits both a teleological totality and "a soul that longs to admire and revere" that totality in theoretical contemplation. Aristotle's approach to understanding phenomena and valuing humanity is a failure because we recognize "that becoming has no goal and that underneath all becoming there is no grand unity in which the individual could immerse himself completely as in an element of supreme value." If our faith in our own value depends on the value of some "infinitely valuable whole," the only "escape" from the conclusion that we completely lack value is "to pass sentence on this whole world of becoming as a deception and to invent a world beyond it, a *true* world."[5] Desperate over our failure to find value in the world of becoming, we construct an other, higher world of being to serve as the basis for faith in ourselves. Such a world, which accommodates the True and the Good as the twin pillars of eternity, is proposed by Plato but is fully developed only in Christianity.

Nietzsche's proclamation of the death of God is the observation "that the belief in the Christian god has become unbelievable."[6] Our attempt to escape from a sense of our own worthlessness and of the worthlessness of existence has failed. The nihilism that Nietzsche is confronted with "includes disbelief in any metaphysical world and forbids itself any belief in a true world. Having reached this standpoint, one grants the reality of becoming as the only reality, forbids oneself every kind of clandestine access to afterworlds and false divinities—but cannot endure this world though one does not want to deny it."[7] When one reaches this third and final form of nihilism, which Nietzsche calls "active" nihilism in order to distinguish it from the resignation of passive nihilism, which simply gives up on the prospect of value, one is in a position to make an authentic return to the world of becoming and embrace it as the only world.[8] Moreover, one is in a position to embrace the world in a certain way. Now dispossessed of the misguided aim of finding meaning in the world and using rational categories to model or represent that meaning as the basis of meaning in human life, one is, according to Nietzsche, in a position to affirm the cycles of generation and corruption that are basic to becoming and, in turn, to affirm the suffering that is inseparable from these cycles. Rather than attempting to deny the reality of suffering by positing an ideal of wholeness or totality in which suffering is finally overcome, one is in a position to dispense with all such "false" illusions and proceed on the basis of a Dionysian awareness of the tragic character of existence, an awareness that makes the formation of "truthful" or "pious" illusions possible.[9]

On this basis alone can one attempt to "endure this world." Such an attempt is not for just anyone but only for those "free spirits," "we men of knowledge" who are "unknown to ourselves," whom Nietzsche takes as his proper audience.[10] Nietzsche makes his appeal not to those who despair over the first two forms or conditions of nihilism specified in section 12 of *The Will to Power*, for such people continue to measure "the value of the world according to categories *that refer to a purely fictitious [fingirte] world.*"[11] Nietzsche draws a dire consequence from Kant's insight into the fundamental limits of the human understanding: if such notions as teleology, wholeness, and truth pertain not to the inner nature of things but are simply "the results of certain perspectives of utility, designed to maintain and increase human constructs of domination," then such notions "have been falsely *projected* into the essence of things."[12] This projection has been undertaken to satisfy a need:

> To imagine another, more valuable world is an expression of hatred for a world that makes one suffer: the *ressentiment* of metaphysicians against actuality is here creative. . . .
>
> The preoccupation with suffering on the part of metaphysicians —is quite naïve. . . . Even morality is so important to them only because they see in it an essential condition for the abolition of suffering.[13]

In this statement of the central theme of *On the Genealogy of Morals*, Nietzsche characterizes the construction of the "true world" of metaphysics as a response to the need for suffering to have a meaning and for it to have the kind of "meaning" that promises us eventual release from suffering. Suffering is "a consequence of error" and "of guilt." The opposition between the "true world" and the world in which suffering occurs "derives from the practical sphere of utility," inasmuch as the representation of suffering as punishment for culpable choices has the power to inspire faith in a "true world" in which error, guilt, and suffering have no place.[14] In *Twilight of the Idols* (1888), Nietzsche suggests that the notion of a "true world" purged of error and suffering has lost its former power to inspire faith and hence to function creatively: "the 'true' world . . . is no longer good for anything, not even obligating—an idea which has become useless and superfluous [*eine unnütz, eine über- flüssig gewordene Idee*]—*consequently*, a refuted idea: let us abolish it!"[15]

Nietzsche's call to abolish the "true world" of the philosophers is a call to return to the faith in the earth and its eternal cycles of change that the young Nietzsche symbolizes in terms of Dionysos in *The Birth of Tragedy* and valorizes under the rubric of "a new and improved physis" in "The Use and Disadvantages of History for Life." In the history essay, Nietzsche lauds the ancient Greek conception of culture as "a new and improved *physis*, without inner and outer, without dissimulation and convention, culture as una- nimity of life, thought, appearance, and will . . . it was through the higher force of their *moral* nature that the Greeks achieved victory over all other cultures, and that every increase in truthfulness must also assist to promote true culture."[16] The young Nietzsche takes the tragic Greeks as an example of what is possible for a culture when it preserves an awareness of the fundamental rootedness of all images (the Apollinian) in an awareness, symbolized by Dionysos, of the ineluctable, irreducible, and hence ultimately incomprehensible inner nature of things. This tragic Dionysian awareness constitutes an affirmation of becoming and an accept- ance of the utter nothingness on which existence is founded. Against the background of this awareness, all image-making— including systematic metaphysics—reveals itself as nothing more than dreamlike illusion. Images founded on the tragic Dionysian awareness of the inner nature of things are to be preferred to the "Socratic cheerfulness" that invents the kind of "true world" derided by Nietzsche in *Twilight of the Idols* and *The Will to Power* because the purported "truth" of such Socratic constructions is purchased at the price of denying the conditions of life and hence of denying life itself.[17] Images rooted in Dionysian awareness hold a redemptive promise for the young Nietzsche. "It is only as an *aesthetic phenomenon* that existence and the world are eternally *justified*."[18] Ten years later, Nietzsche offers a more modest hope for art that corresponds closely to the terms of section 12 of *The Will to Power*: "As an aesthetic phenomenon existence is still *bearable* for us, and art furnishes us with eyes and hands and above all the good conscience to be *able* to turn ourselves into such a phenomenon."[19] What must be overcome, for the Nietzsche of *The Gay Science* as for the Nietzsche of *The Birth of Tragedy*, is "the *religion of comfortableness [Behaglichkeit]*" that represents the world of becoming, inseparable as it is from suffering, as a fallen world to be overcome toward a state of tranquility.[20] Only on the basis of an affirmation of suffering—and of a lack of any ultimate meaning of our suffering—can life be lived in a way that makes it *worth* living.

To live life in this way is to follow a path that is fundamentally opposed to Christianity. It is to affirm the will rather than faith in "higher" values. Christianity, like Buddhism, is the product of "a tremendous collapse and disease of the will"; "the free spirit par excellence" is exhibited by those who "take leave of all faith and every wish for certainty, being practiced in maintaining [themselves] on insubstantial ropes and possibilities and dancing even near abysses."[21] If in the metaphysical tradition this world has been represented as a wrong road, and the suffering of this world as the consequence of error and guilt, in truth "the greatest error that has ever been committed" is to have "believed [that] one possessed a criterion of reality in the forms of reason" such that one could be certain that the "true" world "cannot contradict itself, cannot change, cannot become, has no beginning and no end."[22] This assessment of the "true world" of Platonic metaphysics generally and of Christianity in particular—that it was designed to satisfy a need that it has become impotent to meet, and that the values produced by this metaphysics of the transcendent amount to a "slander of life"[23]—has a number of important consequences for an understanding of the modern age and Descartes's place in it. One need not embrace Nietzsche's entire assessment of the nihilism of the modern age—one need not accept the terms of Nietzsche's critique of reason, for example, or his conviction that violence is a necessary concomitant of cultural ascent—to recognize the incisiveness of his grasp of the contemporary crisis in values and to recognize the *aporia* with which we are presented by his analysis of the role played by modern science in the advent of modern nihilism.

Since Nietzsche, nihilism has served as a basic framework for understanding the predicament of the modern age. Hans Jonas points out, however, that nihilism as a category of historical interpretation does not apply to the modern age alone but is also an illuminating category for understanding the world-devaluing tendency of Gnostic metaphysics. Because the Gnostics conceive of the world as having been created not by God but by an agency opposed to God—the demiurge in Valentinus and the force of darkness in Mani—they consider "the transmundane deity" not to "stand in any positive relation to the sensible world. [This deity] is not the essence of that world, but its negation and cancellation."[24] This sense of a radical opposition between God and the world leads some Gnostics to "the subjectivist argument of traditional moral skepticism: nothing is naturally good or bad, things in themselves are indifferent, and 'only by human opinion are actions good or bad.'"[25] Plotinus sees in this conception of ethical valuation a "moral indifference in the Gnostics" that amounts to "moral nihilism."[26]

In his epilogue to *The Gnostic Religion*, Jonas both draws some fundamental parallels between Gnostic and modern nihilism and points out the key differences between them. The parallels help us to understand the very idea of nihilism. At bottom, as Nietzsche recognizes, the problem of nihilism is a problem of homelessness. When the universe in which we find ourselves exhibits "indifference . . . to human aspirations," the human condition becomes that of "the utter loneliness of man in the sum of things."[27] Here there is an affinity with the Gnostic predicament. Even if the demiurge is not indifferent to our aspirations, it nevertheless places demands on us that are discontinuous with and hence irrelevant to God's demands and the prospects for our salvation. A wedge is driven between human beings and the world, such that both the extreme forms of Gnosticism and modernity (existentialism, for Jonas) face a "cosmic nihilism" in which the world is not a teleological whole that assigns a place to human beings but is instead a prison to which human beings owe no respect.[28] The fundamental difference between the two attitudes toward cosmic nihilism is that whereas "dualism between man and physis [is] the metaphysical background of the nihilistic situation" in general, "Gnostic man is thrown into an antagonistic, anti-divine, and therefore anti-human nature, modern man into an indifferent one."[29] For Jonas, Nietzsche's analysis of nihilism in terms of the death of God therefore illuminates the Gnostic predicament as well as the modern one, although the specific terms of the applicability are different in each case. For the Gnostics, it is "the world (not the alienation from it) [that] must be overcome." This "acosmism" amounts to the view that "'the God of the cosmos is dead'—is dead, that is, as a god, has ceased to be divine for us and therefore to afford the lodestar for our lives."[30] This places the Gnostics in a bleak position as far as worldly values are concerned—the gnosis that puts us in touch with the *deus absconditus* has no relevance to our earthly existence—but for all that, "the gnostic position . . . is the very opposite of an abandonment of transcendence."[31]

In this respect, the nihilism of modernity is a comparatively more dire situation. Nietzsche opens Book 5 of *The Gay Science* with the suggestion that the death of God signifies that "belief in the Christian God has become unbelievable"—that, in Heidegger's

words, "the supersensible world is without effective force."[32]
Where the Gnostics had the promise of salvation through Gnosis,
our contemporary situation—the one in which "nihilism stands at
the door"—is beset with a moral skepticism so extreme as to bring
with it "the suspicion that *all* interpretations of the world are
false."[33] This "radical nihilism" is such that "we lack the least right
to posit a beyond or an in-itself of things that might be 'divine' or
morality incarnate."[34] The freedom of the Gnostic pneuma is a
freedom from the world and toward the transcendent God, whereas
the "freedom" of the modern self is the groundlessness of the will
before the vacant abyss of meaninglessness. The worldly predicament of modern nihilism is more radical in the sense that there
appears to be no prospect of redemption, either inside or outside
the world. To this extent, freedom in the modern context "is of a
desperate kind, and, as a compassless task, inspires dread rather
than exultation."[35]

The most intriguing statement made by Nietzsche concerning
the advent of nihilism in the modern age has Copernicus as its focal
point. "Since Copernicus man has been rolling from the center
toward X."[36] In the *Genealogy*, Nietzsche expands upon this idea:
"Since Copernicus, man seems to have got himself on an inclined
plane—now he is slipping faster and faster away from the center
into—what? Into nothingness? into a penetrating sense of his nothingness?"[37] The section on "The Madman" in *The Gay Science* provides guidance for interpreting these remarks about Copernicus.
Nietzsche asks, "what were we doing when we unchained this earth
from its sun? Whither is it moving now? Whither are we moving?
Away from all suns?"[38] The image of the sun represents, as it does
in Plato's *Republic*, the ideal of a transcendent basis and measure
for value. As Freud recognizes, Copernicus's insight constitutes
one of the primary "blows to the naïve self-love of man" in the
modern world, inasmuch as Copernicus removes human beings
from their former privileged place at the center of creation.[39] Nietzsche's remark in the *Genealogy* invites us to conceive of the

movement on an inclined plane as a movement away from traditional sources of authority and the "extreme overvaluation of man" found in Christianity.[40] Hans Blumenberg sees in these remarks about Copernicus an attempt on Nietzsche's part to take away from reality as much authority as possible to make room for human creativity: "It was not enough for Nietzsche to legitimize resistance against a reality no longer characterized by consideration for man; man's right then remains dependent on reality as he finds it or believes he finds it. His right should consist in imputing the least possible binding force to reality, so as to make room for his own works."[41] The young Nietzsche is as committed to this view as the Nietzsche of the 1880s: "Our salvation [*Heil*] lies not in knowing, but in creating! Our greatness lies in the highest illusions, in the noblest emotion. If the universe is of no concern to us, then we ought to have the right to despise it."[42]

Not only the idea of God as the Christian *idea ton agathon* but also the Cartesian ideals of reason and mastery are called radically into question by Nietzsche's critique of modern nihilism. The focus of Nietzsche's critique of Descartes is his assessment of the status of subjectivity. "The 'subject' is the fiction that many similar states in us are the effect of one substratum: but it is we who first created the similarity of these states."[43] The notion of the subject is itself a representation of the activity of representation. Just as the world projected by modern science is a representation of multiplicity as if it were a unity, the subject is an ideal representation of a multiplicity of states. Heidegger captures the essence of Nietzsche's critique of the representational activity of the subject in the following way:

> It is doubtful—in fact, is to be denied—that what is represented in representation reveals anything at all about reality; for everything real is a becoming. But all re-presenting [*Vor-stellen*], as setting in place [*Fest-stellen*], obviates becoming and shows what is becoming as at a standstill, and hence as it "is" *not*. Representation gives only the semblance of reality. What representation takes to be true and existent is therefore essentially in error when

measured against the real taken as becoming. Truth is an error, but a necessary error.[44]

It is necessary because we would perish without it: "Truth is the kind of error without which a certain species of life could not live. The value for life is ultimately decisive."[45] Thinking is a creative distortion or falsification of experience. There is no such thing as a pure drive for knowledge but "merely a drive toward belief in truth" that makes life bearable.[46] A primary consequence of this radical position is that the idea of truth as correspondence between a subject's representation and the object represented is an error of the tradition that is finally untenable: "But in any case it seems to me that 'the correct perception'—which would mean 'the adequate expression of an object in the subject'—is a contradictory absurdity [*Unding*]."[47] To be "truthful" is not to establish reliable correspondence but rather "to employ the usual metaphors . . . to lie according to a fixed convention, to lie with the herd and in a manner binding upon everyone."[48]

The fiction of the subject is the preeminent modern product of this process of abstraction, in which "an image [gets dissolved] into a concept."[49] In *The Will to Power*, Nietzsche characterizes the Cartesian ego as precisely such a fiction:

> Through thought the ego is posited; but hitherto one believed as ordinary people do, that in 'I think' there was something of immediate certainty, and that this 'I' was the given *cause* of thought, from which by analogy we understood all other causal relationships. However habitual and indispensable this fiction may have become by now—that in itself proves nothing against its imaginary origin: a belief can be a condition of life and nonetheless be false.[50]

Nietzsche's inversion of the philosophical ideal reverses the relationship between ego and thought. If our feeling of power is enhanced by the supposition that the ego controls the process of thinking, in reality the subject or Cartesian ego is itself a product of that process:

> Let the people suppose that knowledge means knowing things entirely; the philosopher must say to himself: When I analyze the process that is expressed in the sentence "I think," I find a whole series of daring assertions that would be difficult, perhaps impossible, to prove; for example, that it is *I* who think, that there must necessarily be something that thinks, that thinking is an activity and operation on the part of a being who is thought of as a cause, that there is an "ego," and, finally, that it is already determined what is to be designated by thinking—that I *know* what thinking is.[51]

By calling our assumptions about the ego and the nature of thinking into question, Nietzsche opens up the prospect of reversing the relationship between the two. "A thought comes when 'it' wishes, and not when 'I' wish, so that it is a falsification of the facts of the case to say that the subject 'I' is the condition of the predicate 'think.' *It* thinks; but that this 'it' is precisely the famous old 'ego' is, to put it mildly, only a supposition, an assertion, and assuredly not an 'immediate certainty.'"[52] To call radically into question the reality of the Cartesian ego and its particular brand of certainty is ultimately to challenge the entire "soul atomism" of Christianity, "which regards the soul as something indestructible, eternal, indivisible, as a monad, as an *atomon*: this belief ought to be expelled from science!"[53] The ideal of a "gay" science, to seek "the thrill of the infinite, the unmeasured" through *exposure* to danger rather than through insulation from it, leaves no room for such a conception of soul, which is the highest modern instance of the sort of fiction whose utility lies in insulating us from suffering and uncertainty and whose employment is therefore fundamentally a denial of life.[54] In place of this conception of soul, Nietzsche allows for the possibility of "new versions and refinements of the soul-hypothesis," such as "'soul as social structure of the drives and affects.'"[55] "Sensualism . . . at least as a regulative hypothesis" inverts the Christian-Cartesian conception of the primacy of soul or mind over body, so as to bring thinking, along with the affects, under the yoke of the will.[56] The resulting primacy of body over thinking gives rise to a conception of the former "as a social structure composed of many souls."[57] Transformed or "refined" in this manner, the idea of soul becomes detached from the debilitating ascetic commitments in virtue of which it can be said that the modern idealistic conception of the subject expresses a "will to nothingness."[58]

In his interpretation of Descartes's place in Nietzsche's account of nihilism, Heidegger focuses on Descartes's appropriation of the medieval notion of the *subiectum*.

> *Sub-iectum* is the Latin translation and interpretation of the Greek *hypo-keimenon* and means what under-lies and lies-at-the-basis-of, what already lies before of itself. Since Descartes and through Descartes, man, the human 'I' . . . [comes] to play the role of the one and only subject proper . . . subjectivity here becomes synonymous with I-ness.[59]

In "The Origin of the Work of Art," Heidegger says that "this translation" from Greek into Latin "is in no way the innocent process it is considered to this day." In it "there is concealed, rather, a transposing of Greek experience into another manner of thinking. . . . The groundlessness of Western thinking begins with this translation."[60] Heidegger accepts the terms of Nietzsche's critique of the modern idea of the subject as a fiction projected onto experience in the interest of security and mastery, and he traces the development of the notion of the subject through a process of linguistic transformation that leads from a Greek conception of things presenting themselves to us to a modern conception of things as being projected through the subject's activity of representation. If for the Roman consciousness *subiectum* signifies "in a distinctive sense that which already lies-before and so lies at the basis of something else," so that "stones, plants, and animals are subjects . . . no less than man is," in Descartes the notion of the *subiectum* undergoes a further "transposing" that assigns to human consciousness the unique position of "lying-before of itself."[61] Heidegger sees in this latter transposition "above all a new determination of the essence of freedom. . . . [T]he new freedom consists in the fact that man himself legislates, chooses what is binding, and binds himself to it."[62]

This conception of a new sense of freedom proper to modernity corresponds to Nietzsche's interpretation of the turn to Cartesian certainty as a specific manifestation of the will to power:

> Logical certainty, transparency, as criterion of truth (*"omne illud verum est, quod clare et distincte percipitur"* [all that is true which is perceived clearly and distinctly]—Descartes): with that, the mechanical hypothesis concerning the world is desired and credible.
>
> But this is a crude confusion: like *simplex sigillum veri* [simplicity is the seal of truth]. How does one know that the real nature of things stands in *this* relation to our intellect?—Could it not be otherwise? that it is the hypothesis that gives the intellect the greatest feeling of power and security, that is most preferred, valued and consequently characterized as true?[63]

Nietzsche interprets the entire apparatus of subjectivity against the background of his conviction that "there is no [pure] drive toward knowledge and truth." The impure nature of subjectivity is to be seen in terms of the affects that it is designed to serve. Heidegger makes implicit sense of this relation to the affective basis of subjectivity when he links subjectivity to a new determination of the essence of freedom. His suggestion that the essence of freedom is now to be understood in terms of human legislation and determination recalls Nietzsche's suggestion that "'freedom of the will' is essentially the affect of superiority in relation to him who must obey."[64] What Nietzsche says here of relations between human beings holds mutatis mutandis for his view of the relationship between modern human beings and nature. In both kinds of relationship, the principle holds that

> every specific body strives to become master over all space and to extend its force (—its will to power) and to thrust back all that resists its extension. But it continually encounters similar efforts on the part of other bodies and ends by coming to an arrangement ("union") with those of them that are sufficiently related to it: thus they then conspire together for power.[65]

For Nietzsche, this principle equally underlies political associations and the endeavor to master nature. In the case of mastering nature, our faith in reason, the fundamental intelligibility of nature, and the possibility of control are forms of faith in aim, unity, and truth specific to modernity. The subject's projection of constant and identifiable causes onto the world is motivated by a desire to comprehend the world and in turn to master it. This projection is, at bottom, a free *invention*.[66] It has a correlate in the projection of the subject as the putative cause of all representations.

Nietzsche's and Heidegger's interpretations have done a great deal to shape the historical reception of Descartes as a wholly secular thinker. Both fail to recognize the significance of faith in Descartes's thought. In particular, the indebtedness of Descartes's conception of freedom to the Augustinian notion of freedom directly contradicts Heidegger's claim of an "essential transposition" in Descartes from Christian faith to subjective representation. Nonetheless, Heidegger's interpretation of Descartes, like Nietzsche's, has tremendous power to illuminate the controversy in contemporary thought over the power of reason to ground values. The value of Heidegger's interpretation of Descartes consists not in being a historically faithful analysis of Descartes's thought but rather in functioning as a symptomology of contemporary disputes over the legitimacy of the modern age.

In this connection, of particular interest for an understanding of Descartes as a moral thinker is the question whether the interpretive presupposition that guides Heidegger in his analysis of Descartes has validity in spite of the distortions in Heidegger's understanding of Descartes. That guiding presupposition is the secularization thesis, which in its general formulation calls for the grounding ideas of modernity to be understood as desacralized versions of concepts out of Christian eschatology. Heidegger applies the secularization thesis to Descartes in his lectures on Nietzsche to locate Descartes in a history of metaphysical thinking that reaches its nadir in the death of God. The secularization thesis proves to be a powerfully suggestive thesis for interpreting modernity and for thinking through the claim that modernity is nihilistic. It is also an extremely controversial thesis. In what follows, I consider the secularization thesis and the controversies surrounding it.

2. THE SECULARIZATION THESIS AND ITS IMPLICATIONS FOR UNDERSTANDING DESCARTES

In the Nietzsche lectures, Heidegger argues that the key to understanding Descartes's conception of human freedom lies in recognizing it as a secularized form of the medieval Christian conception of freedom. He implicitly proposes this interpretation of Descartes's place in the history of metaphysics in the following characterization of Cartesian certainty:

> Man's claim to a ground of truth found and secured by man himself arises from that "liberation" in which he disengages himself from the constraints of biblical Christian revealed truth and church doctrine. Every authentic liberation, however, is not only a breaking of chains and a casting off of bonds, it is also and above all a new determination of the essence of freedom. To be free now means that, in place of the certitude of salvation, which

was the standard for all truth, man posits the kind of certitude by virtue of which and in which he becomes certain of himself as the being that thus founds itself on itself.[67]

When Heidegger wrote these words (1940), the secularization thesis was already well known, having been employed in 1922 by Carl Schmitt as a tool for illuminating the modern notion of political sovereignty. In *Political Theology*, Schmitt argues that the notion of political sovereignty is a secularized version of the idea of divine sovereignty. His conception of political decisionism is a direct consequence of his conception of political authority as supreme over any kind of universal laws or norms, which, in turn, is a direct consequence of his derivation of the idea of political sovereignty from the idea of a God with an absolutely free will.[68] Heidegger employs the thesis in a comparable manner by conceiving of Cartesian cognitive certainty as a secularized version of the medieval certainty of eternal salvation. His claim is not simply that instrumental rationality gains ascendancy once faith in a transcendent God and the promise of eternal salvation have died out but that a discontinuous shift, an "essential transposition," is completed in the thought of Descartes. Implicit in this employment of the secularization thesis is the conviction that the history of Western thought is to be understood as a *Verfallsgeschichte*, a history of fall or decline as a result of which modernity and its Cartesian leitmotif must be understood as deficient. Heidegger sees the development of Cartesian certainty as predicated on the demise of faith in God, and to this extent his analysis of the deficiency of the modern age is closely aligned with Nietzsche's characterization of nihilism in terms of the death of God. In "Hölderlin and the Essence of Poetry," Heidegger characterizes modernity as "the age of the gods who have fled and of the one to come. It is the *destitute* time, because it stands under a double lack and not: the no-longer of the gods who have fled, and the not-yet of the one to come."[69] The flight of the gods is inseparable from modernity's new determination of the essence of freedom. Like Nietzsche's madman, who says not only that God is dead but also that "we have killed him, you and I," Heidegger sees in the insistent self-assertion of Cartesian certainty the death of all transcendent measures and their replacement by the immanent measure of human cognition and the will to mastery. For Nietzsche, the endeavor to master nature "completely and forever with our square little reason" fails to heed Schopenhauer's lesson about the irreducibility of the world will and thereby brings about a "degradation" of existence. Heidegger accepts the basic terms of this critique of modernity and the will to mastery and proposes in the face of this will that "only a god can save us."[70]

This response is in keeping with Heidegger's account of the history of metaphysics as the progressive forgottenness or oblivion of Being and hence as a *Verfallsgeschichte*. To understand the history of the West in terms of the secularization thesis, however, is not necessarily to view that history as one of decline. One may, like Carl Schmitt, see the historical process of secularization as a process of liberation from dogmatism and superstition. There are hints of a similar reception of the idea of secularization in the thought of Hans Blumenberg, although he accepts secularization as a category of historical understanding only in a limited and severely qualified sense. Blumenberg sees secularization not "as the illegitimate liquidation of the sovereignty of religion [*geistlicher Herrschaft*]" but rather "as the liquidation of the illegitimate sovereignty of religion."[71] In debates over the validity of the secularization thesis and the related question whether modernity is to be understood as the product of a history of decline, both sides implicitly accept Heidegger's observation that "Christianity is bereft of the power it had during the Middle Ages to *shape history*."[72] But the two sides disagree fundamentally on the question of the "legitimacy" of the modern age, on the applicability of the secularization thesis as a theoretical tool for understanding modernity, and on the prospects of human rationality to secure an abiding sense of meaning in human life without recourse to extrarational measures. In recent decades, this debate concerning the status of modernity has been most clearly and most polemically expressed in the writings of Karl Löwith and Hans Blumenberg. I now turn to an examination of the dispute between these two thinkers.

As a student of Heidegger, Karl Löwith was deeply influenced by his teacher's account of the history of Western metaphysics as a *Verfallsgeschichte*. Löwith and Hans Jonas, another of Heidegger's students, focus on the problem of the metaphysical void left by Heidegger's proclamation of "the end of philosophy" and his call for an "overcoming of metaphysics." For Löwith and Jonas, the preeminent problem of contemporary thought is that of our relation to the cosmos: in the wake of a progressive reduction of the world in which we live from the divine albeit finite cosmos of the ancient Greeks to the desacralized, boundless mechanism of the moderns, these two thinkers devote themselves to the task of establishing a sense of reverence toward nature that draws its inspiration from the ancient conception of the world as cosmos. Both see in such contemporary positions as Heidegger's existential phenomenology traces of the same subjectivism that Heidegger sees in Nietzsche. Löwith goes so far as to suggest that Husserl, Heidegger, and Jaspers, "notwithstanding their critiques of Descartes, all continue to proceed, like Descartes, within the Christian tradition" that Nietzsche sees as the seedbed of modern subjectivism.[73] This concern over the subjectivism even of contemporary thinkers such as Heidegger leads Löwith and Jonas to rethink Heidegger's call for a "step back" from traditional metaphysical thinking. Rather than counseling a wholesale retreat from metaphysical thinking, they advocate a renewal of metaphysics itself, or at least a contemporary reappropriation of concepts and measures derived from antiquity. For Jonas, the contemporary task of ethics, made incumbent on us by the historical devaluation of nature and the problem of nihilism, demands first of all a philosophy of nature: "A philosophy of mind comprises ethics—and through the continuity of mind with organism and of organism with nature, ethics becomes part of the philosophy of nature. . . . [A]n ethics no longer founded on divine authority must be founded on a principle discoverable in the nature of things, lest it fall victim to subjectivism or other forms of reltivity."[74] Our pervasive sense of meaninglessness is to be overcome through a return to a conception of dwelling according to which human beings are subject to an authoritative cosmic order.

Löwith sees the secularization thesis as a basic methodological tool for rethinking our place in the order of things. He sees in our ancient past the basic elements of a new ethic of dwelling, and, like Nietzsche and Heidegger, he sees the possibility of an authentic human response to the problem of meaninglessness to be predicated on an adequate understanding of the historical genesis of the contemporary situation. The secularization thesis is an account of how the "primordial view of the world" first attained by Heraclitus "got lost in the transition from the Greek cosmos to the Christian saeculum" by means of a historical process in which "the world became suspect, despised, and then secularized [*verweltlicht*]."[75] The result is a split between two senses of 'world', one the physical world established by God and the other the *civitas terrena* of human history. To trace the history of secularization is to seek a link with the historical point before which a split between the human and the natural occurred.

Löwith presents the crux of his version of the secularization thesis in *Meaning in History* (1949), which subsequently appeared in a modified German translation as *Weltgeschichte und Heilsgeschehen: Die theologischen Voraussetzungen der Geschichtsphilosophie*. The subtitle indicates that the theme of the study is "the theological presuppositions of the philosophy of history," that is, that Löwith's central thesis is that the Enlightenment conception of the "philosophy of history," as "a systematic interpretation of universal history in accordance with a principle by which historical events and successions are unified and directed toward an ultimate meaning," is "entirely dependent on theology of history, in particular on the theological concept of history as a history of fulfillment and salvation."[76] Where Heidegger suggests that Cartesian certainty is a secularized form of medieval Christian certainty of salvation, and Schmitt argues that modern political notions like sovereign rule are derived from the Christian notion of absolute divine legislation, Löwith argues that the idea of history as inevitable progress is a secularization of Christian eschatology, which conceives of time as progressing toward an *eschaton* or ideal end.[77]

The main German title of Löwith's text, *Weltgeschichte und Heilsgeschehen*, suggests an original relationship between history and the category of the sacred that has been severed.[78] Löwith believes that by understanding how "philosophy of history originates with the Hebrew and Christian faith in a fulfilment and that it ends with the secularization of its eschatological pattern," we may be able to come to grips with the sense of despair that has been caused in us by "the basic experience of evil and suffering, and . . . man's quest for happiness."[79] Löwith sees in a reflection on the historical roots of our contemporary crisis the prospect of establishing a sense of "wholesomeness," although this is to be achieved "not by an imaginary jump, either into early Christianity (Kierkegaard) or into classical paganism (Nietzsche), but only by the analytical reduction of the modern compound into its original elements."[80] Löwith seeks to understand "the meaning of history as the meaning of suffering by historical action." Such an understanding will overcome "the modern illusion that history can be conceived as a progressive evolution which solves the problem of evil by way of elimination."[81] This illusion, inspired by Hegel's appropriation of Christian eschatology, says that history moves ineluctably in a positive or progressive direction—toward increasing happiness, the progressive elimination of evil and suffering, and the like—because it is moved by a rational principle. The idea of an *eschaton* or "end" of history is attractive because it gives us a way of conceiving of purposes underlying historical events that underlie or transcend those events. Without a relation to such purposes, history becomes reduced to a succession of contingent occurrences without any standard or basis by which to measure and understand them. On Löwith's view, the problem for contemporary philosophy is how to conceive a measure for interpreting and judging historical events in such a way that the measure does not have the status of an absolute that transcends time. The availability or conceivability of such measures seems denied to us by our finitude and the lessons of historical reflection. But if such a measure cannot be transcendent, Löwith argues that it cannot be immanent either: "Historical processes as such do not bear the least evidence of a comprehensive and ultimate meaning. History as such has no outcome. There never has been and never will be an immanent solution to the problem of history, for man's experience is one of steady failure."[82] Thus our Judeo-Christian heritage seems to leave us ill prepared to confront the problem of nihilism. The ideal of salvation, as an ideal that is radically opposed to time, simply devalues history, as in Saint Augustine, and the basic dimension of contingency in history makes the ideal of an immanent measure, presumably derived from human reason, an unattainable illusion.

But our heritage is not exhausted through reference to our Judeo-Christian background. We are equally indebted to a cyclical conception of time developed in classical Greek philosophy. Thus we are heirs not only to a conception of time oriented on a past (original sin) and a future (the Day of Judgment) but also to a conception of time that gives priority to an eternal present. The unpredictability of history and the idea of the inevitability of suffering given prominence in the philosophies of Schopenhauer and Nietzsche lead Löwith to make a place for Stoic resignation in his ideal of a response to the problem of nihilism. But he recognizes that this pagan ideal devalues history, and thus he also makes a place for the assertion of the human will. In doing so, Löwith presents as a programmatic solution to the problem of nihilism the union of resignation and some form of self-assertion. For Löwith, the task is not to forsake self-assertion entirely but rather to establish a sense of proper limits to self-assertion. In this spirit, he turns to Nietzsche's doctrine of eternal recurrence of the same, which he considers to be both rooted in "the old eternity of the cosmic cycle of the pagans" and, if only against Nietzsche's own intention, "deeply marked by a Christian conscience."[83] Nietzsche's paganism consists in his call for the will to "integrate itself with the cyclic law of the cosmos." At the same time, Nietzsche "was so thoroughly Christian and modern that only one thing preoccupied him: the thought of the *future* and the *will* to create it."[84]

Löwith resolves this tension in Nietzsche's thought by giving priority, as Nietzsche himself had, to the comparatively "pagan" elements in the doctrine of eternal return. Notwithstanding the way in which Nietzsche's thought is conditioned by Christianity—in *Meaning in History*, Löwith suggests that Nietzsche's "own *contra Christianos* is an exact replica in reverse of the *contra gentiles* of the Church Fathers"—the doctrine of eternal recurrence is ultimately "a counter*gospel*" indicative of Nietzsche's neopaganism. Nietzsche's writings are a "great attempt to 'translate' man 'back' into the nature of all things," which is to be understood not in terms of a world that transcends time but rather in terms of "the everlasting *physis* of the world and the 'great reason of the body' as what is fundamental and exists always, remains the same and recurs. In this tendency to 'return to nature,' Nietzsche is, in spite of his opposition to a sentimental concept of nature, the Rousseau of the nineteenth century."[85] However much it may be the case that "the modern mind has not made up its mind whether it should be Christian or pagan," that "it sees with one eye of faith and the other of reason" and thereby is subject to a vision that "is necessarily dim in comparison with either Greek or biblical thinking," Löwith sees the prospect of redemption not in any attempt to renew a sense of transcendent measures but rather in a return to a sense of the eternal cycles of the cosmos typified in Stoic thinking.

To embrace the notion of eternal recurrence is not to make a naïve return to the consciousness and life experience of the Stoa. Given the historical nature of self-understanding, such a return would be no more possible (nor, for that matter, would it be any more relevant to the modern condition) than a reappropriation of the Christian ideal of a transcendent God. What is eternal in the cosmos and in humanity is, for Löwith, something selfsame and unchanging, but it is not an identifiable "essence" in the sense sought by the tradition and subsequently repudiated by existential phenomenology. Like Heidegger, Löwith conceives of essence not as a static quality shared by members of a class of beings but instead as the mysterious, hidden principle whereby things come to presence. Hence what we know about an essence like "human nature" is inseparable from the historical manifestations of that nature. Contemplation of human nature or our place in the cosmos must ultimately take the form of a reflection on the rootedness of history in the eternal cycles of nature.

To understand philosophical reflection in these terms is to abandon the hope of a definitive formulation of "human nature," even though such a nature is the presupposition of discourse that is meaningful in the sense of having validity that transcends the immanence of the historical moments out of which the discourse arose. Human nature becomes comparable to *physis*, in the sense that it cannot be experienced directly or definitively but instead manifests its hidden "permanence" through experienced phenomena. Nietzsche's recognition of this elusive sense of permanence or eternity in nature is implicit in his criticism of Schopenhauer for having purported that Platonic Ideas could be derived from the experience of pure becoming. Löwith learns this lesson from Nietzsche, and thus one finds no explicit political manifesto in Löwith's writings but instead only the broad outlines of a political and historical standpoint that Löwith describes as "cosmo-political" in virtue of its commitment to the inscription of the ethico-political realm of human existence within a philosophy of nature.[86]

This program for a modern or postmodern reappropriation of the Greek ideal of the cosmos is motivated by Löwith's critique of modern subjectivism, a critique that has its bearings in Nietzsche's critique of Descartes. Löwith accepts without qualification the proposition, advanced by Nietzsche and endorsed by Heidegger, that "with Descartes the world that had become Christian becomes secular" and "there occurs . . . a liberation of human knowledge and of the man who knows about himself from the authority of the ecclesiastical bond."[87] The transformation in the essence of human freedom of which Heidegger speaks in the Nietzsche lectures is predicated on a "doubt of the God of the Christian faith." The Descartes characterized here is the same Descartes who, as Nietzsche asserts in *Beyond Good and Evil*, "conceded authority to reason alone."[88] I have shown at length in previous chapters that this interpretation fails to acknowledge the indebtedness of Cartesian reason to the God of Christianity. Descartes seeks to vindicate human reason by exploring the extent to which it can be rendered independent of the sorts of authority that he dismisses as "merely" subjective in the early parts of the *Discourse on Method*. His aim is to empower "sceptics and infidels" with an insight into the inner relationship between instrumental rationality and Christian life. He secularizes science in the narrow sense of separating it from ecclesiastical authority, but he does not *oppose* science and Christianity in the way in which as a matter of historical fact they came to be opposed to one another.

By following the basic terms of Nietzsche's and Heidegger's critiques of Descartes, Löwith gives an interpretation of Descartes that is more applicable to the subjective idealism that developed in the wake of Descartes's thought than to Descartes's own philosophical ethos. For the most part, Löwith misses the ambivalence or twilight status of Descartes's thought because he is at pains to provide a thoroughgoing criticism of the philosophy of *nature* inaugurated by Descartes. He sees the seventeenth century as a time when "the world to come began to be understood, not as a kingdom of God beyond this world and its history, but as a kingdom of man, a better world in the future. The other-worldly destiny of man gave way to a worldly purpose. Man no longer 'transcended' to God as the *summum bonum* but to a human world capable of improvement."[89] No longer an Augustinian "*procursus* toward the kingdom of God," the seventeenth century is typified by the endeavor to master nature through mathematical reduction. If we cannot accept the implications of this characterization of the seventeenth century for an understanding of Descartes's conception of the full breadth of human subjectivity, we can nonetheless learn much from it about how Descartes devalues nature in a way that even Patristic and Scholastic thinkers do not.

Löwith takes this ideal of utter subjection to be the preeminent moment in the advent of modern nihilism.

> The practical science outlined by [Francis] Bacon came to be an independent mathematical physical science in the seventeenth century through Descartes, Galileo, and finally Newton. The essential significance of this period is that mathematical physics was finally set free, that is, it was disengaged from everything that was not mechanically and quantitatively determinable. This separation led to the divorce of nature and natural science from the life of the universe and all questions of theology and morality. For the first time, the natural world was transformed from a partner into an object that can be manipulated through calculation and experiment for the purpose of *utilitas* and *potentia*.[90]

The seventeenth-century mathematization of nature amounts to a secularization of nature. For Löwith this is not the first but the *second* fateful moment in the historical process of secularization, the first secularization of nature having occurred in the shift from the Greek conception of a divine cosmos to the Christian conception of *mundus* or terra as a creation that stands at a distance from the divine.[91] This is the most distinctive and revealing feature of Löwith's version of the secularization thesis, for it draws the focus away from a transcendent God and toward the earth as the basis of meaning. Here the special appeal to Löwith of Nietzsche's doctrine of eternal recurrence becomes apparent: in turning toward the cosmos or earth as the source of meaning and the basis for future moral measures and a sense of dwelling, Löwith gives priority to the divine conceived in terms of *physis* rather than in the anthropomorphic and anthropocentric terms of the Christian God. A crucial feature of Löwith's secularization thesis is that anthropocentrism lies at the core of the entire process of secularization, at the core of the shift from Greek cosmos to Christian mundus as well as at the core of the shift from mundus to the mathematico-dynamic world-picture of modern science. The effect is to intensify and consolidate the place of human beings as the zenith of being. In the first shift, the world becomes conceived not only as having been created for human beings—even the Stoics believe this—but also as having the dual status of an instrumentality and an object of contempt.[92] In the second shift, the world becomes understood as a creation without a creator that lies at the feet of human beings, who now have no superior in the order of being. Human beings in this latter sense are *fully* "secularized."[93]

Already in the first of these two moments the problem of secularization manifests itself. "The *philia* of human beings for the cosmos and of the cosmos for itself gets converted into a renunciation and an overcoming of the world, to the point of a *contemptus mundi*, because love for the cosmos is enmity toward God (James 4:4)."[94] This "secularization of the world" gets completed by Augustine, who substitutes inwardness for the Greek faith in the cosmos and in the evidence of the visible world. The turn to inwardness "corresponds to a departure from a world order that circumscribes human beings" and leads directly to a situation in which "human beings are placeless and homeless in the totality of the world."[95] The fact that for us today the world remains the "external" world is a sign that "we are still Christians, even if . . . we do not believe in God and think about the salvation of the soul."[96] Whether we locate the origin of *Reflexionsphilosophie* in Descartes or in Augustine, for Löwith the decisive point is that any philosophical outlook that degrades the world by opposing it to the divine cannot be taken seriously as a basis for the meaningful integration or reintegration of humanity into the nature of things. Properly understood, the world is no more the "total horizon" of our intentional consciousness than it is an object of our contempt. Instead, it is, as it was for the Greeks, "a necessary order and at the same time a rank-ordering, in which mortal human beings take on a definite, i.e., subordinate, place. This world order, which generally encompasses everything, is authoritative even . . . in the small domain of the human world that is subordinated to it, the *polis*."[97] Löwith sees in the reappropriation of a sense of piety for the cosmos the prospect of an ethic of dwelling and of addressing our experience of ourselves "as the greatest wonder and puzzle."[98]

Understood in these terms, not only is Descartes a Christian thinker, but he is also the nihilistic culmination of Christian thought. Whereas "Copernicus and Kepler wanted . . . to contemplate God's ideas in the 'book' of nature," "the decisive turning point took place . . . with F. Bacon's equation of knowledge and power, and with Descartes's like-minded intention to make nature conquerable by means of scientific knowledge for the sake of human welfare."[99] According to Löwith, what makes Descartes decisive is that "his construction of the world had its foundations in a methodological destruction [*Destruktion*] of certainty regarding a well-ordered world, regardless of whether that order be inherent in the world or provided by God."[100] Descartes radicalizes the Christian notion of human transcendence of the world toward God by detaching that transcendence from God completely and thereby making human consciousness absolute. "The ultimate consequence of this method of retreat into oneself, whose goal is the discovery of a rational access to God and the world, is Eddington's thesis that the physicist derives from nature only what he put into it in advance, a thesis that Heisenberg designates 'the essential insight of modern physics.'"[101]

Löwith's critique of Descartes as an exemplary *Christian* thinker, then, is not based on any claims about the role of divine grace, illumination through revelation, or any other aspects of church doctrine in Descartes's thought but instead on an analysis of Descartes's conceptions of method and scientific rationality and on the picture of the relationship between divinity, humanity, and world that results from them. Descartes conceives of humanity as closer to God than to nature. For Löwith this is a characteristically modern modification of Christian metaphysics that, with the exception of Spinoza, runs from Cusanus to Heidegger.[102] To speak of a historical process of secularization is, then, as Löwith understands it, to speak of a process whereby the prospect of authentic dwelling foundered through the desanctification of the cosmos and the progressive elevation of humanity first from a subordinate part of a larger, uncreated cosmic whole to the preeminent being in a divinely created world, then from the preeminent being in God's creation to the preeminent being among all beings. A key commitment underlying this analysis is the belief that authentic dwelling is inseparable from a sense of piety toward nature. Hence even though medieval Christendom is founded on the idea of absolute devotion to something higher than humanity, it drives a wedge between human existence and the topos that for the Greeks was in an essential sense our home.

Löwith's critique of modernity is guided by the conviction that respect for the cosmos is necessary if we are to establish a sense of limits in the deployment of technological power. "Is there for us an authority that could impose limits on progress that in itself is boundless, or is there no end to *human beings making everything that they can make*?"[103] Given Christianity's fundamental evaluation of nature as nonspiritual and hence inferior in the order of things, Löwith deems a Christian or "angelic" ethos incapable of providing such limits. By assimilating human beings to God, Christianity opposes human beings to nature. Modern science and technology do not transform this relationship in any basic way, but they instead simply radicalize it so that nature is no longer viewed in Augustinian terms as reflections of the divine majesty. To the extent, then, that we are inclined to follow thinkers such as Löwith and Hans Jonas in seeking to think through the possibility of "overcoming" technology, recourse to the Christian conception of morality that informs Descartes's thought is ill conceived. If the task is to rethink our relationship to nature in a way that elevates nature rather than demeaning it, Christian tradition—leaving aside such possible exceptions as Saint Francis—is one of the last places we should look for inspiration. What is required for the kind of "overcoming" of technology that is at stake here is, as Heidegger recognized, the ability to say "yes and no" to technology—to acknowledge that technology is both a conceptual and practical legacy that cannot simply be erased from our understanding of things and a way of relating to things that ultimately does violence to them.[104] Löwith's turn to the Greek ideal of the cosmos is an attempt to do justice to the "no" to technology. He sees in Aristotle's subordination of the polis to the eternal cycles of the heavens, and in the Stoics' valorization of a certain sense of eternity, a guiding thread for establishing a sense of respect for nature.

3. BLUMENBERG'S CHALLENGE TO THE SECULARIZATION THESIS

The most important contemporary thinker to challenge Löwith's assessment of modernity is Hans Blumenberg, who argues in *Die Legitimität der Neuzeit* (1966) that the secularization thesis cannot be defended in principle. An important corollary of Blumenberg's position is that the conception of history as inevitable progress cannot adequately be understood as a secularization of biblical eschatology. Blumenberg's primary aim is to reject what his translator calls the "profoundly pessimistic" implications of Löwith's thesis, founded as they are on the interpretation of the history of the West as a *Verfallsgeschichte*, and to defend both the idea of progress and the "legitimacy" of the modern age against charges that modernity is somehow spiritually bankrupt.[105] Löwith and

Hans-Georg Gadamer published reviews of the first edition of *Die Legitimität der Neuzeit* in *Philosophische Rundschau* in 1968, and in response to Löwith's review, Blumenberg substantially revised his text and published it in three installments in the course of the 1970s.[106] Against Löwith, Blumenberg argues that the origin of the modern age is best understood not as a secularization or detachment from a transcendent ground for meaning but rather as a legitimate act of self-assertion in the face of despair over the loss of confidence in the cosmic order that occurred in the late Middle Ages. Blumenberg, like Löwith, sees Descartes as a pivotal figure in the advent of modernity. But where Löwith sees Descartes as a key transitional figure within a fundamentally Christian mode of thought, Blumenberg sees Descartes as one of the early pioneers of a distinctively modern conception of truth that dispenses with anthropocentric teleology and thereby effects a decisive break with the Christian Middle Ages. For all this, Blumenberg argues, Descartes's beginning is not absolutely new but instead consists in a response to a specific problem raised by theology in the late Middle Ages.

At bottom, Blumenberg's challenge to the secularization thesis is that it presupposes something that in principle cannot be demonstrated, namely, "the identity of a substance that endures throughout the process" of secularization. "Without such a substantial identity, no recoverable sense could be attached to the talk of conversion and transformation."[107] The secularization thesis maintains that "the worldly form of what was secularized is . . . a pseudomorph—in other words: an inauthentic manifestation—of its original reality."[108] To say that modernity is secularized is to say that there is an original substance that underlies historical transformations, that the process of secularization is one whereby certain fundamental elements become successively removed from that substance so as to transform it, and that the modern product of this process is a reduced, corrupted, or comparatively "inauthentic manifestation" of the substance whose specific loss or lack is the dimension of the sacred that was fundamental to the substance in its original form.

Blumenberg's critique turns on this notion of an underlying substance that has become obscured through a process of historical transformations in human understanding and awaits rediscovery by a renewed sense of human piety. Blumenberg follows a hint offered by Gadamer, who, in his review of *Die Legitimität der Neuzeit*, suggests—against Blumenberg—that the secularization thesis "performs a legitimate hermeneutic function" to the extent that "it brings to the self-understanding of what has been and what is present a whole dimension of hidden meaning, and thereby shows that the present is and signifies far more than it knows of itself."[109] To suppose that there is a dimension of hidden meaning obscured by our modern self-understanding is to suppose that secularization has not simply effected a loss but has buried or disguised the original substance so that the prospect of redemption would still loom on the horizon. Blumenberg challenges the secularization theorist to demonstrate such a dimension of hidden meaning. He believes that the impossibility of meeting this burden of proof fundamentally undermines the secularization theorist's endeavor to show that "the modern age as worldliness has to be explained as a superficial, foreground appearance."[110] Only against the background of some substantial "hidden meaning" obscured by a superficial self-understanding can the present age be thought to be deficient. Once we recognize that the entire idea of a dimension of hidden meaning is a human construction, Blumenberg believes that we will be liberated from misconceptions about nihilism and will be in a position to see the power of human willing to confer a sense of legitimacy on the human condition.

Blumenberg argues that "if eschatology or messianism were really the substantial point of departure of the modern historical consciousness, then that consciousness would be permanently and inescapably defined by teleological conceptions, by ideas of ends."[111] The fact that this condition fails to be met by modern consciousness is evidence, for Blumenberg, that the secularization thesis is untenable. The very idea of instrumental or technological rationality is intended to serve the end of human mastery of nature, but that rationality itself involves no teleological dimension. There is, in other words, no continuity of substance in the transition from the Middle Ages to modernity because the idea of a transcendent end has no place whatsoever in modern consciousness. For Blumenberg, these are sufficient grounds for concluding that technological consciousness is not the product of a secularization of the medieval conception of truthful discourse as a repeating after God but instead constitutes a clear departure from medieval consciousness.

In his review of the first edition of *Die Legitimität der Neuzeit*, Löwith not only rejects Blumenberg's demand for a demonstration of a continuity of substance but also observes that it contradicts the terms of Blumenberg's own analysis:

> This demand for a demonstration of a continuous substance, or even simply of constants in the course of a historical process, stands in a peculiar contrast with [Blumenberg's] rejection of a substantialistic ontology of history. The point of his critique, of course, is that history is not a "substance of tradition" and that the positing [*Feststellung*] of supposed constants implies a renunciation of knowledge. By rejecting a substantialistic tradition and the basic characteristics that go along with it, while at the same time making these into the conditions for a proof of secularization, [Blumenberg's] historical consciousness saddles his opponent with a burden of proof that he himself considers impossible to meet. For what can be demonstrated in the advance from religious to secular manifestations is [according to Blumenberg] not an identical substance, but rather a functional system of positions that can repeatedly be taken up, altered, and substantiated anew.[112]

Blumenberg's demand for a demonstration that an identical substance underlies these historical transformations is something like a demand for a demonstration of the "dimension of hidden meaning" that Gadamer sees as the hermeneutic motivation for the secularization thesis. It is comparable to the demand for an exhibition of *the* meaning in history, once one has acknowledged that meaning is not a substance but instead is the hidden subject of a process in which nothing more than temporally conditioned manifestations of that substance can be shown. This recognition of a contradiction in the demand for a demonstration of an identical substance brings with it a recognition of a basic contradiction in the second of Blumenberg's two questions about secularization, namely, the question of the "agent" of the process of secularization. This, too, mistakenly attributes a substantialistic ontology to the secularization thesis.[113]

Nevertheless, Blumenberg's own analysis suggests a way of conceptualizing the "agent," if not of the process of secularization, then of the process whereby modernity emerged from the Christian Middle Ages. That agent is humanity and its Promethean predilection for self-assertion. Blumenberg points to two early sources of what would become modern consciousness. The first of these is what Blumenberg refers to as "eschatological disappointment." At the time of Christ's crucifixion, it was thought that the promise of eternal salvation would be fulfilled within a foreseeable future, perhaps within "the actual life of the individual and of his generation."[114] But as generations went by and the promise failed to be fulfilled, the hope of salvation was frustrated and there emerged in its place a sense of "fear of judgment and the destruction of the world."[115] This condition made it necessary for the church to offer interim substitutes for salvation. The offer of these substitutes, against the background of a possibility that one would not be saved but instead would be damned on Judgment Day, had the effect of renewing interest in the world and of offering prospects for a self-assertion toward which Blumenberg sees the human will as always having been inclined.

Where Löwith proposes secularization "of" eschatology, Blumenberg proposes secularization "by" eschatology. Eschatology was initially a solution to the problem of suffering and human finitude. Blumenberg seems implicitly to accept Nietzsche's analysis of the Christian promise of eternal salvation as an answer to the question why we suffer. But the constant deferral of the promise of salvation deprived the promise of its appeal, and in response to this frustration, a new position arose and "reoccupied" the position formerly held by eschatology. Then the question was no longer why we suffer or how we can endure our earthly lot but instead how we can improve our earthly condition. The idea of progress thus took the place of the promise of salvation.[116]

But according to Blumenberg, this moment of reoccupation was not the origin of the notion of progress that dominates the consciousness of the Enlightenment. This aspect of Blumenberg's analysis has important implications for his understanding of Descartes's place in the advent of modernity. Blumenberg sees the origin of the idea of progress not in anything like a secularization of eschatology but instead in a key insight arrived at by ancient astronomers and subsequently developed into a formal doctrine.[117] In the second century BCE, Hipparchus was inspired to compile a catalog of the stars by the discovery of a new star in the constellation Scorpio. Such an appearance called into question the formerly presumed immutability of the heavens. Hipparchus recognized that it would take more than his own lifetime to complete an exhaustive investigation of this question, so he compiled his catalog and left it to future generations.[118] Similarly, Seneca took up the question whether comets are celestial or, as Aristotle maintained, merely atmospheric phenomena. Seneca recognized that, due to the possibility that comets obey periods exceeding an individual human lifetime, "an exact record of comet appearances over long periods of time would be needed to disprove their atmospheric nature."[119] Both Hipparchus and Seneca present findings "leading to the result that astronomical progress is necessarily conditioned by time."[120] Nonetheless, neither arrives at a formal doctrine of progress because the ancient conception of θεωρία remained oriented on the present: "The ancient ideal of theory rests on the conception of reality as the evidence of the moment; it has no dimension of time. It was not until a late date that men recognized how contradictory it is to exalt the exemplary object of that theory, the starry sky, and yet to presuppose time for the techniques of its exact representation."[121]

On Blumenberg's view, these observations about the history of astronomy show that the modern notion of progress has its essential source in something other than a process of secularization and hence that modernity can be shown to possess a certain "legitimacy." Where advocates of the secularization thesis see modernity "as the wrong turning for which the thesis itself is able to prescribe the corrective," Blumenberg argues that the claim of fallenness is incoherent and that modernity is fundamentally "legitimate."[122] The modern age is not simply a derivative of any prior epoch, though it does have an essential relationship with the late Middle Ages and thus in a specific sense is "conditioned" by medieval Christendom. The category of self-assertion is central to Blumenberg's analysis. Whereas the thinking of the Middle Ages led to a specific sense of resignation about the prospects for arriving at truth about the nature of things, modernity, as represented by such thinkers as Descartes, repudiates the pathos of resignation in favor of an affirmation of human rationality. Just as Christian thought constitutes a "reoccupation" of a position formerly occupied by Greek cosmology, modern technological rationality constitutes a "reoccupation" of a Christian view whose capacity to make life worth living had foundered.[123]

In his study of myth, Blumenberg identifies human "contingency in the world" as the fundamental problem confronted by humanity through its history. Our recognition of what Blumenberg calls "the absolutism of reality" is the source of "the deepest conflict that the subject that reflects on its absolute root can have with itself," namely, "the confirmation of its contingency in the world, of its lack of necessity."[124] This conflict takes the form of an acknowledgment of the irreducible gap between "the fact that a subject is a result of a physical process" and the sense of autonomy that the subject craves as a result of the experience of its capacity for abstraction from physical conditions. Myths function as symbolic gestures toward the overcoming of the absolutism of reality. In *The Birth of Tragedy*, Nietzsche proposes that the myth of the Olympian gods made it possible for the early Greeks to endure existence.[125] Blumenberg believes that myths are rhetorical or symbolic coping mechanisms that make it possible to live life. But because the absolutism of reality *is* absolute, it does not make sense on Blumenberg's account to speak of a "final" myth, for example, the presumption of the German Idealists to have conquered the absolutism of reality once and for all. "Myth has always already passed over into the process of reception."[126] Hence Blumenberg dismisses as a vain attempt to realize "an end to myth" Descartes's pretension to establish a definitive morality on the basis of "the guarantee for the accessibility of the world for theory."[127]

Blumenberg attempts to show both the relationship of modernity to the Middle Ages and its clear departure from them by comparing the answers of William of Ockham and Descartes to the problem of "theological absolutism." In contrast to the Greek myth of the demiurge, according to which the demiurge is simply the mechanism whereby eternal form is projected onto the world, the nominalists view the order of things as the arbitrary choice of an inscrutable God. That God's will is absolute and unconstrained by the sorts of rational requirements that make Aquinas's God comprehensible at least in principle means that there is an insuperable gap between God's creative act and any order that human beings may attribute to things. "The gratuitousness of the Creation implies that it can no longer be expected to exhibit any adaptation to the needs of reason. Rather than helping man to reconstruct the order *given* in nature, the principle of economy (Ockham's razor) helps him to reduce nature forcibly to an order *imputed* to it by man."[128] The attribution of absolute freedom to God "implies that there is no limit to what is possible, and this renders meaningless the interpretation of the individual as the repetition of a universal.

Creation is now supposed to mean that every entity comes into existence from nothing," the consequence being that it can no longer be assumed that nature "could become comprehensible for the benefit of man and his reason. Divine spirit and human spirit, creative and cognitive principles, operate as though without taking each other into account."[129]

Henceforth nature could no longer be assumed to be dependable, because it could no longer be assumed to be comprehensible.[130] With the intensification of eschatological disappointment came the sense of an irreducible gap between the world as lived and Christianity's initial promise of redemption. This sense of worldly detachment from God had, in the late Middle Ages, the effect of "endangering and finally destroying the substance of the biblical idea of God, the idea of a God for Whom interest in man and the capacity to be affected by human events and actions had been constitutive."[131] The idea of theological absolutism thus engendered the notion that human beings are not the highest end of creation but instead are merely incidental to God's purposes:

> The incidentalness of man in God's dealings with and for Himself eliminated everything that supported the idea that God's creation of man committed Him, in regard to His Incarnation, to the choice of human nature as the medium of His appearance in the world. On the contrary, this problem was covered by the standard formula of voluntarism, that He could have adopted any other nature and that He adopted this one only because it suited His pure will. This point exhibits most clearly nominalism's difference from the reassuring function of the Epicurean theology, in which the gods, as beings with human form, lead their blissful lives outside the worlds and represent this life to man as his highest possibility in the realization of philosophical wisdom.[132]

The nominalists believe that the hidden God provides certainty only with regard to salvation, not with regard to anything having to do with earthly existence. For Ockham this means that "God owes nothing and cannot owe anything to any being, and neither can He do any wrong. The teleological interpretation of the human striving for knowledge does not support any claim that it should be fulfilled, or even that it should not be deceived."[133] Aquinas, by assuming a "pregiven arrangement between man and the world" in the form of an accessible teleological structure in the order of creation, "kept the problem of knowledge latent," whereas Ockham brings the problem into clear focus and is thereby brought to the point of having to recognize the fundamental threat to the situation of human beings in the world posed by theological absolutism.

The insights of nominalism lead to resignation. Unable to establish the sense of freedom from the world that Epicurus had achieved, nominalists were beset with a sense of the burdensome character of human existence in a world neither made for human beings nor understandable by them according to the Scholastic formula of correspondence with the creative intellect of God. This leads the nominalists to the "extreme of human self-abnegation."[134] Descartes's thought is motivated by the same recognition of divine omnipotence, but he responds in a unique way that Blumenberg identifies as definitive of the modern age. Where nominalism responds to "the provocation of the *transcendent* absolute" in a manner that reproduces the *contemptus mundi* of Gnosticism and Augustinianism, in Descartes this provocation reaches "the point of its most extreme radicalization," where it gives rise to "the uncovering of the immanent absolute."[135] Here God is "no longer the highest and the necessary, nor even the possible point of reference of the human will. On the contrary, He left to man only the alternative of his natural and rational self-assertion."[136] Descartes adopts a "rational deism," from which he deduces "the dependability of the world and our knowledge of it."[137] Henceforth, in place of the self-abnegation of the late Middle Ages, "the idea of method . . . [makes] theoretical domination of nature the condition of the historical 'marcher avec assurance dans cette vie' [to walk with assurance in this life]."[138]

Blumenberg presents a view of the epochal shift to modernity in terms of a strict either-or, with Descartes deciding unequivocally in favor of rational self-assertion. This either-or constitutes an inversion of the Christian conception of the relationship between salvation and history. Where "the original core of Christian teaching . . . makes an absolute lack of interest in the conceptualization and explanation of history a characteristic of the acute situation of its end," modernity opens the possibility of making history into an object of real human concern, precisely because history is no longer seen in the reflected light of the promise of salvation.[139] Descartes paves the way for an interest in history as such by legitimating the idea of investigating nature and, by extension, mastering it.[140]

Blumenberg bases his claim regarding the nature of Cartesian freedom on an interpretation of the First Meditation. That Meditation exhibits an "artificial order of the stages of doubt" that culminates in an artificial device: the deceiving demon hypothesis.[141] The artificiality of this device consists in the fact that the *genius malignus* does not really represent conditions of deception about the nature of things at all. It is not a response to the challenge of skepticism, renewed by Montaigne, but instead it represents the problem posed for human freedom by theological absolutism: "By transforming the theological absolutism of omnipotence into the philosophical hypothesis of the deceptive world spirit, Descartes denies the historical situation to which his initial undertaking is bound and turns it into the methodical freedom of arbitrarily chosen conditions."[142] Where Ockham capitulates in the face of the prospect that an omnipotent God made things entirely differently from the way they appear to us in our finite experience, Descartes seeks a means for representing or modeling the world in a manner sufficient to meet the demands of human self-securing. In this way, "the exigency of self-assertion became the sovereignty of self-foundation":

From the nominalists' hidden God . . . Descartes derives the hypothesis of the *deus fallax* [deceiver God], the *deceptor poten-*

tissimus [most powerful deceiver], Who in pursuit of his intention-
ally universal deception can not only intervene on the side of the
objects but can also have given man himself a nature that even in
regard to what it is most clearly given is capable only of error.[143]

Precisely where Descartes makes a distinction in principle between
the evil genius and a veracious God, Blumenberg proposes that the
two are identical.

This is a peculiar identification. It demands a renunciation of
the Augustinian-Thomistic confidence in our ability to participate
in God's truth. Its emphasis is on the practicistic thread of
Descartes's thinking, but it is focused exclusively on that thread
and not at all on the depth of Descartes's fidelity to the model of
truth articulated by Patristic and Scholastic thought. Moreover,
Descartes's entire approach to the problem of truth and error in the
Fourth Meditation makes futile any attempt to identify God as a
source of deception. As Blumenberg himself sometimes acknowledges, "Descartes . . . sought the guarantee for the accessibility of
the world for theory" not in the internal coherence of clear and distinct perceptions but instead in a veracious God.[144] This suggests
that Descartes's conception of reason is not that of a "zero point" of
absolute subjectivity, as Blumenberg alleges.[145] Instead, it is a point
of removal from worldly experience whose horizon or measure is
the infinite God first appealed to in the Third Meditation. Otherwise
the entire endeavor to secure scientific truth, which is the explicit
motivation of the *Meditations*, would be undermined. Perhaps most
significant in this connection is Descartes's suggestion in the
Second Replies that, even though one can conceive that "the perception whose truth we are so firmly convinced of may appear false
to God or an angel, so that it is, absolutely speaking, false," such a
possibility is simply not to be taken seriously because "the evident
clarity of our perceptions does not allow us to listen to anyone who
makes up this kind of story."[146] Descartes is not satisfied with the
prospect of mere coherence among his clear and distinct percep-

tions. What he demands is "an absolute conception of reality," to whatever extent that can be attained by a finite intelligence.[147]

Blumenberg proposes that Descartes's abandonment of truth as an ideal follows directly from abandonment of the Scholastic idea, inherited from Stoicism, that the world was created for human beings. This dual abandonment explains the shift from the ancient ideal of theoretical contemplation to the modern ideal of using theory to achieve practical ends. The "disassociation of theoretical efficacy from the idea of truth" is "a correlate of the declining anthropocentric consciousness."[148] Copernicus believes that truth is accessible to human beings precisely because the machinery of the world was constructed by God for our benefit.[149] To this extent, Copernicus is not yet a "modern" thinker because he remains resistant to the theoretical implications of theological absolutism. The recognition of divine omnipotence or "the omnipotence proviso" amounts to the recognition that "God can also produce a phenomenon in nature in a different way than is made to appear plausible by a particular explanation." This proviso "throws man back, as far as he is concerned with theoretical truth, to a hopeless position. For him the world would continue to have an unperspicuous structure, whose laws had to remain unknown to him and for which any theoretical exertion would stand under the threat of the revocation of the general condition of its possibility."[150] The omnipotence proviso would appear, then, to frustrate the pursuit of truth. Yet Copernicus, and Galileo after him, resists this implication of divine omnipotence. Descartes responds differently to the omnipotence proviso because he is interested in the practical application of theory precisely where Copernicus and Galileo are not.[151]

In casting Descartes in these terms, Blumenberg proposes that Descartes's position is in accord with Osiander's "epoch-making break with the Middle Ages" rather than with Copernicus's faith in an "accessible truth about the world."[152] Osiander, a Lutheran theologian and preacher, wrote to Copernicus on April 20, 1541, "urging Copernicus to present his astronomical system, not as a true picture of the universe, but rather as a device, true or false, for saving the phenomena."[153] Osiander writes that "I have always felt about hypotheses that they are not articles of faith but the basis of computation; so that even if they are false it does not matter, provided that they reproduce exactly the phenomena of the motions."[154] On the same day, he expands on this idea in a letter to Rheticus, stating that

> there can be different hypotheses for the same apparent motion; that the present hypotheses are brought forward, not because they are in reality true, but because they regulate the computation of the apparent and combined motion as conveniently as may be; that it is possible for someone else to devise different hypotheses; that one man may conceive a suitable system, and another a more suitable, while both systems produce the same phenomena of motion; that each and every man is at liberty to devise more convenient hypotheses; and that if he succeeds, he is to be congratulated. In this way they will be diverted from stern defense and attracted by the charm of inquiry.[155]

Osiander was entrusted to manage the printing of the first edition of Copernicus's *De revolutionibus* in 1543. In the preface, titled "To the Reader Concerning the Hypotheses of this Work," Osiander states that a scientist must remain content with mere hypotheses "since he cannot in any way attain to the true causes."[156]

Blumenberg sees in Descartes's treatment of three world systems an acceptance of the kind of reasoning offered by Osiander. In the *Principles of Philosophy*, Descartes compares the world systems of Ptolemy, Copernicus, and Tycho. But he holds back from any definitive claim as to which of these systems captures the truth because "it is impossible for us to know, simply on the basis of the observed motions, what proper motions should be attributed to any given body."[157] What is needed is a hypothesis that can explain the appearances. Since, as Osiander points out, the "true causes" are inaccessible to us, we must rest satisfied with conjectures that enable us to make sense of the genesis of observed phenomena. This is how Descartes proposes to explain the present world in the *Principles*. He assumes the conservation of "the same quantity of motion in matter" and supposes that the present condition of the world can be accounted for by assuming that all motion is subject to a set of "constant and immutable" laws of nature created by God.[158] Descartes considers the Copernican system to be superior to the two alternatives. But in treating that system as a mere hypothesis, Blumenberg suggests, Descartes is implicitly accepting the proposition that simplicity and clarity cannot be taken as measures of truth. Descartes's refusal to assert the truth of the Copernican view is motivated not by "the author's fearfulness and masked anxiety under the influence of the Galileo affair" but instead by "the rejection of anthropocentrism," which "prevents the human power of imagination from serving as a criterion of the real circumstances in the world."[159]

This is not the only way to understand Descartes's treatment of the Copernican worldview as a hypothesis. There is a clear alternative explanation of Descartes's position that requires no recourse to Blumenberg's "omnipotence proviso." In spite of his insight into the autonomous character of human rationality, Descartes maintains fidelity to a conception of truth *sub specie aeternitatis*. Like Copernicus and Galileo, Descartes is unwilling to abandon the commitment to truth. But he is the beneficiary of insights into the limitations imposed on the pursuit of truth by the perspective character of human finitude. Descartes makes clear reference to the tradition of thinking about this problem in his explanation of the need to hold back from definitive truth claims about scientific hypotheses: "When a sailor on the high seas in calm weather looks out from his own ship and sees other ships a long way off changing their mutual positions, he can often be in doubt whether the motion responsible for this change of position should be attributed to this or that ship, or even to his own." Our judgments about the motions of the planets are subject to the same sort of limitation.[160] Descartes borrows this seafaring metaphor from Nicholas of Cusa, who employs it in *De docta ignorantia* (*On Learned Ignorance*, 1440):

> It is already clear to us that the earth, in truth, is moved, yet it may not appear this way to us, since we detect motion only by a comparison to a fixed point. How would a passenger know that one's ship was being moved, if one did not know that the water was flowing past and if the shores were not visible from the ship in the middle of the water? Since it always appears to every observer, whether on the earth, the sun, or another star, that one is, as if, at an immovable center of things and that all else is being moved, one will always select different poles in relation to oneself, whether one is on the sun, the earth, the moon, Mars, and so forth.[161]

For Cusanus, this recognition of the distorting power of perspective demands not a renunciation of truth but instead only the recognition that truth is a regulative ideal toward which our descriptions can tend but can never attain. Cusanus sees the human quest for truth in terms of a relationship between the finite and the infinite. "Because the infinite escapes all proportion, the infinite as infinite is unknown"; "there can be no proportion between the infinite and the finite."[162] The consequence of this incongruence between a finite intelligence and the infinite truth that is God is that "the intellect, which is not truth, never comprehends truth so precisely but that it could always be comprehended with infinitely more precision."[163]

When Descartes takes up this reasoning, he accepts the premium placed by Cusanus on mathematical symbols in the endeavor to find truth. Where Cusanus proposes that "since our only approach to divine things is through symbols, we can appropriately use mathematical signs because of their incorruptible certitude," Descartes, because of his interest in practical application and the improvement of our earthly estate, seeks to model his conception of clear and distinct perception on the "incorruptible certitude" of mathematics, with the specific hope of finding truth not about the divine but ultimately about physical processes and the ways in which those processes can be controlled in the service of human welfare.[164] Descartes sees that the problems that Cusanus recognizes in connection with the endeavor to know God apply, mutatis mutandis, to the endeavor to know the material world. The need to couch scientific claims in hypothetical terms follows not from the abandonment of final causes in the study of nature—in Blumenberg's terminology, from the abandonment of "anthropocentric teleology"—but instead from a reflection on the limitations of human perspective. It is likewise motivated by Descartes's implicit recognition that the scope of clear and distinct ideas is ultimately extremely limited.

Thus Descartes is not at odds with Copernicus on the question of truth, at least not in the sense in which Blumenberg suggests that he is:

> The question of the laws of a "world as such" is already in the background here [viz. in Part Three of the *Principles*] as the autonomous theme of a reason that by that theme defines itself, for the first time, in an original manner, and that no longer seems to have need of any anthropocentric teleology. This nonneediness is the real difference between the modern age's rationality and Copernicus, a difference that makes his claim to truth, and what that claim presupposed, obsolete, and excludes it, as a transitional episode, from being part of the epoch.[165]

Descartes's departure from Copernicus lies in his embrace of the ideal of practice. He is a "technological" thinker precisely where Copernicus concerns himself exclusively with truth. In this respect, Copernicus adheres to the ancient ideal of theory as contemplation. Descartes's repudiation of teleology in nature reflects a recognition of the limits of human understanding and the hubris involved in supposing that we can know that God made the universe specifically for human beings; "for we should not be so arrogant as to suppose that we can share in God's plans."[166] His treatment of Copernicanism as a mere hypothesis follows from his recognition, inspired by Cusanus, that our interpretations of nature always remain to be improved upon. The pragmatic measure for improvement is the extent to which a given interpretation facilitates the reproduction of observed effects, but the absolute or ideal measure is the extent to which a given interpretation comes closer than previous ones to conformity with the truth that is accessible only to God. The logic of Descartes's position is entirely compatible with the supposition that God is wholly veracious and yet not fully comprehensible to us.

Blumenberg's interpretation of Descartes's definitive and provisional moralities follows directly from his claim about Cartesian self-assertion. Truth no longer plays a role in the project of human existence. The goal of life is no longer to live up to any divinely appointed mission, nor to achieve participation in God's view of things, but simply to augment our material security. This reduces the notion of morality in Descartes's thought to an endeavor "dependent on the given reality."[167] What Descartes calls the definitive morality concerns nothing more than "the adaptation of human behavior to the reality of nature that is mastered by theory."[168]

> Here there arises a sort of intrascientific morality, a rigorism of systematic logic, to which the unbridled appetite for knowledge is bound to be suspect. . . . Descartes gave human knowledge the teleological character of a strenuous exertion, united by the Method, toward the attainment of the definitive morality, which as the epitome of materially appropriate behavior in the world presupposes the perfection of factual knowledge.[169]

In contrast with the old idea of morality concerned with the determination of proper ends for human conduct, Descartes's exclusive devotion to the project of human self-assertion leads him to take for granted a conception of ends understood in terms of human happiness.[170] To this extent, Blumenberg suggests, the definitive morality "may no longer be aptly described as 'morality.'"[171]

The terms of Blumenberg's characterization of Descartes's provisional morality follow the terms of his interpretation of the definitive morality. The aspiration to theoretical knowledge is so absolute for Descartes that he leaves no room whatsoever for reflection, correction, or discussion in the enactment of the provisional morality. One simply submits to the force of prevailing authority and exercises no judgment in the face of it, until such time when the definitive certainties have been acquired. To this extent, the provisional morality involves the

> illusion . . . that the intervening period could be a static phase of holding fast to what had always been obligatory. Descartes took no cognizance of the retroactive effect of the process of theory on the supposed interim of the provisional ethics. . . . The fact that Descartes wanted to stage the preliminary situation as a standstill meant that he was not compelled to think through the anthropological implications of this state.[172]

In accordance with his conception of the human condition as an insurmountable confrontation with contingency, Blumenberg sees human beings as subject to "an immanent deficiency" and hence as incapable in principle of anything like a final, absolutely certain morality.[173] This places human beings in the position of needing rhetoric, which Blumenberg describes as "the effort to produce the accords that have to take the place of the 'substantial' base of regulatory processes in order to make action possible. From this point of view, language is a set of instruments . . . for the production of mutual understanding, agreement, or toleration on which the actor depends."[174] The "illusion" on which Descartes's provisional morality is founded is the supposition, in effect, that rhetoric need play no role whatsoever in the decisions that we make prior to the completion of theory. In reality, Blumenberg believes, "everything that remains, this side of definitive evidence, is rhetoric; rhetoric is the vehicle of the *morale par provision*."[175] Blumenberg assumes, not without some justification, that everyone today knows that the sort of definitive theoretical grounding for conduct sought by Descartes is impossible, due to the nature of our encounter with "the absolutism of reality." What takes the place of the naïve aspiration to a definitive morality is a process of discursive consensus, in which "theory" functions as a progressively self-correcting process with no ultimate end point. This conception of theory is what Blumenberg has in mind when he appeals to the notion of "sufficient rationality" as the basis for the legitimacy of the modern age. Such rationality "is just enough to accomplish the postmedieval self-assertion and to bear the consequences of this emergency self-consolidation."[176] By the standards of this contemporary communicative action model, Descartes's assumption "that the intervening period could be a static phase of holding fast to what had always been obligatory" exhibits no sensitivity to the irreducible role played by rhetoric, that is, by the sort of discursive negotiations between human subjects that can serve as the basis for norms in the absence of definitive knowledge.

What speaks most strongly against Blumenberg's interpretation of the definitive and provisional moralities is that the two share certain key features, in particular the role played by resoluteness and the distinction in principle between actions guided by knowledge and those not so guided. The maxim that requires us to follow the examples set by the wisest and most moderate members of the community implicitly invokes this distinction between wisdom and ignorance, even if prior to the establishment of the definitive morality we cannot be secure in our judgments in this connection. Most significantly, the appeal to religion in the first maxim of the provisional morality so anticipates the way in which theory (cognition) needs recourse to Christian ideals in the development of a full moral ethos, that Christianity seems to function from the start as the surplus of meaning that will motivate and guide the implementation of theory and the program for the mastery of nature.

For all that, Blumenberg's critique of the provisional morality does effectively seize upon a problem that has gained urgency since

Descartes's time, namely, that of blind submission to authority. Devotion to one's religion and the laws of one's country has the character of blind submission to the extent that it does not admit of examination and correction through such activities as discursive consensus making. The deepest problem with a moral code such as the *morale par provision*, from the standpoint of our contemporary sensibilities, is that authorities such as the pope tend to exclude or at least to minimize dissent rather than promoting an open exchange of ideas. This is what leads Jaspers to criticize Descartes for failing to impose upon reason the obligation "to apprehend the positive sources of authority." Descartes would have responded that the special affinity between his philosophy and Christianity should be taken as an indication of the priority of Christianity among religious sources of authority, and the ideal of a Christian king that he articulates in his writings is the earthly correlate of a Christian metaphysics and morality. The provisional morality must function in the absence of any definitive conclusions as to what counts as a "positive" source of authority, and this is why the provisional morality calls for allegiance to the given individual's religious tradition rather than to Christianity in particular. At the same time, Descartes's writings contain clear indications of a hope that all individuals will eventually recognize Christianity as the preeminent religion, even if the complete edifice of reason by itself will never be able to secure this recognition. Blumenberg sees "rhetoric" or discursive consensus as the only positive source of authority available today. In the face of Descartes's invocation of Christianity, Blumenberg would say that any appeal to religion, be it "provisional" or "definitive," is an appeal to the tyranny of an authority that no longer has any proper place in European consciousness. He would class such an appeal to religion together with Löwith's call for a return to ancient faith in the cosmos, namely, as a futile, perhaps romantic gesture toward the prospect of a wholeness that is unavailable to us in principle.

4. DESCARTES, SECULARIZATION, AND THE PROBLEM OF NIHILISM

The debate between Löwith and Blumenberg about the legitimacy of the modern age is a debate concerning the sufficiency of reason to guide moral reflection. Is reason alone sufficient, as Blumenberg claims, to adduce ends for conduct? Or is some form of faith in the cosmos, as Nietzsche and Löwith propose, the source of ends and thus the necessary ground of practical reason? Blumenberg, Nietzsche, Heidegger, and Löwith all see Descartes as the first secular rationalist in the West, and as a result they fail to see a third possibility, embraced by Descartes: the dependence of reason on faith in a transcendent God as the source of meaning and ends in life. By misinterpreting Descartes in this way, each of these thinkers contributes to the mistaken conventional wisdom about Descartes, namely, that he sought to defy transcendent authorities through the turn to reason and autonomous self-assertion. As a result, they fail to see that Descartes's thought contains clues to the resolution of contemporary disputes about secularization, nihilism, and the legitimacy of the modern age.

Blumenberg treats the prospect of wholeness as an unfulfillable dream, as the general form of a "final myth" to which we aspire due to our "eschatological melancholy."[177] He sees Descartes's program for a definitive morality as the expression of a desire for wholeness that can never be satisfied. Descartes, however, is motivated not by eschatological melancholy but rather by a sense of divine appointment derived from Genesis by way of such ecclesiastical figures as Hugh of Saint Victor. The lineage of Descartes's ideal of mastery shows that he is not guided by a commitment to earthly happiness adduced *par prétérition*. His philosophical project is not a defiant gesture against a fugitive God, although it is a rejection of Ockham's resignation in the face of God's incomprehensibility. Unlike Ockham, who believes that divine omnipotence entails a radical gulf between divine truth and the most perspicuous human insights, Descartes adheres to the principle of divine veracity even though it seems incompatible with divine omnipotence. God's immutability and veracity guarantee that laws of nature are both permanent and knowable by human minds.[178] Our prospects for mastering nature presuppose knowledge of these laws, and thus mastery depends on divine veracity. Similarly, Descartes believes that the prospects for a definitive morality depend on a God who is not only immutable and veracious but also inherently good. The distinction between the provisional and definitive moralities depends crucially on the inherent goodness of a transcendent God, since in the absence of such an absolute measure our moral reflections can never move beyond the relativistic terms of discursive consensus-making.

Descartes would not rest satisfied with the rhetorical model of discursive consensus-making offered by Blumenberg, because that model presupposes the inaccessibility in principle of transcendent authorities. Descartes is committed to a conception of truth and goodness *sub specie aeternitatis*, that is, truth and goodness have their source and their measure in the creative intellect of God. The terms of Descartes's conception of reason show why a morality based entirely in reason cannot overcome its status as provisional: reason produces only logical insights, not ends for conduct. Unless reason acknowledges the authority of some extrarational source of meaning, such as Christian faith in Descartes's case, reason can always challenge the putative authority of extrarational sources of meaning such as Christianity. And it must challenge every current discursive consensus, since these are merely provisional and remain to be revised.[179]

The respective claims of faith and reason stand in an uneasy tension in Descartes's thought. Sensitive to the need for what Jaspers calls the "positive sources of authority," Descartes maintains fidelity to a medieval Christian worldview in which the foundational insights of morality are ultimately irreducible to rational insight. Descartes recognizes the dependence of reason on faith in moral reflection, and to this extent his conceptions of reason and the will are not fully secularized. The will finds its measure not in its own arbitrary determinations, nor in instrumental considerations about material welfare, but rather in determinations of truth and goodness that have their measure in the divine intellect. Blumenberg's image of Descartes as an iconoclast in the style of Lucifer or Faust erroneously projects onto Descartes the fully secularized sensibilities of late capitalist technophilia or of anyone who celebrates the death of God proclaimed by Nietzsche's madman. This is to miss the fundamental piety at the core of Descartes's philosophical ethos.

One of the most important lessons that we can learn from Descartes is that reason alone is insufficient to ground an abiding sense of meaning, ends, or propriety in life. The supposition that autonomous reason *can* determine ends for conduct, evident in Kant's thought, is the product of a process of secularization in which human reason and will are conceived in terms that change over time. In the medieval world, reason and will are understood to be subordinate to the divine intellect, whereas in the modern world, they are understood to be self-grounding and self-sufficient. On the modern view, reason and will are secularized versions of divine legislation. As such, they are susceptible to the same charge of arbitrariness that has been lodged against Descartes's conception of God: if God's choices are not guided by an absolute notion of the good that stands higher than his will, but instead are good simply in the sense that God chooses them, then divine choice appears to be completely arbitrary. There is no absolute reason why the commandments are good, for example; they are "good" only in the sense that God happens to have chosen them, and if God had legislated other commandments instead, then those other commandments would be "good." This conclusion follows from Descartes's doctrine of God's free creation of the eternal truths, according to which God's omnipotence entails that he was not constrained to choose the eternal truths but instead chose them freely.[180] Descartes rejects the classical neo-Platonic position, according to which the essences of created things are "attenuations of the essence of the divine understanding—with the consequence that God, in contemplating them, does nothing but contemplate Himself."[181] Descartes instead maintains that divine omnipotence entails that nothing is impossible for God, even if some things appear to human reason to be impossible. God's choice of the eternal truths was absolutely free.[182]

Descartes's doctrine of the free creation of the eternal truths, and his acknowledgement that some things can appear to human beings to be impossible for God even though they are really possible (such as that the sum of one and two could be something other than three) entails the possibility that the true order of being is different than the way it appears to human minds to be. Blumenberg seizes upon this possibility as the basis for his claim that Descartes makes a defiant gesture against God, where Ockham retreats from the world in resignation. From a purely logical standpoint, Blumenberg's claim is unassailable—if nothing is impossible for God, then God can make things in a way completely different from the way they appear to human beings. What we *take* to be true may be completely different than the way things are in the divine intellect. But Descartes staunchly resists the implication that divine omnipotence undermines divine veracity. His attempt to derive laws of nature from God's immutable nature is one sign of this resistance; another is the analysis of truth and error in the Fourth Meditation, particularly when that analysis is interpreted in the light of its Augustinian background. That Descartes is unwilling to accept the logical implications of his doctrine of the free creation of the eternal truths is an indication of the tension or instability in Descartes's thought of which I speak throughout this book. Precisely where autonomous reason threatens to undermine belief in a veracious God, Descartes insists on a view of God and truth that requires recourse to a source of meaning outside of reason. If Blumenberg's claim about a defiant gesture against God has any legitimacy, then we must recognize that his claim holds not for Descartes but for subsequent thinkers for whom God is dead (or irrelevant) and for whom reason holds the promise of sufficiency.

Nietzsche, Heidegger, and Löwith express a concern about the moral status of modernity and despair over the prospects for reason to ground reflection on values. Each sees our age as nihilistic in the sense that we have lost faith in absolute values, and each calls for recourse to a source of meaning that transcends reason. The dispute between Blumenberg and these thinkers hinges on the question whether reason can be sufficient as a guide for the will. Heidegger and Löwith invoke the secularization thesis to account for the loss of meaning or ethical moorings that they consider to be characteristic of nihilism and a product of a historical process of secularization. The terms of the secularization thesis, especially as these are articulated by Löwith, place emphasis on the category of the sacred as the extrarational source of meaning from which we can derive a sense of proper place that reason is incapable of providing. Where thinkers like Heidegger and Nietzsche focus on the loss of transcendent values in the process of secularization, Löwith situates this moment in the process against the background of a prior, more fundamental loss of faith in an immanent cosmos. I call this aspect of Löwith's position the "weak" secularization thesis to distinguish it from his more complex claim about the modern philosophy of history, a "strong" secularization thesis that combines the weak secularization thesis with a supplementary one about the derivation of the philosophy of history from eschatology. At issue in the interpretation of Descartes is the weak secularization thesis.

The weak secularization thesis enables us to understand the sense in which such thinkers as Löwith and Heidegger consider our age to be nihilistic. These thinkers do not share Blumenberg's optimism about the power of reason but instead see a fundamental deficiency or groundlessness at the root of modernity. They trace this deficiency to the rise of modern subjectivity, with its claim to autonomous self-sufficiency and its refusal to acknowledge any authorities that transcend human reason and will. In this respect, Löwith and Heidegger share unexpected affinities with Descartes. Descartes paves the way for Enlightenment conceptions of the sheer autonomy of the human will, but he himself never means to embrace such a conception. The shift from medieval piety to modern self-assertion is not a discontinuous leap, and it is not one that Descartes makes. Instead Descartes must be understood as a "twilight" figure, a thinker torn between a commitment to a veracious if omnipotent and incomprehensible God on the one hand and a commitment to the autonomy of human reason on the other. The problem that Descartes encounters is that by developing his conception of autonomous reason so effectively, he brings rational reflection into conflict with the one positive source of authority that he never intended to undermine—Christianity.

Löwith shares Blumenberg's misgivings about dualism, and thus, like Blumenberg, he does not believe that a tradition such as Christianity has the power to ground moral reflection. But where Blumenberg advocates sufficient rationality, Löwith advocates a turn to faith conceived in nondualistic terms. He stresses the need to inscribe human life within the life of nature and to find meaning in the eternal cycles of the cosmos. His vision is based on the conviction that the death of God, as the death of faith in transcendent measures, is irreversible. Our task is one not of devising or discovering "new" transcendent measures, nor of reestablishing a connection to the transcendent that has been buried over in the course of time, but rather of finding a vocabulary that leaves behind the Kantian distinction between immanent and transcendent altogether in the effort to conceptualize a nonanthropocentric ethic of integration into nature.

On Löwith's view, such a vocabulary holds the promise of articulating for our time an ethos that has some basic affinities with the ethos that speaks through Descartes's writings. It characterizes human beings as a subordinate part of a larger whole in which we are assigned a proper place, which is to say that we are assigned a sense of limits. Such a vocabulary, in other words, promises to realize Heidegger's ideal of ethics as "dwelling."[183] Moreover, it makes a place for both faith and reason, that is, for piety and critique. With his ideal of a cosmo-politics, Löwith demands first a rethinking of *nature* and then a reflection on our place in nature. Löwith bases his ideal on the conviction that modernity is nihilistic, that dualism is fundamentally misguided, and that an ethics for the present age must include a basic moment of resignation in the face of the inalterable conditions of suffering and decay in the world.

Advocates of sufficient rationality see Löwith's ideal as a self-contradictory flight of fancy or as the expression of a failure of will that would rather retreat into quietism than take decisive action.[184] Stanley Rosen argues that the root cause of nihilism is a discontinuity between "rational speech" and human will or desire, and any approach to the problem of meaning that counsels resignation or "silence" in the face of the world is irretrievably nihilistic. Appeals to extrarational authority, whether they be to the authority of a religious tradition such as Christianity or to a naturalism that expresses faith in the cosmos, are, from the standpoint of rational scrutiny, arbitrary and indefensible. Rosen argues that the only possible solution to the problem of nihilism is to preserve or reestablish continuity between rational speech and willing, such that reason is acknowledged to be the sole positive authority over the will. This acknowledgment, for Rosen, entails a basic *dis*continuity between human beings and nature.[185]

Hans Jonas, in contrast, attempts to steer a middle course between the "Scylla" of monistic naturalism and the "Charybdis" of rationalist self-assertion. Jonas accepts the proposition that modernity is nihilistic, and he agrees with Löwith that ethics must be grounded in a philosophy of nature. But he intimates that the complete abandonment of dualism would be a fateful mistake:

> The disruption between man and total reality is at the bottom of nihilism. The illogicality of the rupture, that is, of a dualism without metaphysics, makes its fact no less real, nor its seeming alternative any more acceptable: the stare at isolated selfhood, to which it condemns man, may wish to exchange itself for a

monistic naturalism which, along with the rupture, would abolish also the idea of man as man. Between that Scylla and this her twin Charybdis, the modern mind hovers. Whether a third road is open to it—one by which the dualistic rift can be avoided and yet enough of the dualistic insight saved to uphold the humanity of man—philosophy must find out.[186]

The "dualism without metaphysics" of which Jonas speaks is the secularized dualism of modern consciousness. Untethered from devotion to God, modern consciousness lacks the basis for making determinations about ends in life—we are "rolling from the center toward X." On Jonas's view, what is needed is a metaphysics for the modern mind. But Jonas, like Löwith, resists a return to traditional metaphysical dualism and instead proposes a metaphysics for the technological age that can accommodate the power of reason within the larger framework of a philosophy of nature.

These controversies surrounding modernity—whether our age is nihilistic, whether dualism is the problem or the solution, and whether reason is ultimately "sufficient" to the task of ethical reflection—converge on what Jaspers characterizes as the "enormous task" of contemporary philosophy: rather than seeking to "live by pure reason, in the naïve conviction that everything will come out alright," we "must strive, through reason, to apprehend the positive sources of authority."[187] Descartes's reflection on the nature and limits of reason shows why the fulfillment of this task is very difficult to envision. Instrumental rationality and the restricted sense of wisdom at work in modern technology are ill equipped to provide an authoritative sense of meaning. Yet at the same time, Descartes's reflections also suggest that reason cannot demonstrate the authority of an extrarational source of meaning such as Christianity. As much as Descartes is committed to the authority of Christian doctrine, he recognizes the limits of reason and thus denies theology the status of a science. The problem with which Descartes leaves us is how to conceive of "the positive sources of authority" so that they are amenable to rational scrutiny without being mere postulates or subsidiaries of reason.

Is nihilism the defining predicament of modernity, or is it simply the price we pay for a failure of rational will? Does dualism inevitably jeopardize the dignity of nature by denuding nature of inherent value, or is dualism potentially compatible with a sense of reverence toward nature? Is practical reason fully autonomous, or is it inherently dependent on a higher, extrarational source of meaning and value? The vehement disagreements that prevail today regarding each of these questions are signs of a fundamental ambivalence in our culture about the nature and limits of reason. That our ambivalence bears traces of Descartes's own should not be surprising. We are struggling with the same fundamental problems that Descartes confronted. We are still, if only against our own intention, Cartesians.

The philosophy of a thinker who demonstrated no respect for nature and no sense of the historical character of consciousness would seem to be the last place to look for guidance in the endeavor to understand our contemporary situation. But Descartes knew that dwelling is irreducible to rational speech, and he knew that ends are not simply derived *par prétérition*. He had a sense of the rootedness of human existence in infinity, and in this regard we still have much to learn from him.

NOTES

1. Friedrich Nietzsche, *Götzen-Dämmerung*, in *Kritische Studienausgabe*, ed. Giorgio Colli and Mazzino Montinari, 15 vols. (Munich: Deutscher Taschenbuch Verlag, Berlin/New York: de Gruyter, 1980), 6.80; *Twilight of the Idols*, "How the 'True World' Finally Became a Fable," in *The Portable Nietzsche*, trans. Walter Kaufmann (New York: Penguin, 1982), p. 485. Subsequent references to Nietzsche's *Kritische Studienausgabe* will be to "KSA" plus volume and page number.

2. Nietzsche, *Die fröhliche Wissenschaft*, KSA 3.480 f.; *The Gay*

Science, trans. Walter Kaufmann (New York: Vintage/Random House, 1974), bk. 3, sec. 125, p. 181.

3. Nietzsche, *Nachlaß* (November 1887–März 1888), KSA 13.46f., *The Will to Power*, trans. Walter Kaufmann and R. J. Hollingdale (New York: Vintage/Random House, 1968), bk. 1, sec. 12, p. 12.

4. Nietzsche, *Nachlaß* (November 1887–März 1888), KSA 13.46f., *Will to Power*, bk. 1, sec. 12, p. 13 f.

5. Nietzsche, *Nachlaß* (November 1887–März 1888), KSA 13.47f., *Will to Power*, bk. 1, sec. 12, p. 13.

6. Nietzsche, *Die fröhliche Wissenschaft*, KSA 3.573; *Gay Science*, bk. 5, sec. 343, p. 279.

7. Nietzsche, *Nachlaß* (November 1887–März 1888), KSA 13.48, *Will to Power*, bk. 1, sec. 12, p. 13.

8. On the distinction between "active" and "passive" nihilism, see *Nachlaß* (Herbst 1887), KSA 12.350 f., *Will to Power*, bk. 1, sec. 22, p. 17; on "active nihilism," see *Nachlaß* (Sommer 1886–Herbst 1887), KSA 12.216, *Will to Power*, bk. 1, sec. 55, p. 38. Nihilism in the active sense is not our ineluctable fate but instead "represents a pathological transitional stage" on the way to the cultural renewal that Nietzsche anticipates under the rubric of "a revaluation of all values" (*Nachlaß* [Herbst 1887], KSA 12.351, *Will to Power*, bk. 1, sec. 13, p. 14).

9. See Friedrich Nietzsche, "Ueber Wahrheit und Lüge im aussermoralischen Sinne," in *Gesammelte Werke*, 23 vols. (Munich: Musarion, 1920–1929), 6.98 f. (subsequent references to this edition are to "Musarion" plus volume and page number), "On Truth and Lies in a Nonmoral Sense," *Philosophy and Truth: Selections from Nietzsche's Notebooks of the Early 1870's*, ed. and trans. Daniel Breazeale (New Jersey/London: Humanities Press International, 1992), p. 96 f.; "Vom Nutzen und Nachtheil der Historie für das Leben," KSA 1.296, "On the Use and Disadvantages of History for Life," in *Untimely Meditations*, trans. R. J. Hollingdale (Cambridge: Cambridge University Press), 1987, p. 95.

10. Nietzsche, preface to *On the Genealogy of Morals*, KSA 5.247, in *Basic Writings of Nietzsche*, trans. Walter Kaufmann (New York: Modern Library, 1992), p. 451.

11. Nietzsche, *Nachlaß* (November 1887–März 1888), KSA 13.49, *Will to Power*, bk. 1, sec. 12, p. 13.

12. Nietzsche, *Nachlaß* (November 1887–März 1888), KSA 13.49, *Will to Power*, bk. 1, sec. 12, p. 14.

13. Nietzsche, *Nachlaß* (Sommer 1887), KSA 12.327 f., *Will to Power*, bk. 3, sec. 579, p. 311.

14. Ibid. Cf. *Nachlaß* (Herbst 1887), KSA 12.366, *Will to Power*, bk. 3, sec. 585, p. 317: "*The fiction of a world* that corresponds to our desires: psychological trick and interpretation with the aim of associating everything we honor and find pleasant with this true world."

15. Nietzsche, *Götzen-Dämmerung*, KSA 6.81, "How the 'True World' Finally Became a Fable," *Twilight of the Idols*, in *Portable Nietzsche*, p. 485 (italics in original). Cf. *Nachlaß* (Herbst 1887), KSA 12.365, *Will to Power*, bk. 3, sec. 585, p. 317 ("'Will to truth'—*as the impotence of the will to create*"), and *Nachlaß* (Früjahr 1888), KSA 13.281, *Will to Power*, bk. 3, sec. 583, p. 314 ("It is of cardinal importance that one should abolish the *true* world").

16. Nietzsche, "Vom Nutzen und Nachtheil der Historie für das Leben," KSA 1.334, "On the Use and Disdavantages of History for Life," p. 123.

17. On Nietzsche's critique of Socratic cheerfulness, see *Die Geburt der Tragödie*, KSA 1.97 ff., *Birth of Tragedy*, sec. 15, in *Basic Writings of Nietzsche*, pp. 93 ff. By this point in *Birth of Tragedy*, Nietzsche has criticized Socrates as "the opponent of Dionysus" whose "great Cyclops eye . . . was denied the pleasure of gazing into the Dionysian abysses"; see sec. 12, KSA 1.88, *Birth of Tragedy*, p. 86, and sec. 14, KSA 1.92, *Birth of Tragedy*, p. 89.

18. Nietzsche, *Die Geburt der Tragödie*, KSA 1.47, *Birth of Tragedy*, sec. 5, p. 52 (italics in original); see also KSA 1.17, *Birth of Tragedy*, "Attempt at a Self-Criticism," p. 22, and KSA 1.152, *Birth of Tragedy*, sec. 24, p. 141.

19. Nietzsche, *Die fröhliche Wissenschaft*, KSA 3.464, *Gay Science*, bk. 2, sec. 107, p. 163 f. Cf. bk. 4, sec. 289 and 290, where Nietzsche speaks dismissively of "an overall philosophical justification of [one's] way of living" and calls for "a new justice" and "new philosophers" who can attain self-satisfaction through the art of "giving style" to their character—but not through anything like philosophical justification (*Die fröhliche Wissenschaft*, KSA 3.529 f., *Gay Science*, p. 231 f.).

20. Nietzsche, *Die fröhliche Wissenschaft*, KSA 3.567, *Gay Science*, bk. 4, sec. 338, p. 270.

21. Nietzsche, *Die fröhliche Wissenschaft*, KSA 3.582 f., *Gay Science*, bk. 5, sec. 347, p. 289 f.

22. Nietzsche, *Nachlaß* (Frühjahr 1888), KSA 13.337, *Will to Power*, bk. 3, sec. 584, p. 315.

23. Ibid., p. 316.

24. Hans Jonas, *The Gnostic Religion: The Message of the Alien God and the Beginnings of Chrisitanity*, 2d ed. (Boston: Beacon Press, 1991), p. 271.

25. Ibid., p. 272.

26. Ibid., p. 270. On the grounding of human moral opinions in the action of the demiurge, see p. 272; on Plotinus's criticism of Gnosticism, cf. p. 328 f.

27. Ibid., p. 322.

28. Ibid., pp. 325, 327.

29. Ibid., p. 338.

30. Ibid., pp. 329, 331.

31. Ibid., p. 332.

32. Martin Heidegger, "Nietzsches Wort 'Gott ist tot,'" in *Holzwege*, 6th ed. (Frankfurt: Klostermann, 1980), p. 212; "The Word of Nietzsche: 'God is Dead,'" in *The Question Concerning Technology and Other Essays*, trans. William Lovitt (New York: Harper Colophon, 1980), p. 61 (translation altered).

33. Nietzsche, *Nachlaß* (Herbst 1885–Herbst 1886), KSA 12.125 f., *Will to Power*, bk. 1, sec. 1, p. 7.

34. Nietzsche, *Nachlaß* (Herbst 1887), KSA 12.571, *Will to Power*, bk. 1, sec. 3, p. 9.

35. Jonas, *Gnostic Religion*, p. 332. On the distinction between *psyche* and *pneuma*, see p. 44.

36. Nietzsche, *Nachlaß* (Herbst 1885–Herbst 1886), KSA 12.27, *Will to Power*, bk. 1, sec. 1, p. 8.

37. Nietzsche, *Zur Genealogie der Moral*, KSA 5.404, Third Essay, in *On the Genealogy of Morals*, sec. 25, p. 591.

38. Nietzsche, *Die fröhliche Wissenschaft*, KSA 3.481, *Gay Science*, bk. 3, sec. 125, p. 181.

39. Freud, Lecture 28, in *Introductory Lectures on Psycho-Analysis*,

trans. James Strachey (New York: Norton, 1989), p. 353. The other two "blows" are dealt by Darwin and Freud/psychoanalysis.

40. Nietzsche, *Nachlaß* (November 1887–März 1888), KSA 13.69, *Will to Power*, bk. 1, sec. 30, p. 20.

41. Hans Blumenberg, *Die Legitimität der Neuzeit*, rev. ed. (Frankfurt: Suhrkamp, 1988), p. 163 f., *The Legitimacy of the Modern Age*, trans. Robert M. Wallace (Cambridge, MA/London: MIT Press, 1983), p. 141 f.

42. Friedrich Nietzsche, "Der Philosoph. Betrachtungen über den Kampf von Kunst und Erkenntnis," Musarion 6.35, "The Philosopher: Reflections on the Struggle Between Art and Knowledge," in *Philosophy and Truth*, p. 33.

43. Nietzsche, *Nachlaß* (Herbst 1887), KSA 12.465, *Will to Power*, bk. 3, sec. 485, p. 269; see also *Nachlaß* (Herbst 1885–Herbst 1886), KSA 12.140, *Will to Power*, bk. 3, sec. 556, p. 302.

44. Martin Heidegger, *Nietzsche*, 3d ed., 2 vols. (Pfullingen: Neske, 1961), 2.184; *Nietzsche, Volume Four: Nihilism*, trans. Frank Capuzzi and David Farrell Krell (San Francisco: Harper and Row, 1982), p. 131 f. (translation altered).

45. Nietzsche, *Nachlaß* (April–Juni 1885), KSA 11.506, *Will to Power*, bk. 3, sec. 493, p. 272.

46. Nietzsche, "Ueber Wahrheit und Lüge," Musarion 6.96, "On Truth and Lies in a Nonmoral Sense," p. 95. Cf. *Nachlaß* (Ende 1886–Frühjahr 1887), KSA 12.318, *Will to Power*, sec. 487, p. 269: "But that a belief, however necessary it may be for the preservation of a species, has nothing to do with truth, one knows from the fact that, e.g., we have to believe in time, space, and motion, without feeling compelled to grant them absolute reality."

47. Nietzsche, "Ueber Wahrheit und Lüge," Musarion 6.85 (also KSA 1.884), "On Truth and Lies in a Nonmoral Sense," p. 86. This claim follows from Nietzsche's analysis of perception as a process of metaphor formation in which "there is a complete overleaping of one sphere, right into the middle of another one." See "Ueber Wahrheit und Lüge im aussermoralischen Sinne," Musarion 6.79 (also KSA 1.879), "On Truth and Lies in a Nonmoral Sense," p. 82.

48. Nietzsche, "Ueber Wahrheit und Lüge," Musarion 6.81 f. (also KSA 1.881), "On Truth and Lies in a Nonmoral Sense," p. 84.

49. Nietzsche, "Ueber Wahrheit und Lüge," Musarion 6.82 (also KSA 1.881), "On Truth and Lies in a Nonmoral Sense," p. 84.

50. Nietzsche, *Nachlaß* (Juni–Juli 1885), KSA 11.597 f., *Will to Power*, sec. 483, p. 267 f.

51. Nietzsche, *Jenseits von Gut und Böse*, KSA 5.29 f., *Beyond Good and Evil*, part 1, sec. 16, p. 213.

52. Nietzsche, *Jenseits von Gut und Böse*, KSA 5.31, *Beyond Good and Evil*, in *Basic Writings of Nietzche*, Part 1, sec. 17, p. 214.

53. Nietzsche, *Jenseits von Gut und Böse*, KSA 5.27, *Beyond Good and Evil*, part 1, sec. 12, p. 210.

54. Nietzsche, *Jenseits von Gut und Böse*, KSA 5.160, *Beyond Good and Evil*, part 7, sec. 224, p. 343; cf. *Nachlaß* (Ende 1886–Frühjahr 1887), KSA 12.297, *Will to Power*, bk. 3, sec. 644, p. 342.

55. Nietzsche, *Jenseits von Gut und Böse*, KSA 5.27, *Beyond Good and Evil*, part 1, sec. 12, p. 210.

56. Nietzsche, *Jenseits von Gut und Böse*, KSA 5.29, *Beyond Good and Evil*, part 1, sec. 15, p. 212.

57. Nietzsche, *Jenseits von Gut und Böse*, KSA 5.33, *Beyond Good and Evil*, part 1, sec. 19, p. 216. Cf. Nachlaß (August–September 1885), KSA 11.650, *Will to Power*, bk. 3, sec. 490, p. 270 f.: "My hypotheses: The subject as multiplicity. . . . The continual transitoriness and fleetingness of the subject. 'Mortal soul'."

58. See Third Essay, in *Zur Genealogie der Moral*, particularly sec. 1 and 28, KSA 5.339, 5.412; *On the Genealogy of Morals*, pp. 533, 599.

59. Heidegger, *Nietzsche*, 2.141 f., *Nietzsche: Nihilism*, p. 96 (translation altered).

60. Heidegger, "Der Ursprung des Kunstwerkes," in *Holzwege*, p. 7, "The Origin of the Work of Art," in *Poetry, Language, Thought*," trans. Albert Hofstadter (New York: Harper and Row, 1975), p. 23 (translation altered).

61. Heidegger, *Nietzsche* 2.142, *Nietzsche: Nihilism*, p. 96 f.

62. Heidegger, *Nietzsche* 2.143, *Nietzsche: Nihilism*, p. 97 f.

63. Nietzsche, *Nachlaß* (Herbst 1887), KSA 12.386 f., *Will to Power*, bk. 3, sec. 533, p. 289 f.

64. Nietzsche, *Jenseits von Gut und Böse*, KSA 5.32, *Beyond Good and Evil*, part 1, sec. 19, p. 215.

65. Nietzsche, *Nachlaß* (Frühjahr 1888), KSA 13.373 f., *Will to Power*, sec. 636, p. 340.

66. Nietzsche, *Nachlaß* (Ende 1886–Frühjahr 1887), KSA 12.314, *Will to Power*, sec. 624, p. 334.

67. Heidegger, *Nietzsche*, 2.142 f., *Nietzsche: Nihilism*, p. 97; see also *Nietzsche*, 2.425.

68. See Carl Schmitt, *Political Theology: Four Chapters on the Concept of Sovereignty*, trans. George Schwab (Cambridge/London: MIT Press, 1985).

69. Martin Heidegger, "Hölderlin und das Wesen der Dichtung," in *Erläuterungen zu Hölderlins Dichtung*, 5th ed. (Frankfurt: Klostermann, 1981), p. 47, "Hölderlin and the Essence of Poetry," in *Existence and Being*, ed. Werner Brock (Washington, DC: Regnery/Gateway, 1988), p. 289 (translation altered). Heidegger's invocation of Hölderlin's notion of the needy or destitute time ("Wozu Dichter in dürftiger Zeit?" from the seventh strophe of "Brot und Wein") recalls Nietzsche's reference to "the one thing [that] is needful [*Eins ist Noth*]," which for Nietzsche is "a new justice" or "to 'give style' to one's character—a great and rare art!" (*Die fröhliche Wissenschaft*, KSA 3.529 f., *Gay Science*, bk. 4, sec. 289–90, p. 232).

70. Nietzsche, *Die fröhliche Wissenschaft*, KSA 3.625, *Gay Science*, bk. 5, sec. 373, p. 335; "Nur ein Gott kann uns noch retten," *Der Spiegel* (May 31, 1976), and "'Only a God Can Save Us': *Der Spiegel*'s Interview with Martin Heidegger," in *The Heidegger Controversy: A Critical Reader*, ed. Richard Wolin (Cambridge: MIT Press, 1993), pp. 91–116.

71. See Hermann Lübbe, "Säkularisierung as geschichtsphilosophischer Kategorie," in *Die Philosophie und die Frage nach dem Fortschritt. Verhandlungen des Siebten Deutschen Kongresses für Philosophie, Münster in Westfalen, 1964*, ed. Helmut Kuhn and Franz Wiedmann (Munich: Anton Pustet, 1964), p. 225. Cf. p. 233: On either interpretation, "im Problem der Säkularisierung hat es die Theologie mit dem Problem der *Entchristlichung* einer Kultur christlicher Herkunft zu tun."

72. Heidegger, *Nietzsche*, 2.144, *Nietzsche: Nihilism*, p. 99.

73. Karl Löwith, "Der Weltbegriff der neuzeitlichen Philosophie," *Sitzungsberichte der Heidelberger Akademie der Wissenschaften, Philosophisch-historischer Klasse* 44 (1960): 7, 19.

74. Hans Jonas, "Epilogue: Nature and Ethics," in *The Phenomenon*

of Life: Toward a Philosophical Biology (Chicago/London: The University of Chicago Press, 1982).

75. Löwith, "Der Weltbegriff der neuzeitlichen Philosophie," p. 22 f. The *saeculum* is the idea of mundane or earthly time, to which Christianity radically opposed its ideal of salvation; in a literal sense, it can refer to a measure of time such as a generation or a human life span. Of the saeculum and secularization, C. F. von Weizsäcker says:

> The word "secularization" derives from the Latin word *saeculum*, which means century. In traditional Christian language, *saeculum* means the time in which we are actually living today, as opposed to God's eternity: hence it also means everything which belongs to this world and which to that extent does not belong directly to God. Secularization was for a long time a juristic concept which designated the transference of ecclesiastical goods into secular hands. Thus men talked of a secularized monastery. In our century, many authors have begun to use the word secularization in a more general way as a description of the process by which the modern world has developed (*The Relevance of Science: Creation and Cosmogony*, Gifford Lectures 1959–60 [New York/Evanston: Harper and Row, 1964], p. 162).

76. Karl Löwith, *Weltgeschichte und Heilsgeschehen. Die theologischen Voraussetzungen der Geschichtsphilosophie*, in *Sämtliche Schriften*, 9 vols. (Stuttgart: Metzler, 1981–1988), 2.11; *Meaning in History*, (Chicago/London: The University of Chicago Press/Phoenix Books, 1949), p. 1. See also Karl Löwith, *Der europaische Nihilismus: Betrachtungen zur geistigen Vorgeschichte des europäischen Krieges* (1940), in *Sämtliche Schriften*, 2.473–601, *European Nihilism: Reflections on the Spiritual and Historical Background of the European War, Martin Heidegger and European Nihilism*, ed. Richard Wolin, trans. Gary Steiner (New York: Columbia University Press, 1995), pp. 171–234.

77. See Löwith, *Weltgeschichte und Heilsgeschehen*, 2.199, 2.214; *Meaning in History*, pp. 186, 200.

78. Löwith, *Meaning in History*, p. 225n1. *Weltgeschichte* means "world history." *Heilsgeschehen* is more difficult to translate because the term *Heil* can mean "healing," "wholeness," or "salvation." *Heils-*

geschichte refers to the retrieval of wholeness or completion that is at stake in Löwith's critique of modernity.

79. Löwith, *Weltgeschichte und Heilsgeschehen*, 2.12 f., *Meaning in History*, p. 2 f.

80. Löwith, *Meaning in History*, p. 3; cf. *Weltgeschichte und Heils-geschehen*, 2.13, where the parenthetical references to Kierkegaard and Nietzsche have been removed.

81. Löwith, *Weltgeschichte und Heilsgeschehen*, 2.13, *Meaning in History*, p. 3.

82. Löwith, *Weltgeschichte und Heilsgeschehen*, 2.205, *Meaning in History*, p. 191.

83. Löwith, *Weltgeschichte und Heilsgeschehen*, 2.235, 2.237; *Meaning in History*, pp. 219, 221.

84. Löwith, *Weltgeschichte und Heilsgeschehen*, 2.237, *Meaning in History*, p. 221.

85. Löwith, *Weltgeschichte und Heilsgeschehen*, 2.237; *Meaning in History*, p. 220; *Nietzsches Philosophie der ewigen Wiederkehr des Gleichen*, in *Sämtliche Schriften*, 6.337; *Nietzsche's Philosophy of the Eternal Recurrence of the Same*, trans. J. Harvey Lomax (Berkeley: University of California Press, 1997), p. 187.

86. Löwith, "Welt und Menschenwelt" (1960), *Welt und Menschenwelt*, in *Sämtliche Schriften*, 1.303.

87. Löwith, *Nietzsches Philosophie*, 6.274, *Nietzsche's Philosophy of the Eternal Recurrence*, p. 138.

88. Nietzsche, *Jenseits von Gut und Böse*, KSA 5.113, *Beyond Good and Evil*, part 5, sec. 191, p. 294.

89. Karl Löwith, "Das Verhängnis des Fortschritts," *Weltgeschichte und Heilsgeschehen: Zur Kritik der Geschichtsphilosophie*, in *Sämtliche Schriften*, 2.397, "The Fate of Progress," in *Nature, History, and Existentialism and Other Essays in the Philosophy of History*, ed. Arnold Levinson (Evanston, IL: Northwestern University Press, 1966), p. 149.

90. Löwith, "Das Verhängnis des Fortschritts," 2.404, "The Fate of Progress," p. 156.

91. See Löwith, "Das Verhängnis des Fortschritts," 2.396, "The Fate of Progress," p. 149.

92. On the Stoic doctrine of προνοία (providence), see Epictetus,

The Discourses as Reported by Arrian, Books 1–2, Greek-English, trans. W. A. Oldfather (Cambridge, MA/London: Harvard University Press, 2000), bk. 1, chap. 16, pp. 106 ff.

93. Löwith, *Gott, Mensch und Welt in der Philosophie der Neuzeit—G. B. Vico—Paul Valery*, in *Sämtliche Schriften*, 9.4.

94. Ibid., 9.10.

95. Ibid., 9.11 f.

96. Ibid., 9.11.

97. Ibid., 9.7.

98. Ibid., 9.12.

99. Ibid., 9.14.

100. Ibid., 9.13.

101. Ibid., 9.15.

102. Ibid., 9.19.

103. Ibid., 9.408.

104. On Heidegger's idea of a "yes and no" to technology, see "Wozu Dichter?" in *Holzwege*, p. 299; "What are Poets For?" *Poetry, Language, Thought*, trans. Albert Hofstadter (New York: Harper Colophon, 1975), p. 125; "Die Zeit des Weltbildes," in *Holzwege*, p. 95, "The Age of the World Picture," in *Question Concerning Technology*, p. 137 f.

105. Robert M. Wallace, translator's introduction to *Legitimacy of the Modern Age*, p. xvi; cf. Wallace, "Progress, Secularization and Modernity: The Löwith-Blumenberg Debate," *New German Critique* 22 (1981): 67 f.

106. See *Philosophische Rundschau* 15 (1968): 195–201 (Löwith), 201–209 (Gadamer). The English translation (*Legitimacy of the Modern Age*) is based on the revised edition of *Die Legitimität der Neuzeit*. References to Löwith's review in the present discussion are to Löwith, *Sämtliche Schriften*, 2.452–59, where his review is reprinted.

107. Blumenberg, *Die Legitimität der Neuzeit*, p. 24, *Legitimacy of the Modern Age*, p. 16.

108. Blumenberg, *Die Legitimität der Neuzeit*, p. 25, *Legitimacy of the Modern Age*, p. 18.

109. Gadamer, review of *Die Legitimität der Neuzeit*, p. 201 f.

110. Blumenberg, *Die Legitimität der Neuzeit*, p. 24, *Legitimacy of the Modern Age*, p. 17.

111. Blumenberg, *Die Legitimität der Neuzeit,* p. 45, *Legitimacy of the Modern Age*, p. 35.

112. Löwith, review of *Die Legitimität der Neuzeit*, in *Sämtliche Schriften*, 2.453 f.

113. See Blumenberg, *Die Legitimität der Neuzeit,* p. 25 f., *Legitimacy of the Modern Age*, p. 18.

114. Blumenberg, *Die Legitimität der Neuzeit,* p. 51, *Legitimacy of the Modern Age*, p. 42.

115. Blumenberg, *Die Legitimität der Neuzeit,* p. 54, *Legitimacy of the Modern Age*, p. 44.

116. Blumenberg, *Die Legitimität der Neuzeit,* p. 61, *Legitimacy of the Modern Age*, p. 49.

117. The other key historical event that Blumenberg cites as a basis for the idea of progress is the *querelle des anciens et des modernes* regarding the relative merits of the art and literature of antiquity and of modernity. "Here the idea of progress arises from protest against the status of permanent prototypes as obligatory ideals" (*Die Legitimität der Neuzeit*, p. 42, *Legitimacy of the Modern Age*, p. 33).

118. Hans Blumenberg, "On a Lineage of the Idea of Progress," *Social Research* 41 (1974): 8 f.

119. Ibid., p. 15.

120. Ibid., p. 18.

121. Ibid., p. 17.

122. See Blumenberg, *Die Legitimität der Neuzeit*, p. 133, *Legitimacy of the Modern Age*, p. 119: "Not only does the secularization thesis explain the modern age; it explains it as the wrong turning for which the thesis itself is able to prescribe the corrective."

123. Blumenberg, *Die Legitimität der Neuzeit*, p. 79, *Legitimacy of the Modern Age*, p. 69.

124. Hans Blumenberg, *Arbeit am Mythos* (Frankfurt: Suhrkamp, 1979), p. 298; *Work on Myth*, trans. Robert M. Wallace (Cambridge, MA/London: MIT Press, 1985), p. 269; cf. *Arbeit am Mythos*, p. 295, *Work on Myth*, p. 266.

125. Nietzsche, *Die Geburt der Tragödie*, KSA 1.35, *Birth of Tragedy*, sec. 3, p. 42.

126. Blumenberg, *Arbeit am Mythos*, p. 299, *Work on Myth*, p. 270.

127. Blumenberg, *Arbeit am Mythos*, p. 296, *Work on Myth*, p. 268.

128. Blumenberg, *Die Legitimität der Neuzeit*, p. 170, *Legitimacy of the Modern Age*, p. 154.

129. Blumenberg, *Die Legitimität der Neuzeit*, p. 169 f., *Legitimacy of the Modern Age*, p. 153 f.

130. Blumenberg, *Die Legitimität der Neuzeit*, p. 183, *Legitimacy of the Modern Age*, p. 163.

131. Blumenberg, *Die Legitimität der Neuzeit*, p. 198 f., *Legitimacy of the Modern Age*, p. 175.

132. Blumenberg, *Die Legitimität der Neuzeit*, p. 200, *Legitimacy of the Modern Age*, p. 176 f.

133. Blumenberg, *Die Legitimität der Neuzeit*, p. 214, *Legitimacy of the Modern Age*, p. 188.

134. Blumenberg, *Die Legitimität der Neuzeit*, p. 221, *Legitimacy of the Modern Age*, p. 193; Robert M. Wallace, "Hans Blumenberg on Descartes and the Modern Age," *Annals of Scholarship* 5 (1987): 44.

135. Blumenberg, *Die Legitimität der Neuzeit*, p. 202, *Legitimacy of the Modern Age*, p. 178.

136. Blumenberg, *Die Legitimität der Neuzeit*, p. 203, *Legitimacy of the Modern Age*, p. 178. Blumenberg defines self-assertion as "an existential program [*ein Daseinsprogramm*], according to which man posits his existence in a historical situation and indicates to himself how he is going to deal with the reality surrounding him and what use he will make of the possibilities that are open to him." Modernity's self-assertion involves "a new concentration on man's self-interest" (*Die Legitimität der Neuzeit*, pp. 178, 201; *Legitimacy of the Modern Age*, pp. 138, 178).

137. Blumenberg, *Die Legitimität der Neuzeit*, p. 204, *Legitimacy of the Modern Age*, p. 179.

138. Blumenberg, *Die Legitimität der Neuzeit*, p. 42, *Legitimacy of the Modern Age*, p. 33.

139. Blumenberg, *Die Legitimität der Neuzeit*, p. 52, *Legitimacy of the Modern Age*, p. 42 f.

140. See Blumenberg, "On a Lineage of the Idea of Progress," p. 26.

141. Blumenberg, *Die Legitimität der Neuzeit*, p. 208, *Legitimacy of the Modern Age*, p. 183.

142. Blumenberg, *Die Legitimität der Neuzeit*, p. 208 f., *Legitimacy of the Modern Age*, p. 184.

143. Blumenberg, *Die Legitimität der Neuzeit*, p. 213, *Legitimacy of the Modern Age*, p. 187.

144. Blumenberg, *Arbeit am Mythos*, p. 296, *Work on Myth*, p. 268. But cf. *Die Legitimität der Neuzeit*, p. 227, *Legitimacy of the Modern Age*, p. 198.

145. Blumenberg, *Arbeit am Mythos*, p. 412, *Work on Myth*, p. 377; *Die Legitimität der Neuzeit,* p. 442, *Legitimacy of the Modern Age*, p. 379. Cf. Jacques Derrida, "Cogito et histoire de la folie," in *L'écriture et la différence* (Paris: Éditions du Seuil, 1967), p. 86, "Cogito and the History of Madness," in *Writing and Difference*, trans. Alan Bass (Chicago: The University of Chicago Press, 1978), p. 56: The "zero point" (*point-zéro*) of subjectivity in Descartes is the point at which "determined meaning and nonmeaning come together in their common origin."

146. Descartes, Author's Replies to the Second Set of Objections, AT 7.145 f., CSM 2.103 f.

147. Bernard Williams, *Descartes: The Project of Pure Enquiry* (Harmondsworth: Penguin, 1978), p. 66. Cf. p. 200: "We cannot understand Descartes if we break the connection between the search for certainty and the search for truth, or the connection between knowledge and the correspondence of the ideas to reality." Like Blumenberg, Frankfurt tries to break the connection between reason and truth in Descartes by appealing to divine omnipotence. See Harry Frankfurt, "Descartes on the Creation of the Eternal Truths," *Philosophical Review* 86 (1977): 48–50; cf. *Demons, Dreamers, and Madmen: The Defense of Reason in Descartes's "Meditations"* (Indianapolis: Bobbs-Merrill, 1970), p. 180. I return to this problem below.

148. Blumenberg, *Die Legitimität der Neuzeit*, p. 234, *Legitimacy of the Modern Age*, p. 205.

149. Hans Blumenberg, *Die Genesis der kopernikanischen Welt*, 2d ed. (Frankfurt: Suhrkamp, 1985), p. 367; *The Genesis of the Copernican World*, trans. Robert M. Wallace (Cambridge, MA/London: MIT Press, 1987), p. 312.

150. Blumenberg, *Die Legitimität der Neuzeit*, p. 462, *Legitimacy of the Modern Age*, p. 394.

151. See Blumenberg, *Die Legitimität der Neuzeit*, pp. 462 ff., *Legitimacy of the Modern Age*, pp. 394 ff.

152. Blumenberg, *Die Genesis der kopernikanischen Welt*, p. 367 f., *Genesis of the Copernican World*, p. 312 f.

153. Edward Rosen, introduction to *Three Copernican Treatises*, trans. and intro. Edward Rosen (New York: Columbia University Press, 1939), p. 22.

154. Cited in ibid., p. 22.

155. Cited in ibid., p. 23.

156. Cited in ibid., p. 24.

157. Descartes, *Principles*, Part 3, sec. 15, AT 8A.85, CSM 1.250.

158. Ibid., Part 2, sec. 36 and 37, AT 8A.61 f., CSM 1.240.

159. Blumenberg, *Die Legitimität der Neuzeit*, p. 236, *Legitimacy of the Modern Age*, p. 206 f.

160. Descartes, *Principles*, Part 3, sec. 15, AT 8A.85, CSM 1.250.

161. Nicholas of Cusa, *On Learned Ignorance*, bk. 2, chap. 12, in *Selected Spiritual Writings*, trans. H. Lawrence Bond (New York/Mahwah, NJ: Paulist Press, 1997), p. 160 f.

162. Ibid., bk. 1, chap. 1, p. 88; bk. 2, chap. 2, p. 133.

163. Ibid., bk. 1, chap. 3, p. 91.

164. Ibid., bk. 1, chap. 11, p. 101.

165. Blumenberg, *Die Genesis der kopernikanischen Welt*, p. 370, *Genesis of the Copernican World*, p. 315.

166. Descartes, *Principles*, Part 1, sec. 28, AT 8.15, CSM 1.202.

167. Blumenberg, *Die Legitimität der Neuzeit*, p. 238, *Legitimacy of the Modern Age*, p. 209

168. Blumenberg, *Die Legitimität der Neuzeit*, p. 239, *Legitimacy of the Modern Age*, p. 209.

169. Blumenberg, *Die Legitimität der Neuzeit*, p. 466, *Legitimacy of the Modern Age*, p. 397.

170. Blumenberg, *Die Legitimität der Neuzeit*, p. 274, *Legitimacy of the Modern Age*, p. 239.

171. Blumenberg, *Die Legitimität der Neuzeit*, p. 239, *Legitimacy of the Modern Age*, p. 209.

172. Hans Blumenberg, "An Anthropological Approach to the Contemporary Significance of Rhetoric," in *After Philosophy: End or Transformation?* ed. Kenneth Baynes, James Bohman, and Thomas McCarthy (Cambridge, MA/London: MIT Press, 1987), p. 434.

173. Ibid., p. 433.

174. Ibid., p. 433; cf. p. 437.

175. Ibid., p. 435.

176. Blumenberg, *Die Legitimität der Neuzeit*, p. 109, *Legitimacy of the Modern Age*, p. 99.

177. Blumenberg, *Arbeit am Mythos*, p. 689, *Work on Myth*, p. 636.

178. See Descartes, *Principles*, Part 2, sec. 36 and 42, AT 8A.61, 8A.66; CSM 1.240, 1.243. Nadler points out the fundamental difficulties involved in Descartes's claim to derive the laws of nature from a God whose nature Descartes admits to be incomprehensible. See Steven Nadler, "Scientific Certainty and the Creation of the Eternal Truths: A Problem in Descartes," *Southern Journal of Philosophy* 25 (1987): 183–86.

179. Even if we ultimately decide that discursive consensus-making is the best possible form of moral reflection, we must still come to grips with a key implication of Descartes's thinking: that the extrarational ability to adduce ends for conduct is the necessary if unacknowledged presupposition of a successful discourse ethics. I have argued at length for this conclusion in "The Perils of a Total Critique of Reason: Rethinking Heidegger's Influence," *Philosophy Today* 47 (2003): 93–111.

180. See Descartes, letter to Mersenne, April 15, 1630, AT 1.145, CSM 3.23; letter to Mersenne, May 6, 1630, AT 1.149f., CSM 3.24; letter to [Mersenne], May 27, 1630, AT 1.151f., CSM 3.25.

181. Émile Bréhier, "The Creation of the Eternal Truths in Descartes's System," in *Descartes: A Collection of Critical Essays*, ed. Willis Doney (Garden City, NJ: Anchor/Doubleday, 1967): 195f.

182. See Descartes, letter to [Mesland], May 2, 1644, AT 4.118f., CSM 3.235; *Conversation with Burman*, AT 5.159f., CSM 3.343, letter for [Arnauld], July 29, 1648, AT 5.224, CSM 3.359.

183. Heidegger makes the connection between ethics and dwelling in the "Letter on 'Humanism,'" where he offers an etymological analysis of the term ethos: "ηθος means abode [*Aufenthalt*] dwelling place [*Ort des Wohnens*]. This word names the open region within which human beings dwell." Thus Heraclitus's statement ηθος ανθρώπω δαίμων, which is often translated as "man's character is his daimon," really means that "human beings dwell, insofar as they are human beings, in the nearness of God" (Martin Heidegger, "Brief über den 'Humanismus,'" in *Wegmarken*, 2d ed. (Frankfurt: Klostermann, 1978), p. 351; "Letter on

'Humanism,'" in *Pathmarks*, ed. William McNeill (Cambridge: Cambridge University Press, 1998), p. 269 [translation altered]). Conceived in these terms, ethics is a life project in which we seek to realize our proper place in the larger cosmic scheme of things.

184. See, for example, Bernard Yack, "Myth and Modernity: Hans Blumenberg's Reconstruction of Modern Theory," *Political Theory* 15 (1987): 257.

185. Stanley Rosen, *Nihilism: A Philosophical Essay* (New Haven/London: Yale University Press, 1969), pp. 230, 233.

186. Jonas, *Gnostic Religion*, p. 340.

187. Karl Jaspers, *Three Essays: Leonardo, Descartes, Max Weber*, trans. Ralph Manheim (New York: Harcourt, Brace, & World, 1964), p. 150.

BIBLIOGRAPHY

Abercrombie, Nigel. *The Origins of Jansenism*. Oxford: Clarendon, 1936.

Aquinas, Saint Thomas. *Basic Writings of Saint Thomas Aquinas*. Edited by Anton C. Pegis. 2 vols. Indianapolis/Cambridge: Hackett, 1997.

———. *On Faith and Reason*. Edited by Stephen F. Brown. Indianapolis/Cambridge: Hackett, 1999.

———. *St. Thomas Aquinas on Politics and Ethics*. Translated by Paul E. Sigmund. New York: Norton, 1988.

———. *Summa Contra Gentiles. Book One: God*. Translated by Anton C. Pegis. Notre Dame, IN/London: University of Notre Dame Press, 1975.

———. *The "Summa Theologica" of St. Thomas Aquinas*. Translated by Fathers of the English Dominican Province. 20 vols. New York/Cincinnati/Chicago: Benziger Brothers, 1912–1925.

———. *Truth*. Translated by Robert W. Mulligan, James V. McGlynn, and Robert W. Schmidt. 3 vols. Indianapolis/Cambridge: Hackett, 1995.

Aristotle. *Introduction to Aristotle*. Edited by Richard McKeon. New York: Modern Library, 1992.

Armogathe, Jean-Robert. *Theologica Cartesiana: L'explication physique de l'Eucharistie chez Descartes et Dom Desgabets*. The Hague: Nijhoff, 1977.

Augustine, Saint. *The Catholic and Manichaean Ways of Life*. Translated by Donald A. Gallagher and Idella J. Gallagher. Washington, DC: Catholic University Press, 1966.

———. *The City of God against the Pagans*. Edited and translated by R. W. Dyson. Cambridge: Cambridge University Press, 1998.

———. *Confessions*. Translated by R. S. Pine-Coffin. London: Penguin, 1961.

———. *The Essential Augustine*. Edited by Vernon J. Bourke. Indianapolis: Hackett, 1984.

———. *On Free Choice of the Will*. Translated by Thomas Williams. Indianapolis: Hackett, 1993.

———. *The Immortality of the Soul. The Magnitude of the Soul. On Music. The Advantage of Believing. On Faith in Things Unseen*. Translated by Ludwig Schopp et al. In *Fathers of the Church*, vol. 4. Washington, DC: Catholic University of America Press, 1992.

———. *Tractates on the Gospel of John 28–54*, in *Fathers of the Church*, vol. 88. Translated by John W. Rettig. Washington, DC: Catholic University of America Press, 1993.

———. *The Trinity*. Translated by Stephen McKenna. Boston: St. Paul Editions, 1965.

Bacon, Francis. *Francis Bacon*. Edited by Brian Vickers. Oxford/New York: Oxford University Press, 1996.

———. *The New Organon*. Edited by Lisa Jardine and Michael Silverthorne. Cambridge: Cambridge University Press, 2000.

———. *The Works of Francis Bacon*. Edited by James Spedding, Robert Leslie Ellis, and Douglas Denon Heath. 14 vols. London: Longman and Co., 1857–1874.

Baillet, Adrien. *La vie de Monsieur Des-Cartes*. 2 vols. New York/London: Garland, 1987.

Berns, Laurence. "Francis Bacon and the Conquest of Nature." *Interpretation* 7 (1978): 1–26.

Blackwell, Richard J. *Galileo, Bellarmine, and the Bible. Including a Translation of Foscarini's Letter on the Motion of the Earth*. Notre Dame, IN: University of Notre Dame Press, 1991.

Bluhm, William T. "Political Theory and Ethics." In *Discourse on the Method and Meditations on First Philosophy*, edited by David Weissman. New Haven, CT: Yale University Press, 1996, pp. 306–29.

Blumenberg, Hans. "An Anthropological Approach to the Contemporary Significance of Rhetoric." In *After Philosophy: End or Transformation?* edited by Kenneth Baynes, James Bohman, and Thomas McCarthy. Cambridge, MA/London: MIT Press, 1987, pp. 429–58.

———. *Arbeit am Mythos*. Frankurt: Suhrkamp, 1979.

———. *The Genesis of the Copernican World*. Translated by Robert M. Wallace. Cambridge, MA/London: MIT Press, 1987.

———. *Die Genesis der kopernikanischen Welt*. 2d ed. Frankfurt: Suhrkamp, 1985.

———. *The Legitimacy of the Modern Age*. Translated by Robert M. Wallace. Cambridge, MA/London: MIT Press, 1983.

———. *Die Legitimität der Neuzeit*. Rev. ed. Frankfurt: Suhrkamp, 1988.

———. "On a Lineage of the Idea of Progress." *Social Research* 41 (1974): 5–27.

———. "'Säkularisation': Kritik einer Kategorie historischer Illegitimität." In *Die Philosophie und die Frage nach dem Fortschritt, Verhandlungen des Siebten Deutschen Kongresses für Philosophie, Münster in Westfalen, 1964*. Edited by Helmut Kuhn and Franz Wiedmann. Munich: Anton Pustet, 1964, pp. 240–65.

———. *Work on Myth*. Translated by Robert M. Wallace. Cambridge, MA/London: MIT Press, 1985.

Bodin, Jean. *Six Books of the Commonwealth*. Abridged and translated by Michael Tooley. New York: Barnes and Noble, 1967.

Boutroux, Émile. *Historical Studies in Philosophy*. Translated by Fred Rothwell. London: MacMillan, 1912.

Box, Ian. "Bacon's Moral Philosophy." In *The Cambridge Companion to Bacon*, edited by Markku Peltonen. Cambridge: Cambridge University Press, 1996, pp. 260–82.

Bréhier, Émile. "The Creation of the Eternal Truths in Descartes's System." In *Descartes: A Collection of Critical Essays*, edited by Willis Doney. Garden City, NY: Anchor/Doubleday, 1967, pp. 192–208.

Briggs, John C. *Francis Bacon and the Rhetoric of Nature*. Cambridge, MA: Harvard University Press, 1989.

Bruno, Giordano. *The Expulsion of the Triumphant Beast*. Translated by Arthur D. Imerti. New Brunswick, NJ: Rutgers University Press, 1964.

Bury, J. B. *The Idea of Progress: An Inquiry into Its Origin and Growth.* London: Macmillan, 1924.

Canons and Decrees of the Council of Trent. Translated by H. J. Schroeder. Rockford, IL: Tan Books, 1978.

Cassirer, Ernst. *Descartes: Lehre—Persönlichkeit—Wirkung.* Stockholm: Bermann-Fischer, 1939.

Caton, Hiram. *The Origin of Subjectivity: An Essay on Descartes.* New Haven: Yale University Press, 1973.

———. "The Problem of Descartes' Sincerity." *Philosophical Forum* 2 (1971): 355–70.

Combès, Joseph. *Le dessein de la sagesse Cartésienne.* Lyon/Paris: Emmanuel Vitte, 1960.

Comenius, Johannes. *The Labyrinth of the World and the Paradise of the Heart.* Translated with an introduction by Howard Louthan and Andrea Sterk. New York/Mahwah, NJ: Paulist Press, 1998.

Cottingham, John. *Philosophy and the Good Life: Reason and the Passions in Greek, Cartesian and Psychoanalytic Ethics.* Cambridge: Cambridge University Press, 1998.

Derrida, Jacques. "Cogito and the History of Madness." In *Writing and Difference*, translated by Alan Bass. Chicago: University of Chicago Press, 1978, pp. 31–63.

———. "Cogito et histoire de la folie." In *L'écriture et la différence.* Paris: Éditions du Seuil, 1967, pp. 51–97.

Descartes, René. *Correspondance avec Élisabeth et autres letters.* Edited by Jean-Marie Beyssade and Michelle Beyssade. Paris: Flammarion, 1989.

———. *Descartes' Conversation with Burman.* Translated by John Cottingham. Oxford, UK: Clarendon, 1976.

———. *Descartes: His Moral Philosophy and Psychology.* Translated with an introduction by John J. Blom. New York: New York University Press, 1978.

———. *Discourse de la Méthode: Texte et commentaire.* Edited by Étienne Gilson. 5th ed. Paris: Vrin, 1976.

———. *Le Monde, ou Traité de la lumière.* Translatcd with an introduction by Michael Sean Mahoney. French-English ed. New York: Abaris Books, 1979.

————. *Oeuvres de Descartes*. Edited by Charles Adam and Paul Tannery. Rev. ed. 12 vols. Paris: Vrin, 1964–1976.

————. *The Passions of the Soul*. Translated by Stephen Voss. Introduction by Geneviève Rodis-Lewis. Indianapolis/Cambridge: Hackett, 1989.

————. *The Philosophical Writings of Descartes*. Translated by John Cottingham, Robert Stoothoff, and Dugald C. Murdoch. 3 vols. Cambridge: Cambridge University Press, 1984–1991.

Descartes, René, and Martin Schoock. *La Querelle d'Utrecht*. Edited by Theo Verbeek. Preface by Jean-Luc Marion. Paris: Les impressions nouvelles, 1988.

Doeuff, Michèle Le. *The Philosophical Imaginary*. Translated by Colin Gordon. Stanford: Stanford University Press, 1989.

Dupré, Louis. *Passage to Modernity: An Essay in the Hermeneutics of Nature and Culture*. New Haven: Yale University Press, 1993.

Ellis, Peter F. *The Yahwist: The Bible's First Theologian*. London: Geoffrey Chapman, 1969.

Epictetus. *The Discourses as Reported by Arrian, Books I–II*. Translated by W. A. Oldfather. Greek-English. Cambridge, MA/London: Harvard University Press, 2000.

Farrington, Benjamin. *The Philososophy of Francis Bacon: An Essay on Its Development from 1603 to 1609 with a New Translation of Fundamental Texts*. Liverpool: Liverpool University Press, 1964.

Frankfurt, Harry. *Demons, Dreamers, and Madmen: The Defense of Reason in Descartes's "Meditations."* Indianapolis: Bobbs-Merrill, 1970.

————. "Descartes on the Creation of the Eternal Truths." *Philosophical Review* 86 (1977): 36–57.

Freud, Sigmund. *Civilization and Its Discontents*. Translated by James Strachey. New York: Norton, 1984.

————. *Introductory Lectures on Psycho-Analysis*. Translated by James Strachey. New York: Norton, 1989.

Gäbe, Lüder. *Descartes' Selbstkritik: Untersuchungen zur Philosophie des jungen Descartes*. Hamburg: Meiner, 1972.

Gadamer, H. G. Review of Hans Blumenberg, *Die Legitimität der Neuzeit. Philosophische Rundschau* 15 (1968): 201–209.

Galilei, Galileo. *Discoveries and Opinions of Galileo.* Translated by Stillman Drake. New York: Anchor/Doubleday, 1957.

Gaukroger, Stephen. *Descartes: An Intellectual Biography.* Oxford: Clarendon, 1995.

Gilson, Étienne. *The Christian Philosophy of Saint Augustine.* Translated by L. E. M. Lynch. New York: Random House, 1960.

———. *The Philosophy of St. Thomas Aquinas.* Translated by Edward Bullough. New York: Dorset, 1948.

———. *The Spirit of Mediaeval Philosophy.* Translated by A. H. C. Downes. Notre Dame, IN/London: University of Notre Dame Press, 1991.

Gouhier, Henri. "Descartes et la religion. Note méthodologique." In *Cartesio nel terzo centenario nel 'Discorso del Metodo.'* Milan: Società Editrice "Vita e Pensiero," 1937, pp. 417–24.

———. *Essais sur Descartes.* Paris: Vrin, 1937.

———. *La pensée religieuse de Descartes.* 2d ed. Paris: Vrin, 1972.

Gueroult, Martial. *Descartes' Philosophy Interpreted According to the Order of Reasons.* Translated by Roger Ariew. 2 vols. Minneapolis: University of Minnesota Press, 1984–1985.

Haldane, Elizabeth S. *Descartes: His Life and Times.* London: John Murray, 1905.

Hamelin, O. *Le système de Descartes.* 2d ed. Paris: Alcan, 1921.

Harries, Karsten. "Descartes, Perspective, and the Angelic Eye." *Yale French Studies* 49 (1973): 28–42.

Heidegger, Martin. "The Age of the World Picture." In *The Question Concerning Technology and Other Essays*, translated by William Lovitt. New York: Harper Colophon, 1977, pp. 115–54.

———. "Brief über den 'Humanismus.'" In *Wegmarken*, 2d ed. Frankfurt: Klostermann, 1978.

———. "Einleitung zu: 'Was ist Metaphysik?' Der Rückgang in den Grund der Metaphysik." In *Wegmarken*, 2d ed. Frankfurt: Klostermann, 1978, pp. 361–77.

———. "Hölderlin and the Essence of Poetry." In *Existence and Being*, edited by Werner Brock. Washington, DC: Regnery/Gateway, 1988, pp. 270–91.

———. "Hölderlin und das Wesen der Dichtung." In *Erläuterungen zu Hölderlins Dichtung*, 5th ed. Frankfurt: Klostermann, 1981, pp. 33–48.

———. "Introduction to 'What is Metaphysics?'" In *Pathmarks*, edited by William McNeill. Cambridge: Cambridge University Press, 1998, pp. 277–90.

———. "Letter on 'Humanism.'" In *Pathmarks*, edited by William McNeill. Cambridge: Cambridge University Press, 1998.

———. *Nietzsche*. 3d ed. 2 vols. Pfullingen: Neske, 1961.

———. *Nietzsche,* vol. 4, *Nihilism*. Translated by Frank A. Capuzzi. Edited by David Farrell Krell. San Francisco: Harper and Row, 1982.

———. "Nietzsches Wort 'Gott ist tot.'" In *Holzwege*, 6th ed. Frankfurt: Klostermann, 1980, pp. 205–63.

———. "Nur ein Gott kann uns noch retten." *Der Spiegel* (May 31, 1976).

———. "'Only a God Can Save Us': *Der Spiegel*'s Interview with Martin Heidegger." In *The Heidegger Controversy: A Critical Reader*, edited by Richard Wolin. Cambridge, MA/London: MIT Press, 1993, pp. 91–116.

———. "The Origin of the Work of Art." In *Poetry, Language, Thought*, translated by Albert Hofstadter. New York: Harper Colophon, 1975, pp. 15–87.

———. "Der Ursprung des Kunstwerkes." In *Holzwege*, 6th ed. Frankfurt: Klostermann, 1978, pp. 1–72.

———. "What are Poets For?" In *Poetry, Language, Thought*. Translated by Albert Hofstadter. New York: Harper Colophon, 1975, pp. 89–142.

———. "The Word of Nietzsche: 'God is Dead.'" In *The Question Concerning Technology and Other Essays*, translated by William Lovitt. New York: Harper Colophon, 1980, pp. 53–112.

———. "Wozu Dichter?" In *Holzwege*, 6th ed. Frankfurt: Klostermann, 1980, pp. 265–316.

———. "Die Zeit des Weltbildes." In *Holzwege*, 6th ed. Frankfurt: Klostermann, 1980, pp. 73–110.

Hiebert, Theodore. *The Yahwist's Landscape: Nature and Religion in Early Israel*. New York/Oxford: Oxford University Press, 1996.

Hobbes, Thomas. *Leviathan*. Harmondsworth, UK: Penguin, 1985.

Hugh of Saint Victor. *On the Sacraments of the Christian Faith*. Translated by Roy J. Deferrari. Cambridge, MA: The Medieval Academy of America, 1951.

Hugo de S. Victore. *De sacramentis Christianæ fidei*. In *Patrologia Latina*, vol. 176. Paris: J.-P. Migne, 1854.

Jacob, Margaret C. *The Radical Enlightenment: Pantheists, Freemasons and Republicans*. London: George Allen & Unwin, 1981.

Janowski, Zbigniew. *Cartesian Theodicy: Descartes' Quest for Certitude*. Dordrecht: Kluwer, 2000.

Jaspers, Karl. *The Great Philosophers*. Vol. 4, *The Disturbers: Descartes, Pascal, Lessing, Kierkegaard, Nietzsche. Philosophers in Other Realms: Einstein, Weber, Marx*. Edited by Michael Ermarth and Leonard H. Ehrlich. New York: Harcourt Brace, 1995.

———. *Three Essays: Leonardo, Descartes, Max Weber*. Translated by Ralph Manheim. New York: Harcourt, Brace, & World, 1964.

Jedin, Hubert. *A History of the Council of Trent*. Translated by Dom Ernest Graf. 2 vols. Vol. 1, *The Struggle for the Council*. Vol. 2, *The First Sessions at Trent, 1545–47*. St. Louis: B. Herder, 1963 (vol. 1), 1961 (vol. 2).

Jonas, Hans. "Epilogue: Nature and Ethics." In *The Phenomenon of Life: Toward a Philosophical Biology*. Chicago/London: The University of Chicago Press, 1982, pp. 282–84.

———. *The Gnostic Religion: The Message of the Alien God and the Beginnings of Christianity*. 2d ed. Boston: Beacon Press, 1991.

———. "The Practical Uses of Theory." In *The Phenomenon of Life: Toward a Philosophical Biology*. Chicago/London: The University of Chicago Press, 1982, pp. 188–210.

———. "Seventeenth Century and After: The Meaning of the Scientific and Technological Revolution." In *Philosophical Essays: From Ancient Creed to Technological Man*. Chicago/London: The University of Chicago Press, 1974, pp. 45–80.

Kant, Immanuel. *Critique of Judgment*. Translated by Werner S. Pluhar. Indianapolis: Hackett, 1987.

———. *Critique of Practical Reason*. Translated by Lewis White Beck. 3d ed. Upper Saddle River, NJ: Library of Liberal Arts/Prentice Hall, 1993.

———. *Critique of Pure Reason*. Translated by Norman Kemp Smith. New York: Humanities Press, 1950.

———. *Grounding for the Metaphysics of Morals*, Translated by James W. Ellington. 2d ed. Indianapolis/Cambridge: Hackett, 1985.

Kay, Jeanne. "Concepts of Nature in the Hebrew Bible." *Environmental Ethics* 10 (1988): 309–27.

Keefe, T. "Descartes's 'Morale Définitive' and the Autonomy of Ethics." *Romanic Review* 64 (1973): 85–98.

———. "Descartes's 'Morale Provisoire': A Reconsideration." *French Studies* 26 (1972): 129–42.

Koyré, Alexandre. *Descartes und die Scholastik*. Bonn: Bouvier Verlag Herbert Grundemann, 1971.

Lalande, André. "Sur quelques textes de Bacon et de Descartes." *Revue de Métaphysique et de Morale* 19 (1911): 296–311.

Laporte, Jean. *Le rationalisme de Descartes*, revised ed. Paris: Presses universitaires de France, 1950.

Lefebvre, M. H. "De la morale provisoire a la générosité." In *Descartes*, Cahiers de Royamount, Philosophie no. 2. Paris: Les Éditions de Minuit, 1957, pp. 237–55.

Leroy, Maxime. *Descartes, le philosophe au masque*. 2 vols. Paris: Éditions Rieder, 1929.

Levi, Anthony. *French Moralists: The Theory of the Passions 1585–1649*. Oxford: Clarendon, 1964.

Löwith, Karl. "Besprechung des Buches *Die Legitimität der Neuzeit* von Hans Blumenberg." In *Sämtliche Schriften*, 9 vols. Stuttgart: Metzler, 1981–1988. Vol. 2: *Weltgeschichte und Heilsgeschehen: Zur Kritik der Geschichtsphilosophie*, pp. 452–59.

———. *Der europaische Nihilismus: Betrachtungen zur geistigen Vorgeschichte des europäischen Krieges*. In *Sämtliche Schriften*, 9 vols. Stuttgart: Metzler, 1981–1988. Vol. 2: *Weltgeschichte und Heilsgeschehen: Zur Kritik der Geschichtsphilosophie*, pp. 473–540.

———. *European Nihilism: Reflections on the Spiritual and Historical Background of the European War*. In *Martin Heidegger and European Nihilism*. Edited by Richard Wolin. Translated by Gary Steiner. New York: Columbia University Press, 1995, pp. 171–234.

———. "The Fate of Progress." In *Nature, History, and Existentialism and Other Essays in the Philosophy of History*, edited by Arnold Levinson. Evanston, IL: Northwestern University Press, 1966, pp. 145–61.

———. *Gott, Mensch und Welt in der Philosophie der Neuzeit—G. B. Vico—Paul Valery*. In *Sämtliche Schriften*, 9 vols. Stuttgart: Metzler, 1981–1988. Vol. 9.

————. *Meaning in History*. Chicago/London: The University of Chicago Press/Phoenix Books, 1949.

————. *Nietzsche's Philosophy of the Eternal Recurrence of the Same*. Translated by J. Harvey Lomax. Berkeley: University of California Press, 1997.

————. *Nietzsches Philosophie der ewigen Wiederkehr des Gleichen*. In *Sämtliche Schriften*, 9 vols. Stuttgart: Metzler, 1981–1988. Vol. 6.

————. "Das Verhängnis des Fortschritts." In *Sämtliche Schriften*, 9 vols. Stuttgart: Metzler, 1981–1988. Vol. 2: *Weltgeschichte und Heilsgeschehen: Zur Kritik der Geschichtsphilosophie*, pp. 392–410.

————. "Welt und Menschenwelt." In *Sämtliche Schriften*, 9 vols. Stuttgart: Metzler, 1981–1988. Vol. 1: *Welt und Menschenwelt: Beiträge zur Anthropologie*, pp. 295–328.

————. "Der Weltbegriff der neuzeitlichen Philosophie." *Sitzungsberichte der Heidelberger Akademie der Wissenschaften, Philosophisch-historischer Klasse* 44 (1960): 7–23.

————. *Weltgeschichte und Heilsgeschehen. Die theologischen Voraussetzungen der Geschichtsphilosophie*. In *Sämtliche Schriften*, 9 vols. Stuttgart: Metzler, 1981–88. Vol. 2: *Weltgeschichte und Heilsgeschehen: Zur Kritik der Geschichtsphilosophie*, pp. 7–239.

Loyola, Saint Ignàcio de. *The Spiritual Exercises of St. Ignatius*. Translated by Anthony Mottola. Garden City, NY: Image/Doubleday, 1964.

Lübbe, Hermann. "Säkularisierung als geschichtsphilosophischer Kategorie." In *Die Philosophie und die Frage nach dem Fortschritt. Verhandlungen des Siebten Deutschen Kongresses für Philosophie, Münster in Westfalen, 1964*, edited by Helmut Kuhn and Franz Wiedmann. Munich: Anton Pustet, 1964.

Machaivelli, Niccolò. *The Prince*. Translated with an introduction by Harvey C. Mansfield Jr. Chicago: University of Chicago Press, 1985.

Marion, Jean-Luc. "Generosity and Phenomenology: Remarks on Michel Henry's Interpretation of the Cartesian *Cogito*." In *Essays in the Philosophy and Science of René Descartes*, edited by Stephen Voss. New York/Oxford: Oxford University Press, 1993, pp. 52–74.

————. *Sur la théologie blanche de Descartes: Analogie, création des vérités éternelles et fondement*. Paris: Presses universitaires de France, 1981.

Maritain, Jacques. *The Dream of Descartes Together with Some Other Essays.* Translated by Mabelle L. Andison. New York: Philosophical Library, 1944.

————. *Three Reformers: Luther—Descartes—Rousseau.* Rev. ed. New York: Scribner's Sons, 1929.

Marshall, John. *Descartes's Moral Theory.* Ithaca, NY/London: Cornell University Press, 1998.

Marx, Karl. "Estranged Labour." In *The Marx-Engels Reader*, edited by Richard C. Tucker. 2d ed. New York: Norton, 1978, pp. 71–80.

Mesnard, Pierre. *Essai sur la morale de Descartes.* Paris: Boivin & Cie, 1936.

Mettrie, Julian Offray de la. *Man Machine and Other Writings.* Edited by Ann Thomson. Cambridge: Cambridge University Press, 1996.

More, Henry. *Philosophical Writings of Henry More.* Edited by Flora Isabel Mackinnon. New York: AMS Press, 1969.

Moule, C. F. D. Moule. *Man and Nature in the New Testament.* Philadelphia: Fortress Press, 1967.

Nadler, Steven M. "Arnauld, Descartes, and Transubstantiation: Reconciling Cartesian Metaphysics and Real Presence." *Journal of the History of Ideas* 49 (1988): 229–46.

————. "Scientific Certainty and the Creation of the Eternal Truths: A Problem in Descartes." *Southern Journal of Philosophy* 25 (1987): 175–92.

Nicholas of Cusa. *On Learned Ignorance.* In *Selected Spiritual Writings*, translated by H. Lawrence Bond. New York/Mahwah, NJ: Paulist Press, 1997, pp. 85–206.

Nietzsche, Friedrich. *Beyond Good and Evil.* In *Basic Writings of Nietzsche*, translated by Walter Kaufmann. New York: Modern Library, 1992, pp. 179–435.

————. *The Birth of Tragedy.* In *Basic Writings of Nietzsche*, translated by Walter Kaufmann. New York: Modern Library, 1992, pp. 1–144.

————. *The Gay Science.* Translated by Walter Kaufmann. New York: Vintage/Random House, 1974.

————. *On the "Genealogy of Morals."* In *Basic Writings of Nietzsche*, translated by Walter Kaufmann. New York: Modern Library, 1992, pp. 437–599.

————. *Gesammelte Werke.* 23 vols. Munich: Musarion, 1920–1929.

———. "The Philosopher: Reflections on the Struggle Between Art and Knowledge." In *Philosophy and Truth: Selections from Nietzsche's Notebooks of the Early 1870's*, edited and translated by Daniel Breazeale. London: Humanities Press International, 1992, pp. 3–58.

———. *Sämtliche Schriften. Kritische Studienausgabe*. Edited by Giorgio Colli and Mazzino Montinari. 15 vols. Munich: Deutscher Taschenbuch Verlag, Berlin/New York: de Gruyter, 1980.

———. *Thus Spoke Zarathustra*. In *The Portable Nietzsche*, edited and translated by Walter Kaufmann. New York: Penguin, 1976, pp. 103–439.

———. "On Truth and Lies in a Nonmoral Sense." In *Philosophy and Truth: Selections from Nietzsche's Notebooks of the Early 1870's*, edited and translated by Daniel Breazeale. New Jersey/London: Humanities Press International, 1992, pp. 79–97.

———. *Twilight of the Idols*. In *The Portable Nietzsche*, edited and translated by Walter Kaufmann. New York: Penguin, 1976, pp. 463–563.

———. "On the Use and Disadvantages of History for Life." In *Untimely Meditations*, translated by R. J. Hollingdale. Cambridge: Cambridge University Press, 1987, pp. 59–123.

———. *The Will to Power*. Translated by Walter Kaufmann and R. J. Hollingdale. New York: Vintage/Random House, 1968.

Popkin, Richard H. *The History of Scepticism from Erasmus to Spinoza*. Berkeley: University of California Press, 1979.

———. "The Religious Background of Seventeenth-Century Philosophy." *Journal of the History of Philosophy* 25 (1987): 35–50.

Prauss, Gerold. *Knowing and Doing in Heidegger's 'Being and Time.'* Translated by Gary Steiner and Jeffrey S. Turner. Amherst, NY: Humanity Books, 1999.

Regius, Henricus. *Brevis explicatio mentis humanae*. New ed. Utrecht: Th. ab Ackersdijck and G. à Zyll, 1657.

Röd, Wolfgang. *Descartes: Die Genese des cartesianischen Rationalismus*. 2d ed. Munich: C. H. Beck, 1982.

Rodis-Lewis, Geneviève. *Descartes: His Life and Thought*. Translated by Jane Marie Todd. Ithaca, NY/London: Cornell University Press, 1998.

———. "Liberté et égalité chez Descartes." *Archives de Philosophie* 53 (1990): 421–30.

————. "Maîtrise des passions et sagesse chez Descartes." In *Descartes.* Cahiers de Royaumont, Philosophie no. 2. Paris: Les éditions de minuit, 1957, pp. 208–36.

————. "From Metaphysics to Physics." Translated by Frederick P. Van de Pitte. In *Essays on the Philosophy and Science of René Descartes,* edited by Stephen Voss. New York/Oxford: Oxford University Press, 1993, pp. 242–58.

————. *La Morale de Descartes.* Paris: Presses universitaires de France, 1957.

Rosen, Stanley. *Nihilism: A Philosophical Essay.* New Haven/London: Yale University Press, 1969.

Rossi, Paolo. *Philosophy, Technology, and the Arts in the Early Modern Era.* Translated by Salvator Attanasio. Edited by Benjamin Nelson. New York: Harper Torchbooks, 1970.

Schmaltz, Tad M. "What Has Cartesianism To Do with Jansenism?" *Journal of the History of Ideas* 60 (1999): 37–56.

Schmitt, Carl. *Political Theology: Four Chapters on the Concept of Sovereignty.* Translated by George Schwab. Cambridge/London: MIT Press, 1985.

Sedgwick, Alexander. *Jansenism in Seventeenth-Century France: Voices from the Wilderness.* Charlottesville: University Press of Virginia, 1977.

Smith, Norman. *Studies in the Cartesian Philosophy.* New York: Russell and Russell, 1962.

Specht, Rainer. *Descartes.* Reinbek bei Hamburg: Rowohlt, 1966.

————. "Über Descartes' politische Ansichten." *Der Staat* 3 (1964): 281–94.

Steiner, Gary. "Descartes on the Moral Status of Animals." *Archiv für Geschichte der Philosophie* 80 (1998): 268–91.

————. "The Perils of a Total Critique of Reason: Rethinking Heidegger's Influence." *Philosophy Today* 47 (2003): 93–111.

Three Copernican Treatises. Translated with an introduction by Edward Rosen. New York: Columbia University Press, 1939.

Tugendhat, Ernst. *Self-Consciousness and Self-Determination.* Translated by Paul Stern. Cambridge: MIT Press, 1986.

Verbeek, Theo. *Descartes and the Dutch: Early Reactions to Cartesian Philosophy, 1637–1650.* Carbondale/Edwardsville: Southern Illinois University Press, 1992.

Vrooman, Jack. *René Descartes: A Biography.* New York: G. P. Putnam's Sons, 1970.

Wallace, Robert M. "Hans Blumenberg on Descartes and the Modern Age." *Annals of Scholarship* 5 (1987): 37–63.

———. "Progress, Secularization and Modernity: The Löwith-Blumenberg Debate." *New German Critique* 22 (1981): 63–79.

Watson, Richard A. "Transubstantiation among the Cartesians." In *Problems of Cartesianism*, edited by Thomas M. Lennon, John M. Nicholas, and John W. Davis. Montreal: McGill-Queen's University Press, 1982, pp. 127–48.

Weaver, Rebecca Harden. *Divine Grace and Human Agency: A Study of the Semi-Pelagian Controversy.* Macon, GA: Mercer University Press, 1996.

Weizsäcker, C. F. von. *The Relevance of Science: Creation and Cosmogony.* Gifford Lectures 1959–1960. New York/Evanston: Harper and Row, 1964.

White Jr., Lynn. "The Historical Roots of Our Ecological Crisis." In *Ecology and Religion in History*, edited by David Spring and Eileen Spring. New York: Harper Torchbooks, 1974, pp. 15–31.

Williams, Bernard. *Descartes: The Project of Pure Enquiry.* Harmondsworth: Penguin, 1978.

Yack, Bernard. "Myth and Modernity: Hans Blumenberg's Reconstruction of Modern Theory." *Political Theory* 15 (1987): 244–61.

INDEX